PRACTICE BOOK
Conceptual Physical Science

THIRD EDITION

Paul G. Hewitt

John Suchocki

Leslie A. Hewitt

PEARSON

Addison
Wesley

San Francisco   Boston   New York
Capetown   Hong Kong   London   Madrid   Mexico City
Montreal   Munich   Paris   Singapore   Sydney   Tokyo   Toronto

Cover Credit: Art Wolfe/Getty Images

ISBN: 0-321-05180-7

5 6 7 8 9 10 TCS 06
www.aw.com/physics

Table of Contents
Conceptual Physical Science Third Edition—Practice Book

Part 1—Mechanics
Chapter 1: Patterns of Motion and Equilibrium
The Equilibrium Rule: $\Sigma F = 0$ 1–2
Free Fall Speed 3
Acceleration of Free Fall 4

Chapter 2: Newton's Laws of Motion
Newton's First Law and Friction 5
Non-Accelerated Motion 6
A Day at the Races with Newton's Second Law: $a = F/m$ 7
Dropping Masses and Accelerating Cart 8–10
Bronco and Newton's Second Law 11
Newton's Third Law 13
Nellie and Newton's Third Law 14
Vectors and the Parallelogram Rule 15–16
Force Vectors and the Parallelogram Rule 17
Force-Vector Diagrams 18

Chapter 3: Momentum and Energy
Momentum 19
Systems 20
Impulse—Momentum 21
Conservation of Momentum 22
Work and Energy 23–24
Conservation of Energy 25
Energy and Momentum 26

Chapter 4: Newton's Law of Universal Gravitation
The Inverse-Square Law—Weight 27
Ocean Tides 28

Chapter 5: Projectile and Satellite Motion
Projectile Motion 29–30
Tossed-Ball Vectors 31–32
Circular Orbits 33
Elliptical Orbits 34
Mechanics Overview 35

Chapter 6: Fluid Mechanics
Archimedes' Principle 37–38
More Archimedes' Principle 39–40
Gases 41

Chapter 7: Thermal Energy and Thermodynamics
Temperature Mix 43
Absolute Zero 44
Thermal Expansion 45–46

Chapter 8: Heat Transfer and Change of Phase
Transmission of Heat 47
Change of Phase 48–49

Chapter 9: Static and Current Electricity
Electric Potential 51
Series Circuits 52
Parallel Circuits 53
Compound Circuits 54

Chapter 10: Magnetism and Electromagnetic Induction
Magnetism.. 55
Field Patterns 56
Faraday's Law 57
E&M Induction—The Transformer.. 58

Chapter 11: Waves and Sound
Vibration and Wave Fundamentals 59–60
Shock Waves.. 61–62

Chapter 12: Light Waves
Color 63-64
Interference Patterns.. 65
Diffraction and Interference 66

Chapter 13: Properties of Light
Reflection 67–68
Refraction 69–72
Wave-Particle Duality 73

Part 2—Chemistry
Chapter 14: Atoms and the Periodic Table
Subatomic Particles.. 75
Melting Points of the Elements 77
Densities of the Elements... 78

Chapter 15: Visualizing the Atom
Losing Valence Electrons.. 79

Chapter 16: The Atomic Nucleus
Radioactivity 81–82
Radioactive Half-Life.. 83
Nuclear Fission and Fusion.. 85
Nuclear Reactions 86

Chapter 17: Elements of Chemistry
The Submicroscopic.. 87
Balancing Chemical Equations... 89
Physical and Chemical Changes... 90

Chapter 18: Mixtures
Solutions.. 91
Pure Mathematics 93

Chapter 19: How Atoms Bond
Chemical Bonds.. 95
Shells and the Covalent Bond 97–98
Bond Polarity 99–100

Chapter 20: Molecular Attractions
Atoms to Molecules.. 101–102

Chapter 21: Chemical Reactions
Relative Masses... 103–105
Exothermic and Endothermic Reactions.. 107–108

Chapter 22: Acids and Bases
Donating and Accepting Hydrogen Bonds... 109–110

Chapter 23: Oxidation and Reduction
Loss and Gain of Electrons 111

Chapter 24: Organic Compounds
Structures of Organic Compounds 113
Polymers.. 115

Part 3—Earth and Space Science
Chapter 25: Minerals and How We Use Them
Chemical Structure and Formulas of Minerals 117–118

Chapter 26: Rocks
The Rock Cycle 119
Igneous Rock Differentiation: How to Make Granite 120

Chapter 27: The Dynamic Earth
Faults 121
Structural Geology 122
Plate Boundaries 123
Sea-Floor Spreading 124
Plate Boundaries and Magma Generation 125

Chapter 28: Occurrence and Movement of Water
Groundwater Flow and Contaminant Transport 127
Aquifer Hydraulics 128

Chapter 29: Surface Processes
Stream Flow 129
Stream Velocity 130
Glacial Movement 131

Chapter 30: A Brief History of the Earth
Relative Time—What Came First? 133
Age Relationships 135
Unconformities and Age Relationships 136
Radiometric Dating 137
Our Earth's Hot Interior 138

Chapter 31: The Atmosphere, the Oceans, and Their Interactions
The Earth's Seasons 139–140
Short and Long Wavelength 141
Driving Forces of Air Motion 142

Chapter 32: Weather
Air Temperature and Pressure Patterns 143–144
Surface Weather Maps 145–146
Chilly Winds 147

Chapter 33: The Solar System
Earth-Moon-Sun Alignment 149
Pinhole Image Formation 150

Chapter 34 The Stars and Beyond
Stellar Parallax 151

Chapter 35 Special and General Relativity
Time Dilation and the Twin Trip 153–156
Relativistic Time Dilation 157

Appendices
Appendix B Rotational Mechanics
Mobile Torques 159
Torques and See-Saws 160

Appendix C Vectors
Vectors and Sailboats 161–162

Answers to the Practice Sheets 164–202

Answers to Odd-Numbered Exercises and Problems from the Textbook 203–247

Welcome to the Conceptual Physical Science
Practice Book

These practice sheets supplement *Conceptual Physical Science, Third Edition.* Their purpose is as the name implies—practice—not testing. It is easier to learn science by doing it—by practicing. AFTER you've worked through a sheet, check your responses with the reduced answer pages at the back of the book. You'll find that doing and learning physical science is enjoyable.

We think that these practice sheets can be an important part of the way you learn science and carry your knowledge of science with you throughout your life. We welcome your ideas, criticisms, and suggestions.

Enjoy!

At the end of this book are answers and solutions to the odd-numbered exercises and problems in the textbook.

Paul G. Hewitt

John Suchocki

Leslie A. Hewitt

CONCEPTUAL **Physical Science** PRACTICE SHEET

Chapter 1: Patterns of Motion and Equilibrium
The Equilibrium Rule: ΣF = 0

1. Gymnast Nellie Newton hangs from a variety of positions as shown. Since she is not accelerating, the net force on her is zero. This means the upward pull of the rope(s) equals the downward pull of gravity. She weighs 300 N. Show the scale reading for each case.

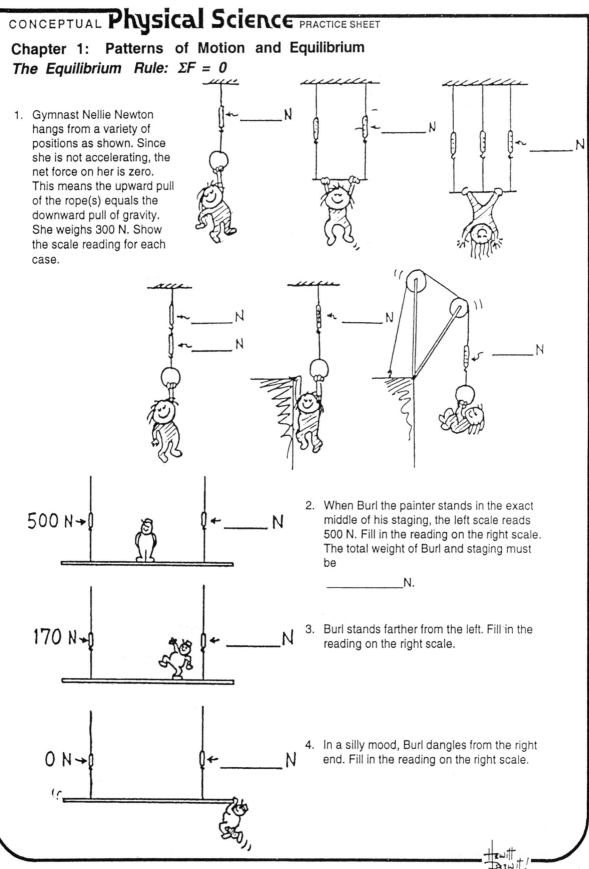

2. When Burl the painter stands in the exact middle of his staging, the left scale reads 500 N. Fill in the reading on the right scale. The total weight of Burl and staging must be

_____N.

3. Burl stands farther from the left. Fill in the reading on the right scale.

4. In a silly mood, Burl dangles from the right end. Fill in the reading on the right scale.

Chapter 1: Patterns of Motion and Equilibrium
The Equilibrium Rule: ΣF = 0

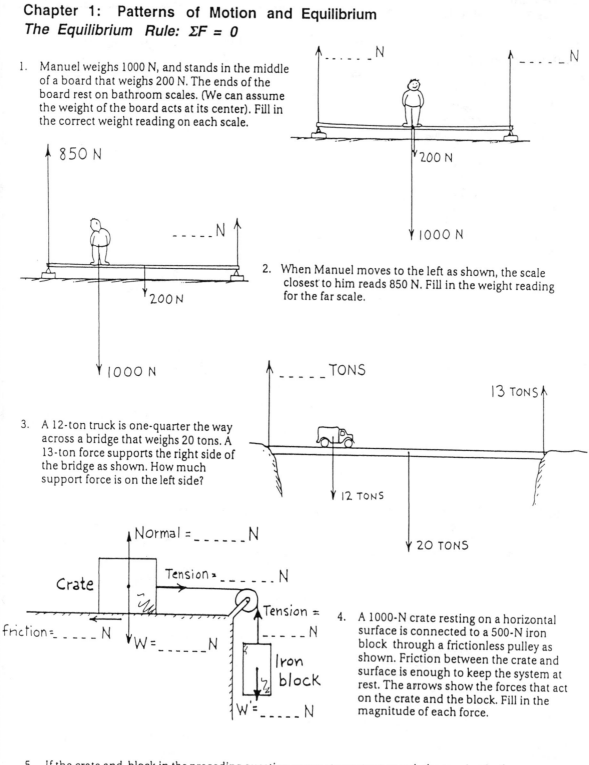

1. Manuel weighs 1000 N, and stands in the middle of a board that weighs 200 N. The ends of the board rest on bathroom scales. (We can assume the weight of the board acts at its center). Fill in the correct weight reading on each scale.

850 N

_ _ _ _ _ N

200 N

1000 N

_ _ _ _ _ N

_ _ _ _ _ N

200 N

1000 N

2. When Manuel moves to the left as shown, the scale closest to him reads 850 N. Fill in the weight reading for the far scale.

_ _ _ _ _ TONS

13 TONS

3. A 12-ton truck is one-quarter the way across a bridge that weighs 20 tons. A 13-ton force supports the right side of the bridge as shown. How much support force is on the left side?

12 TONS

20 TONS

Normal = _ _ _ _ _ _ N

Tension = _ _ _ _ _ _ N

Crate

Tension = _ _ _ _ _ N

friction = _ _ _ _ _ N

W = _ _ _ _ _ N

Iron block

W' = _ _ _ _ _ N

4. A 1000-N crate resting on a horizontal surface is connected to a 500-N iron block through a frictionless pulley as shown. Friction between the crate and surface is enough to keep the system at rest. The arrows show the forces that act on the crate and the block. Fill in the magnitude of each force.

5. If the crate and block in the preceding question move at constant speed, the tension in the rope (is the same) (increases) (decreases).

   The sliding system is then in (static equilibrium) (dynamic equilibrium).

CONCEPTUAL **Physical Science** PRACTICE SHEET

Chapter 1: Patterns of Motion and Equilibrium
Free Fall Speed

1. Aunt Minnie gives you $10 per second for 4 seconds. How much money do you have
   after 4 seconds? _____

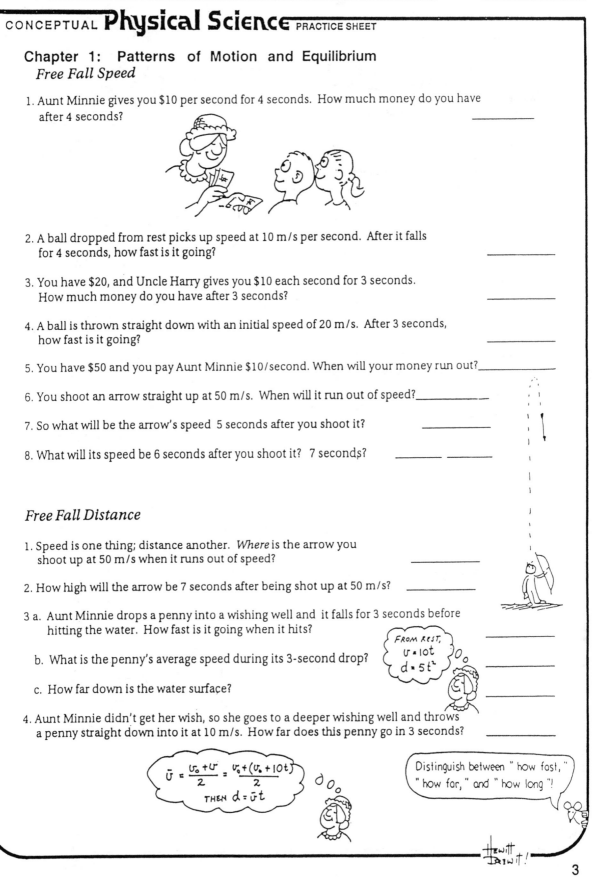

2. A ball dropped from rest picks up speed at 10 m/s per second. After it falls
   for 4 seconds, how fast is it going? _____

3. You have $20, and Uncle Harry gives you $10 each second for 3 seconds.
   How much money do you have after 3 seconds? _____

4. A ball is thrown straight down with an initial speed of 20 m/s. After 3 seconds,
   how fast is it going? _____

5. You have $50 and you pay Aunt Minnie $10/second. When will your money run out? _____

6. You shoot an arrow straight up at 50 m/s. When will it run out of speed? _____

7. So what will be the arrow's speed 5 seconds after you shoot it? _____

8. What will its speed be 6 seconds after you shoot it? 7 seconds? _____ _____

Free Fall Distance

1. Speed is one thing; distance another. *Where* is the arrow you
   shoot up at 50 m/s when it runs out of speed? _____

2. How high will the arrow be 7 seconds after being shot up at 50 m/s? _____

3 a. Aunt Minnie drops a penny into a wishing well and it falls for 3 seconds before
   hitting the water. How fast is it going when it hits? _____

   b. What is the penny's average speed during its 3-second drop? _____

   FROM REST,
   $v = 10t$
   $d = 5t^2$

   c. How far down is the water surface? _____

4. Aunt Minnie didn't get her wish, so she goes to a deeper wishing well and throws
   a penny straight down into it at 10 m/s. How far does this penny go in 3 seconds? _____

$$\bar{v} = \frac{v_0 + v}{2} = \frac{v_0 + (v_0 + 10t)}{2}$$
THEN $d = \bar{v}t$

Distinguish between " how fast, "
" how far, " and " how long "!

Hewitt
Drew it !

3

Acceleration of Free Fall

A rock dropped from the top of a cliff picks up speed as it falls. Pretend that a speedometer and odometer are attached to the rock to show readings of speed and distance at 1-second intervals. Both speed and distance are zero at time = zero (see sketch). Note that after falling 1 second the speed reading is 10 m/s and the distance fallen is 5 m. The readings for succeeding seconds of fall are not shown and are left for you to complete. So draw the position of the speedometer pointer and write in the correct odometer reading for each time. Use $g = 10$ m/s^2 and neglect air resistance.

> **YOU NEED TO KNOW:**
> Instantaneous speed of fall from rest:
> $$v = gt$$
> Distance fallen from rest:
> $$d = \frac{1}{2}gt^2$$

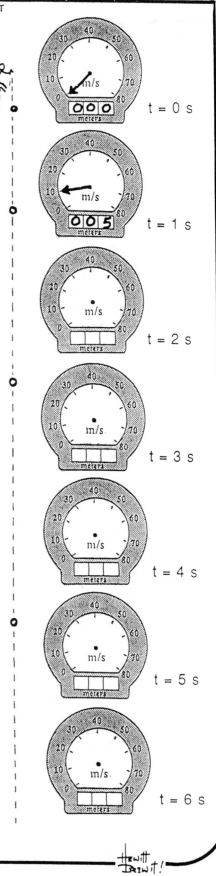

1. The speedometer reading increases by the same amount, _____ m/s, each second. This increase in speed per second is called

   _____.

2. The distance fallen increases as the square of the _____.

3. If it takes 7 seconds to reach the ground, then its speed at impact is _____ m/s, the total distance fallen is _____ m, and its acceleration of fall just before impact is _____ m/s^2.

4

Name _____ Date _____

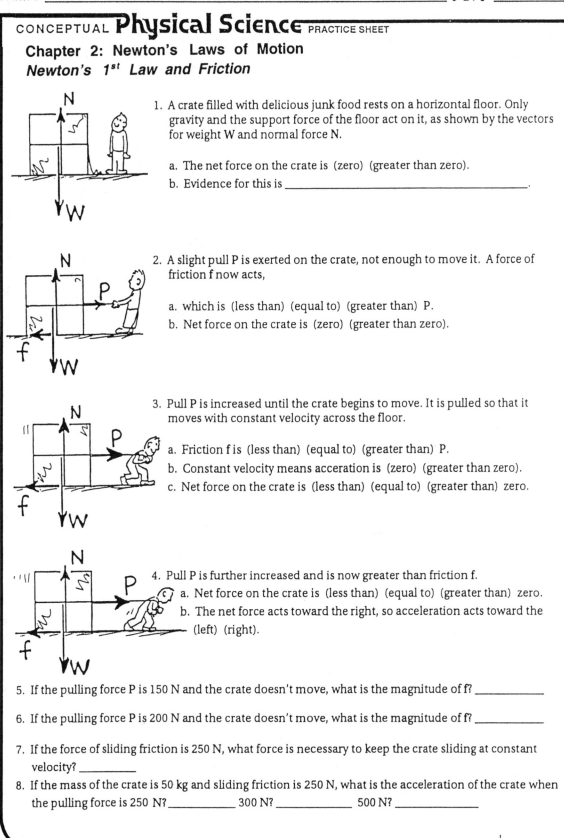

CONCEPTUAL **Physical Science** PRACTICE SHEET

Chapter 2: Newton's Laws of Motion
Newton's 1ˢᵗ Law and Friction

1. A crate filled with delicious junk food rests on a horizontal floor. Only gravity and the support force of the floor act on it, as shown by the vectors for weight W and normal force N.

   a. The net force on the crate is (zero) (greater than zero).
   b. Evidence for this is _____.

2. A slight pull P is exerted on the crate, not enough to move it. A force of friction f now acts,

   a. which is (less than) (equal to) (greater than) P.
   b. Net force on the crate is (zero) (greater than zero).

3. Pull P is increased until the crate begins to move. It is pulled so that it moves with constant velocity across the floor.

   a. Friction f is (less than) (equal to) (greater than) P.
   b. Constant velocity means acceration is (zero) (greater than zero).
   c. Net force on the crate is (less than) (equal to) (greater than) zero.

4. Pull P is further increased and is now greater than friction f.
   a. Net force on the crate is (less than) (equal to) (greater than) zero.
   b. The net force acts toward the right, so acceleration acts toward the (left) (right).

5. If the pulling force P is 150 N and the crate doesn't move, what is the magnitude of f? _____

6. If the pulling force P is 200 N and the crate doesn't move, what is the magnitude of f? _____

7. If the force of sliding friction is 250 N, what force is necessary to keep the crate sliding at constant velocity? _____

8. If the mass of the crate is 50 kg and sliding friction is 250 N, what is the acceleration of the crate when the pulling force is 250 N? _____ 300 N? _____ 500 N? _____

5

Non-Accelerated Motion

1. The sketch shows a ball rolling at constant velocity along a level floor. The ball rolls from the first position shown to the second in 1 second. The two positons are 1 meter apart. Sketch the ball at successive 1-second intervals all the way to the wall (neglect resistance).

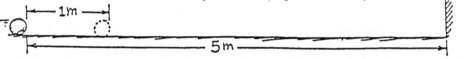

   a. Did you draw successive ball positions evenly spaced, farther apart, or closer together? Why?

   _____

   b. The ball reaches the wall with a speed of _____ m/s and takes a time of _____ seconds.

2. Table I shows data of sprinting speeds of some animals. Make whatever computations are necessary to complete the table.

   Table I

ANIMAL	DISTANCE	TIME	SPEED
CHEETAH	75 m	3 s	25 m/s
GREYHOUND	160 m	10 s	
GAZELLE	1 km		100 km/h
TURTLE		30 s	1 cm/s

Accelerated Motion

3. An object starting from rest gains a speed $v = at$ when it undergoes uniform acceleration. The distance it covers is $d = 1/2\ at^2$. Uniform acceleration occurs for a ball rolling down an inclined plane. The plane below is tilted so a ball picks up a speed of 2 m/s each second; then its acceleration $a = 2$ m/s². The positions of the ball are shown at 1-second intervals. Complete the six blank spaces for distance covered, and the four blank spaces for speeds.

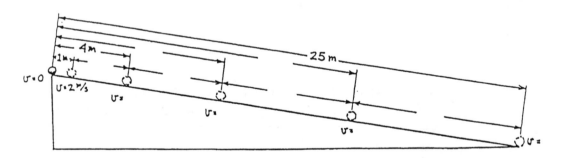

   a. Do you see that the total distance from the starting point increases as the square of the time? This was discovered by Galileo. If the incline were to continue, predict the ball's distance from the starting point for the next 3 seconds.

   _____

   b. Note the increase of distance between ball positions with time. Do you see an odd-integer pattern (also discovered by Galileo) for this increase? If the incline were to continue, predict the successive distances between ball positions for the next 3 seconds.

   _____

Name _____   Date _____

Chapter 2: Newton's Laws of Motion
A Day at the Races with Newton's Second Law: a = F/m

In each situation below, Cart A has a mass of **1 kg**. The mass of Cart B varies as indicated.
Circle the correct answer (A, B, or Same for both).

1. Cart A is pulled with a force of **1 N**. Cart B also has a mass of **1 kg** and is pulled with a force of **2 N**. Which undergoes the greater acceleration?

    A   B   Same for both

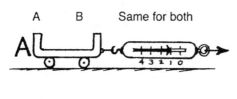

2. Cart A is pulled with a force of **1 N**. Cart B has a mass of **2 kg** and is also pulled with a force of **1 N**. Which undergoes the greater acceleration?

    A   B   Same for both

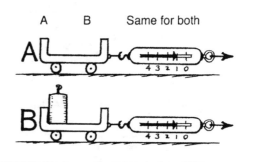

3. Cart A is pulled with a force of **1 N**. Cart B has a mass of **2 kg** and is pulled with a force of **2 N**. Which undergoes the greater acceleration?

    A   B   Same for both

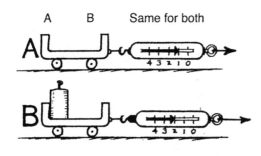

4. Cart A is pulled with a force of **1 N**. Cart B has a mass of **3 kg** and is pulled with a force of **3 N**. Which undergoes the greater acceleration?

    A   B   Same for both

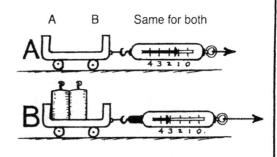

5. This time Cart A is pulled with a force of **4 N**. Cart B has a mass of **4 kg** and is pulled with a force of **4 N**. Which undergoes the greater acceleration?

    A   B   Same for both

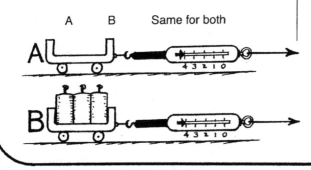

6. Cart A is pulled with a force of **2 N**. Cart B has a mass of **4 kg** and is pulled with a force of **3 N**. Which undergoes the greater acceleration?

    A   B   Same for both

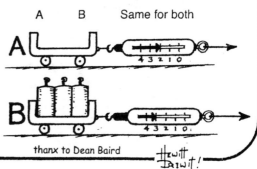

thanx to Dean Baird

Name _____ Date _____

Chapter 2: Newton's Laws of Motion
Dropping Masses and Accelerating Cart

1. Consider the simple case of a 1-kg cart being pulled by a 10-N applied force. According to Newton's 2nd law, acceleration of the cart is

$$a = \frac{F}{m} = \frac{10\,N}{1\,kg} = 10\,m/s^2$$

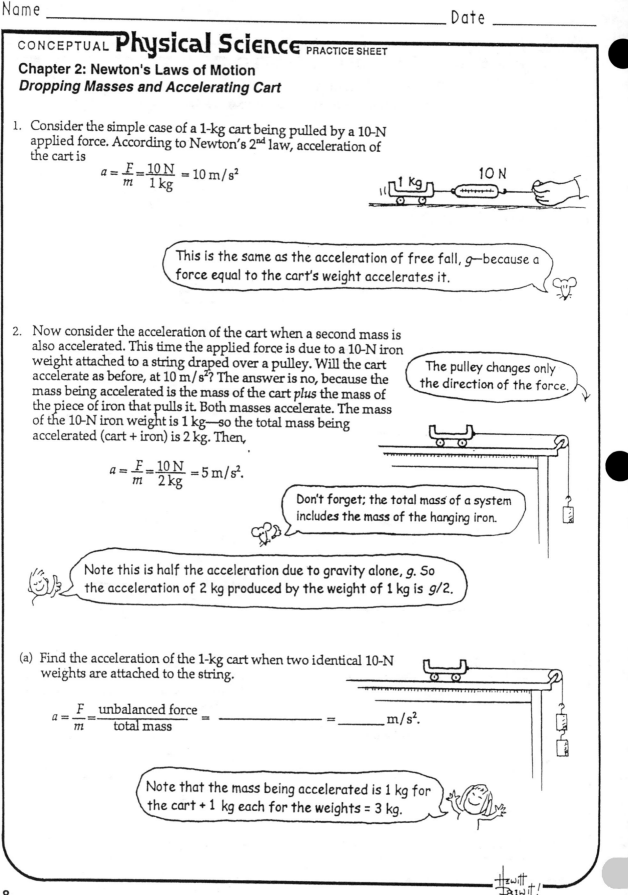

This is the same as the acceleration of free fall, *g*—because a force equal to the cart's weight accelerates it.

2. Now consider the acceleration of the cart when a second mass is also accelerated. This time the applied force is due to a 10-N iron weight attached to a string draped over a pulley. Will the cart accelerate as before, at 10 m/s²? The answer is no, because the mass being accelerated is the mass of the cart *plus* the mass of the piece of iron that pulls it. Both masses accelerate. The mass of the 10-N iron weight is 1 kg—so the total mass being accelerated (cart + iron) is 2 kg. Then,

The pulley changes only the direction of the force.

$$a = \frac{F}{m} = \frac{10\,N}{2\,kg} = 5\,m/s^2.$$

Don't forget; the total mass of a system includes the mass of the hanging iron.

Note this is half the acceleration due to gravity alone, *g*. So the acceleration of 2 kg produced by the weight of 1 kg is *g*/2.

(a) Find the acceleration of the 1-kg cart when two identical 10-N weights are attached to the string.

$$a = \frac{F}{m} = \frac{unbalanced\ force}{total\ mass} = \underline{\hspace{2cm}} = \underline{\hspace{1cm}} m/s^2.$$

Note that the mass being accelerated is 1 kg for the cart + 1 kg each for the weights = 3 kg.

8

Chapter 2: Newton's Laws of Motion
Dropping Masses and Accelerating Cart—continued

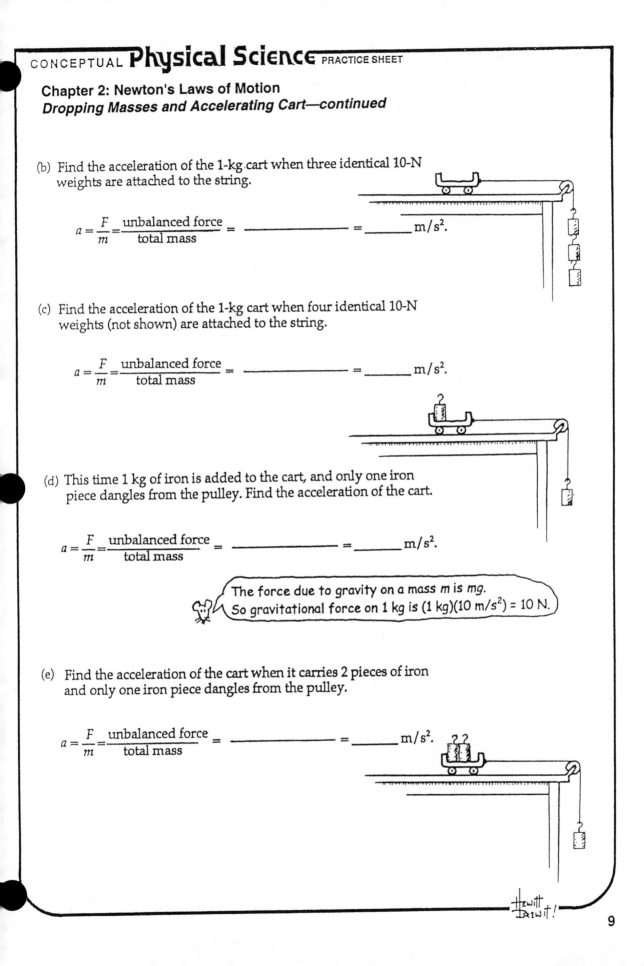

(b) Find the acceleration of the 1-kg cart when three identical 10-N weights are attached to the string.

$$a = \frac{F}{m} = \frac{\text{unbalanced force}}{\text{total mass}} = \underline{\hspace{3cm}} = \underline{\hspace{2cm}} \text{ m/s}^2.$$

(c) Find the acceleration of the 1-kg cart when four identical 10-N weights (not shown) are attached to the string.

$$a = \frac{F}{m} = \frac{\text{unbalanced force}}{\text{total mass}} = \underline{\hspace{3cm}} = \underline{\hspace{2cm}} \text{ m/s}^2.$$

(d) This time 1 kg of iron is added to the cart, and only one iron piece dangles from the pulley. Find the acceleration of the cart.

$$a = \frac{F}{m} = \frac{\text{unbalanced force}}{\text{total mass}} = \underline{\hspace{3cm}} = \underline{\hspace{2cm}} \text{ m/s}^2.$$

The force due to gravity on a mass *m* is *mg*.
So gravitational force on 1 kg is (1 kg)(10 m/s^2) = 10 N.

(e) Find the acceleration of the cart when it carries 2 pieces of iron and only one iron piece dangles from the pulley.

$$a = \frac{F}{m} = \frac{\text{unbalanced force}}{\text{total mass}} = \underline{\hspace{3cm}} = \underline{\hspace{2cm}} \text{ m/s}^2.$$

Chapter 2: Newton's Laws of Motion
Dropping Masses and Accelerating Cart—continued

(f) Find the acceleration of the cart when it carries 3 pieces of iron
and only one iron piece dangles from the pulley.

$$a = \frac{F}{m} = \frac{\text{unbalanced force}}{\text{total mass}} = \underline{\hspace{3cm}} = \underline{\hspace{2cm}} \text{ m/s}^2.$$

(g) Find the acceleration of the cart when it carries 3 pieces of iron
and 4 iron pieces dangle from the pulley.

$$a = \frac{F}{m} = \frac{\text{unbalanced force}}{\text{total mass}} = \underline{\hspace{3cm}} = \underline{\hspace{2cm}} \text{ m/s}^2.$$

How does this compare with the acceleration of (2) above, and why?

Mass of cart is 1 kg. Mass of 10-N iron is also 1 kg.

(h) Draw your own combination of masses and find the acceleration.

$$a = \frac{F}{m} = \frac{\text{unbalanced force}}{\text{total mass}} = \underline{\hspace{3cm}} = \underline{\hspace{2cm}} \text{ m/s}^2.$$

CONCEPTUAL **Physical Science** PRACTICE SHEET

Chapter 2: Newton's Laws
Bronco and Newton's Second Law

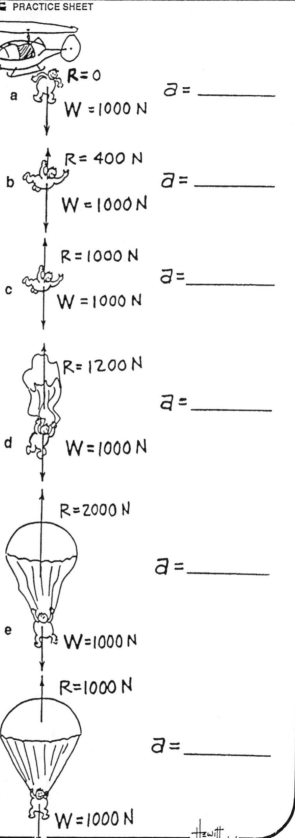

Bronco skydives and parachutes from a stationary helicopter. Various stages of fall are shown in positions *a* through *f*. Using Newton's 2nd law,

$$a = \frac{F_{NET}}{m} = \frac{W-R}{m}$$

find Bronco's acceleration at each position (answer in the blanks to the right). You need to know that Bronco's mass *m* is 100 kg so his weight is a constant 1000 N. Air resistance *R* varies with speed and cross-sectional area as shown.

Circle the correct answers.

1. When Bronco's speed is least, his acceleration is

    (least) (most).

2. In which position(s) does Bronco experience a downward acceleration?

    (a) (b) (c) (d) (e) (f)

3. In which position(s) does Bronco experience an upward acceleration?

    (a) (b) (c) (d) (e) (f)

4. When Bronco experiences an upward acceleration, his velocity is

    (still downward) (upward also).

5. In which position(s) is Bronco's velocity constant?

    (a) (b) (c) (d) (e) (f)

6. In which position(s) does Bronco experience terminal velocity?

    (a) (b) (c) (d) (e) (f)

7. In which position(s) is terminal velocity greatest?

    (a) (b) (c) (d) (e) (f)

8. If Bronco were heavier, his terminal velocity would be

    (greater) (less) (the same).

a R = 0
W = 1000 N
$a =$ _____

b R = 400 N
W = 1000 N
$a =$ _____

c R = 1000 N
W = 1000 N
$a =$ _____

d R = 1200 N
W = 1000 N
$a =$ _____

R = 2000 N
$a =$ _____

e W = 1000 N

R = 1000 N

f W = 1000 N
$a =$ _____

CONCEPTUAL **Physical Science** PRACTICE SHEET

Chapter 2: Newton's Laws of Motion
Newton's Third Law

Your thumb and finger pull on each other when you stretch a rubber band between them. This pair of forces, thumb on finger and finger on thumb, make up an action-reaction pair of forces, both of which are equal in magnitude and oppositely directed. Draw the reaction vector and state in words the reaction force for each of the examples **a** through **g**. Then make up your own example in **h**.

Thumb pulls finger

Finger pulls thumb

Foot hits ball

a _____

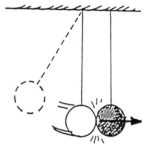

White ball strikes black ball

b _____

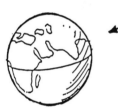

Earth pulls on moon

c _____

Tires push backward on road

d _____

Wings push air downward

e _____

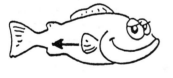

Fish pushes water backward

f _____

Helen touches Hyrum

g _____

h _____

_____

YOU CAN'T TOUCH
WITHOUT BEING TOUCHED—
NEWTON'S THIRD LAW

Nellie and Newton's Third Law

Nellie Newton holds an apple weighing 1 newton at rest on the palm of her hand. *Circle the correct answers:*

1. To say the weight (W) of the apple is 1 N is to say that a downward gravitational force of 1 N is exerted on the apple by

   (the Earth)   (her hand).

2. Nellie's hand supports the apple with normal force N, which acts in a direction opposite to W. We can say N

   (equals W)   (has the same magnitude as W).

3. Since the apple is at rest, the net force on the apple is

   (zero)   (nonzero).

4. Since N is equal and opposite to W, we   (can)   (cannot)

   say that N and W comprise an action-reaction pair. The reason is because action and reaction

   (act on the same object)   (act on different objects),   and here we see N and W

   (both acting on the apple)   (acting on different objects).

5. In accord with the rule, "If ACTION is A acting on B, then REACTION is B acting on A,"
   if we say action is the Earth pulling down on the apple, reaction is

   (the apple pulling up on the Earth)   (N, Nellie's hand pushing up on the apple).

6. To repeat for emphasis, we see that N and W are equal and opposite to each other

   (and comprise an action-reaction pair)   (but do *not* comprise an action-reaction pair).

> To identify a pair of action-reaction forces in any situation, first identify the pair of interacting objects involved. Something is interacting with something else. In this case the whole Earth is interacting (gravitationally) with the apple. So the Earth pulls downward on the apple (call it action), while the apple pulls upward on the Earth (reaction).

> Simply put, Earth pulls on apple (action); apple pulls on Earth (reaction).

> Better put, apple and Earth *pull on each other* with equal and opposite forces that comprise a *single* interaction.

7. Another pair of forces is N [shown] and the downward force of the apple against Nellie's

   hand [not shown]. This pair of forces   (is)   (isn't)   an action-reaction pair.

8. Suppose Nellie now pushes upward on the apple with a force of 2 N. The apple

   (is still in equilibrium)   (accelerates upward),   and compared with W, the magnitude of N is

   (the same)   (twice)   (not the same, and not twice).

9. Once the apple leaves Nellie's hand, N is   (zero)   (still twice the magnitude of W),

   and the net force on the apple is   (zero)   (only W)   (still W - N, which is a negative force).

Name _____ Date _____

Chapter 2: Newton's Laws of Motion
Vectors and the Parallelogram Rule

1. When vectors A and B are at an angle to each other, they add to produce the resultant C by the *parallelogram rule*. Note that C is the diagonal of a parallelogram where A and B are adjacent sides. Resultant C is shown in the first two diagrams, *a* and *b*. Construct the resultant C in diagrams *c* and *d*. Note that in diagram *d* you form a rectangle (a special case of a parallelogram).

a   b   c   d

2. Below we see a top view of an airplane being blown offcourse by wind in various directions. Use the parallelogram rule to show the resulting speed and direction of travel for each case. In which case does the airplane travel fastest across the ground? _____ Slowest? _____

a   wind   b   wind   c   wind   d   wind

3. To the right we see top views of 3 motorboats crossing a river. All have the same speed relative to the water, and all experience the same water flow.

Construct resultant vectors showing the speed and direction of the boats.

a. Which boat takes the shortest path to the opposite shore?_____

b. Which boat reaches the opposite shore first? _____

c. Which boat provides the fastest ride? _____

a

b

c

Hewitt
Drew it!

15

Vectors

Use the parallelogram rule to carefully construct the resultants for the eight pairs of vectors.

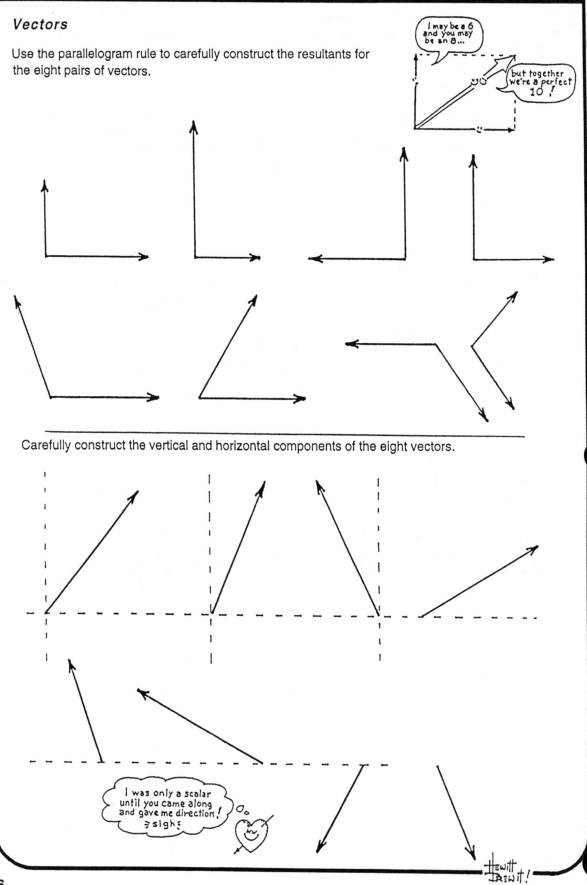

Carefully construct the vertical and horizontal components of the eight vectors.

CONCEPTUAL **Physical Science** PRACTICE SHEET

Chapter 2: Newton's Laws of Motion
Force Vectors and the Parallelogram Rule

1. The heavy ball is supported in each case by two strands of rope. The tension in each strand is shown by the vectors. Use the parallelogram rule to find the resultant of each vector pair.

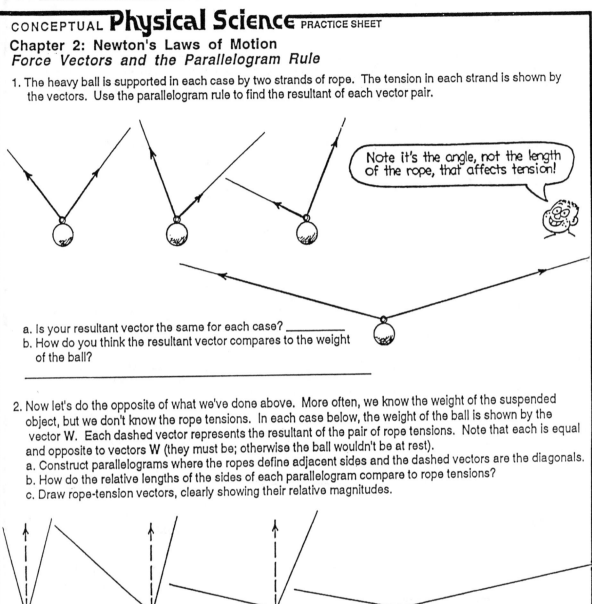

Note it's the angle, not the length of the rope, that affects tension!

    a. Is your resultant vector the same for each case? _____
    b. How do you think the resultant vector compares to the weight of the ball?

_____

2. Now let's do the opposite of what we've done above. More often, we know the weight of the suspended object, but we don't know the rope tensions. In each case below, the weight of the ball is shown by the vector **W**. Each dashed vector represents the resultant of the pair of rope tensions. Note that each is equal and opposite to vectors **W** (they must be; otherwise the ball wouldn't be at rest).
    a. Construct parallelograms where the ropes define adjacent sides and the dashed vectors are the diagonals.
    b. How do the relative lengths of the sides of each parallelogram compare to rope tensions?
    c. Draw rope-tension vectors, clearly showing their relative magnitudes.

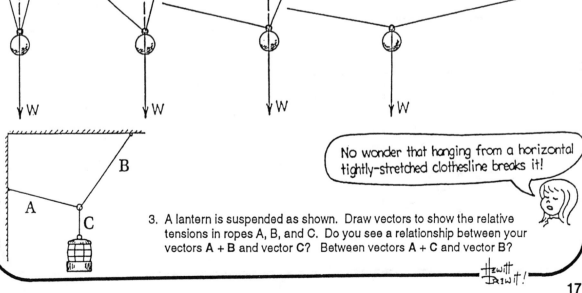

No wonder that hanging from a horizontal tightly-stretched clothesline breaks it!

3. A lantern is suspended as shown. Draw vectors to show the relative tensions in ropes A, B, and C. Do you see a relationship between your vectors A + B and vector C? Between vectors A + C and vector B?

Hewitt
Drawit!

Force-Vector Diagrams

In each case, a rock is acted on by one or more forces. Draw an accurate vector diagram showing all forces acting on the rock, and no other forces. Use a ruler, and do it in pencil so you can correct mistakes. The first two are done as examples. Show by the parallelogram rule in 2 that the vector sum of **A** + **B** is equal and opposite to **W** (that is, **A** + **B** = -**W**). Do the same for 3 and 4. Draw and label vectors for the weight and normal forces in 5 to 10, and for the appropriate forces in 11 and 12.

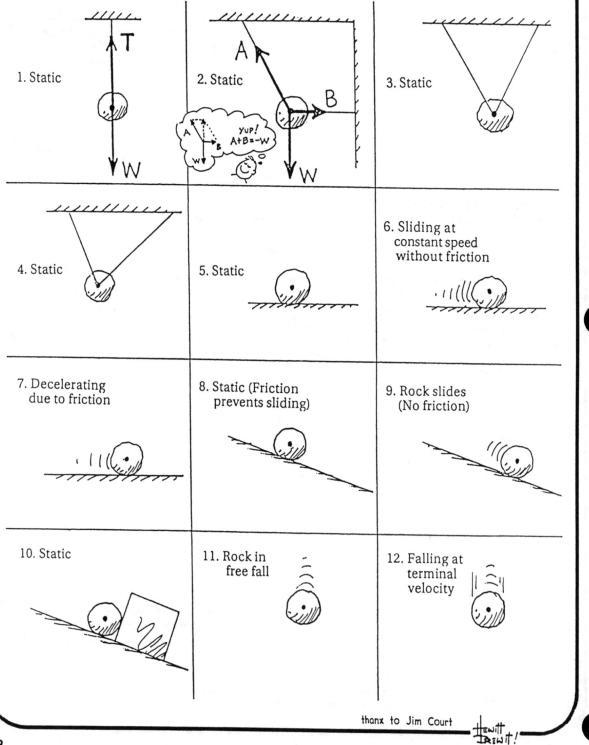

1. Static

2. Static

3. Static

4. Static

5. Static

6. Sliding at constant speed without friction

7. Decelerating due to friction

8. Static (Friction prevents sliding)

9. Rock slides (No friction)

10. Static

11. Rock in free fall

12. Falling at terminal velocity

thanx to Jim Court

CONCEPTUAL **Physical Science** PRACTICE SHEET

Chapter 3: Momentum and Energy
Momentum

1. A moving car has momentum. If it moves twice as fast, its momentum
   is _____ as much.

2. Two cars, one twice as heavy as the other, move down a hill at the same speed. Compared to the
   lighter car, the momentum of the heavier car is _____ as much.

3. The recoil momentum of a gun that kicks is
   (more than) (less than) (the same as)
   the momentum of the gases and bullet it fires.

4. If a man firmly holds a gun when fired, then the momentum of the
   bullet and expelled gases is equal to the recoil momentum of the
   (gun alone) (gun-man system) (man alone).

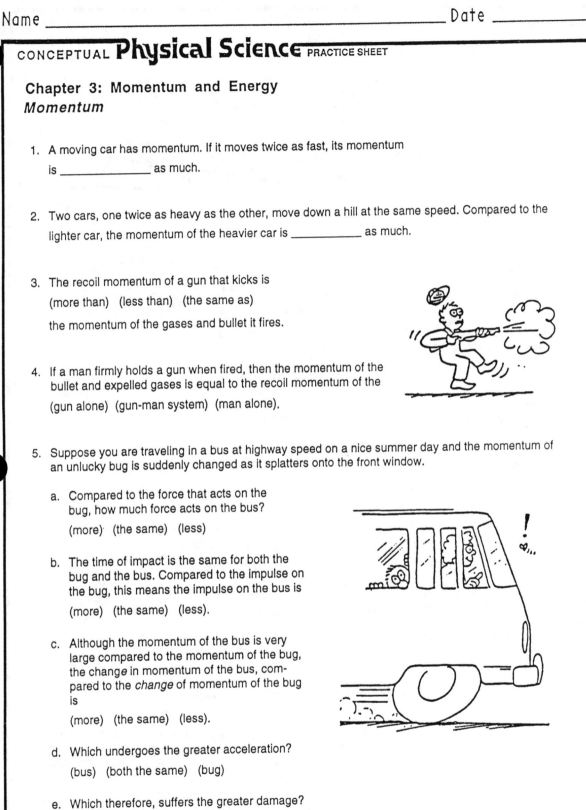

5. Suppose you are traveling in a bus at highway speed on a nice summer day and the momentum of
   an unlucky bug is suddenly changed as it splatters onto the front window.

   a. Compared to the force that acts on the
      bug, how much force acts on the bus?
      (more) (the same) (less)

   b. The time of impact is the same for both the
      bug and the bus. Compared to the impulse on
      the bug, this means the impulse on the bus is
      (more) (the same) (less).

   c. Although the momentum of the bus is very
      large compared to the momentum of the bug,
      the change in momentum of the bus, com-
      pared to the *change* of momentum of the bug
      is
      (more) (the same) (less).

   d. Which undergoes the greater acceleration?
      (bus) (both the same) (bug)

   e. Which therefore, suffers the greater damage?
      (bus) (both the same) (the bug of course!)

Systems

Momentum conservation (and Newton's 3rd law) apply to *systems* of bodies. Here we identify some systems.

1. When the compressed spring is released, Blocks A and B will slide apart. There are 3 systems to consider here, indicated by the closed dashed lines below — System A, System B, and System A+B. Ignore the vertical forces of gravity and the support force of the table.

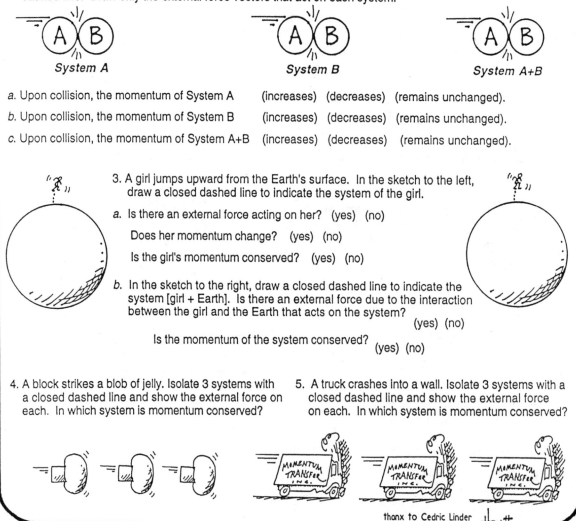

a. Does an external force act on System A?   (yes) (no)

   Will the momentum of System A change?   (yes) (no)

b. Does an external force act on System B?   (yes) (no)

   Will the momentum of System B change?   (yes) (no)

c. Does an external force act on System A+B?   (yes) (no)

   Will the momentum of System A+B change?   (yes) (no)

2. Billiard ball A collides with billiard ball B at rest. Isolate each system with a closed dashed line. Draw only the external force vectors that act on each system.

      System A   System B   System A+B

a. Upon collision, the momentum of System A   (increases) (decreases) (remains unchanged).

b. Upon collision, the momentum of System B   (increases) (decreases) (remains unchanged).

c. Upon collision, the momentum of System A+B (increases) (decreases) (remains unchanged).

3. A girl jumps upward from the Earth's surface. In the sketch to the left, draw a closed dashed line to indicate the system of the girl.

a. Is there an external force acting on her? (yes) (no)

   Does her momentum change? (yes) (no)

   Is the girl's momentum conserved? (yes) (no)

b. In the sketch to the right, draw a closed dashed line to indicate the system [girl + Earth]. Is there an external force due to the interaction between the girl and the Earth that acts on the system?

                      (yes) (no)

   Is the momentum of the system conserved?

                      (yes) (no)

4. A block strikes a blob of jelly. Isolate 3 systems with a closed dashed line and show the external force on each. In which system is momentum conserved?

5. A truck crashes into a wall. Isolate 3 systems with a closed dashed line and show the external force on each. In which system is momentum conserved?

thanx to Cedric Linder

CONCEPTUAL **Physical Science** PRACTICE SHEET

Chapter 3: Momentum and Energy
Impulse—Momentum

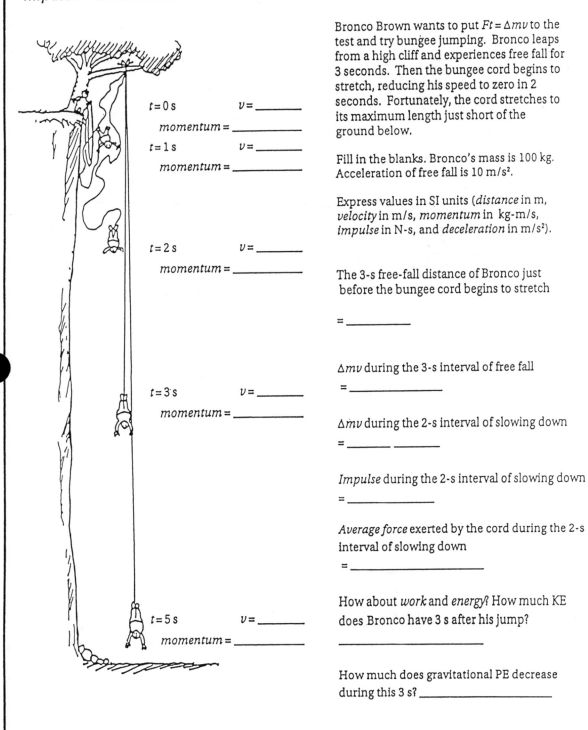

$t = 0$ s $v =$ _____
momentum = _____

$t = 1$ s $v =$ _____
momentum = _____

$t = 2$ s $v =$ _____
momentum = _____

$t = 3$ s $v =$ _____
momentum = _____

$t = 5$ s $v =$ _____
momentum = _____

Bronco Brown wants to put $Ft = \Delta mv$ to the test and try bungee jumping. Bronco leaps from a high cliff and experiences free fall for 3 seconds. Then the bungee cord begins to stretch, reducing his speed to zero in 2 seconds. Fortunately, the cord stretches to its maximum length just short of the ground below.

Fill in the blanks. Bronco's mass is 100 kg. Acceleration of free fall is 10 m/s².

Express values in SI units (*distance* in m, *velocity* in m/s, *momentum* in kg-m/s, *impulse* in N-s, and *deceleration* in m/s²).

The 3-s free-fall distance of Bronco just before the bungee cord begins to stretch

= _____

Δmv during the 3-s interval of free fall

= _____

Δmv during the 2-s interval of slowing down

= _____ _____

Impulse during the 2-s interval of slowing down

= _____

Average force exerted by the cord during the 2-s interval of slowing down

= _____

How about *work* and *energy*? How much KE does Bronco have 3 s after his jump?

_____

How much does gravitational PE decrease during this 3 s? _____

What two kinds of PE are changing during the slowing-down interval?

_____

Conservation of Momentum

Granny whizzes around the rink and is suddenly confronted with Ambrose at rest directly in her path. Rather than knock him over, she picks him up and continues in motion without "braking."

Consider both Granny and Ambrose as two parts of one system. Since no outside forces act on the system, the momentum of the system before collision equals the momentum of the system after collision.

a. Complete the before-collision data in the table below.

BEFORE COLLISION

Granny's mass	80 kg
Granny's speed	3 m/s
Granny's momentum	_____
Ambrose's mass	40 kg
Ambrose's speed	0 m/s
Ambrose's momentum	_____
Total momentum	_____

b. After collision, does Granny's speed increase or decrease?

_____

c. After collision, does Ambrose's speed increase or decrease?

_____

d. After collision, what is the total mass of Granny + Ambrose?

_____

e. After collision, what is the total momentum of Granny + Ambrose?

_____

f. Use the conservation of momentum law to find the speed of Granny and Ambrose together after collision.
(Show your work in the space below.)

New speed = _____

Name _____ Date _____

CONCEPTUAL **Physical Science** PRACTICE SHEET

Chapter 3: Momentum and Energy
Work and Energy

1. How much work (energy) is needed to lift an object that weighs 200 N to a height of 4 m?

_____

2. How much power is needed to lift the 200-N object to a height of 4 m in 4 s?

_____

3. What is the power output of an engine that does 60 000 J of work in 10 s?

_____

4. The block of ice weighs 500 newtons.

   a. Neglecting friction, how much force is needed to push it up the incline?

   _____

   b. How much work is required to push it up the incline compared with lifting the block vertically 3?

   _____

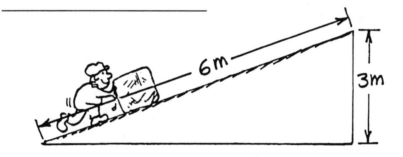

5. All the ramps are 5 m high. We know that the KE of the block at the bottom of the ramp will be equal to the loss of PE (conservation of energy). Find the speed of the block at ground level in each case. [Hint: Do you recall from earlier chapters how long it takes something to fall a vertical distance of 5 m from a positon of rest (assume g = 10 m/s²)? And how much speed a falling object acquires in this time? This gives you the answer to Case 1. Discuss with your classmates how energy conservation gives you the answers to Cases 2 and 3.]

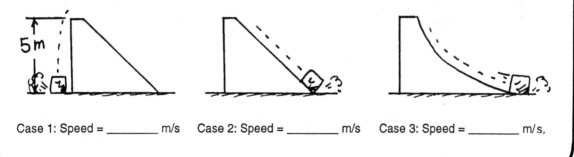

Case 1: Speed = _____ m/s   Case 2: Speed = _____ m/s   Case 3: Speed = _____ m/s,

6. Which block gets to the bottom of the incline first?
   Assume no friction. (Be careful!) Explain your answer.

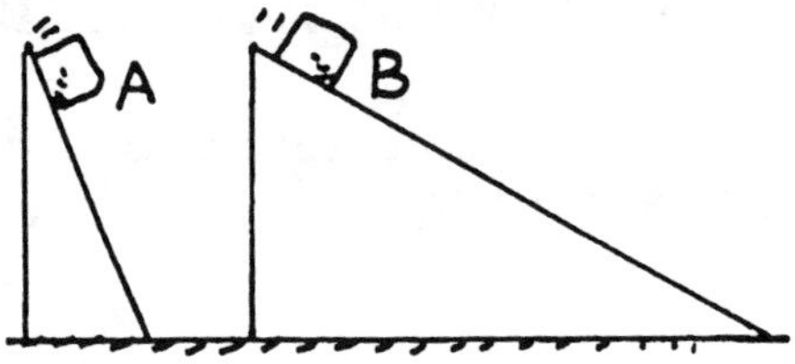

   _____

   _____

   _____

7. The KE and PE of a block freely sliding down a ramp are shown in only one place in the sketch.
   Fill in the missing values.

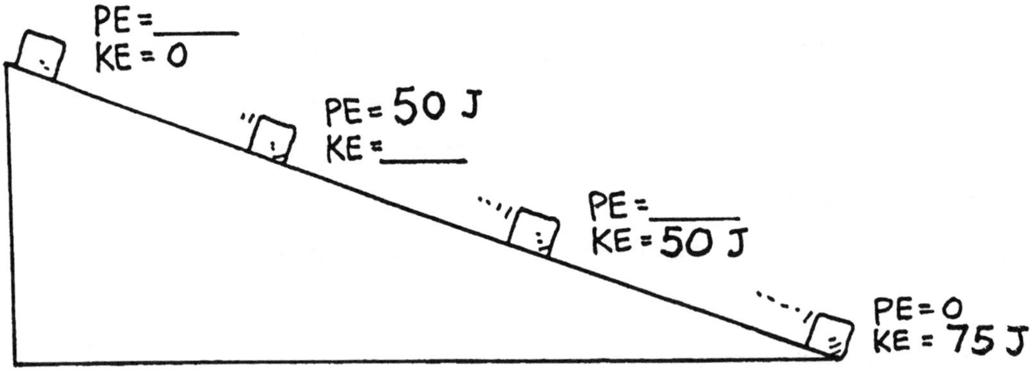

PE = _____
KE = 0

PE = 50 J
KE = _____

PE = _____
KE = 50 J

PE = 0
KE = 75 J

8. A big metal bead slides due to gravity
   along an upright friction-free wire. It
   starts from rest at the top of the wire
   as shown in the sketch. How fast is it
   traveling as it passes

   Point B?_____

   Point D?_____

   Point E?_____

   At what point does it have the

   maximum speed?_____

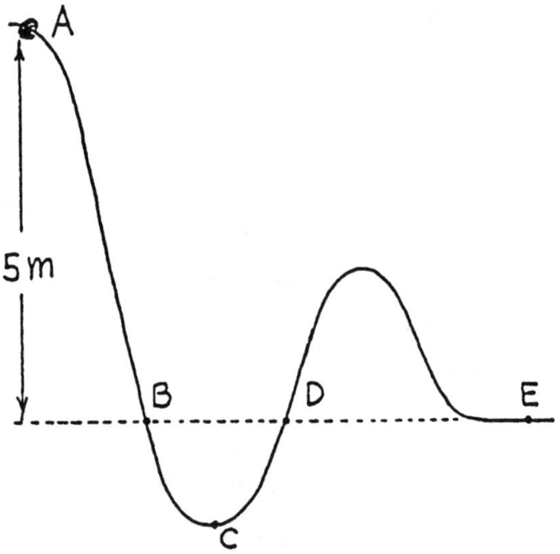

A

5 m

B   D   E

C

9. Rows of wind-powered generators are used in various
   windy locations to generate electric power. Does the power
   generated affect the speed of the wind? Would locations
   behind the 'windmills' be windier if they weren't there?
   Discuss this in terms of energy conservation with your
   classmates.

   _____

   _____

   _____

   _____

CONCEPTUAL Physical Science PRACTICE SHEET

Chapter 3: Momentum and Energy
Conservation of Energy

Fill in the blanks for the six systems shown.

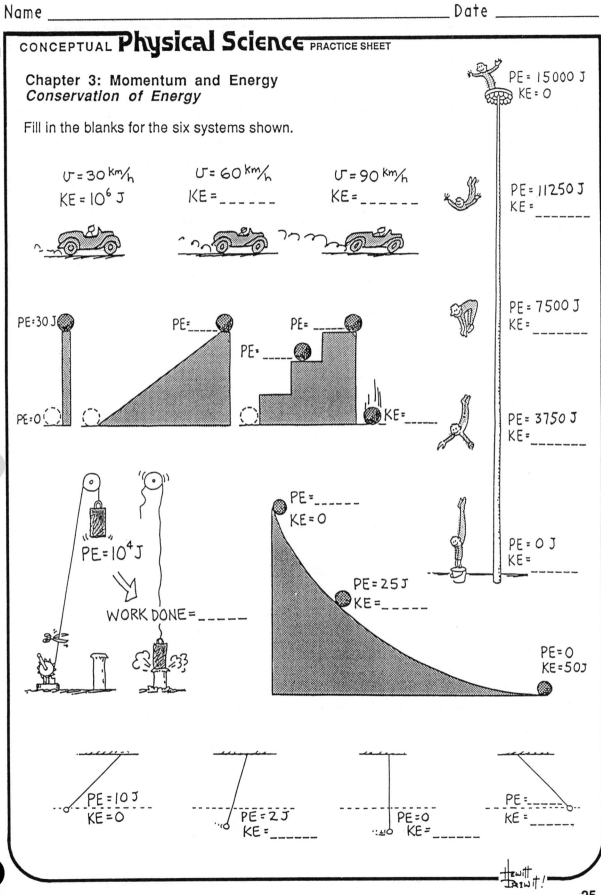

$v = 30 \frac{km}{h}$
$KE = 10^6 J$

$v = 60 \frac{km}{h}$
$KE = _____$

$v = 90 \frac{km}{h}$
$KE = _____$

PE = 15000 J
KE = 0

PE = 11250 J
KE = _____

PE = 7500 J
KE = _____

PE = 3750 J
KE = _____

PE = 0 J
KE = _____

PE = 30 J

PE = 0

PE = _____

PE = _____

PE = _____

KE = _____

$PE = 10^4 J$

WORK DONE = _____

PE = _____
KE = 0

PE = 25 J
KE = _____

PE = 0
KE = 50 J

PE = 10 J
KE = 0

PE = 2 J
KE = _____

PE = 0
KE = _____

PE = _____
KE = _____

Energy and Momentum

A Honda Civic and a Lincoln Town Car are initially at rest on a horizontal parking lot at the edge of a steep cliff. For simplicity, we assume that the Town Car has twice as much mass as the Civic. Equal constant forces are applied to each car and they accelerate across equal distances (we ignore the effects of friction). When they reach the far end of the lot the force is suddenly removed, whereupon they sail through the air and crash to the ground below. (The cars are beat up to begin with, and this is a scientific experiment!)

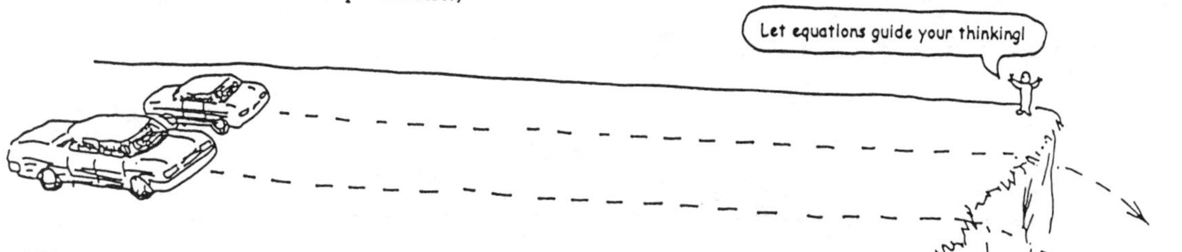

Let equations guide your thinking!

1. Which car has the greater acceleration ? (Think $a = F/m$)

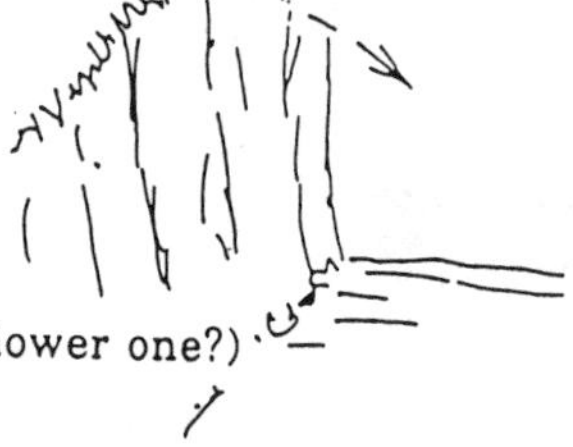

   _____

2. Which car spends more time along the surface of the lot? (The faster or slower one?)

   _____

3. Which car has the larger impulse imparted to it by the applied force? (Think Impulse = Ft)

   Defend your answer.

   _____

4. Which car has the greater momentum at the cliff's edge? (Think $Ft = \Delta mv$) Defend your answer.

   _____

   Impulse = Δ momentum
   $Ft = \Delta mv$

5. Which car has the greater work done on it by the applied force? (Think $W = Fd$)
   Defend your answer in terms of the distance traveled.

   Work = Fd = ΔKE = $\Delta \frac{1}{2}mv^2$

   _____

6. Which car has the greater kinetic energy at the edge of the cliff? (Think $W = \Delta KE$)
   Does your answer follow from your explanation of 5?
   Does it contradict your answer to 3? Why or why not?

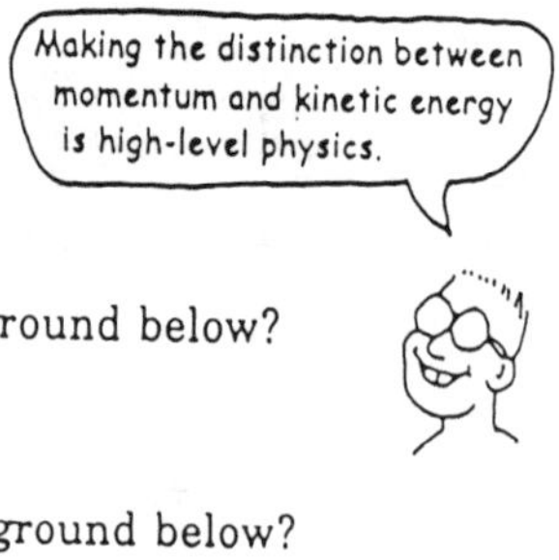

   Making the distinction between momentum and kinetic energy is high-level physics.

   _____

7. Which car spends more time in the air, from the edge of the cliff to the ground below?

   _____

8. Which car lands farthest horizontally from the edge of the cliff onto the ground below?

   _____

   Challenge: Suppose the slower car crashes a horizontal distance of 10 m from the ledge. Then at what horizontal distance does the faster car hit?

CONCEPTUAL **Physical Science** PRACTICE SHEET

Chapter 4: Newton's Law of Universal Gravitation
The Inverse-Square Law — Weight

1. Paint spray travels radially away from the nozzle of the can in straight lines. Like gravity, the strength (intensity) of the spray obeys an inverse-square law. Complete the diagram by filling in the blank spaces.

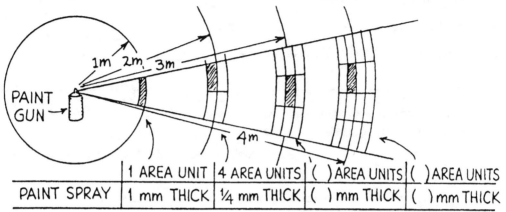

	1 AREA UNIT	4 AREA UNITS	( ) AREA UNITS	( ) AREA UNITS
PAINT SPRAY	1 mm THICK	¼ mm THICK	( ) mm THICK	( ) mm THICK

2. A small light source located 1 m in front of an opening of area 1 m² illuminates a wall behind. If the wall is 1 m behind the opening (2 m from the light source), the illuminated area covers 4 m². How many square meters will be illuminated if the wall is

   5 m from the source?_____

   10 m from the source? _____

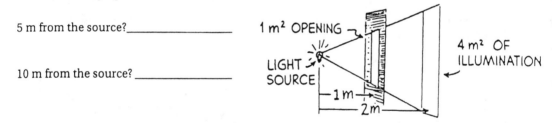

1 m² OPENING

LIGHT SOURCE

4 m² OF ILLUMINATION

1m

2m

3. If we stand on a weighing scale and find that we are pulled toward the earth with a force of 500 N,

   then we weigh _____ N. Strictly speaking, we weigh _____ N relative to the earth. How much does the earth weigh? If we tip the scale upside down and repeat the weighing process, we can say

   that we and the earth are still pulled together with a force of _____ N, and therefore, relative to us, the whole 6 000 000 000 000 000 000 000 000-kg earth weighs _____ N! Weight, unlike mass, is a relative quantity.

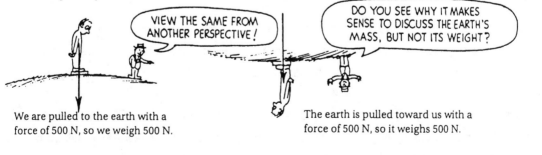

VIEW THE SAME FROM ANOTHER PERSPECTIVE!

DO YOU SEE WHY IT MAKES SENSE TO DISCUSS THE EARTH'S MASS, BUT NOT ITS WEIGHT?

We are pulled to the earth with a force of 500 N, so we weigh 500 N.

The earth is pulled toward us with a force of 500 N, so it weighs 500 N.

Chapter 4: Newton's Law of Universal Gravitation
Ocean Tides

1. Consider two equal-mass blobs of water, A and B, initially at rest in the Moon's gravitational field. The vector shows the gravitational force of the Moon on A.

   a. Draw a force vector on B due to the Moon's gravity.

   b. Is the force on B more or less than the force on A? _____

   c. Why?_____

   d. The blobs accelerate toward the Moon. Which has the greater acceleration? (A) (B)

   e. Because of the different accelerations, with time

   (A gets farther ahead of B) (A and B gain identical speeds) and the distance between A and B

   (increases) (stays the same) (decreases).

   f. If A and B were connected by a rubber band, with time the rubber band would

   (stretch) (not stretch).

   g. This (stretching) (non-stretching) is due to the (difference) (non-difference) in the Moon's gravitational pulls.

   h. The two blobs will eventually crash into the Moon. To orbit around the Moon instead of crashing into it, the blobs should move

   (away from the Moon) (tangentially). Then their accelerations will consist of changes in

   (speed) (direction).

2. Now consider the same two blobs located on opposite sides of the Earth.

   a. Because of differences in the Moon's pull on the blobs, they tend to

   (spread away from each other) (approach each other).

   b. Does this spreading produce ocean tides? (Yes) (No)

   c. If Earth and Moon were closer, gravitational force between them would be

   (more) (the same) (less), and the difference in gravitational forces on the near and far parts

   of the ocean would be (more) (the same) (less).

   d. Because the Earth's orbit about the Sun is slightly elliptical, Earth and Sun are closer in December

   than in June. Taking the Sun's tidal force into account, on a world average, ocean tides are greater in

   (December) (June) (no difference).

CONCEPTUAL **Physical Science** PRACTICE SHEET

Chapter 5: Projectile and Satellite Motion
Projectile Motion

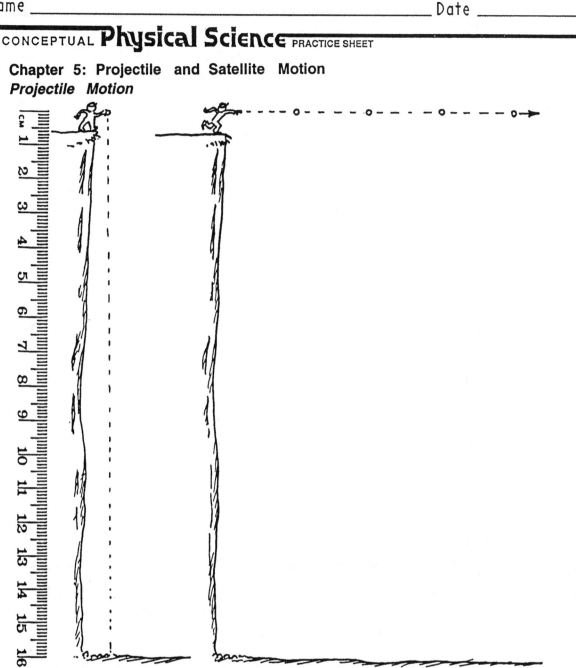

1. Above left: Use the scale 1 cm: 5 m and draw the positions of the dropped ball at 1-second intervals. Neglect air drag and assume $g = 10$ m/s². Estimate the number of seconds the ball is in the air.

   _____ seconds.

2. Above right: The four positions of the thrown ball with *no gravity* are at 1-second intervals. At 1 cm: 5 m, carefully draw the positions of the ball *with* gravity. Neglect air drag and assume $g = 10$ m/s². Connect your positions with a smooth curve to show the path of the ball. How is the motion in the vertical direction affected by motion in the horizontal direction?

   _____

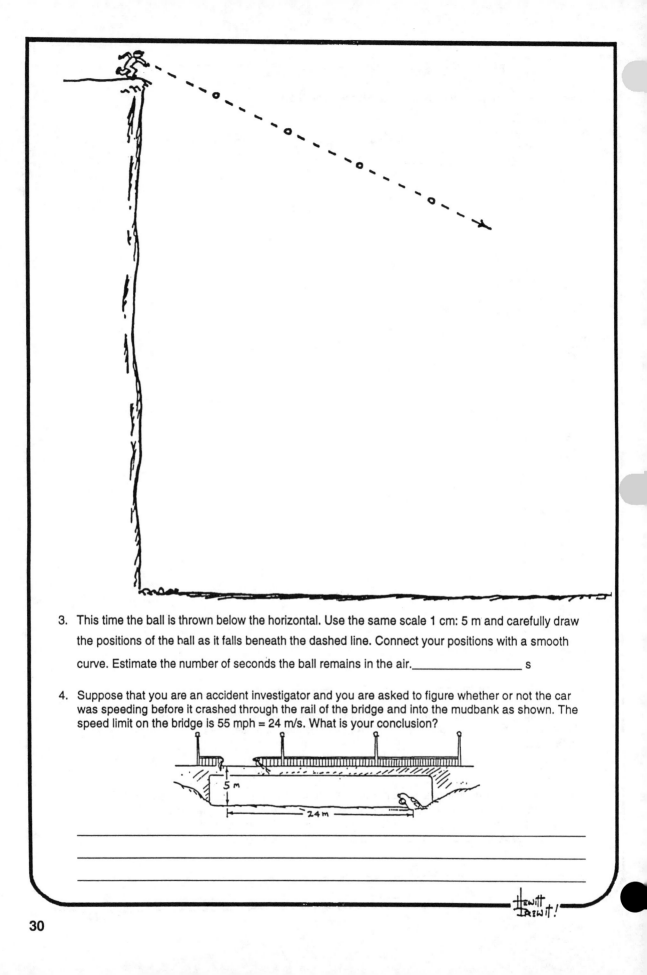

3. This time the ball is thrown below the horizontal. Use the same scale 1 cm: 5 m and carefully draw the positions of the ball as it falls beneath the dashed line. Connect your positions with a smooth curve. Estimate the number of seconds the ball remains in the air._____ s

4. Suppose that you are an accident investigator and you are asked to figure whether or not the car was speeding before it crashed through the rail of the bridge and into the mudbank as shown. The speed limit on the bridge is 55 mph = 24 m/s. What is your conclusion?

5 m

24 m

_____

_____

_____

CONCEPTUAL **Physical Science** PRACTICE SHEET

Chapter 5: Projectile and Satellite Motion
Tossed-Ball Vectors

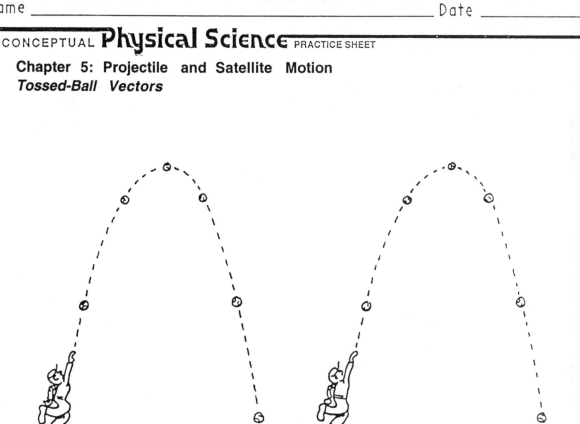

1. Draw sample vectors to represent the force of gravity on the ball in the positions shown above (after it leaves the thrower's hand). Neglect air drag.

2. Draw sample bold vectors to represent the velocity of the ball in the positions shown above. With lighter vectors, show the horizontal and vertical components of velocity for each position.

3. (a) Which velocity component in the previous question remains constant ? Why?

   _____

   (b) Which velocity component changes along the path? Why?

   _____

4. It is important to distinguish between force and velocity vectors. Force vectors combine with other force vectors, and velocity vectors combine with other velocity vectors. Do velocity vectors combine with force vectors? _____

Chapter 5: Projectile and Satellite Motion
Tossed-Ball Vectors

A ball tossed upward has initial velocity components 30 m/s vertical, and 5 m/s horizontal. The position of the ball is shown at 1-second intervals. Air resistance is negligible, and $g = 10$ m/s^2. Fill in the boxes, writing in the values of velocity *components* ascending, and your calculated *resultant velocities* descending.

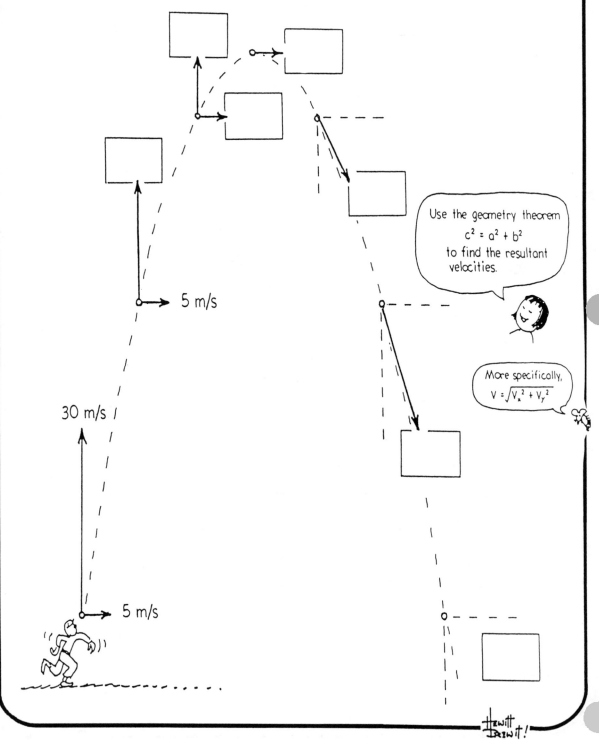

5 m/s

30 m/s

5 m/s

Use the geometry theorem
$$c^2 = a^2 + b^2$$
to find the resultant velocities.

More specifically,
$$V = \sqrt{V_x^2 + V_y^2}$$

Name _____ Date _____

Chapter 5: Projectile and Satellite Motion
Circular Orbits

1. Figure A shows "Newton's Mountain," so high that its top is above the drag of the atmosphere. The cannonball is fired and hits the ground as shown.

   a. You draw the path the cannonball might take if it were fired a little bit faster.

   b. Repeat for a still greater speed, but still less than 8 km/s.

   c. Then draw the orbital path it would take if its speed were 8 km/s.

   d. What is the shape of the 8 km/s curve?

   _____

   Figure A

   e. What would be the shape of the orbital path if the cannonball were fired at a speed of about 9 km/s?

   _____

2. Figure B shows a satellite in circular orbit.

   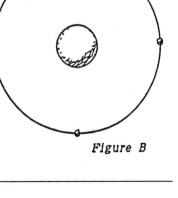

   a. At each of the four positions draw a vector that represents the gravitational *force* exerted on the satellite.

   b. Label the force vectors *F*.

   c. Then draw at each position a vector to represent the *velocity* of the satellite at that position, and label it *V*.

   Figure B

   d. Are all four *F* vectors the same length? Why or why not?

   _____

   e. Are all four *V* vectors the same length? Why or why not?

   _____

   f. What is the angle between your *F* and *V* vectors? _____

   g. Is there any component of *F* along *V*? _____

   h. What does this tell you about the work the force of gravity does on the satellite?

   _____

   i. Does the KE of the satellite in Figure B remain constant, or does it vary? _____

   j. Does the PE of the satellite remain constant, or does it vary?

   _____

Elliptical Orbits

3. Figure C shows a satellite in elliptical orbit.

a. Repeat the procedure you used for the circular orbit, drawing vectors **F** and **V** for each position, including proper labeling. Show equal magnitudes with equal lengths, and greater magnitudes with greater lengths, but don't bother making the scale accurate.

b. Are your vectors **F** all the same magnitude? Why or why not?

_____

_____

c. Are your vectors **V** all the same magnitude? Why or why not?

_____

_____

_____

_____

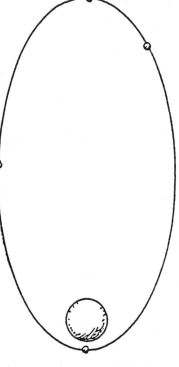

d. Is the angle between vectors **F** and **V** everywhere the same, or does it vary?

_____

e. Are there places where there is a component of **F** along **V**?

_____

_____

f. Is work done on the satellite when there is a component of **F** along and in the same direction of **V** and if so, does this increase or decrease the KE of the satellite?

_____

Figure C

g. When there is a component of **F** along and opposite to the direction of **V**, does this increase or decrease the KE of the satellite?

_____

_____

_____

Be very very careful when placing both velocity and force vectors on the same diagram. Not a good practice, for one may construct the resultant of the vectors -- ouch!

h. What can you say about the sum KE + PE along the orbit?

_____

_____

CONCEPTUAL **Physical Science** PRACTICE SHEET

Mechanics Overview

1. The sketch shows the elliptical path described by a satellite about the earth. In which of the marked positions, A - D, (put S for "same everywhere") does the satellite experience the maximum

    a.   gravitational force?_____

    b.   speed? _____

    c.   velocity? _____

    d.   momentum?_____

    e.   kinetic energy?_____

    f.   gravitational potential energy?_____

    g.   total energy (KE + PE)?_____

    h.   acceleration?_____

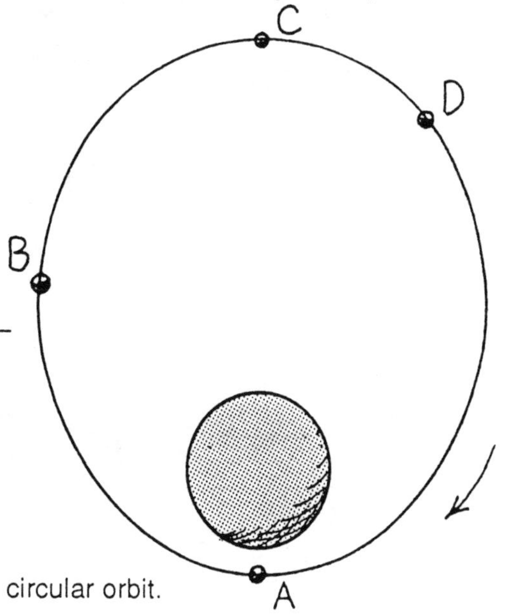

2. Answer the above questions for a satellite in circular orbit.

    a. _____   b._____   c._____   d._____   e._____   f. _____   g._____   h._____   i._____

3. In which position(s) is there momentarily no work done on the satellite by the force of gravity? Why?

    _____

4. Work changes energy. Let the equation for work, $W = Fd$, guide your thinking on these: Defend your answers in terms of $W = Fd$.

    a.   In which position will a several-minutes thrust of rocket engines do the most work on the satellite and give it the greatest change in kinetic energy?

    _____

    b.   In which position will a several-minute thrust of rocket engines do the most work on the *exhaust gases* and give the *exhaust gases* the greatest change in kinetic energy?

    _____

    c.   In which position will a several-minutes thrust of rocket engines give the satellite the least boost in kinetic energy?

    _____

Name _____ Date _____

CONCEPTUAL **Physical Science** PRACTICE SHEET

Chapter 6: Fluid Mechanics
Archimedes' Principle

1. Consider a balloon filled with 1 liter of water (1000 cm³) in equilibrium in a container of water, as shown in Figure 1.

   a. What is the mass of the 1 liter of water?

   _____

   b. What is the weight of the 1 liter of water?

   _____

   c. What is the weight of water displaced by the balloon?

   _____

   d. What is the buoyant force on the balloon?

   _____

   e. Sketch a pair of vectors in Figure 1: one for the weight of the balloon and the other for the buoyant force that acts on it. How do the size and directions of your vectors compare?

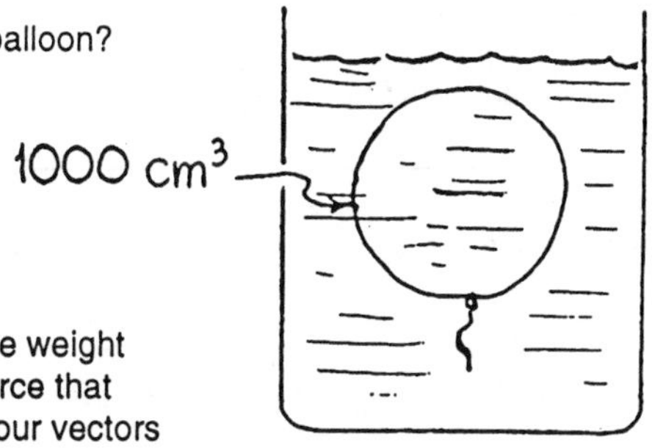

   _____

   WATER DOES NOT SINK IN WATER!

   1000 cm³

   Figure 1

2. As a thought experiment, pretend we could remove the water from the balloon but still have it remain the same size of 1 liter. Then inside the balloon is a vacuum.

   a. What is the mass of the liter of nothing?

   _____

   b. What is the weight of the liter of nothing?

   _____

   c. What is the weight of water displaced by the massless balloon?

   _____

   d. What is the buoyant force on the massless balloon?

   _____

   ANYTHING THAT DISPLACES 9.8 N OF WATER EXPERIENCES 9.8 N OF BUOYANT FORCE.

   CUZ IF YOU PUSH 9.8 N OF WATER ASIDE THE WATER PUSHES BACK ON YOU WITH 9.8 N!

   e. In which direction would the massless balloon be accelerated?

   _____

3. Assume the balloon is replaced by a 0.5-kilogram piece of wood that has exactly the same volume (1000 cm³), as shown in Figure 2. The wood is held in the same submerged position beneath the surface of the water.

a. What volume of water is displaced by the wood?

_____

b. What is the mass of the water displaced by the wood?

_____

c. What is the weight of the water displaced by the wood?

_____

d. How much buoyant force does the surrounding water exert on the wood?

_____

e. When the hand is removed, what is the net force on the wood?

_____

f. In which direction does the wood accelerate when released? _____

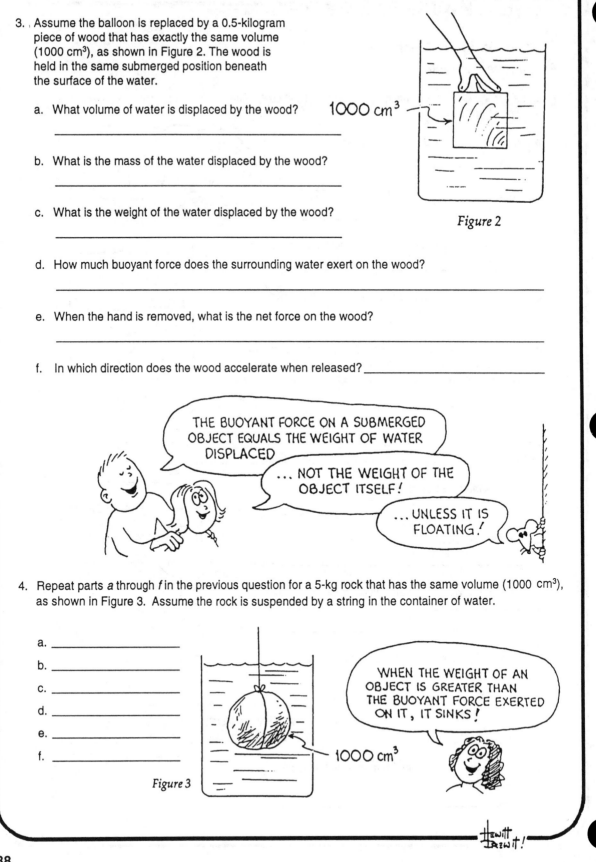

1000 cm³

Figure 2

THE BUOYANT FORCE ON A SUBMERGED OBJECT EQUALS THE WEIGHT OF WATER DISPLACED

... NOT THE WEIGHT OF THE OBJECT ITSELF!

... UNLESS IT IS FLOATING!

4. Repeat parts *a* through *f* in the previous question for a 5-kg rock that has the same volume (1000 cm³), as shown in Figure 3. Assume the rock is suspended by a string in the container of water.

a. _____

b. _____

c. _____

d. _____

e. _____

f. _____

Figure 3

WHEN THE WEIGHT OF AN OBJECT IS GREATER THAN THE BUOYANT FORCE EXERTED ON IT, IT SINKS!

1000 cm³

CONCEPTUAL **Physical Science** PRACTICE SHEET

Chapter 6: Fluid Mechanics
More Archimedes' Principle

1. The water lines for the first three cases are shown. Sketch in the appropriate water lines for cases *d* and *e*, and make up your own for case *f*.

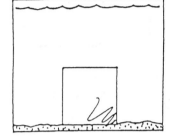

a. DENSER THAN WATER

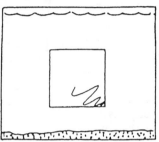

b. SAME DENSITY AS WATER

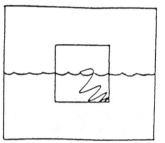

c. 1/2 AS DENSE AS WATER

d. 1/4 AS DENSE AS WATER

e. 3/4 AS DENSE AS WATER

f._____AS DENSE AS WATER

2. If the weight of a ship is 100 million N, then the water it displaces weighs_____ .

If cargo weighing 1000 N is put on board then the ship will sink down until an extra

_____ of water is displaced.

3. The first two sketches below show the water line for an empty and a loaded ship. Draw in the appropriate water line for the third sketch.

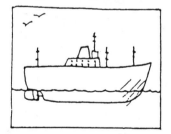

a. SHIP EMPTY

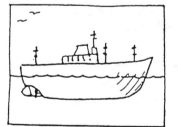

b. SHIP LOADED WITH 50
    TONS OF IRON

c. SHIP LOADED WITH 50
    TONS OF STYROFOAM

39

4. Here is a glass of ice water with an ice cube floating in it. Draw the water line after the ice cube melts. (Will the water line rise, fall, or remain the same?)

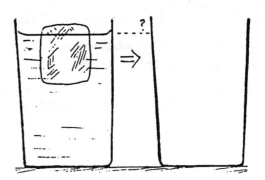

_____

_____

_____

_____

_____

5. The air-filled balloon is weighted so it sinks in water. Near the surface, the balloon has a certain volume. Draw the balloon at the bottom (inside the dashed square) and show whether it is bigger, smaller, or the same size.

   a. Since the weighted balloon sinks, how does its overall density compare to the density of water?

   _____

   b. As the weighted balloon sinks, does its density increase, decrease, or remain the same?

   _____

   c. Since the weighted balloon sinks, how does the buoyant force on it compare to its weight?

   _____

   d. As the weighted balloon sinks deeper, does the buoyant force on it increase, decrease, or remain the same?

   _____

6. What would be your answers to Questions _a, b, c,_ and _d_ for a rock instead of an air-filled balloon?

   a. _____

   b. _____

   c. _____

   d. _____

CONCEPTUAL **Physical Science** PRACTICE SHEET

Chapter 6: Fluid Mechanics
Gases

1. A principle difference between a liquid and a gas is that when a liquid is under pressure, its volume

   (increases) (decreases) (doesn't change noticeably)

   and its density

   (increases) (decreases) (doesn't change noticeably).

   When a gas is under pressure, its volume

   (increases) (decreases) (doesn't change noticeably)

   and its density

   (increases) (decreases) (doesn't change noticeably).

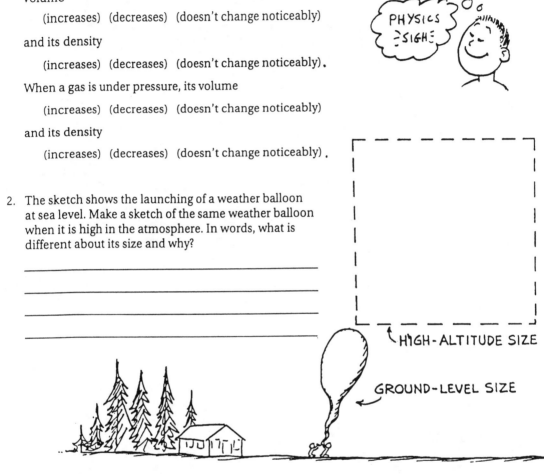

2. The sketch shows the launching of a weather balloon at sea level. Make a sketch of the same weather balloon when it is high in the atmosphere. In words, what is different about its size and why?

   _____

   _____

   _____

   _____

   HIGH-ALTITUDE SIZE

   GROUND-LEVEL SIZE

3. A hydrogen-filled balloon that weighs 10 N must displace_____N of air in order to float in air.

   If it displaces less than_____N it will be buoyed up with less than_____N and sink.

   If it displaces more than_____N of air it will move upward.

4. Why is the cartoon more humorous to physics types than to non-physics types? What physics has occurred?

   _____

   _____

   _____

   _____

   RATS TO YOU TOO, DANIEL BERNOULLI!

Name _____ Date _____

CONCEPTUAL **Physical Science** PRACTICE SHEET

Chapter 7: Thermal Energy and Thermodynamics
Temperature Mix

1. You apply heat to 1 L of water and raise its temperature by 10°C. If you add the same quantity of heat to 2 L of water, how much will the temperature rise? To 3 L of water? *Record your answers on the blanks in the drawing at the right.*

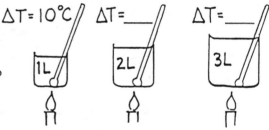

$\Delta T = 10°C$ $\Delta T = $____ $\Delta T = $____

1L   2L   3L

2. A large bucket contains 1 L of 20°C water.

20°C

    a. What will be the temperature of the mixture when 1 L of 20°C water is added?

    _____

    b. What will be the temperature of the mixture when 1 L of 40°C water is added?

    _____

    c. If 2 L of 40°C water were added, would the temperature of the mixture be greater or less than 30°C?

    _____

3. A red-hot iron kilogram mass is put into 1 L of cool water. Mark each of the following statements true (T) of false (F). (Ignore heat transfer to the container.)

    a. The increase in the water temperature is equal to the decrease in the iron's temperature.

    _____

    b. The quantity of heat gained by the water is equal to the quantity of heat lost by the iron. _____

    _____

    c. The iron and the water will both reach the same temperature._____

    d. The final temperature of the iron and water is about halfway between the initial temperatures of each._____

4. *True or False*: When Queen Elizabeth throws the last sip of her tea over Queen Mary's rail, the ocean gets a little warmer._____

Chapter 7: Thermal Energy and Thermodynamics
Absolute Zero

A mass of air is contained so that the volume can change but the pressure remains constant. Table I shows air volumes at various temperatures when the air is heated slowly.

1. Plot the data in Table I on the graph, and connect the points.

Table I

TEMP. (°C)	VOLUME (mL)
0	50
25	55
50	60
75	65
100	70

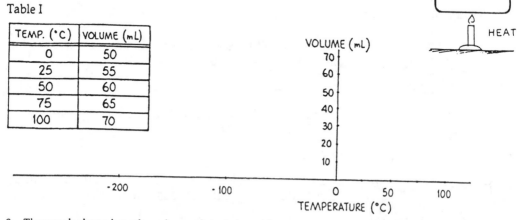

2. The graph shows how the volume of air varies with temperature at constant pressure. The straightness of the line means that the air expands uniformly with temperature. From your graph, you can predict what will happen to the volume of air when it is cooled.

Extrapolate (extend) the straight line of your graph to find the temperature at which the volume of the air would become zero. Mark this point on your graph. Estimate this temperature: _____

3. Although air would liquify before cooling to this temperature, the procedure suggests that there is a lower limit to how cold something can be. This is the absolute zero of temperature.

Careful experiments show that absolute zero is _____ °C.

4. Scientists measure temperature in *kelvins* instead of degrees Celsius, where the absolute zero of temperature is 0 kelvins. If you relabeled the temperature axis on the graph in Question 1 so that it shows temperature in kelvins, would your graph look like the one below? _____

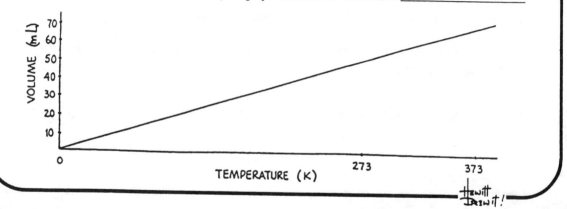

CONCEPTUAL **Physical Science** PRACTICE SHEET

Chapter 7: Thermal Energy and Thermodynamics
Thermal Expansion

$$\Delta \ell = \tfrac{1}{10^5}\, \ell_\circ \Delta T$$

1. Steel expands by about 1 part in 100,000 for each 1°C increase in temperature.

   a. How much longer will a piece of steel 1000 mm long (1 meter) be when its temperature is increased by 10 °C?_____

   b. How much longer will a piece of steel 1000 m long (1 kilometer) be when its temperature is increased by 10 °C?_____

   c. You place yourself between a wall and the end of a 1-m steel rod when the opposite end is securely fastened as shown. No harm comes to you if the temperature of the rod is increased a few degrees. Discuss the consequences of doing this with a rod many meters long?

   _____

   _____

2. The **Eiffel Tower** in Paris is 298 meters high. On a cold winter night it is shorter than on a hot summer day. What is its change in height for a 30°C temperature difference?

   _____

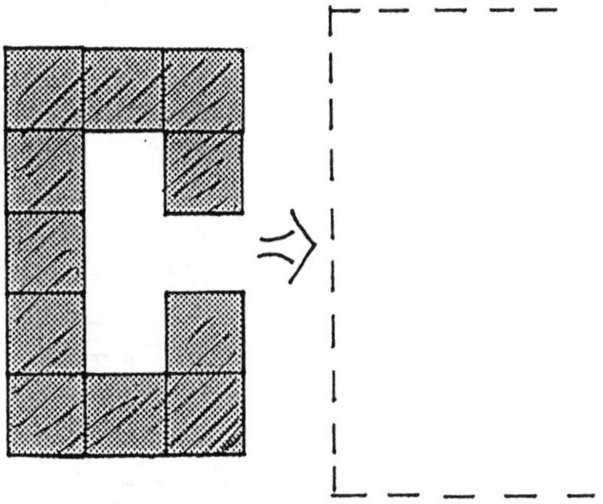

3. Consider a gap in a piece of metal. Does the gap become wider or narrower when the metal is heated? [Consider the piece of metal made up of 11 blocks — if the blocks are individually heated, each is slightly larger. Make a sketch of them, slightly enlarged, beside the sketch shown.]

   _____

4. The equatorial radius of the earth is about 6370 km. Consider a 40,000-km long steel pipe that forms a giant ring that fits snugly around the equator of the earth. Suppose people all along its length breathe on it so as to raise its temperature 1°C. The pipe gets longer. It is also no longer snug. How high does it stand above the ground? (Hint: Concentrate on the radial distance.)

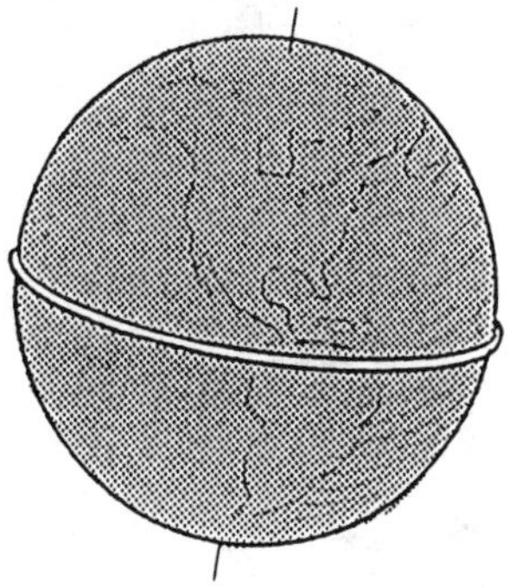

_____

Chapter 7: Thermal Energy and Thermodynamics
Thermal Expansion

1. The weight hangs above the floor from the copper wire. When a candle is moved along the wire and heats it, what happens to the height of the weight above the floor? Why?

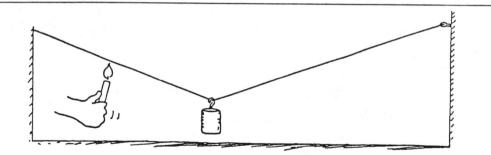

2. The levels of water at 0°C and 1°C are shown below in the first two flasks. At these temperatures there is microscopic slush in the water. There is slightly more slush at 0°C than at 1°C. As the water is heated, some of the slush collapses as it melts, and the level of the water falls in the tube. That's why the level of water is slightly lower in the 1°C-tube. Make rough estimates and sketch in the appropriate levels of water at the other temperatures shown. What is important about the level when the water reaches 4°C?

3. The diagram at right shows an ice-covered pond. Mark the probable temperatures of water at the top and bottom of the pond.

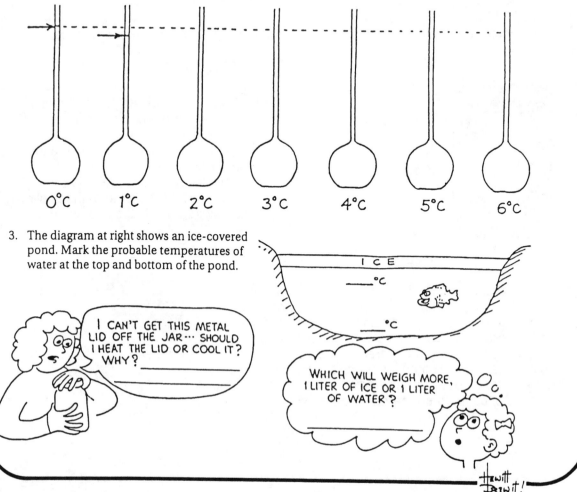

CONCEPTUAL **Physical Science** PRACTICE SHEET

Chapter 8: Heat Transfer and Change of Phase
Transmission of Heat

1. The tips of both brass rods are held in the gas flame.
   Mark the following true (T) or false (F).

   a. Heat is conducted only along Rod A._____

   b. Heat is conducted only along Rod B._____

   c. Heat is conducted equally along both

      Rod A and Rod B._____

   d. The idea that "heat rises" applies to heat transfer by *convection*, not by *conduction*. _____

2.  Why does a bird fluff its feathers to keep warm on a cold day?

   _____

3. Why does a down-filled sleeping bag keep you warm on a cold night? Why is it useless if the down is wet?

   _____

   _____

4. What does *convection* have to do with the holes in the shade of the desk lamp?

   _____

5. When hot water rapidly evaporates, the result can be dramatic. Consider 4 g of boiling water spread over a large surface so that 1 g rapidly evaporates. Suppose further that the surface and surroundings are very cold so that all 540 calories for evaporation come from the remaining 3 g of water.

   a. How many calories are taken from each gram of water?

      _____

   b. How many calories are released when 1 g of 100°C water cools to 0°C?

      _____

   c. How many calories are released when 1 g of 0°C water changes to 0°C ice?

      _____

   d. What happens in this case to the remaining 3 g of boiling water when 1 g rapidly evaporates?

      _____

      _____

CONCEPTUAL **Physical Science** PRACTICE SHEET

Chapter 6: Thermal Energy
Change of Phase

All matter can exist in the solid, liquid, or gaseous phases. The solid phase exists at relatively low temperatures, the liquid phase at higher temperatures, and the gaseous phase at still higher temperatures. Water is the most common example, not only because of its abundance but also because the temperatures for all three phases are common. Study Section 8.10 in your textbook and then answer the following:

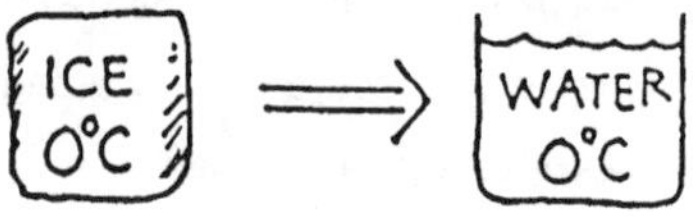

1. How many calories are needed to change 1 gram of 0°C ice to water?

   _____

2. How many calories are needed to change the temperature of 1 gram of water by 1°C?

   _____

3. How many calories are needed to melt 1 gram of 0°C ice and turn it to water at a room temperature of 23°C?

   _____

4. A 50-gram sample of ice at 0°C is placed in a glass beaker that contains 200 g of water at 20°C.

   a. How much heat is needed to melt the ice? _____

   b. By how much would the temperature of the water change if it gave up this much heat to the ice? _____

   c. What will be the final temperature of the mixture? (Disregard any heat absorbed by the glass or given off by the surrounding air.) _____

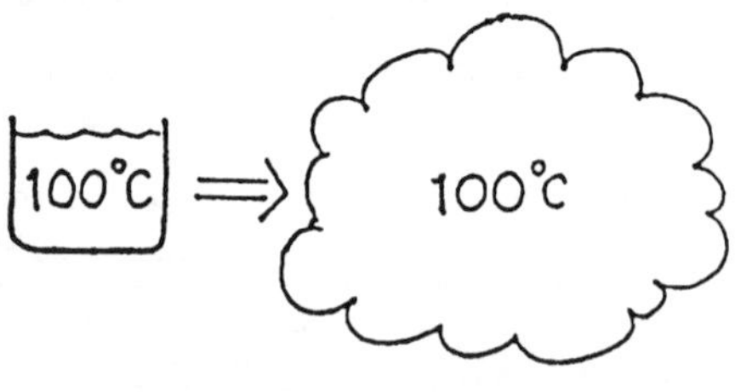

5. How many calories are needed to change 1 gram of 100°C boiling water to 100°C steam?

   _____

6. Fill in the number of calories at each step below for changing the state of 1 gram of 0°C ice to 100°C steam.

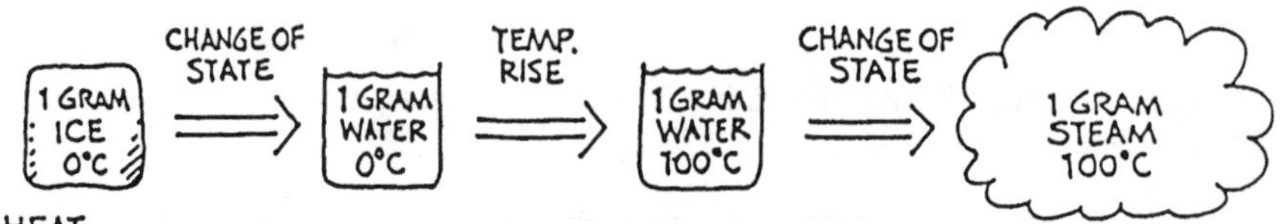

   CHANGE OF STATE   TEMP. RISE   CHANGE OF STATE

   1 GRAM ICE 0°C ⟹ 1 GRAM WATER 0°C ⟹ 1 GRAM WATER 100°C ⟹ 1 GRAM STEAM 100°C

   HEAT NEEDED = _____ CAL + _____ CAL + _____ CAL = _____ CAL

7. One gram of steam at 100°C condenses, and the water cools to 22°C.

   a. How much heat is released when the steam
      condenses?_____

   b. How much heat is released when the water cools from 100°C to 22°C?

   _____

   c. How much heat is released altogether? _____

8. In a household radiator 1000 g of steam at 100°C condenses, and the water cools to 90°C.

   a. How much heat is released when the steam condenses?

   _____

   b. How much heat is released when the water cools from 100°C to 90°C?

   _____

   c. How much heat is released altogether?

   _____

9. Radioactive minerals in common granite release 0.01 cal/kg of energy per year. If a 1-kg chunk of 50°C granite is thermally insulated, so all this energy heats it, how many years does it take to reach its melting temperature of 700°C? (Assume the specific heat of granite is 200 cal/kg°C.)

   _____

10. How many years would be required if the chunk of granite had a mass of 1 million kg? Why?

   _____

11. To calculate the time it takes to melt the 700°C granite, what other information would you need?

   _____

12. So we see that radioactivity keeps the earth's interior hot. After energy due to radioactivity eventually migrates to the earth's surface, in what form does it leave the earth?

   _____

13. To get water from the ground, even in the hot desert, dig a hole about a half meter wide and a half meter deep. Place a cup at the bottom. Spread a sheet of plastic wrap over the hole and place stones along the edge to hold it secure. Weight the center of the plastic with a stone so it forms a cone shape. Why will water collect in the cup? (Physics can save your life if you're ever stranded in a desert!)

   _____

   _____

   _____

   _____

   _____

CONCEPTUAL **Physical Science** PRACTICE SHEET

Chapter 9: Static and Current Electricity
Electric Potential

Just as PE transforms to KE for a mass lifted against the gravitation field (left), the electric PE of an electric charge transforms to other forms of energy when it changes location in an electric field (right). In both cases, how does the KE acquired compare to the decrease in PE?

_____

Complete the statements.

A force compresses the spring. The work done in compression is the product of the average force and the distance moved. W = Fd. This work increases the PE of the spring.

Similarly, a force pushes the charge (call it a test charge) closer to the charged sphere. The work done in moving the test charge is the

product of the average _____ and the _____ moved.

W = _____. This work _____ the PE of the test charge.

If the test charge is released, it will be repelled and fly past the starting point. Its gain in KE

at this point is _____ to its decrease in PE.

At any point, a greater amount of test charge means a greater amount of PE. But not a greater amount of PE *per amount* of charge. The quantities PE (measured in joules) and PE/charge (measured in volts) are different concepts.

By definition: **Electric Potential = PE/charge.** 1 volt = 1 joule/1 coulomb. So 1 C of charge with a PE of 1 J has an electric potential of 1 V. And 2 C of

charge with a PE of 2 J has an electric potential of _____V.

If a conductor connected to the terminal of a battery has an electric potential of 12 V, then

each coulomb of charge on the conductor has a PE of _____J.

You do very little work in rubbing a balloon on your hair to charge it. The PE of several thousand billion electrons (about one-millionth coulomb [10^{-6}C]) transferred may be a thousandth of a joule [10^{-3}J]. Impressively, however, the electric potential of the balloon is about _____VI

Why is contact with a balloon charged to thousands of volts not as dangerous as contact with household 110 V? _____

_____

51

Chapter 9: Static and Current Electricity
Series Circuits

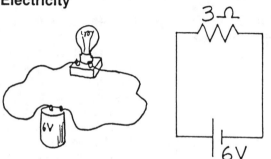

1. The simple circuit is a 6-V battery that pushes charge through a single lamp that has a resistance of 3 Ω. According to Ohm's law, the current in the lamp (and therefore the whole circuit) is _____A.

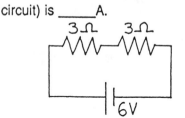

2. If a second identical lamp is added, the 6-V battery must push charge through a total resistance of _____Ω. The current in the circuit is then _____A.

3. If a third identical lamp is added in series, the total resistance of the circuit (neglecting any internal resistance in the battery) is _____Ω.

4. The current through all three lamps in series is _____A. The current through each individual lamp is _____A.

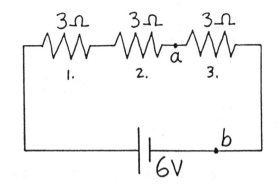

5. Does current in the lamps occur simultaneously, or does charge flow first through one lamp, then the other, and finally the last, in turn? _____

6. Does current flow *through* a resistor, or *across* a resistor?_____ Is voltage established *through* a resistor, or *across* a resistor?_____

7. The voltage across all three lamps in series is 6 V. The voltage (or commonly, *voltage drop*) across each individual lamp is _____V.

8. Suppose a wire connects points *a* and *b* in the circuit. The voltage drop across lamp 1 is now _____V, across lamp 2 is _____V, and across lamp 3 is _____V. So the current through lamp 1 is now _____A, through lamp 2 is _____A, and through lamp 3 is _____A. The current in the battery (neglecting internal battery resistance) is _____A.

9. Which circuit dissipates more power, the 3-lamp circuit or the 2-lamp circuit? (Another way of asking this is which circuit would glow brightest; which would be best seen on a dark night from a great distance?) Defend your answer.

_____

_____

_____

CONCEPTUAL **Physical Science** PRACTICE SHEET

Chapter 9: Static and Current Electricity
Parallel Circuits

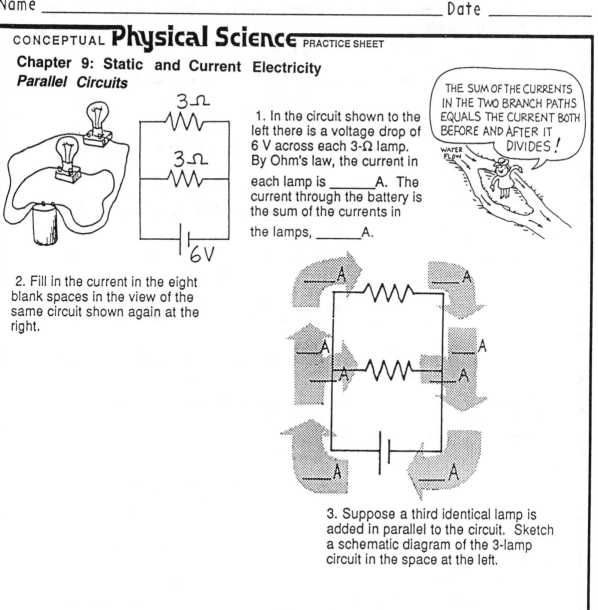

THE SUM OF THE CURRENTS IN THE TWO BRANCH PATHS EQUALS THE CURRENT BOTH BEFORE AND AFTER IT DIVIDES!

WATER FLOW

1. In the circuit shown to the left there is a voltage drop of 6 V across each 3-Ω lamp. By Ohm's law, the current in each lamp is _____A. The current through the battery is the sum of the currents in the lamps, _____A.

2. Fill in the current in the eight blank spaces in the view of the same circuit shown again at the right.

3. Suppose a third identical lamp is added in parallel to the circuit. Sketch a schematic diagram of the 3-lamp circuit in the space at the left.

4. For the three identical lamps in parallel, the voltage drop across each lamp is _____V. The current through each lamp is _____A. The current through the battery is now _____A. Is the circuit resistance now greater or less than before the third lamp was added? Explain.

_____

5. Which circuit dissipates more power, the 3-lamp circuit or the 2-lamp circuit? (Another way of asking this is which circuit would glow brightest; which would be best seen on a dark night from a great distance?) Defend your answer and compare this to the similar case for 2- and 3-lamp series circuits.

_____

_____

Compound Circuits

The table beside circuit *a* below shows the current through each resistor, the voltage across each resistor, and the power dissipated as heat in each resistor. Find the similar correct values for circuits *b, c,* and *d,* and put your answers in the tables shown.

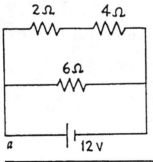

RESISTANCE	CURRENT ×	VOLTAGE =	POWER
2 Ω	2 A	4 V	8 W
4 Ω	2 A	8 V	16 W
6 Ω	2 A	12 V	24 W

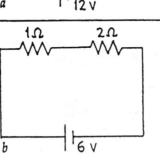

RESISTANCE	CURRENT ×	VOLTAGE =	POWER
1 Ω			
2 Ω			

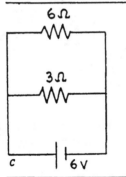

RESISTANCE	CURRENT ×	VOLTAGE =	POWER
6 Ω			
3 Ω			

RESISTANCE	CURRENT ×	VOLTAGE =	POWER
2 Ω			
2 Ω			
1 Ω			

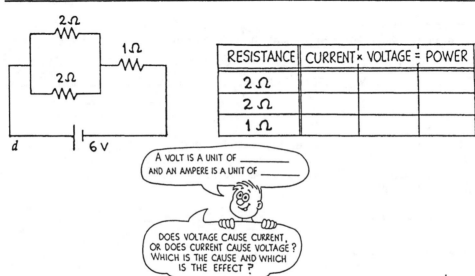

A VOLT IS A UNIT OF _____
AND AN AMPERE IS A UNIT OF _____

DOES VOLTAGE CAUSE CURRENT, OR DOES CURRENT CAUSE VOLTAGE? WHICH IS THE CAUSE AND WHICH IS THE EFFECT?

CONCEPTUAL **Physical Science** PRACTICE SHEET

Chapter 10: Magnetism and Electromagnetic Induction
Magnetism

Fill in each blank with the appropriate word.

1. Attraction or repulsion of charges depends on their *signs*, positives or negatives. Attraction or repulsion of magnets depends on their magnetic _____:
   _____ or _____.

   YOU HAVE A MAGNETIC PERSONALITY !

2. Opposite poles attract; like poles _____.

3. A magnetic field is produced by the _____ of electric charge.

4. Clusters of magnetically aligned atoms are magnetic_____.

5. A magnetic _____ surrounds a current-carrying wire.

6. When a current-carrying wire is made to form a coil around a piece of iron, the result is an

   _____.

7. A charged particle moving in a magnetic field experiences a deflecting _____ that is maximum when the charge moves
   _____ to the field.

8. A current-carrying wire experiences a deflecting
   _____that is maximum when the
   wire and magnetic field are _____ to one another.

9. A simple instrument designed to detect electric current is the_____ ;
   when calibrated to measure current, it is an _____ ; when calibrated
   to measure voltage, it is a _____.

   THEN TO REALLY MAKE THINGS "SIMPLE," THERE'S THE RIGHT-HAND RULE !

10. The largest size magnet in the world is the _____
    _____ itself.

Field Patterns

1. The illustration below is similar to Figure 10.3 in your textbook. Iron filings trace out patterns of magnetic field lines about a bar magnet. In the field are some magnetic compasses. The compass needle in only one compass is shown. Draw in the needles with proper orientation in the other compasses.

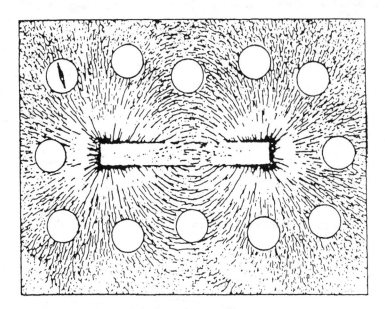

2. The illustration below is similar to Figure 10.12b in your textbook. Iron filings trace out the magnetic field pattern about the loop of current-carrying wire. Draw in the compass needle orientations for all the compasses.

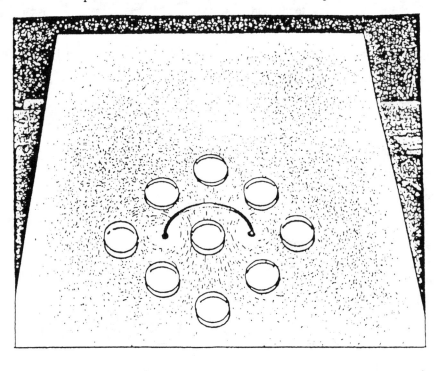

CONCEPTUAL **Physical Science** PRACTICE SHEET

Chapter 10: Magnetism and Electromagnetic Induction
Faraday's Law

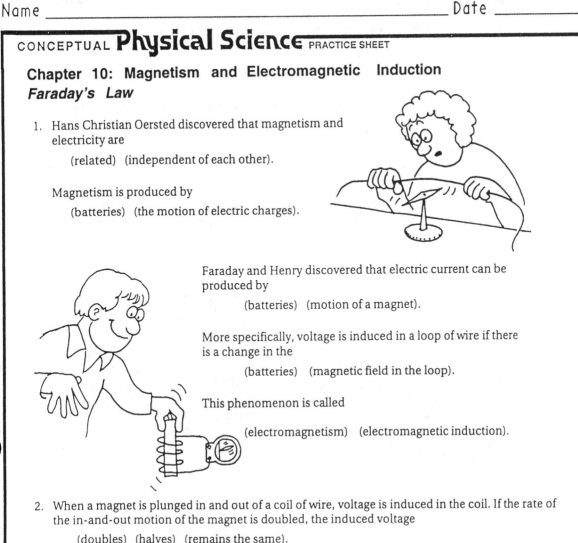

1. Hans Christian Oersted discovered that magnetism and electricity are

    (related) (independent of each other).

    Magnetism is produced by

    (batteries) (the motion of electric charges).

    Faraday and Henry discovered that electric current can be produced by

    (batteries) (motion of a magnet).

    More specifically, voltage is induced in a loop of wire if there is a change in the

    (batteries) (magnetic field in the loop).

    This phenomenon is called

    (electromagnetism) (electromagnetic induction).

2. When a magnet is plunged in and out of a coil of wire, voltage is induced in the coil. If the rate of the in-and-out motion of the magnet is doubled, the induced voltage

    (doubles) (halves) (remains the same).

    If instead the number of loops in the coil is doubled, the induced voltage

    (doubles) (halves) (remains the same).

3. A rapidly changing magnetic field in any region of space induces a rapidly changing

    (electric field) (magnetic field) (gravitational field)

    which in turn induces a rapidly changing

    (magnetic field) (electric field) (baseball field).

    This generation and regeneration of electric and magnetic fields makes up

    (electromagnetic waves) (sound waves) (both of these).

PHYSICS
≡ SIGH ≡

Chapter 10: Magnetism and Electromagnetic Induction
E&M Induction — the Transformer

A changing magnetic field is produced in a coil of wire when a bar magnet is plunged in and out of the coil. This induces an electric pressure in the coil called _____.

If the number of loops in the coil are increased, the induced voltage is _____.

The physical movement of a bar magnet is one way to produce a changing magnetic field. Another is to use a stationary electromagnet powered with _____ current.

The square iron core (right) becomes an electromagnet when current flows through the primary loop. This magnetic field is enclosed by the secondary loop. If the current is ac, it induces an alternating magnetic field that induces voltage in the secondary loop. In (a) the voltage induced in the secondary equals the input voltage. (b) An extra secondary encloses the same changing magnetic field and voltage is induced in it also. (c) The induced voltages combine when the two secondaries are combined. Write in the induced voltage where indicated.

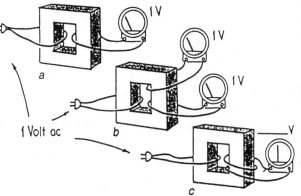

1 Volt ac

Consider a more practical transformer with a 200-turn primary and a 1000-turn secondary (left). Suppose the primary is connected to a 120-volt alternating source, and the secondary is connected to an electrical device with a resistance of 600 ohms.

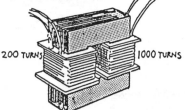

200 TURNS   1000 TURNS

What will be the voltage output of the secondary?_____V

What current will flow in the secondary circuit?_____A

Knowing the voltage and current, what will be the power in the secondary?_____W

Neglecting small heat losses, and knowing that energy is conserved, what is the power in the primary?_____W

What is the current drawn by the primary?_____A

From this we see that the voltage is stepped up in the secondary, and compared to the current in the primary, is the current stepped up or down?_____

Can a transformer step up voltage?_____

Can a transformer step up current?_____

Can a transformer step up energy and or power?_____

CONCEPTUAL **Physical Science** PRACTICE SHEET

Chapter 11: Waves and Sound
Vibration and Wave Fundamentals

1. A sine curve that represents a transverse wave is drawn below. With a ruler, measure the wavelength and amplitude of the wave.

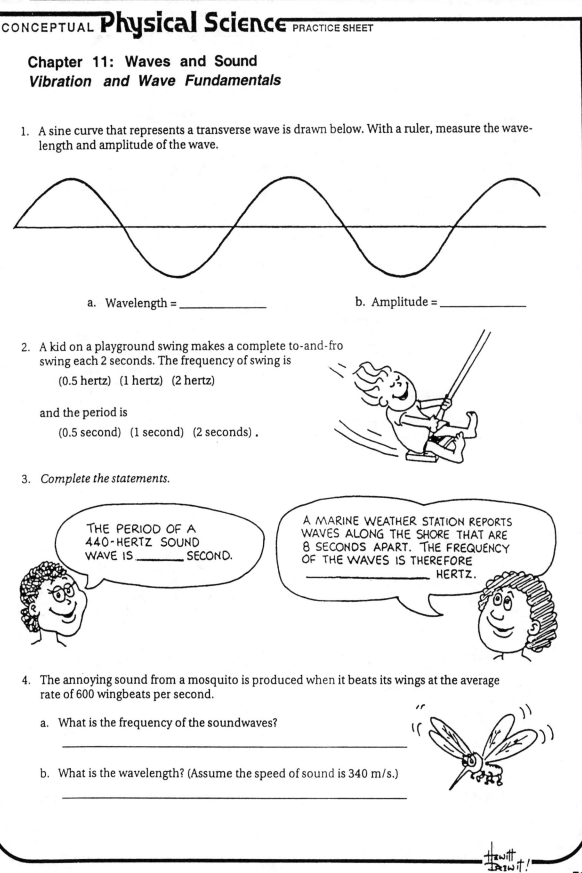

  a. Wavelength = _____   b. Amplitude = _____

2. A kid on a playground swing makes a complete to-and-fro swing each 2 seconds. The frequency of swing is

    (0.5 hertz) (1 hertz) (2 hertz)

    and the period is

    (0.5 second) (1 second) (2 seconds) .

3. *Complete the statements.*

    THE PERIOD OF A 440-HERTZ SOUND WAVE IS _____ SECOND.

    A MARINE WEATHER STATION REPORTS WAVES ALONG THE SHORE THAT ARE 8 SECONDS APART. THE FREQUENCY OF THE WAVES IS THEREFORE _____ HERTZ.

4. The annoying sound from a mosquito is produced when it beats its wings at the average rate of 600 wingbeats per second.

    a. What is the frequency of the soundwaves?

    _____

    b. What is the wavelength? (Assume the speed of sound is 340 m/s.)

    _____

5. A machine gun fires 10 rounds per second. The speed of the bullets is 300 m/s.

   a. What is the distance in the air between the flying bullets?_____

   b. What happens to the distance between the bullets if the rate of fire is increased?

   _____

6. Consider a wave generator that produces 10 pulses per second. The speed of the waves is 300 cm/s.

   a. What is the wavelength of the waves? _____

   b. What happens to the wavelength if the frequency of pulses is increased?

   _____

7. The bird at the right watches the waves. If the portion of a wave between 2 crests passes the pole each second, what is the speed of the wave?

   _____

   What is its period?

   _____

8. If the distance between crests in the above question were 1.5 meters apart, and 2 crests pass the pole each second, what would be the speed of the wave?

   _____

   What would be its period?

   _____

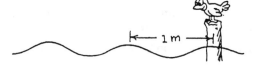

9. When an automobile moves toward a listener, the sound of its horn seems relatively

   (low pitched) (normal)

   (high pitched) .

   and when moving away from the listener, its horn seems

   (low pitched) (normal)

   (high pitched) .

10. The changed pitch of the Doppler effect is due to changes in

    (wave speed) (wave frequency) .

CONCEPTUAL **Physical Science** PRACTICE SHEET

Chapter 11: Waves and Sound
Shock Waves

The cone-shaped shock wave produced by a supersonic aircraft is actually the result of overlapping spherical waves of sound, as indicated by the overlapping circles in Figure 11.32 in your textbook. Sketches *a, b, c, d,* and *e,* at the left show the "animated" growth of only one of the many spherical sound waves (shown as an expanding circle in the two-dimensional sketch). The circle originates when the aircraft is in the position shown in *a.* Sketch *b* shows both the growth of the circle and position of the aircraft at a later time. Still later times are shown in *c, d,* and *e.* Note that the circle grows and the aircraft moves farther to the right. Note also that the aircraft is moving farther than the sound wave. This is because the aircraft is moving faster than sound.

Careful examination will reveal how fast the aircraft is moving compared to the speed of sound. Sketch *e* shows that in the same time the sound travels from O to A, the aircraft has traveled from O to B — twice as far. You can check this with a ruler.

Circle the answer.

1. Inspect sketches *b* and *d.* Has the aircraft traveled twice as far as sound in the same time in these postions also?

   (yes) (no)

2. For greater speeds, the angle of the shock wave would be

   (wider) (the same) (narrower).

DURING THE TIME THAT SOUND TRAVELS FROM O TO A, THE PLANE TRAVELS TWICE AS FAR --- FROM O TO B.

SO IT'S FLYING AT TWICE THE SPEED OF SOUND!

3. Use a ruler to estimate the speeds of the aircraft that produce the shock waves in the two sketches below.

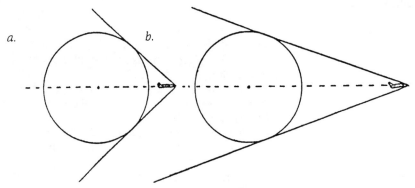

a. b.

Aircraft *a* is traveling about _____ times the speed of sound.

Aircraft *b* is traveling about _____ times the speed of sound.

4. Draw your own circle (anywhere) and estimate the speed of the aircraft to produce the shock wave shown below.

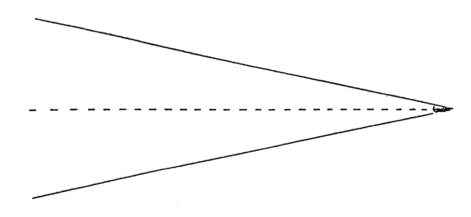

The speed is about _____ times the speed of sound.

5. In the space below, draw the shock wave made by a supersonic missile that travels at four times the speed of sound.

CONCEPTUAL **Physical Science** PRACTICE SHEET

Chapter 12: Light Waves
Color

The sketch to the right shows the shadow of an instructor in front of a white screen in a dark room. The light source is red, so the screen looks red and the shadow looks black. Color the sketch, or label the colors with pen or pencil.

A green lamp is added and makes a second shadow. The shadow cast by the red lamp is no longer black, but is illuminated by green light. So it is green. Color or mark it green. The shadow cast by the green lamp is not black because it is illuminated by the red lamp. Indicate its color. Do the same for the background, which receives a mixture of red and green light.

A blue lamp is added and three shadows appear. Indicate the appropriate colors of the shadows and the background.

The lamps are placed closer together so the shadows overlap. Indicate the colors of all screen areas.

Color

If you have colored markers, have a go at these.

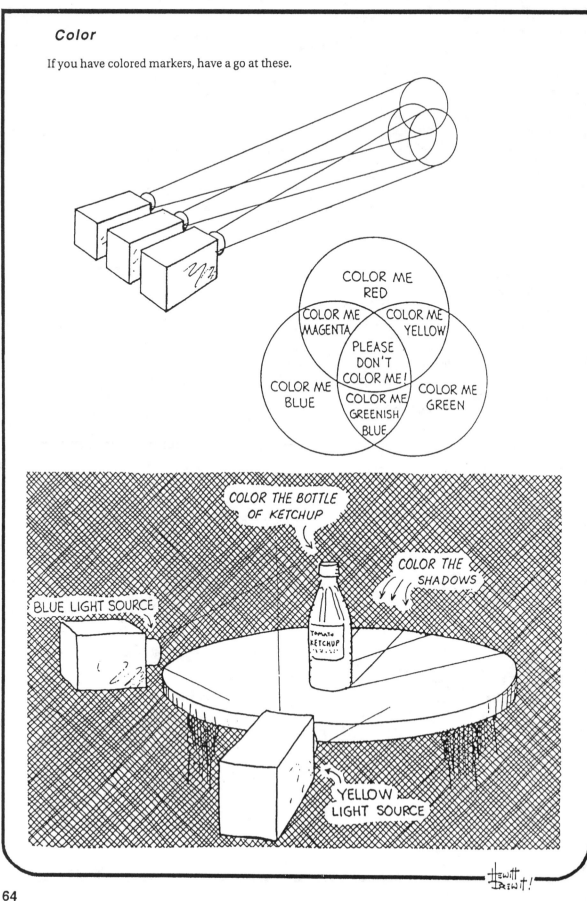

CONCEPTUAL **Physical Science** PRACTICE SHEET

Chapter 12: Light Waves
Interference Patterns

The illustration is a schematic depiction of coherent monochromatic light incident upon a thin slit at O that diffracts to thin slits M and N where it emerges to form an interference pattern on a screen S. Carefully count the number of wavelengths along the following paths between the double slits and the screen.

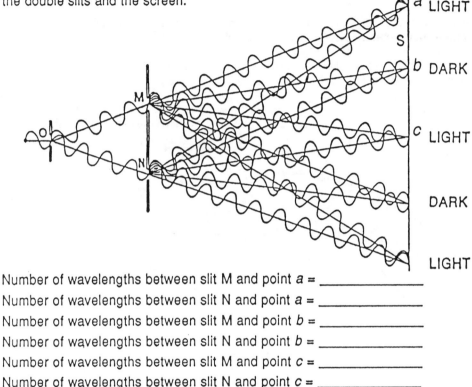

Number of wavelengths between slit M and point *a* = _____
Number of wavelengths between slit N and point *a* = _____
Number of wavelengths between slit M and point *b* = _____
Number of wavelengths between slit N and point *b* = _____
Number of wavelengths between slit M and point *c* = _____
Number of wavelengths between slit N and point *c* = _____

When the number of wavelengths along each path is the same or differs by one or more whole wavelengths, is interference constructive or destructive? _____

When the number of wavelengths differs by a half wavelength (or odd multiples of a half wavelength) is interference constructive or destructive?_____

If the light used were higher in frequency, would the fringes of light and dark areas be more widely or more closely spaced?_____

If the spacing between slits were reduced, would the fringes of light and dark areas be more widely or more closely spaced?_____

If a greater number of equally-spaced slits, instead of two slits, were illuminated, would an interference pattern still be produced? (Give an example.)

_____

_____

CONCEPTUAL **Physical Science** PRACTICE SHEET

Chapter 12: Light Waves
Diffraction and Interference

Shown below are concentric solid and dashed circles, each different in radius by 1 cm.
Consider the circular pattern a top view of water waves, where the solid circles are crests and the
dashed circles are troughs.

a. Draw another set of the same concentric circles with a compass. Choose any part of the paper
    for your center (except the present central point). Let the circles run off the edge of the paper.

b. Find where a dashed line crosses a solid line and draw a large dot at the intersection. Do this
    for ALL places where a solid and dashed line intersect.

c. With a wide felt marker, connect the dots with smooth lines. These *nodal lines* lie in regions
    where the waves have cancelled — where the crest of one wave overlaps the trough of another

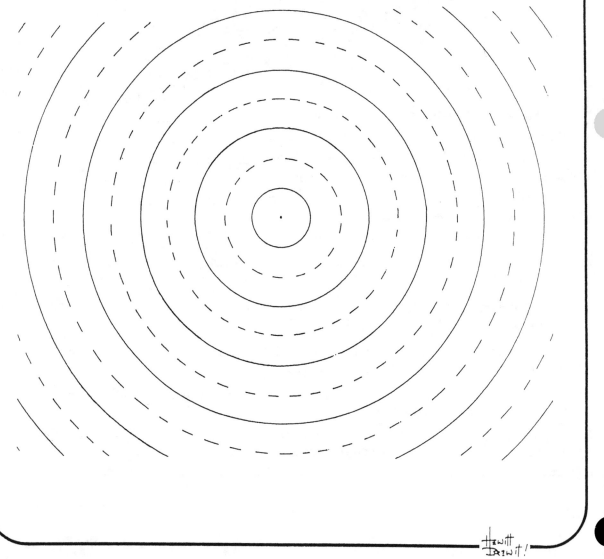

CONCEPTUAL **Physical Science** PRACTICE SHEET

Chapter 13: Properties of Light
Reflection

1. Light from a flashlight shines on a mirror and illuminates one of the cards. Draw the reflected beam to indicate the illuminated card.

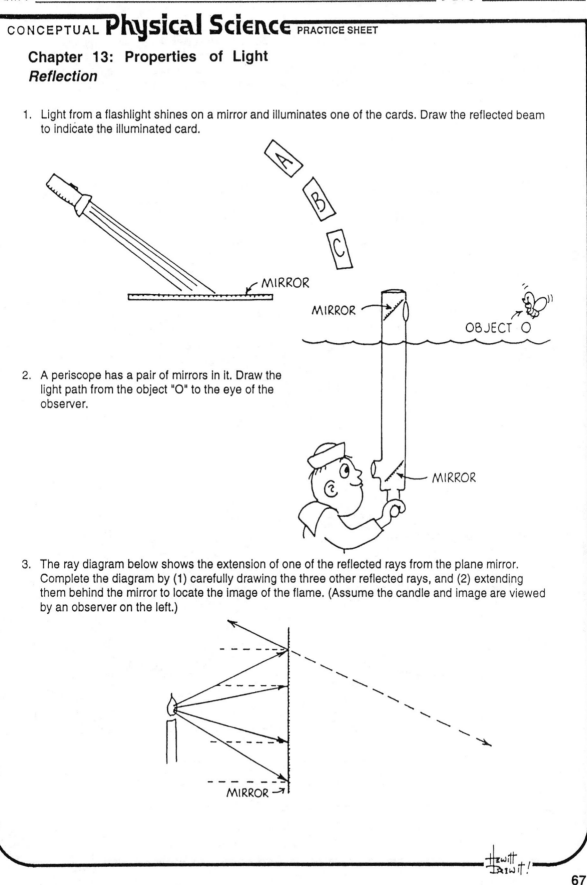

2. A periscope has a pair of mirrors in it. Draw the light path from the object "O" to the eye of the observer.

3. The ray diagram below shows the extension of one of the reflected rays from the plane mirror. Complete the diagram by **(1)** carefully drawing the three other reflected rays, and **(2)** extending them behind the mirror to locate the image of the flame. (Assume the candle and image are viewed by an observer on the left.)

Reflection

4. The ray diagram below shows the reflection of one of the rays that strikes the parabolic mirror. Notice that the law of reflection is obeyed, and the angle of incidence (from the normal, the dashed line) equals the angle of reflection (from the normal). Complete the diagram by drawing the reflected rays of the other three rays that are shown. (Do you see why parabolic mirrors are used in automobile headlights?)

5. A girl takes a photograph of the bridge as shown. Which of the two sketches correctly shows the reflected view of the bridge? Defend your answer.

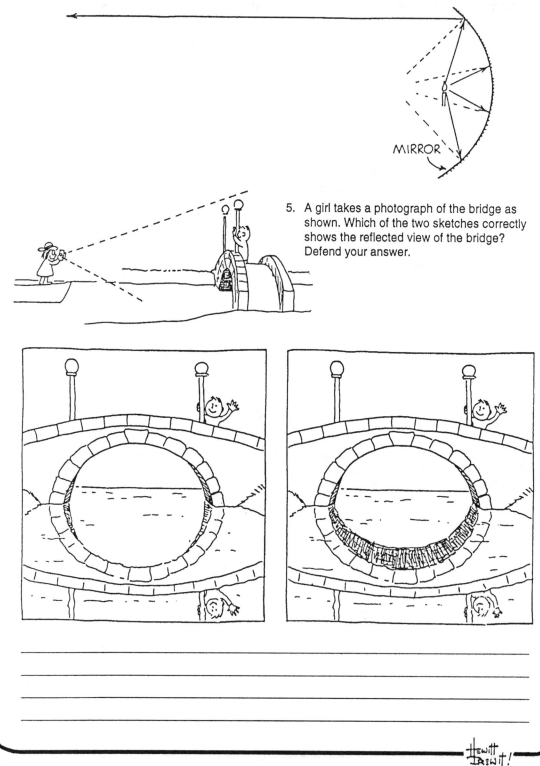

_____

_____

_____

_____

CONCEPTUAL **Physical Science** PRACTICE SHEET

Chapter 13: Properties of Light
Refraction

1. A pair of toy cart wheels are rolled obliquely from a smooth surface onto two plots of grass —
   a rectangular plot as shown at the left, and a triangular plot as shown at the right. The ground is
   on a slight incline so that after slowing down in the grass, the wheels speed up again when
   emerging on the smooth surface. Finish each sketch and show some positions of the wheels
   inside the plots and on the other side. Clearly indicate their paths and directions of travel.

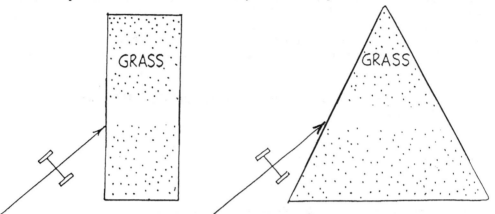

2. Red, green, and blue rays of light are incident upon a glass prism as shown. The average speed of
   red light in the glass is less than in air, so the red ray is refracted. When it emerges into the air it
   regains its original speed and travels in the direction shown. Green light takes longer to get
   through the glass. Because of its slower speed it is refracted as shown. Blue light travels even
   slower in glass. Complete the diagram by estimating the path of the blue ray.

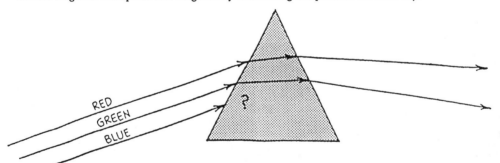

3. Below we consider a prism-shaped hole in a piece of glass — that is, an "air prism." Complete the
   diagram, showing likely paths of the beams of red, green, and blue light as they pass through this
   "prism" and back to glass.

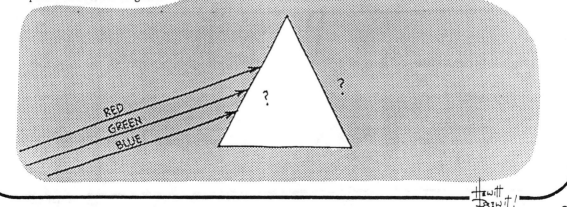

4. Light of different colors diverges when emerging from a prism. Newton showed that with a second prism he could make the diverging beams become parallel again. Which placement of the second prism will do this?

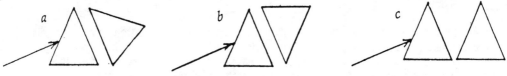

5. The sketch shows that due to refraction, the man sees the fish closer to the water surface than it actually is.

   a. Draw a ray beginning at the fish's eye to show the line of sight of the fish when it looks upward at 50° to the normal at the water surface. Draw the direction of the ray after it meets the surface of the water.

   b. At the 50° angle, does the fish see the man, or does it see the reflected view of the starfish at the bottom of the pond? Explain.

   _____

   c. To see the man, should the fish look higher or lower than the 50° path?

   _____

   d. If the fish's eye were barely above the water surface, it would see the world above in a 180° view, horizon to horizon. The fisheye view of the world above as seen beneath the water, however, is very different. Due to the 48° critical angle of water, the fish sees a normally 180° horizon-to-horizon view compressed within an angle of _____.

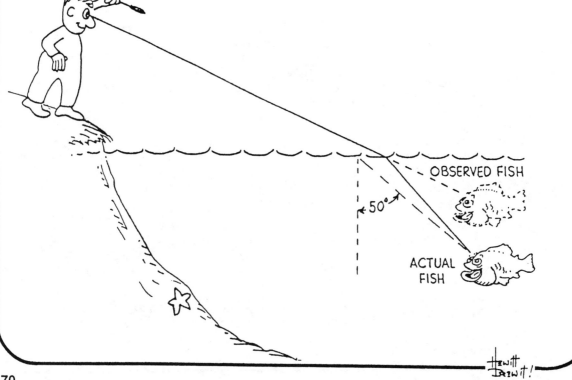

OBSERVED FISH

50°

ACTUAL FISH

Name _____ Date _____

Chapter 13: Properties of Light
Refraction

1. The sketch to the right shows a light ray moving from air into water, at 45° to the normal. Which of the three rays indicated with capital letters is most likely the light ray that continues inside the water?

_____

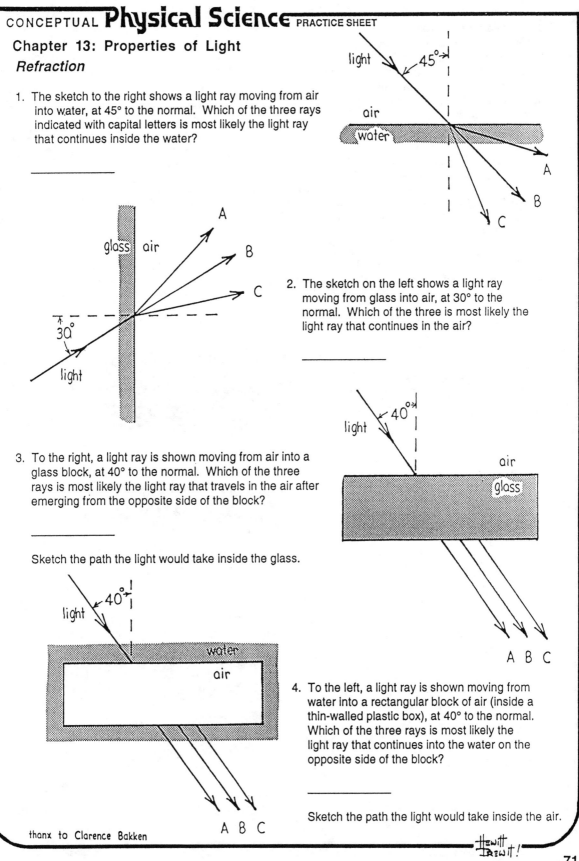

2. The sketch on the left shows a light ray moving from glass into air, at 30° to the normal. Which of the three is most likely the light ray that continues in the air?

_____

3. To the right, a light ray is shown moving from air into a glass block, at 40° to the normal. Which of the three rays is most likely the light ray that travels in the air after emerging from the opposite side of the block?

_____

Sketch the path the light would take inside the glass.

4. To the left, a light ray is shown moving from water into a rectangular block of air (inside a thin-walled plastic box), at 40° to the normal. Which of the three rays is most likely the light ray that continues into the water on the opposite side of the block?

_____

Sketch the path the light would take inside the air.

thanx to Clarence Bakken

71

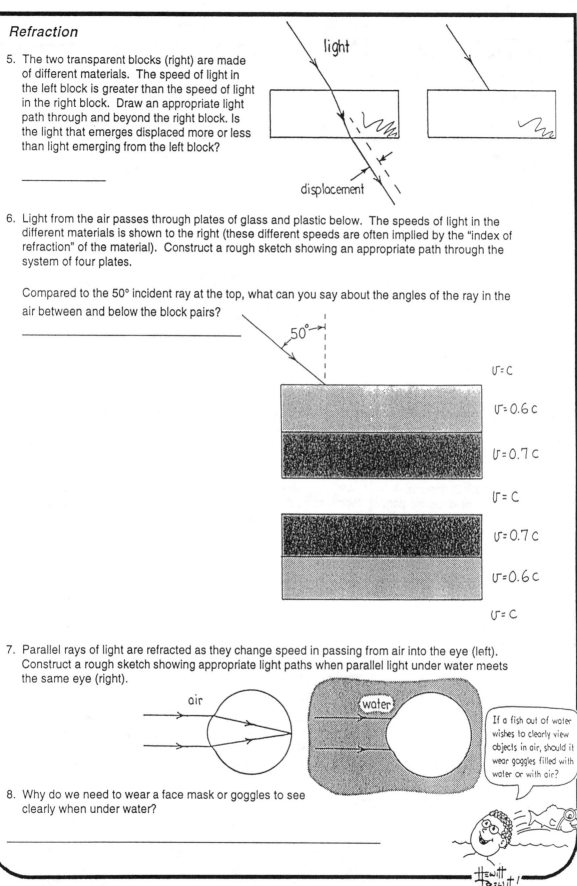

Refraction

5. The two transparent blocks (right) are made of different materials. The speed of light in the left block is greater than the speed of light in the right block. Draw an appropriate light path through and beyond the right block. Is the light that emerges displaced more or less than light emerging from the left block?

_____

6. Light from the air passes through plates of glass and plastic below. The speeds of light in the different materials is shown to the right (these different speeds are often implied by the "index of refraction" of the material). Construct a rough sketch showing an appropriate path through the system of four plates.

Compared to the 50° incident ray at the top, what can you say about the angles of the ray in the air between and below the block pairs?

_____

7. Parallel rays of light are refracted as they change speed in passing from air into the eye (left). Construct a rough sketch showing appropriate light paths when parallel light under water meets the same eye (right).

If a fish out of water wishes to clearly view objects in air, should it wear goggles filled with water or with air?

8. Why do we need to wear a face mask or goggles to see clearly when under water?

_____

Name _____ Date _____

Chapter 13: Properties of Light
Wave-Particle Duality

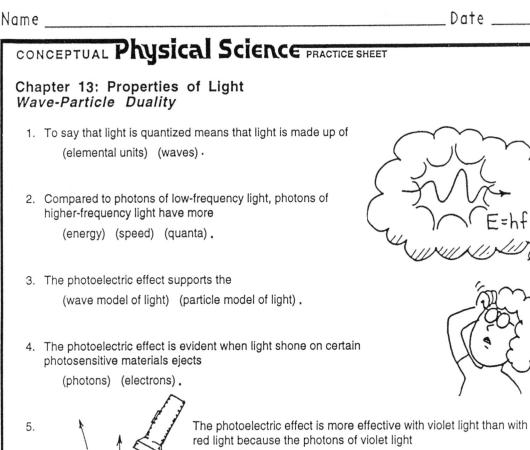

1. To say that light is quantized means that light is made up of

   (elemental units) (waves) ·

2. Compared to photons of low-frequency light, photons of higher-frequency light have more

   (energy) (speed) (quanta) .

3. The photoelectric effect supports the

   (wave model of light) (particle model of light) .

4. The photoelectric effect is evident when light shone on certain photosensitive materials ejects

   (photons) (electrons) .

5. The photoelectric effect is more effective with violet light than with red light because the photons of violet light

   (resonate with the atoms in the material)

   (deliver more energy to the material)

   (are more numerous) .

6. According to De Broglie's wave model of matter, a beam of light and a beam of electrons

   (are fundamentally different) (are similar) .

7. According to De Broglie, the greater the speed of an electron beam, the

   (greater is its wavelength) (shorter is its wavelength) .

8. The discreteness of the energy levels of electrons about the atomic nucleus is best understood by considering the electron to be a

   (wave) (particle) .

9. Heavier atoms are not appreciably larger in size than lighter atoms. The main reason for this is the greater nuclear charge

   (pulls surrounding electrons into tighter orbits)

   (holds more electrons about the atomic nucleus)

   (produces a denser atomic structure) .

10. Whereas in the everyday macroworld the study of motion is called *mechanics,* in the microworld the study of quanta is called

    (Newtonian mechanics) (quantum mechanics) .

A QUANTUM MECHANIC!

Name _____ Date _____

CONCEPTUAL **Physical Science** PRACTICE SHEET

Chapter 14: Atoms and the Periodic Table
Subatomic Particles

Three fundamental particles of the atom are the _____, _____, and

_____ . At the center of each atom lies the atomic _____, which

consists of _____ and _____. The **atomic number** refers to the

number of _____ in the nucleus. All atoms of the same element have the

same number of _____, hence, the same atomic number.

Isotopes are atoms that have the same number of _____ but a different

number of _____. An isotope is identified by its **atomic mass number**, which

is the total number of _____ and _____ in the nucleus. A carbon isotope

that has 6 _____ and 6 _____ is identified as carbon-12, where 12 is

the atomic mass number. A carbon isotope having 6 _____ and 8 _____,

on the other hand, is carbon-14.

1. Complete the following table:

Isotope	Number of...		
	Electrons	Protons	Neutrons
Hydrogen-1	1		
Chlorine-36		17	
Nitrogen-14			7
Potassium-40	19		
Arsenic-75		33	
Gold-197			118

2. Which results in a more valuable product — *adding* or *substracting* protons from gold nuclei?

3. Which has more mass, a helium atom or a neon atom?

4. Which has a greater number of atoms, a gram of helium or a gram of neon?

CONCEPTUAL **Physical Science** PRACTICE SHEET

Chapter 14: Atoms and the Periodic Table
Melting Points of the Elements

There is a remarkable degree of organization in the periodic table. As discussed in your textbook, elements within the same atomic group (vertical column) share similar properties. Also, the chemical reactivity of an element can be deduced from its position in the periodic table. Two additional examples of the periodic table's organization are the melting points and densities of the elements.

The periodic table below shows the melting points of nearly all the elements. Note the melting points are not randomly oriented, but, with only a few exceptions, either gradually increase or decrease as you move in any particular direction. This can be clearly illustrated by color coding each element according to its melting point.

Use colored pencils to color in each element according to its melting point. Use the suggested color legend. Color lightly so that symbols and numbers are still visible.

Color	Temperature Range, °C	Color	Temperature Range, °C
Violet	-273 — -50	Yellow	1400 — 1900
Blue	-50 — 300	Orange	1900 — 2900
Cyan	300 — 700	Red	2900 — 3500
Green	700 — 1400		

| 1 | 2 | 3 | 4 | 5 | 6 | 7 | 8 | 9 | 10 | 11 | 12 | 13 | 14 | 15 | 16 | 17 | 18 |

Melting Points of the Elements (°C)

H -259																	He -272
Li 180	Be 1278											B 2079	C 3550	N -210	O -218	F -219	Ne -248
Na 97	Mg 648											Al 660	Si 1410	P 44	S 113	Cl -100	Ar -189
K 63	Ca 839	Sc 1541	Ti 1660	V 1890	Cr 1857	Mn 1244	Fe 1535	Co 1495	Ni 1453	Cu 1083	Zn 419	Ga 30	Ge 937	As 817	Se 217	Br -7	Kr -156
Rb 39	Sr 769	Y 1522	Zr 1852	Nb 2468	Mo 2617	Tc 2172	Ru 2310	Rh 1966	Pd 1554	Ag 961	Cd 320	In 156	Sn 231	Sb 630	Te 449	I 113	Xe -111
Cs 28	Ba 725	La 921	Hf 2227	Ta 2996	W 3410	Re 3180	Os 3045	Ir 2410	Pt 1772	Au 1064	Hg -38	Tl 303	Pb 327.	Bi 271	Po 254	At 302	Rn -71
Fr 27	Ra 700	Ac 1050	--	--	--	--	—	--									

Lanthanides:	Ce 799	Pr 931	Nd 1021	Pm 1168	Sm 1077	Eu 822	Gd 1313	Tb 1356	Dy 1412	Ho 1474	Er 1159	Tm 1545	Yb 819	Lu 1663

Actinides:	Th 1750	Pa 1600	U 1132	Np 640	Pu 641	Am 994	Cm 1340	Bk --	Cf --	Es .	Fm --	Md --	No --	Lr —

1. Which elements have the highest melting points?

_____

2. Which elements have the lowest melting points?

_____

3. Which atomic groups tend to go from higher to lower melting points reading from top to bottom? (Identify each group by its group number.)

_____

4. Which atomic groups tend to go from lower to higher melting points reading from top to bottom?

_____

Chapter 14: Atoms and the Periodic Table
Densities of the Elements

The periodic table below shows the densities of nearly all the elements. As with the melting points, the densities of the elements either gradually increase or decrease as you move in any particular direction. Use colored pencils to color in each element according to its density. Shown below is a suggested color legend. Color lightly so that symbols and numbers are still visible. (Note: All gaseous elements are marked with an asterisk and should be the same color. Their densities, which are given in units of g/L, are much less than the densities non-gaseous elements, which are given in units of g/mL.)

Color	Density (g/mL)		Color	Density (g/mL)
Violet	gaseous elements		Yellow	16 — 12
Blue	5 — 0		Orange	20 — 16
Cyan	8 — 5		Red.	23 — 20
Green	12 — 8			

| 1 | 2 | 3 | 4 | 5 | 6 | 7 | 8 | 9 | 10 | 11 | 12 | 13 | 14 | 15 | 16 | 17 | 18 |

Densities of the Elements (g/mL)

1	2	3	4	5	6	7	8	9	10	11	12	13	14	15	16	17	18
H * 0.09																	He * 0.18
Li 0.5	Be 1.8											B 2.3	C 2.0	N * 1.25	O * 1.43	F * 1.70	Ne * 0.90
Na 1.0	Mg 1.7											Al 2.7	Si 2.3	P 1.8	S 2.1	Cl * 3.21	Ar * 1.78
K 0.9	Ca 1.6	Sc 3.0	Ti 4.5	V 6.1	Cr 7.2	Mn 7.3	Fe 7.8	Co 8.9	Ni 8.9	Cu 9.0	Zn 7.1	Ga 6.1	Ge 5.3	As 5.7	Se 4.8	Br * 7.59	Kr * 3.73
Rb 1.5	Sr 2.5	Y 4.5	Zr 6.5	Nb 8.5	Mo 6.8	Tc 11.5	Ru 12.4	Rh 12.4	Pd 12.0	Ag 10.5	Cd 8.7	In 7.3	Sn 5.7	Sb 6.7	Te 6.2	I 4.9	Xe * 5.89
Cs 1.9	Ba 3.5	La 6.2	Hf 13.3	Ta 16.6	W 19.3	Re 21.0	Os 22.6	Ir 22.4	Pt 21.5	Au 18.9	Hg 13.5	Tl 11.9	Pb 11.4	Bi 9.7	Po 9.3	At --	Rn * 9.73
Fr --	Ra 5.0	Ac 10.1	Unq --	Unp --	Unh --	Uns --	Uno --	Une --									

* density of gaseous phase in g/L

Lanthanides:	Ce 6.7	Pr 6.7	Nd 6.8	Pm 7.2	Sm 7.5	Eu 5.2	Gd 7.9	Tb 8.2	Dy 8.6	Ho 8.8	Er 9.1	Tm 9.3	Yb 6.9	Lu 9.8
Actinides:	Th 11.7	Pa 15.4	U 19.0	Np 20.1	Pu 19.8	Am 13.7	Cm 13.5	Bk 14	Cf --	Es --	Fm --	Md --	No --	Lr --

1. Which elements are the most dense?

_____

2. How variable are the densities of the lanthanides compared to the densities of the actinides?

_____

3. Which atomic groups tend to go from higher to lower densities reading from top to bottom? (Identify each group by its group number).

_____

4. Which atomic groups tend to go from lower to higher densities reading from top to bottom?

_____

CONCEPTUAL **Physical Science** PRACTICE SHEET

Chapter 15: Visualizing the Atom
Losing Valence Electrons

The shell model described in Section 15.4 can be used to explain a wide variety of properties of atoms. Using the shell model, for example, we can explain how atoms within the same group tend to lose (or gain) the same number of electrons. Let's consider the case of three group 1 elements: lithium, sodium, and potassium. Look to a periodic table and find the nuclear charge of each of these atoms:

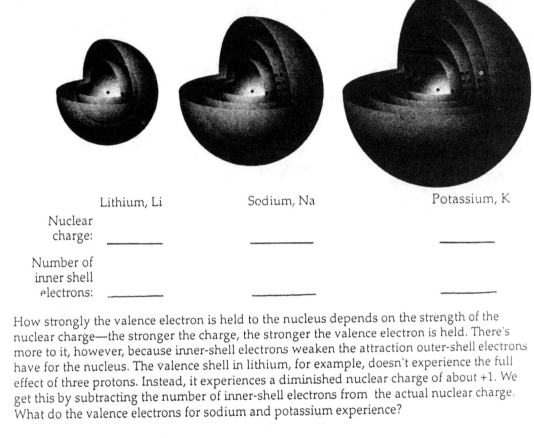

| Lithium, Li | Sodium, Na | Potassium, K |

Nuclear charge: _____   _____   _____

Number of inner shell electrons: _____   _____   _____

How strongly the valence electron is held to the nucleus depends on the strength of the nuclear charge—the stronger the charge, the stronger the valence electron is held. There's more to it, however, because inner-shell electrons weaken the attraction outer-shell electrons have for the nucleus. The valence shell in lithium, for example, doesn't experience the full effect of three protons. Instead, it experiences a diminished nuclear charge of about +1. We get this by subtracting the number of inner-shell electrons from the actual nuclear charge. What do the valence electrons for sodium and potassium experience?

Diminished nuclear charge: _____   _____   _____

Question: Potassium has a nuclear charge many times greater than that of lithium. Why is it actually *easier* for a potassium atom to lose its valence electron than it is for a lithium atom to lose its valence electron?

Hint: Remember from Chapter **9** what happens to the electric force as distance is increased!

CONCEPTUAL **Physical Science** PRACTICE SHEET

Chapter 16: The Atomic Nucleus
Radioactivity

1. *Complete the following statements.*

    a. A lone neutron spontaneously decays into a proton plus an

       _____ .

    b. Alpha and beta rays are made of streams of particles, whereas
       gamma rays are streams of _____ .

    c. An electrically charged atom is called an_____.

    d. Different _____of an element are chemically identical but differ in the number
       of neutrons in the nucleus.

    e. Transuranic elements are those beyond atomic number_____.

    f. If the amount of a certain radioactive sample decreases by half in four weeks, in four more
       weeks the amount remaining should be _____the original amount.

    g. Water from a natural hot spring is warmed by_____inside the earth.

2. The gas in the little girl's balloon is made up of former alpha and beta particles produced by radioactive decay.

    a. If the mixture is electrically neutral, how many more beta
       particles than alpha particles are in the balloon?

       _____

       _____

    b. Why is your answer not "same"?

       _____

       _____

    c. Why are the alpha and beta particles no longer harmful to the child?

       _____

       _____

    d. What element does this mixture make?

       _____

Radioactivity

Draw in a decay-scheme diagram below, similar to Figure 16.16 in your text. In this case you begin at the upper right with U-235 and end up with a different isotope of lead. Use the table at the left and identify each element in the series by its chemical symbol.

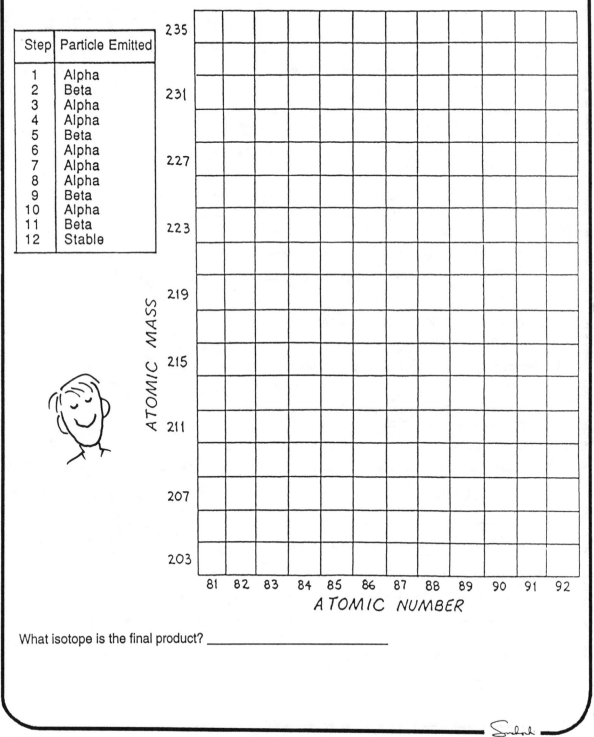

Step	Particle Emitted
1	Alpha
2	Beta
3	Alpha
4	Alpha
5	Beta
6	Alpha
7	Alpha
8	Alpha
9	Beta
10	Alpha
11	Beta
12	Stable

ATOMIC MASS

ATOMIC NUMBER

What isotope is the final product? _____

CONCEPTUAL **Physical Science** PRACTICE SHEET

Chapter 16: The Atomic Nucleus
Radioactive Half-Life

You and your classmates will now play the "half-life game."
Each of you should have a coin to shake inside cupped
hands. After it has been shaken for a few seconds, the
coin is tossed on the table or on the floor. Students with
tails up fall out of the game. Only those who consistently
show heads remain in the game. Finally everybody has
tossed a tail and the game is over.

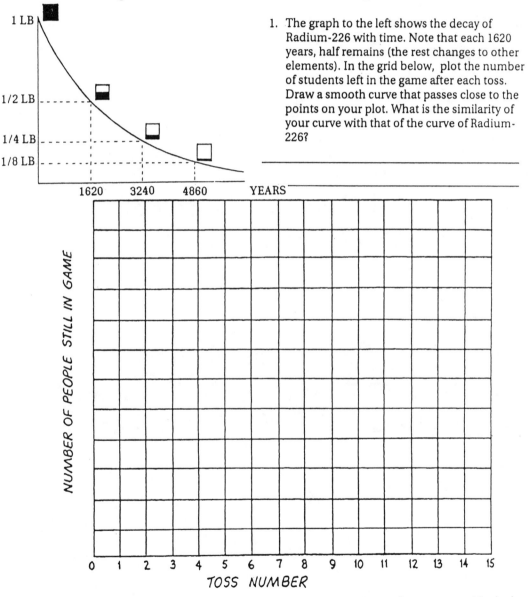

1. The graph to the left shows the decay of
Radium-226 with time. Note that each 1620
years, half remains (the rest changes to other
elements). In the grid below, plot the number
of students left in the game after each toss.
Draw a smooth curve that passes close to the
points on your plot. What is the similarity of
your curve with that of the curve of Radium-
226?

_____

_____

2. Was the person to last longest in the game *lucky*, with some sort of special powers to guide the long
survival? What test could you make to decide the answer to this question?

_____

CONCEPTUAL **Physical Science** PRACTICE SHEET

Chapter 16: The Atomic Nucleus
Nuclear Fission and Fusion

1. Complete the table for a chain reaction in which two neutrons from each step individually cause a new reaction.

EVENT	1	2	3	4	5	6	7
NO. OF REACTIONS	1	2	4				

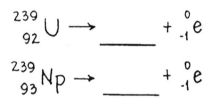

2. Complete the table for a chain reaction where three neutrons from each reaction cause a new reaction.

EVENT	1	2	3	4	5	6	7
NO. OF REACTIONS	1	3	9				

3. Complete these beta reactions, which occur in a breeder reactor.

$$^{239}_{92}U \longrightarrow \underline{\hspace{1cm}} + {}^{0}_{-1}e$$

$$^{239}_{93}Np \longrightarrow \underline{\hspace{1cm}} + {}^{0}_{-1}e$$

4. Complete the following fission reactions.

$$^{1}_{0}n + {}^{235}_{92}U \longrightarrow {}^{143}_{54}Xe + {}^{90}_{38}Sr + \underline{\hspace{1cm}}({}^{1}_{0}n)$$

$$^{1}_{0}n + {}^{235}_{92}U \longrightarrow {}^{152}_{60}Nd + \underline{\hspace{1cm}} + 4({}^{1}_{0}n)$$

$$^{1}_{0}n + {}^{239}_{94}Pu \longrightarrow \underline{\hspace{1cm}} + {}^{97}_{40}Zr + 2({}^{1}_{0}n)$$

5. Complete the following fusion reactions.

$$^{2}_{1}H + {}^{2}_{1}H \longrightarrow {}^{3}_{2}He + \underline{\hspace{1cm}}$$

$$^{2}_{1}H + {}^{3}_{1}H \longrightarrow {}^{4}_{2}He + \underline{\hspace{1cm}}$$

KNOW NUKES!

CONCEPTUAL **Physical Science** PRACTICE SHEET

Chapter 16: The Atomic Nucleus
Nuclear Reactions

Complete these nuclear reactions.

1. $^{230}_{90}Th \longrightarrow ^{226}_{88}Ra + \underline{\hspace{1cm}}$

THORIUM LATE; I OVERTHLEPT?

2. $^{218}_{85}At \longrightarrow \underline{\hspace{1cm}} + ^{4}_{2}He$

3. $^{14}_{6}C \longrightarrow \underline{\hspace{1cm}} + ^{14}_{7}N$

4. $^{80}_{35}Br \longrightarrow ^{80}_{36}Kr + \underline{\hspace{1cm}}$

5. $^{214}_{83}Bi \longrightarrow ^{4}_{2}He + \underline{\hspace{1cm}}$

6. $^{212}_{83}Bi \longrightarrow ^{0}_{-1}e + \underline{\hspace{1cm}}$

7. $^{80}_{35}Br \longrightarrow ^{0}_{-1}e + \underline{\hspace{1cm}}$

8. $^{80}_{35}Br \longrightarrow ^{0}_{+1}e + \underline{\hspace{1cm}}$

NUCLEAR PHYSICS··· IT'S THE SAME TO ME WITH THE FIRST TWO LETTERS INTERCHANGED?

9. $^{1}_{1}H + ^{7}_{3}Li \longrightarrow ^{4}_{2}He + \underline{\hspace{1cm}}$

10. $^{2}_{1}H + ^{3}_{1}H \longrightarrow ^{4}_{2}He + \underline{\hspace{1cm}}$

Name _____ Date _____

CONCEPTUAL **Physical Science** PRACTICE SHEET

Chapter 17: Elements of Chemistry
The Submicroscopic

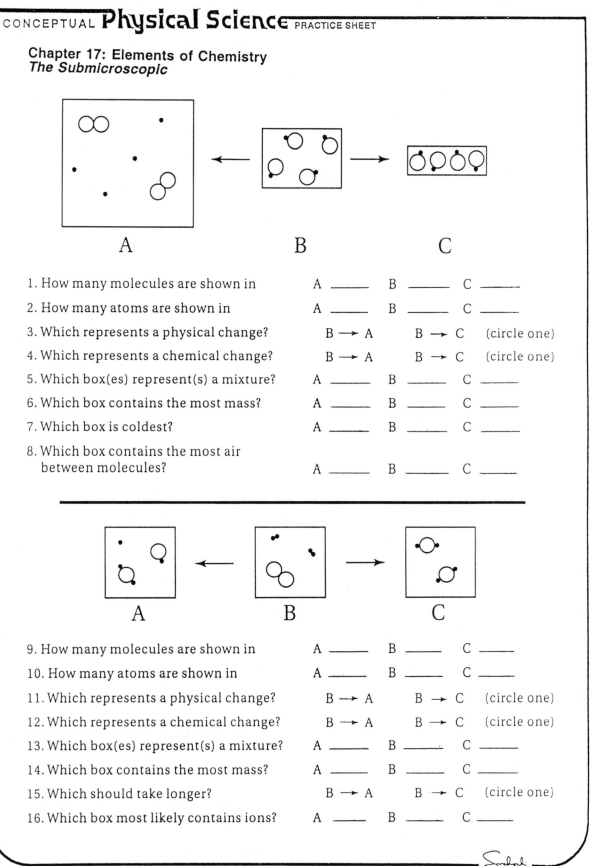

1. How many molecules are shown in   A _____   B _____   C _____

2. How many atoms are shown in   A _____   B _____   C _____

3. Which represents a physical change?   B → A   B → C   (circle one)

4. Which represents a chemical change?   B → A   B → C   (circle one)

5. Which box(es) represent(s) a mixture?   A _____   B _____   C _____

6. Which box contains the most mass?   A _____   B _____   C _____

7. Which box is coldest?   A _____   B _____   C _____

8. Which box contains the most air
    between molecules?   A _____   B _____   C _____

9. How many molecules are shown in   A _____   B _____   C _____

10. How many atoms are shown in   A _____   B _____   C _____

11. Which represents a physical change?   B → A   B → C   (circle one)

12. Which represents a chemical change?   B → A   B → C   (circle one)

13. Which box(es) represent(s) a mixture?   A _____   B _____   C _____

14. Which box contains the most mass?   A _____   B _____   C _____

15. Which should take longer?   B → A   B → C   (circle one)

16. Which box most likely contains ions?   A _____   B _____   C _____

Name _____ Date _____

Chapter 17: Elements of Chemistry
Balancing Chemical Equations

In a balanced chemical equation the number of times each element appears as a reactant is equal to the number of times it appears as a product. For example,

$$2 \ H_2 \ + \ O_2 \ ---> \ 2 \ H_2O$$

Recall that *coefficients* (the integer appearing before the chemical formula) indicate the number of times each chemical formula is to be counted and *subscripts* indicate when a particular element occurs more than once within the formula.

Check whether or not the following chemical equations are balanced.

$$3 \ NO \ ---> \ N_2O \ + \ NO_2$$ ☐ balanced; ☐ unbalanced

$$SiO_2 \ + \ 4 \ HF \ ---> \ SiF_4 \ + \ 2 \ H_2O$$ ☐ balanced; ☐ unbalanced

$$4 \ NH_3 \ + \ 5 \ O_2 \ ---> \ 4 \ NO \ + \ 6 \ H_2O$$ ☐ balanced; ☐ unbalanced

Unbalanced equations are balanced by changing the coefficients. Subscripts, however, should never be changed because this changes the chemical's identity—H_2O is water, but H_2O_2 is hydrogen peroxide! The following steps may help guide you:

1. Focus on balancing only one element at a time. Start with the left-most element and modify the coefficients such that this element appears on both sides of the arrow the same number of times.

2. Move to the next element and modify the coefficients so as to balance this element. Do not worry if you incidentally unbalance the previous element. You will come back to it in subsequent steps.

3. Continue from left to right balancing each element individually.

4. Repeat steps 1 - 3 until all elements are balanced.

Use the above methodology to balance the following chemical equations.

____N_2O + ____N_2 ---> ____O_2

____$NaClO_3$ ---> ____$NaCl$ + ____O_2

____$MnCl_2$ + ____Al ---> ____Mn + ____$AlCl_3$

____K + ____H_2O ---> ____H_2 + ____KOH

____Al_2O_3 + ____C ---> ____Al + ____CO_2

____NH_3 + ____F_2 ---> ____NH_4F + ____NF_3

This is just one of the many methods that chemists have developed to balance chemical equations.

Knowing how to balance a chemical equation is a useful technique, but understanding why a chemical equation needs to be balanced in the first place is far more important.

Chapter 17: Elements of Chemistry
Physical and Chemical Changes

1. What distinguishes a chemical change from a physical change?

2. Based upon observations alone, why is distinguishing a chemical change from a physical change not always so straight-forward?

Try your hand at catagorizing the following processes as either chemical or physical changes. Some of these examples are debatable! Be sure to discuss your reasoning with fellow classmates or your instructor.

(circle one)

3. A cloud grows dark. _ chemical   physical

4. Leaves produce oxygen. _ _ _ _ _ _ _ _ _ _ _ _ _ _ _ _ _ _ chemical   physical

5. Food coloring is added to water. _ _ _ _ _ _ _ _ _ _ _ _ chemical   physical

6. Tropical coral reef dies. _ _ _ _ _ _ _ _ _ _ _ _ _ _ _ _ _ chemical   physical

7. Dead coral reef is pounded by waves into beach sand. _ _ _ _ chemical   physical

8. Oil and vinegar separate. _ _ _ _ _ _ _ _ _ _ _ _ _ _ _ _ chemical   physical

9. Soda drink goes flat. _ _ _ _ _ _ _ _ _ _ _ _ _ _ _ _ _ _ _ chemical   physical

10. Sick person develops a fever. _ _ _ _ _ _ _ _ _ _ _ _ _ chemical   physical

11. Compost pit turns into mulch. _ _ _ _ _ _ _ _ _ _ _ _ chemical   physical

12. A computer is turned on. _ _ _ _ _ _ _ _ _ _ _ _ _ _ _ _ chemical   physical

13. An electrical short melts a computer's integrated circuits. _ chemical   physical

14. A car battery runs down. _ _ _ _ _ _ _ _ _ _ _ _ _ _ _ _ chemical   physical

15. A pencil is sharpened. _ _ _ _ _ _ _ _ _ _ _ _ _ _ _ _ _ chemical   physical

16. Mascara is applied to eyelashes. _ _ _ _ _ _ _ _ _ _ _ _ chemical   physical

17. Sunbather gets tan lying in the sun. _ _ _ _ _ _ _ _ _ _ chemical   physical

18. Invisible ink turns visible upon heating. _ _ _ _ _ _ _ _ chemical   physical

19. A light bulb burns out. _ _ _ _ _ _ _ _ _ _ _ _ _ _ _ _ chemical   physical

20. Car engine consumes a tank of gasoline. _ _ _ _ _ _ _ _ chemical   physical

21. B vitamins turn urine yellow. _ _ _ _ _ _ _ _ _ _ _ _ _ chemical   physical

CONCEPTUAL **Physical Science** PRACTICE SHEET

Chapter 18: Mixtures
Solutions

1. Use these terms to complete the following sentences. Some terms may be used
   more than once.

solution	solvent	solute
dissolve	concentrated	dilute
saturated	concentration	mole
molarity	solubility	soluble
insoluble	precipitate	supersaturated

Sugar is _____ in water for the two can be mixed homogeneously to form a _____.

The _____ of sugar in water is so great that _____ homogeneous mixtures are easily

prepared. Sugar, however, is not infinitely _____ in water for when too much of this

_____ is added to water, which behaves as the _____, the solution becomes

_____. At this point any additional sugar is _____ for it will not _____. If

the temperature of a saturated sugar solution is lowered, the _____ of the sugar in water is also

lowered. If some of the sugar comes out of solution, it is said to form a _____. If, however, the

sugar remains in solution despite the decrease in solubility, then the solution is said to be

_____. Adding only a small amount of sugar to water results in a _____ solution.

The _____ of this solution or any solution can be measure in terms of _____, which

tells us the number of solute molecules per liter of solution. If there are 6.022×10^{23} molecules in 1 liter

of solution, then the _____ of the solution is 1 _____ per liter.

2. Temperature has a variety of effects on the solubilites of various solutes. With some solutes, such as
   sugar, solubility increases with increasing temperature. With other solutes, such as sodium chloride
   (table salt), changing temperature has no significant effect. With some solutes, such as lithium
   sulfate, Li_2SO_4, the solubility actually decreases with increasing temperature.

   a. Describe how you would prepare a supersaturated solution of lithium sulfate.

   _____

   b. How might you cause a saturated solution of lithium sulfate to form a precipitate?

   _____

CONCEPTUAL **Physical Science** PRACTICE SHEET

Chapter 18: Mixtures
Pure Mathematics

Using a scientist's definition of pure, identify whether each of the following is 100% pure:

	100% pure?	
Freshly squeezed orange juice	Yes	No
Country air	Yes	No
Ocean water . . . . ,. . .	Yes	No
Fresh drinking water	Yes	No
Skim milk	Yes	No
Stainless steel	Yes	No
A single water molecule . . . . ._	Yes	No

A glass of water contains on the order of a trillion trillion (1×10^{24}) molecules. If the water in this were 99.9999% pure, you could calculate the percent of impurities by subtracting from 100.0000%

$$
\begin{array}{r}
100.0000\% \text{ water } + \text{ impurity molecules} \\
-\ 99.9999\% \text{ water molecules} \\
\hline
0.0001\% \text{ impurity molecules}
\end{array}
$$

Pull out your calculator and calculate the number of impurity molecules in the glass of water. Do this by finding 0.0001% of 1×10^{24}, which is the same as multiplying 1×10^{24} by 0.000001.

$$(1 \times 10^{24})(0.000001) = \underline{\hspace{4cm}}$$

How many impurity molecules are there in a glass of water that's 99.9999% pure?

a) 1,000 (one thousand: 10^3)   b) 1,000,000 (one million: 10^6)

c) 1,000,000,000 (one billion: 10^9)   d) 1,000,000,000,000,000,000 (one million trillion: 10^{18}).

How does your answer make you feel about drinking water that is 99.9999 percent free of some poison, such as a pesticide?

_____

For every one impurity molecule, how many water molecules are there? (Divide the number of water molecules by the number of impurity molecules.)

_____

Would you describe these impurity molecules within water that's 99.9999% pure as "rare" or "common"?

_____

A friend argues that he or she doesn't drink tap water because it contains thousands of molecules of some impurity in each glass. How would you respond in defense of the water's purity, if it indeed does contain thousands of molecules of some impurity per glass?

_____

Name ______________________________ Date __________

CONCEPTUAL **Physical Science** PRACTICE SHEET

Chapter 19: How Atoms Bond
Chemical Bonds

1. Based upon their positions in the periodic table, predict whether each pair of elements will form an ionic, covalent, or neither (atomic number in parenthesis)

a. Gold (79) and Platinum (78) ______ b. Rubidium (37) and Iodine (53) ______

c. Sulfur (16) and Chlorine (17) ______ d. Sulfur (16) and Magnesium (12) ______

e. Calcium (20) and Chlorine (17) ______ f. Germanium(32) and Arsenic (33) ______

g. Iron (26) and Chromium (24) ______ h. Chlorine (17) and Iodine (53) ______

i. Carbon (6) and Bromine (35) ______ j. Barium (56) and Astatine (85) ______

2. The most common ions of lithium, magnesium, aluminum, chlorine, oxygen, and nitrogen and their respective charges are as follows:

Positively Charged Ions	Negatively Charged Ions
Lithium ion: Li^{1+}	Chloride ion: Cl^{1-}
Barium ion: Ba^{2+}	Oxide ion: O^{2-}
Aluminum ion: Al^{3+}	Nitride ion: N^{3-}

Use this information to predict the chemical formulas for the following ionic compounds:

a. Lithium Chloride:______ b. Barium Chloride: ______ c. Aluminum Chloride: ______

d. Lithium Oxide:______ e. Barium Oxide: ______ f. Aluminum Oxide: ______

g. Lithium Nitride:______ h. Barium Nitride: ______ i. Aluminum Nitride: ______

j. How are elements that form positive ions grouped in the periodic table relative to elements that form negative ions?______________________________

3. Predict whether the following chemical structures are polar or nonpolar:

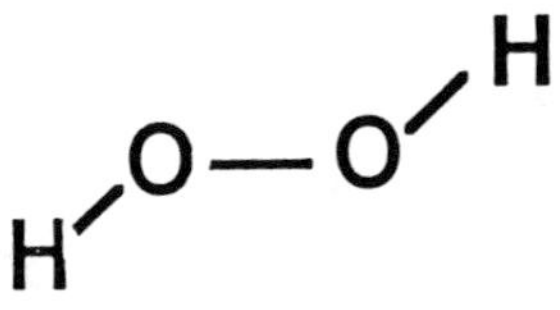

____

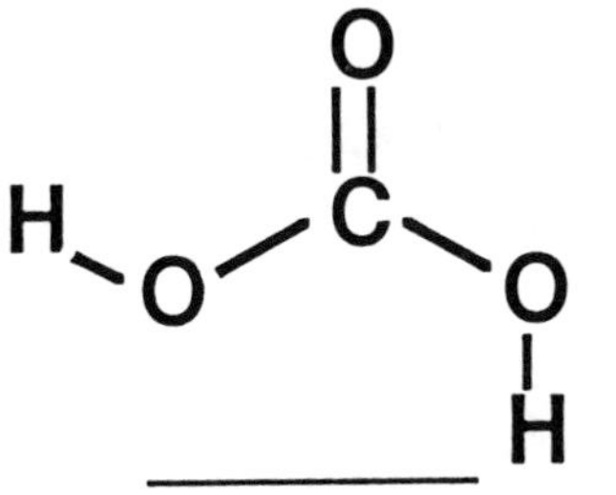

____

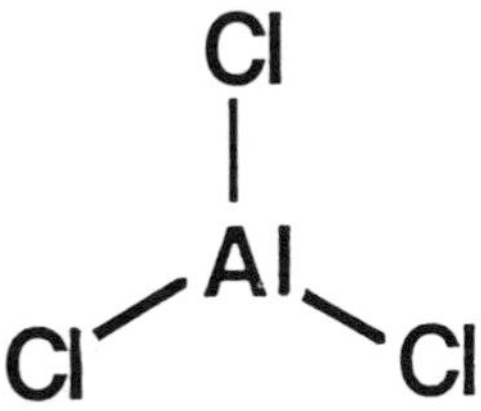

____

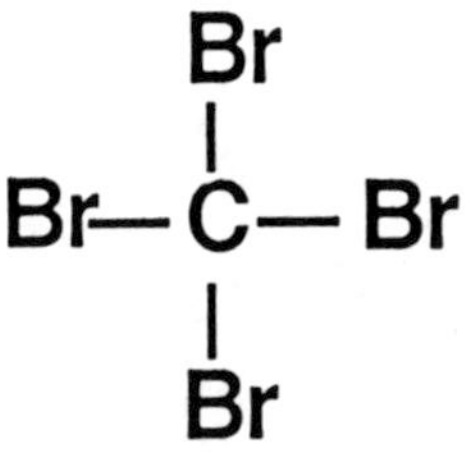

____

____

____

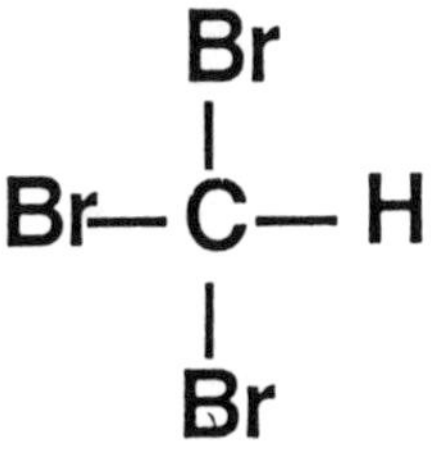

____

Name _____ Date _____

Chapter 19: How Atoms Bond
Shells and the Covalent Bond

When atoms bond covalently their atomic shells overlap so that shared electrons can occupy both shells at the same time.

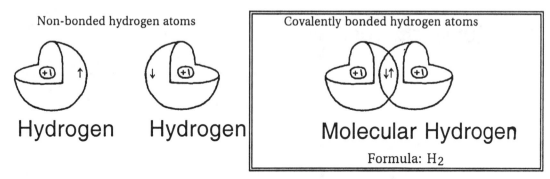

Fill each shell model shown below with enough electrons to make each atom electrically neutral. Use arrows to represent electrons. Within the box draw a sketch showing how the two atoms bond covalently. Draw hydrogen shells more than once when necessary so that no electrons remain unpaired. Write the name and chemical formula for each compound.

A.

Hydrogen   Carbon

Name of Compound: Formula:

B.

Hydrogen   Nitrogen

Name of Compound: Formula:

C.

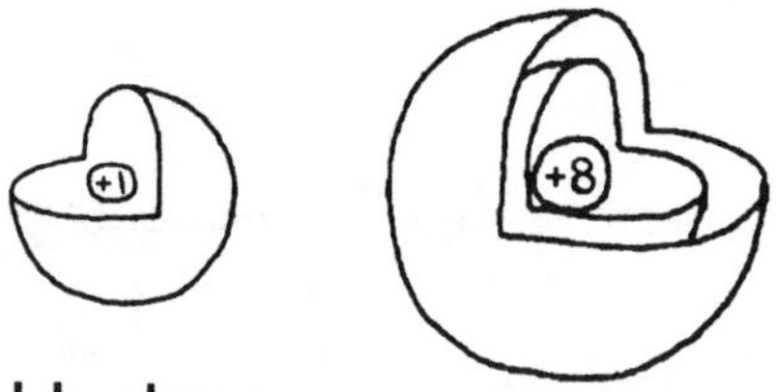

Hydrogen   Oxygen

Name of Compound: Formula:

D.

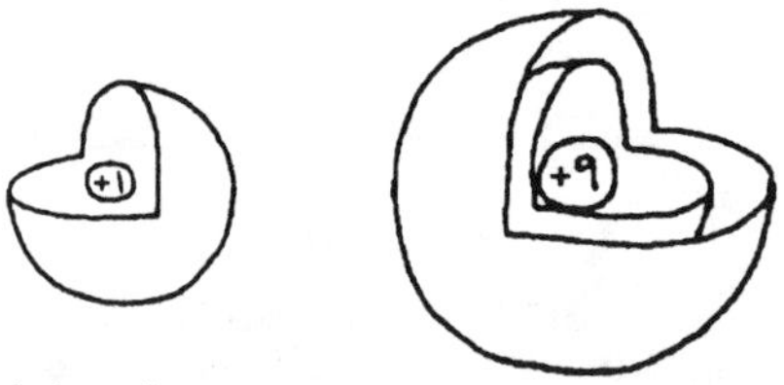

Hydrogen   Fluorine

Name of Compound: Formula:

E.

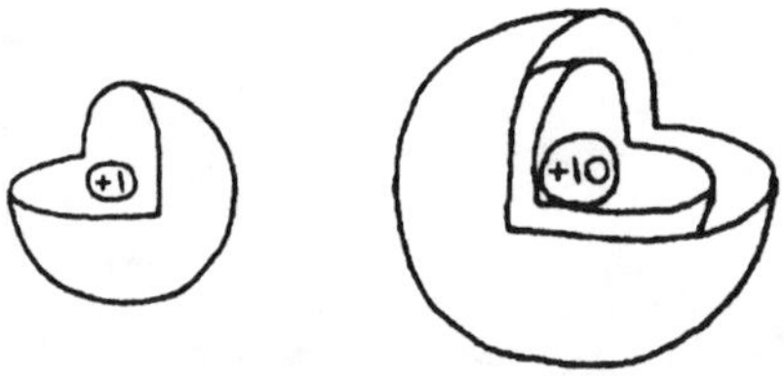

Hydrogen   Neon

Name of Compound: Formula:

1. Note the relative positions of carbon, nitrogen, oxygen, fluorine, and neon in the periodic table. How does this relate to the number of times each of these elements is able to bond with hydrogen?

----

2. How many times is the element boron (atomic number 5) able to bond with hydrogen? Use the shell model to help you with your answer.

CONCEPTUAL **Physical Science** PRACTICE SHEET

Chapter 19: How Atoms Bond
Bond Polarity

Pretend you are one of two electrons being shared by a hydrogen atom and a fluorine atom. Say, for the moment, you are centrally located between the two nuclei. You find that both nuclei are attracted to you, hence, because of your presence the two nuclei are held together.

You are here.

H : F

1. Why are the nuclei of these atoms attracted to you?_____

2. What type of chemical bonding is this?_____

You are held within hydrogen's 1st shell and at the same time within fluorine's 2nd shell. Draw a sketch using the shell models below to show how this is possible. Represent yourself and all other electrons usings arrows. Note your particular location.

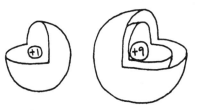

Hydrogen Fluorine

Your Sketch

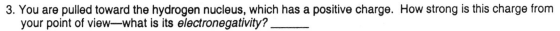

According to the laws of physics, if the nuclei are both attracted to you, then you are attracted to both of the nuclei.

3. You are pulled toward the hydrogen nucleus, which has a positive charge. How strong is this charge from your point of view—what is its *electronegativity*? _____

4. You are also attracted to the fluorine nucleus. What is its electronegativity?____

You are being shared by the hydrogen and fluorine nuclei. But as a moving electron you have some choice as to your location.

5. Consider the electronegativities you experience from both nuclei. Which nucleus would you tend to be closest to? _____

Stop pretending you are an electron and observe the hydrogen-fluorine bond from outside the hydrogen fluoride molecule. Bonding electrons tend to congregate to one side because of the differences in effective nuclear charges. This makes one side slightly negative in character and the opposite side slightly positive. Indicate this on the following structure for hydrogen fluoride using the symbols $\delta-$ and $\delta+$

$$H \quad : \quad F$$

By convention, bonding electrons are not shown. Instead, a line is simply drawn connecting the two bonded atoms. Again indicate the slightly negative and positive ends.

$$H - F$$

6. Would you describe hydrogen fluoride as a polar or nonpolar molecule?_____

7. If two hydrogen fluoride molecules were thrown together would they stick or repel? (Hint: what happens when you throw two small magnets together?)_____

8. Place bonds between the hydrogen and fluorine atoms to show many hydrogen fluoride molecules grouped together. Each element should be bonded only once. Circle each molecule and indicate the slightly negative and slightly positive ends.

H	F	H	F	H	F	H	F	H	F
F	H	F	H	F	H	F	H	F	H
H	F	H	F	H	F	H	F	H	F
F	H	F	H	F	H	F	H	F	H
H	F	H	F	H	F	H	F	H	F
F	H	F	H	F	H	F	H	F	H

The interactions that occur between molecules is the subject of Chapter 20 in your textbook. Onward !

Chapter 20: Molecular Attractions
Atoms to Molecules

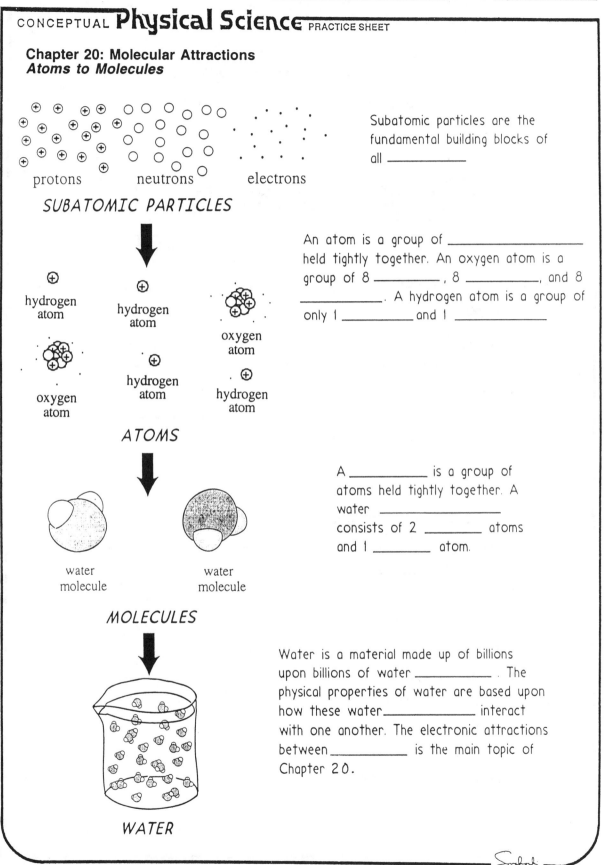

protons   neutrons   electrons

SUBATOMIC PARTICLES

Subatomic particles are the fundamental building blocks of all _____

hydrogen atom

hydrogen atom

oxygen atom

oxygen atom

hydrogen atom

hydrogen atom

ATOMS

An atom is a group of _____ held tightly together. An oxygen atom is a group of 8 _____, 8 _____, and 8 _____. A hydrogen atom is a group of only 1 _____ and 1 _____

water molecule

water molecule

MOLECULES

A _____ is a group of atoms held tightly together. A water _____ consists of 2 _____ atoms and 1 _____ atom.

WATER

Water is a material made up of billions upon billions of water _____ . The physical properties of water are based upon how these water_____ interact with one another. The electronic attractions between_____ is the main topic of Chapter 20.

Chapter 20: Molecular Attractions
Atoms to Molecules

There are four basic types of electrical interactions discussed in Chapter 20.

Electrical Attraction	abbreviation
ion-dipole	i-d
dipole-dipole	d-d
dipole-induced dipole	d-id
induced dipole-induced dipole	id-id

Guess which electrical interaction plays the most significant role in each of the following phenomena? Discuss your answers with your course instructor or fellow classmates.

Salt dissolves in water.. _____

Water droplets stick to glass.. _____

Soap is used to dissolve grime... _____

Your skin is cooled as you perspire.. _____

A fish finds oxygen underwater... _____

A soft drink has fizz.. _____

Plastic wrap sticks to glass.. _____

Soap is rinsed off your hand... _____

Water creeps up a capillary tube.. _____

Tar is a solid at room temperature.. _____

Alcohol mixes with water.. _____

Gasoline is a liquid at room temperature...................................... _____

Tar dissolves in gasoline.. _____

Food cooked on Teflon doesn't stick.. _____

A needle floats on water... _____

Terpentine is used to dilute an oil-based paint.............................. _____

Sugar dissolves in water.. _____

A thin stream of water is deflected by a charged rod.................... _____

Vinegar and oil separate into two layers....................................... _____

Calcium deposits build up in pipes... _____

Oxygen dissolves in perfluorocarbon.. _____

A sugar solution becomes supersaturated.................................... _____

CONCEPTUAL **Physical Science** PRACTICE SHEET

Chapter 21: Chemical Reactions
Relative Masses

In any chemical reaction, a specific number of atoms or molecules react to form a specific number of product atoms or molecules. Since we cannot count out atoms or molecules individually, we instead calculate the number of them in a given bulk using their relative masses.

Assume a baseball is 8 times more massive than a tennis ball.

What is true about the number of balls on each scale shown above?

The atomic masses listed in the periodic table are **relative masses**. Knowing the relative mass of an element we have a handle on the number of atoms within a bulk quantity of that element.

Look to the periodic table to deduce what is true about the number of atoms on each scale shown above?

How many grams of hydrogen fluoride can be formed from the reaction of 18.998 grams of fluorine with 1.008 grams of hydrogen? (Note: Both fluorine and hydrogen occur as diatomic molecules. Their molecular formula are F_2 and H_2, respectively.)

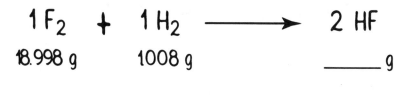

$$1\,F_2 \quad + \quad 1\,H_2 \quad \longrightarrow \quad 2\,HF$$

18.998 g   1008 g   _____ g

Just as we count shoes by pairs and eggs by dozens, we count atoms and molecules by **moles**. One mole equals 6.02×10^{23} (also known as Avogadro's number). Why is Avogadro's number so large when atoms and molecules are so small?

For reasons discussed in your textbook, the atomic mass of an element when expressed in grams is equal to one mole. For example, there is one mole of carbon atoms in 12.011 grams of carbon (C, atomic mass = 12.011). Likewise, the formula mass of a compound when expressed in grams is equal to one mole. For example, there is one mole of water molecules in 18.00 grams of water (H_2O, formula mass = 18.00).

Assume the containers shown below hold fluorine in its diatomic molecular state. In moles, write down the number of atoms and molecules contained in each.

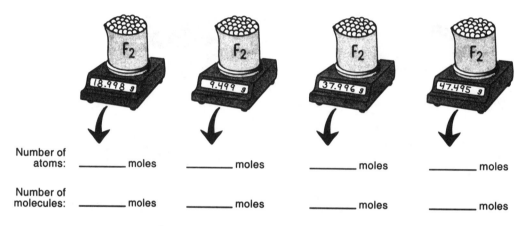

Number of
atoms: _____ moles   _____ moles   _____ moles   _____ moles

Number of
molecules: _____ moles   _____ moles   _____ moles   _____ moles

Multiply each value in moles by Avogadro's number to derive the count of individual atoms and molecules held by each container. Use scientific notation.

Number of
atoms: _____   _____   _____   _____

Number of
molecules: _____   _____   _____   _____

How many grams of hydrogen fluoride can be formed from the reaction of 37.996 grams of fluorine with 1.008 grams of hydrogen?

$$1\,F_2 \quad + \quad 1\,H_2 \longrightarrow \quad 2\,HF$$

37.996 g   1008 g   _____ g

CONCEPTUAL **Physical Science** PRACTICE SHEET

Chapter 21: Chemical Reactions
Relative Masses

On each line "a" indicate the mass of hydrogen fluoride, HF, that can form from the given masses of fluorine, F_2, and hydrogen, H_2. Below each mass on line "b" indicate the corresponding number of moles.

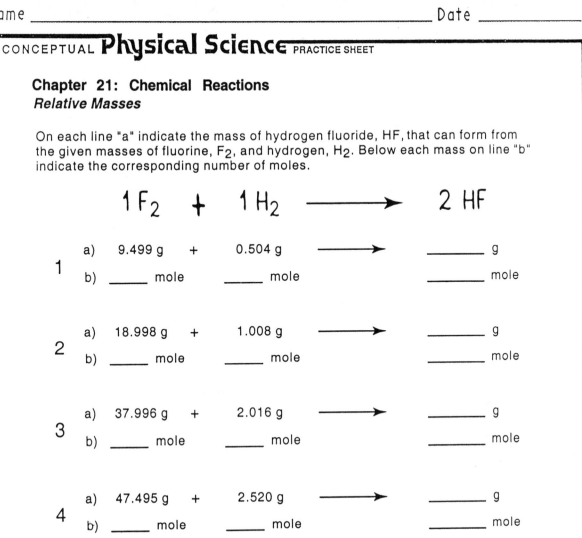

$$1\,F_2 \quad + \quad 1\,H_2 \longrightarrow 2\,HF$$

1
a) 9.499 g   +   0.504 g ⟶ _____ g
b) _____ mole   _____ mole   _____ mole

2
a) 18.998 g   +   1.008 g ⟶ _____ g
b) _____ mole   _____ mole   _____ mole

3
a) 37.996 g   +   2.016 g ⟶ _____ g
b) _____ mole   _____ mole   _____ mole

4
a) 47.495 g   +   2.520 g ⟶ _____ g
b) _____ mole   _____ mole   _____ mole

What do lines 1b, 2b, 3b, and 4b have in common with the coefficients of the chemical equation shown above?

How many grams of hydrogen fluoride can be formed from the reaction of 37.996 grams of fluorine, F_2, with 2.520 grams of hydrogen, H_2?

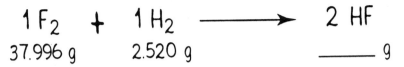

$$1\,F_2 \quad + \quad 1\,H_2 \longrightarrow 2\,HF$$
37.996 g   2.520 g   _____ g

In the preceding reaction, which is too much: 37.996 grams of fluorine, F_2, or 2.520 grams of hydrogen, H_2? Explain.

CONCEPTUAL **Physical Science** PRACTICE SHEET

Chapter 21: Chemical Reactions
Exothermic and Endothermic Reactions

During a chemical reaction atoms are neither created nor destroyed. Instead atoms rearrange—they change partners. This rearrangement of atoms necessarily involves the input and output of energy. First, energy must be supplied to break chemical bonds that hold atoms together. Separated atoms then form new chemical bonds, which involves the release of energy. In an **exothermic** reaction more energy is released than is consumed. Conversely, in an **endothermic** reaction more energy is consumed than is released.

TABLE A   Bond Energies.

Bond	Bond Energy*	Bond	Bond Energy*
H—H	436	Cl—Cl	243
H—C	414	N—N	159
H—N	389	O=O	498
H—O	464	O=C	803
H—Cl	431	N≡N	946

*In kJ/mol

Table A shows bond energies—the amount of energy required to break a chemical bond, and also the amount of energy released when a bond is formed.   Use these bond energies to determine whether the following chemical reactions are exothermic or endothermic.

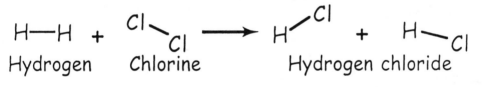

Total Amount of Energy	Total Amount of Energy
Required to Break Bonds	Released Upon Bond Formation
_____kJ/mol	_____kJ/mol

   Net Energy Change of Reaction:_____kJ/mole (absorbed/released)
                                                                   -circle one-

1. Is this reaction exothermic or endothermic?

2. Write the balanced equation for this reaction using chemical formulas and coefficients. If it is exothermic write "Energy" as a product. If it is endothermic write "Energy" as a reactant.

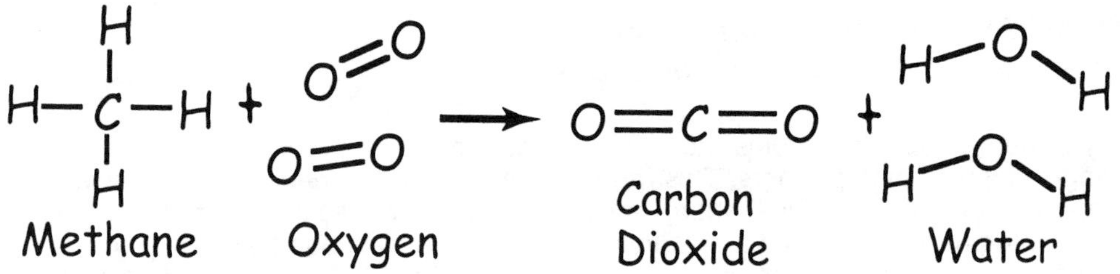

H—C—H + O=O / O=O → O=C=O + H—O—H (×2)

Methane   Oxygen   Carbon Dioxide   Water

Total Amount of Energy
Required to Break Bonds

_____kJ/mol

Total Amount of Energy
Released Upon Bond Formation

_____kJ/mol

Net Energy Change of Reaction:_____kJ/mole (absorbed/released)
-circle one-

3. Is this reaction exothermic or endothermic?

4. Write the balanced equation for this reaction using chemical formulas and coefficients. If it is exothermic write "Energy" as a product. If it is endothermic write "Energy" as a reactant.

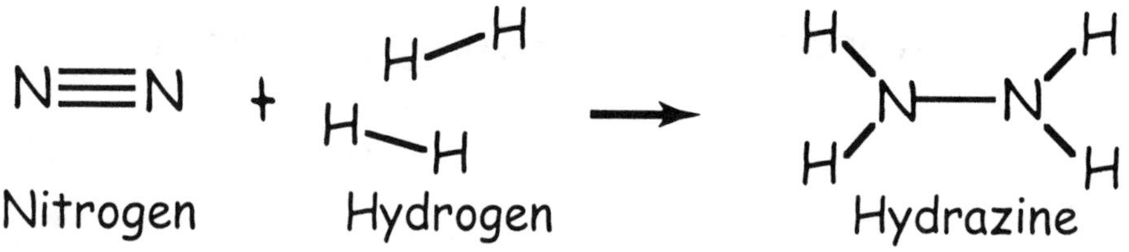

N≡N + H—H / H—H → hydrazine structure

Nitrogen   Hydrogen   Hydrazine

Total Amount of Energy
Required to Break Bonds

_____kJ/mol

Total Amount of Energy
Released Upon Bond Formation

_____kJ/mol

Net Energy Change of Reaction:_____kJ/mole (absorbed/released)
-circle one-

5. Is this reaction exothermic or endothermic?

6. Write the balanced equation for this reaction using chemical formulas and coefficients. If it is exothermic write "Energy" as a product. If it is endothermic write "Energy" as a reactant.

Chapter 22: Acids and Bases
Donating and Accepting Hydrogen Ions

A chemical reaction that involves the transfer of a hydrogen ion from one molecule to another is classified as an acid-base reaction. The molecule that donates the hydrogen ion behaves as an acid. The molecule that accepts the hydrogen ion behaves as a base.

On paper, the acid-base process can be depicted through a series of frames:

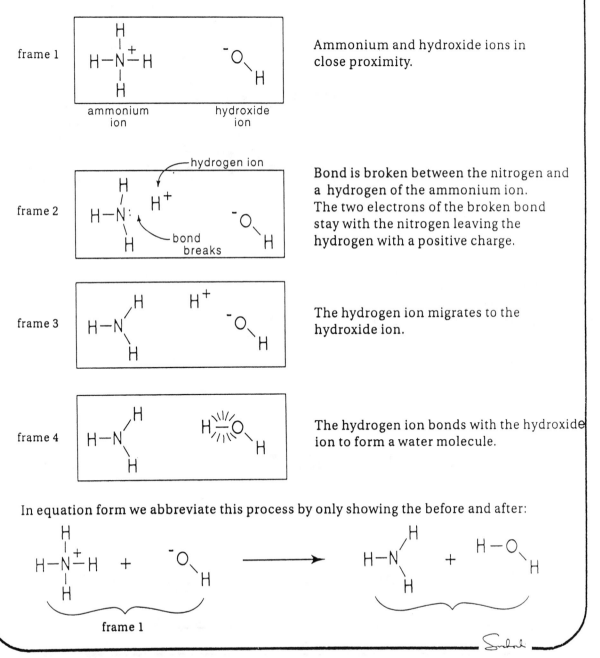

frame 1 — Ammonium and hydroxide ions in close proximity.

frame 2 — Bond is broken between the nitrogen and a hydrogen of the ammonium ion. The two electrons of the broken bond stay with the nitrogen leaving the hydrogen with a positive charge.

frame 3 — The hydrogen ion migrates to the hydroxide ion.

frame 4 — The hydrogen ion bonds with the hydroxide ion to form a water molecule.

In equation form we abbreviate this process by only showing the before and after:

Donating and Accepting Hydrogen Ions continued:

We see from the previous reaction that because the ammonium ion donated a
hydrogen ion, it behaved as an acid. Conversely, the hydroxide ion by accepting
a hydrogen ion behaved as a base. How do the ammonia and water molecules
behave during the reverse process?

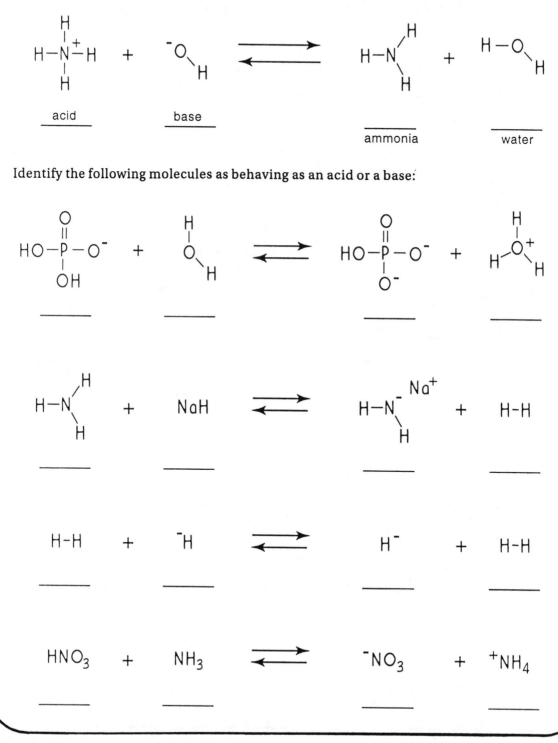

Identify the following molecules as behaving as an acid or a base:

CONCEPTUAL **Physical Science** PRACTICE SHEET

Chapter 23: Oxidation and Reduction
Loss and Gain of Electrons

A chemical reaction that involves the transfer of an electron is classified as an oxidation-reduction reaction. Oxidation is the process of losing an electrons, while reduction is the process of gaining them. Any chemical that causes another chemical to lose electrons (become oxidized) is called an oxidizing agent. Conversely, any chemical that causes another chemical to gain electrons is called a reducing agent.

1. What is the relationship between an atom's ability to behave as an oxidizing agent and its electron affinity?

2. Relative to the periodic table, which elements tend to behave as strong oxidizing agents?

3. Why don't the noble gases behave as oxidizing agents?

4. How is it that an oxidizing agent is itself reduced?

5. Is it possible to have an endothermic oxidation-reduction reaction? If so, cite examples.

6. Specify whether each reactant is about to be oxidized or reduced.

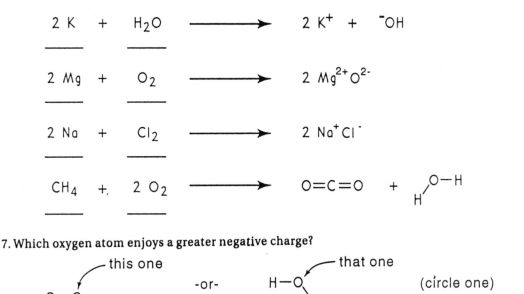

$$2\ K\ +\ H_2O\ \longrightarrow\ 2\ K^+\ +\ {}^-OH$$

$$2\ Mg\ +\ O_2\ \longrightarrow\ 2\ Mg^{2+}O^{2-}$$

$$2\ Na\ +\ Cl_2\ \longrightarrow\ 2\ Na^+Cl^-$$

$$CH_4\ +\ 2\ O_2\ \longrightarrow\ O=C=O\ +\ \underset{H}{\overset{}{}}\!\!\diagdown^{O-H}$$

7. Which oxygen atom enjoys a greater negative charge?

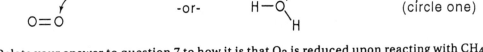

― this one   ― that one

O=O   -or-   H—O   (circle one)
                                    H

8. Relate your answer to question 7 to how it is that O_2 is reduced upon reacting with CH_4 to form carbon dioxide and water.

CONCEPTUAL **Physical Science** PRACTICE SHEET

Chapter 24: Organic Compounds
Structures of Organic Compounds

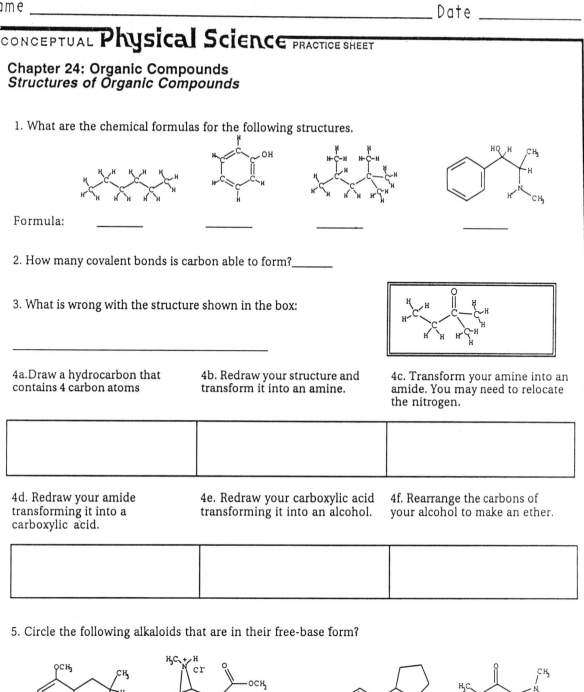

1. What are the chemical formulas for the following structures.

Formula: _____   _____   _____   _____

2. How many covalent bonds is carbon able to form?_____

3. What is wrong with the structure shown in the box:

_____

4a. Draw a hydrocarbon that contains 4 carbon atoms

4b. Redraw your structure and transform it into an amine.

4c. Transform your amine into an amide. You may need to relocate the nitrogen.

4d. Redraw your amide transforming it into a carboxylic acid.

4e. Redraw your carboxylic acid transforming it into an alcohol.

4f. Rearrange the carbons of your alcohol to make an ether.

5. Circle the following alkaloids that are in their free-base form?

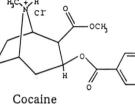   

Mescaline   Cocaine   Nicotine   Caffeine

6. How might you convert a free-base alkaloid into a salt?

7. Why are alkaloids less water soluble in their free-base form?

8. Which should have a greater tendency to vaporize upon heating: an alkaloid in its free-base form or one in its salt form? Why?

Chapter 24: Organic Compounds
Polymers

1. Circle the monomers that may be useful for forming an addition polymer and draw a box around the ones that may be useful for forming a condensation polymer.

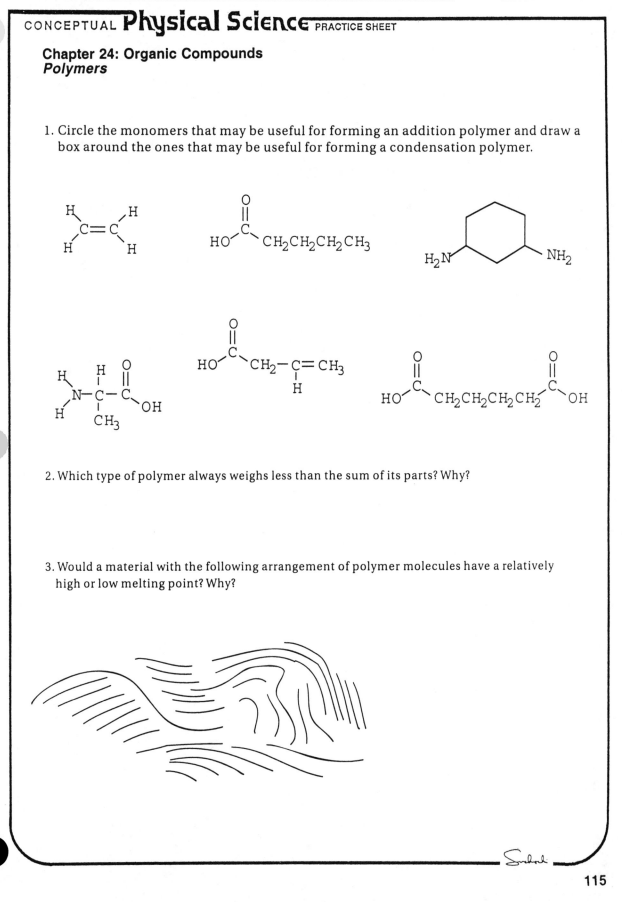

2. Which type of polymer always weighs less than the sum of its parts? Why?

3. Would a material with the following arrangement of polymer molecules have a relatively high or low melting point? Why?

Name _____ Date _____

Chapter 25: Minerals and How We Use Them
Chemical Structure and Formulas of Minerals

Out of the more than 3400 minerals, only about two dozen are abundant. Minerals are classified by their chemical composition and internal atomic structure and are divided into groups. For this exercise we explore the following mineral groups: *carbonates, sulfides, sulfates,* and *halides.*

For each mineral structure diagrammed below, look for a pattern in the structure, count the number of atoms (ions) in each, and fill in the blanks.

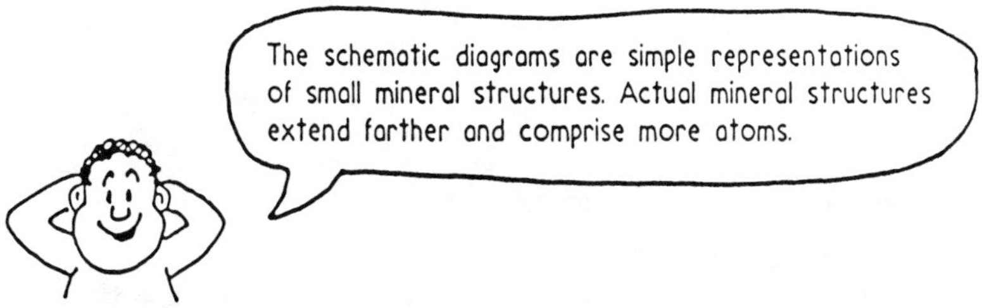

> The schematic diagrams are simple representations of small mineral structures. Actual mineral structures extend farther and comprise more atoms.

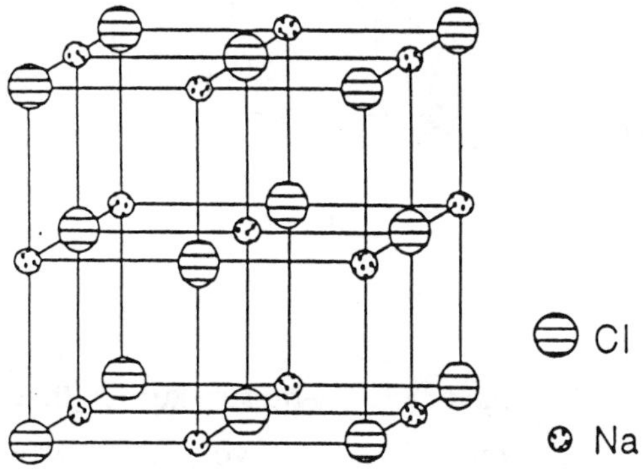

⊖ Cl

☉ Na

1. Circle pairs of Na and Cl ions in the structure and add any ion(s) needed to complete pairing. This mineral structure contains _____ Na ions and _____ Cl ions. The mineral's formula is _____. This mineral belongs to the _____ group.

2. This mineral structure contains _____ Ca atoms, ____ C atoms, and _____ O atoms. The mineral's formula is _____. This mineral belongs to the _____ group.

◯ Ca

● C

◦ O

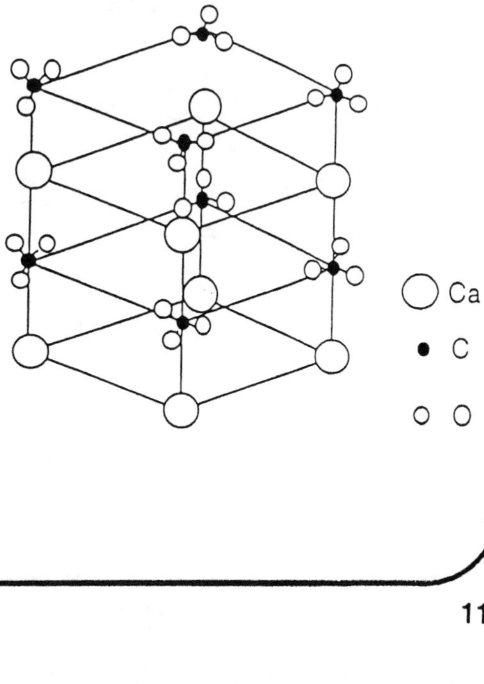

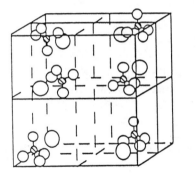

3. This mineral structure contains _____ Ca atoms, _____ S atoms, and _____ O ions.   The mineral's formula is _____ This mineral belongs to the _____ group.

○ Ca

⊘ S

○ O

4. Complete the structure by adding the needed atom(s). This mineral structure contains _____ Fe atoms and _____ S atoms. The mineral's formula is _____. This mineral belongs to the _____ group.

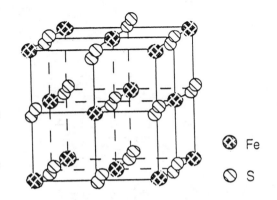

⊛ Fe

⊘ S

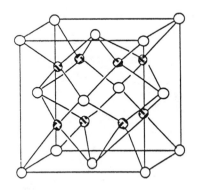

○ Ca

⊘ F

5. Complete the mineral structure so that each Ca atom is linked to two F atoms. Now the mineral structure contains _____ Ca atoms and _____ F atoms. The mineral's formula is _____.
This mineral belongs to the _____ group.

Leslie

CONCEPTUAL **Physical Science** PRACTICE SHEET

Chapter 26: Rocks
The Rock Cycle

Complete the illustration, which depicts the different paths in the rock cycle. Insert arrows to show direction of pathways.

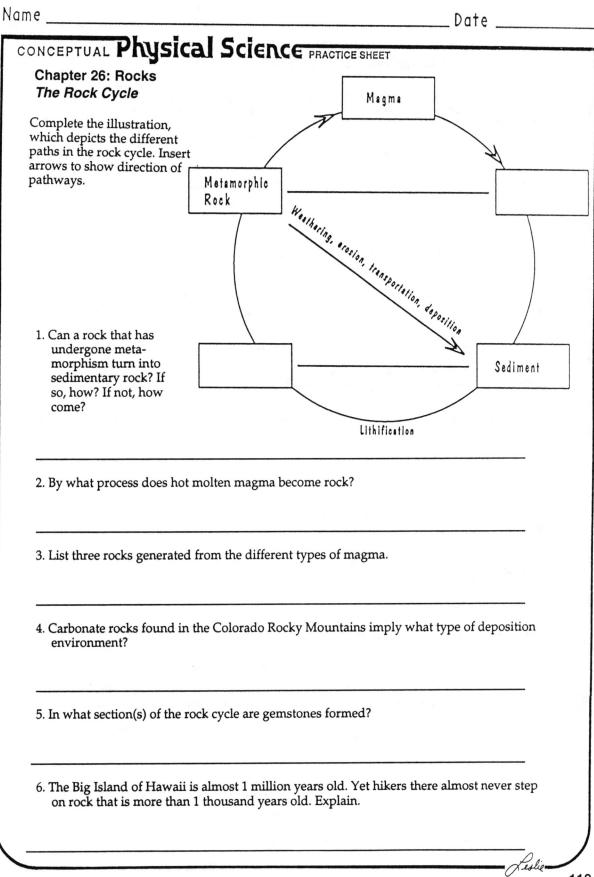

1. Can a rock that has undergone meta-morphism turn into sedimentary rock? If so, how? If not, how come?

_____

2. By what process does hot molten magma become rock?

_____

3. List three rocks generated from the different types of magma.

_____

4. Carbonate rocks found in the Colorado Rocky Mountains imply what type of deposition environment?

_____

5. In what section(s) of the rock cycle are gemstones formed?

_____

6. The Big Island of Hawaii is almost 1 million years old. Yet hikers there almost never step on rock that is more than 1 thousand years old. Explain.

_____

Chapter 26: Rocks
Igneous Rock Differentiation: How to Make Granite

A mineral is called a high temperature mineral if its melting/freezing temperature is relatively high. A mineral is called a low temperature mineral if its melting/freezing temperature is relatively low.

Suppose we start with solid, basaltic rock. If it is heated, it will partially melt.

1. Is the type of mineral left behind (that doesn't liquefy) a high temperature or low temperature mineral?

_____

Do you think granite could form in this manner?

2. Which type will melt to form a liquid?

_____

3. Will the resulting liquid be higher or lower in silicon content than the original rock? Why?

_____

4. If this liquid is separated from the original rock and then cooled relatively quickly, what is the name of the rock that will most likely form?

_____

5. Repeat steps 1 through 4 for the rock formed in question 4. What is the name of the resulting rock if the liquid is allowed to cool very slowly?

_____

Now consider a magma chamber that contains completely molten basaltic magma. Let's allow this magma to cool very slowly.

6. Which type of minerals will be the first to form, low temperature or high temperature minerals?

_____

7. Will the remaining liquid be higher or lower in silicon content than the original liquid? Why?

_____

Assume that the newly formed crystals settle to the bottom of the magma chamber so that there is no chemical interaction between the newly formed crystals and the remaining liquid.

8. If this process continues, will the low temperature minerals eventually crystallize?

_____

9. If so, would a rock formed from these minerals be higher or lower in silicon content than a basalt?

_____

Leslie

CONCEPTUAL **Physical Science** PRACTICE SHEET

Chapter 27: The Dynamic Earth
Faults

Three block diagrams are illustrated below. Draw arrows on each diagram to show the direction of movement. Answer the questions next to each diagram.

A.

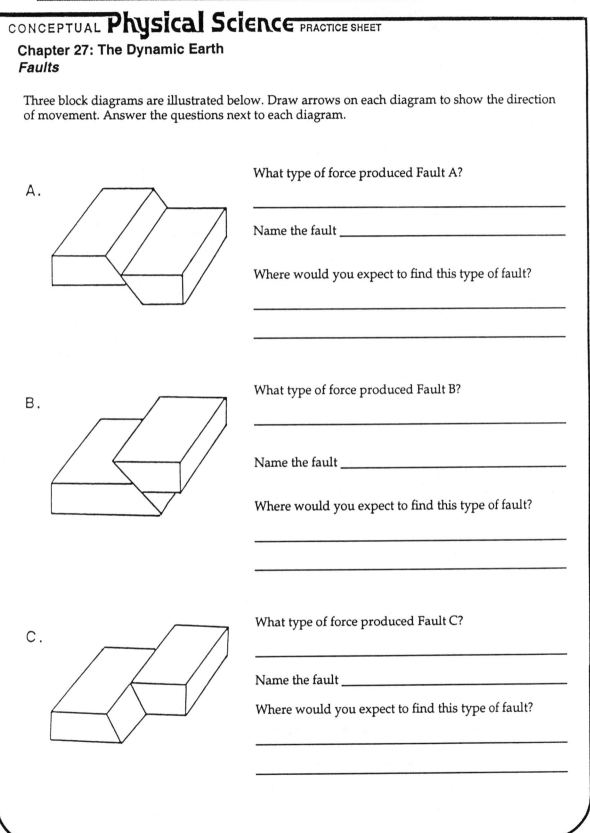

What type of force produced Fault A?

_____

Name the fault _____

Where would you expect to find this type of fault?

_____

_____

B.

What type of force produced Fault B?

_____

Name the fault _____

Where would you expect to find this type of fault?

_____

_____

C.

What type of force produced Fault C?

_____

Name the fault _____

Where would you expect to find this type of fault?

_____

_____

Name _____ Date _____

CONCEPTUAL Physical Science PRACTICE SHEET

Chapter 27: The Dynamic Earth
Structural Geology

Much subsurface information is learned by oil companies when wells are drilled. Some of this information leads to the discovery of oil, and some reveals subsurface structures such as folds and/or faults in the Earth's crust.

Four oil wells that have been drilled to the same depth are shown on the cross section below. Each well encounters contacts between different rock formations at the depths shown in the table below. Rock formations are labeled A — F, with A as the youngest rock formation and F as the oldest rock formation.

	Depth to Contact (in meters)			
Contact	Oil well #1	Oil well #2	Oil well #3	Oil well #4
A-B	200	not encountered	200	not encountered
B-C	400	100	400	100
C-D	600	300	600	300
D-E	800	500	800	500
E-F	1000	700	1000	700

1. In the cross section below, Contacts D - E and E – F are plotted for Oil Wells 1 and 2. Plot the remainder of the data for all four wells, labeling each point you plot.

2. Draw lines to connect the contacts between the rock formations (as is done for Contacts D - E and E – F for Oil Wells 1 and 2).

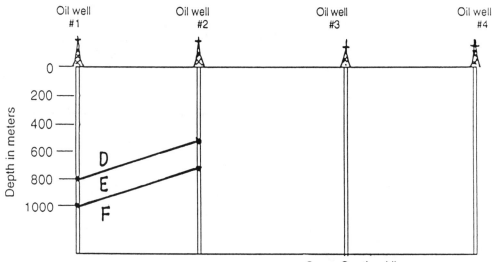

Cross Section View

Questions

1. What explanation can you offer for no sign of formation A in Wells 2 and 4?

_____

2. What geological structures are revealed? Label them on the cross section.

_____

Name:______________________________ Date:__________

CONCEPTUAL **Physical Science** PRACTICE SHEET

Chapter 27: The Dynamic Earth
Plate Boundaries

Draw arrows on the plate boundaries **A**, **B**, and **C**, to show the relative direction of movement.

Type of plate boundary for **A**? ______________

What type of force generates this type of boundary?

____

Is this a site of crustal formation, destruction, or crustal transport?

____

A.

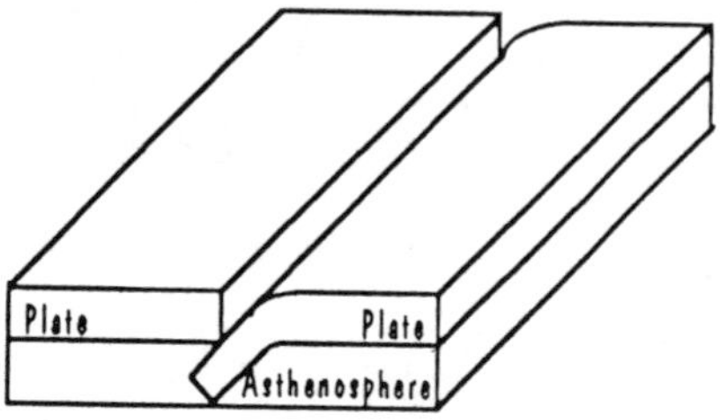

Plate
Plate
Asthenosphere

Type of plate boundary for **B**? ______________

What type of force generates this type of boundary?

____

Is this a site of crustal formation, destruction, or crustal transport?

____

B.

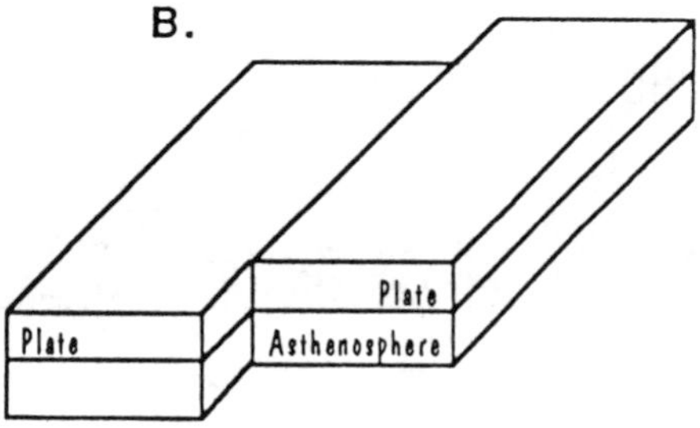

Plate
Plate
Asthenosphere

Type of plate boundary for **C**? ______________

What type of force generates this type of boundary?

____

Is this a site of crustal formation, destruction, or crustal transport?

____

C.

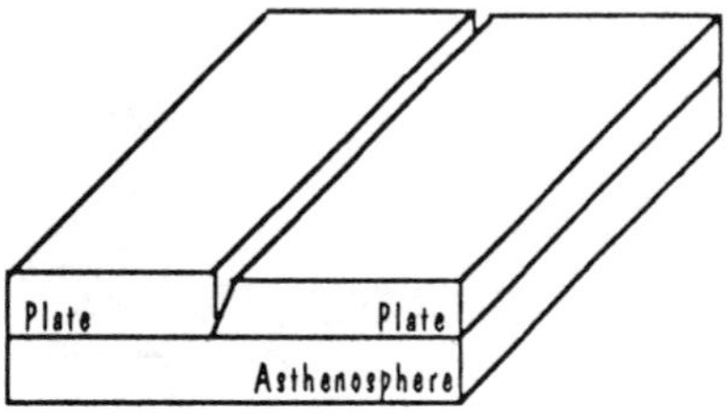

Plate
Plate
Asthenosphere

Draw arrows on the transform faults below to indicate relative motion.

Draw arrows on the transform faults below to indicate relative motion.

|| Mid-ocean spreading ridge —— Transform fault

Geology is a down-to-earth science!

thanx to Bob Abrams Leslie

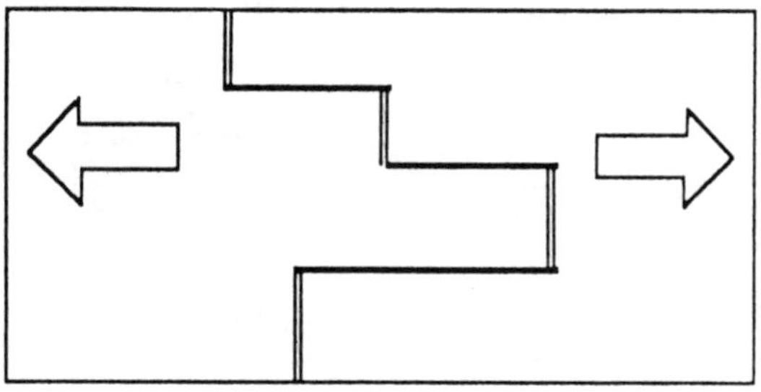

Chapter 27: The Dynamic Earth
Sea-Floor Spreading

The rate of sea-floor spreading is from 1 to 10 centimeters per year. If we know the distance and age between two points on the ocean floor, we can determine the rate of spreading. Diagrams A, B, and C show stages of sea-floor spreading. Spreading begins at A, continues to B where rocks at location **P** begin to spread to the farther-apart positions we see in C. At C newer rock at the ocean crest **S** dated at 10 million years. Using the scale: 1 mm = 50 km, use a ruler on C to find the

1. separation rate of the two continental landmasses in the past 10 million years, in cm/yr _____

2. age of the sea floor at **P** in Diagram C (1 cm/yr = 10 km/million years) _____

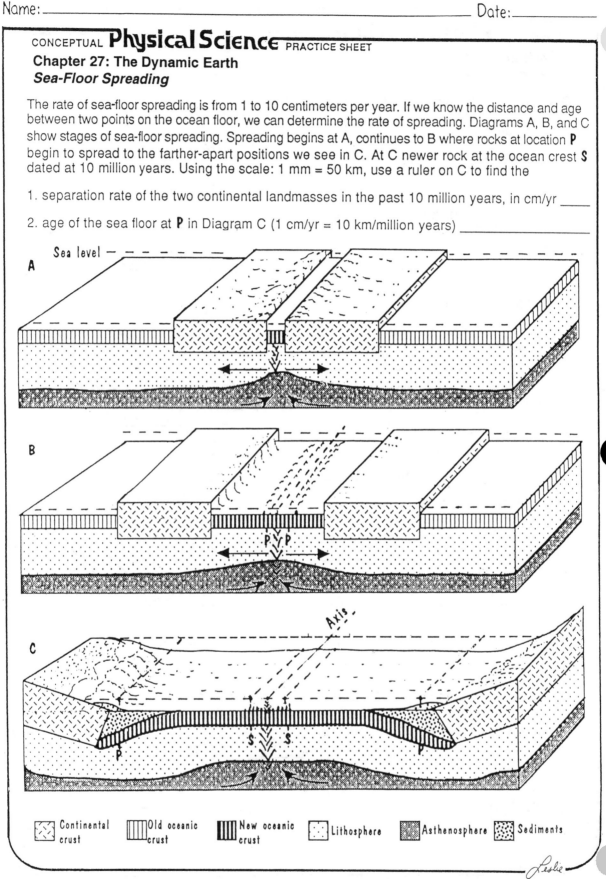

Continental crust   Old oceanic crust   New oceanic crust   Lithosphere   Asthenosphere   Sediments

CONCEPTUAL **Physical Science** PRACTICE SHEET

Chapter 27: The Dynamic Earth
Plate Boundaries and Magma Generation

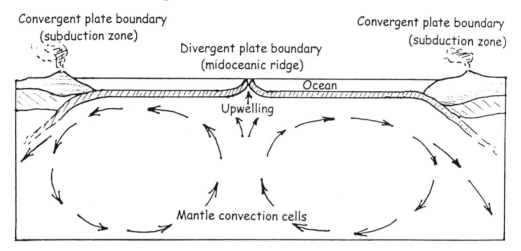

Partial melting occurs in the mantle at divergent and convergent plate boundaries when the melting point of mantle rocks is lowered.

1. What is the mechanism that lowers the melting point of mantle rock at divergent boundaries?

_____

_____

_____

_____

_____

2. What is the mechanism that lowers the melting point of mantle rock at convergent boundaries?

_____

_____

_____

_____

_____

Leslie

CONCEPTUAL **Physical Science** PRACTICE SHEET

Chapter 28: Occurrence and Movement of Water
Groundwater Flow and Contaminant Transport

The occupants of Houses 1, 2, and 3 wish to drill wells for domestic water supply. Note that the locations of all houses are between lakes A and B, at different elevations.

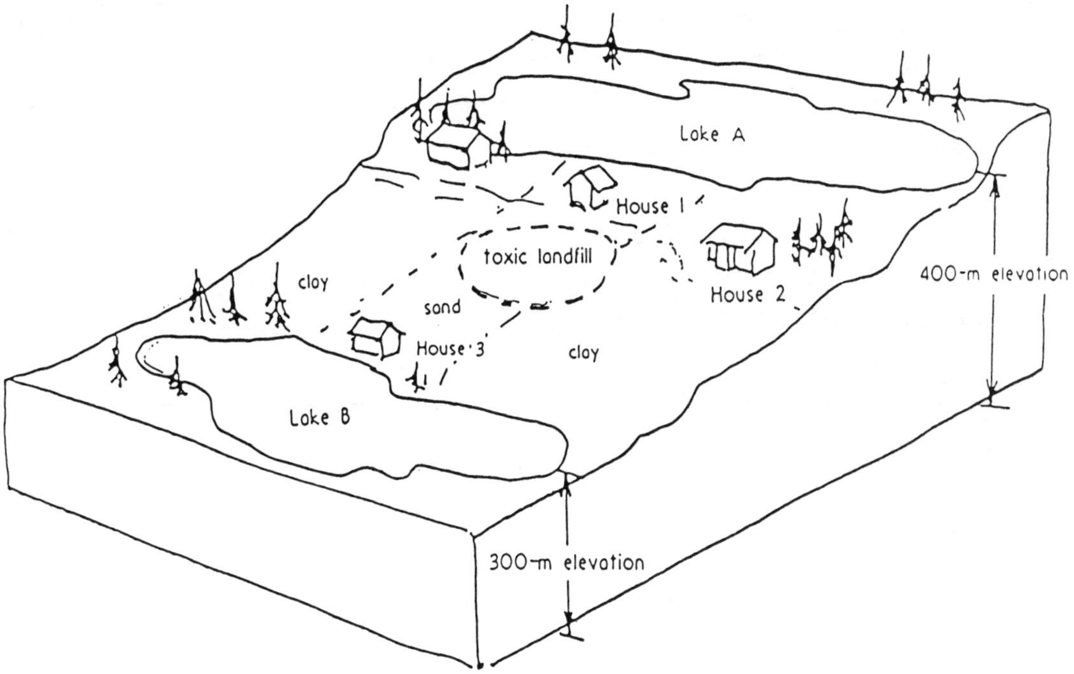

1. Show by sketching dashed lines on the drawing, the likely direction of groundwater flow beneath all the houses.

2. Which of the wells drilled beside Houses 1, 2, and 3 are likely to yield an abundant water supply?

_____

3. Do any of the three need to worry about the toxic landfill contaminating their water supply? Explain.

_____

4. Why don't the homeowners simply take water directly from the lakes?

_____

5. Suggest a potentially better location for the landfill. Defend your choice.

_____

_____

_____

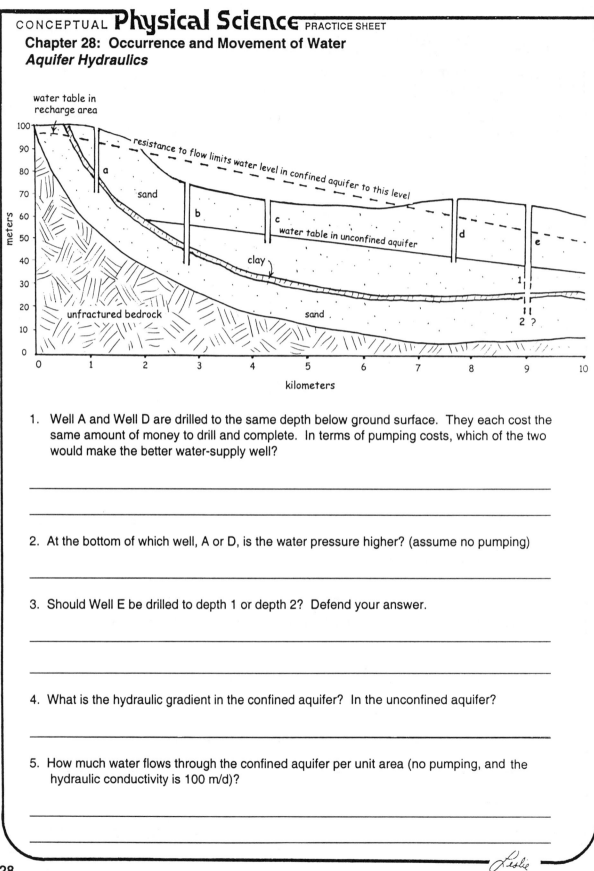

1. Well A and Well D are drilled to the same depth below ground surface. They each cost the same amount of money to drill and complete. In terms of pumping costs, which of the two would make the better water-supply well?

_____

_____

2. At the bottom of which well, A or D, is the water pressure higher? (assume no pumping)

_____

3. Should Well E be drilled to depth 1 or depth 2? Defend your answer.

_____

_____

4. What is the hydraulic gradient in the confined aquifer? In the unconfined aquifer?

_____

5. How much water flows through the confined aquifer per unit area (no pumping, and the hydraulic conductivity is 100 m/d)?

_____

_____

CONCEPTUAL **Physical Science** PRACTICE SHEET

Chapter 29: Surface Processes
Stream Flow

The diagram below illustrates a stream. Coarse sediment grains will be deposited primarily at one type of location, and finer sediment grains at another. On the diagram, mark the likely locations of each.

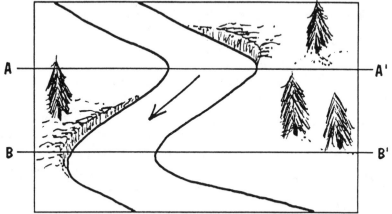

Over time, the shape of the stream will change. Draw a likely new shape in the box below.

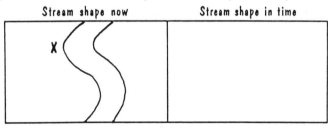

Stream shape now   Stream shape in time

As the shape of the stream changes, the type of sediment deposited changes. At point X, how will the vertical sequence of rocks appear in terms of grain size? Sketch the sequence in the space to the right.

The diagrams below illustrate several types of bedding planes. Name the type of bedding below each diagram, and show arrows on the diagrams to show flow direction.

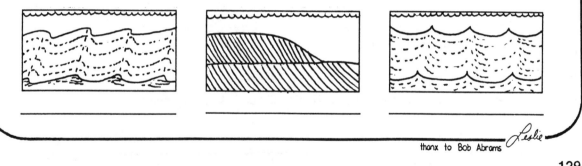

thanx to Bob Abrams *Leslie*

Stream Velocity

Let's explore how the average velocity of streams and rivers can change. Recall in Chapter 35 that the volume of water that flows past a given location over any given length of time depends both on the stream velocity and the cross-sectional area of the stream. We say

$$Q = A \times V$$

where Q is the volumetric flow rate, A is the cross-sectional area of the stream, and V its average velocity.

Consider the stream shown below, with rectangular cross-sectional areas

A = width × depth

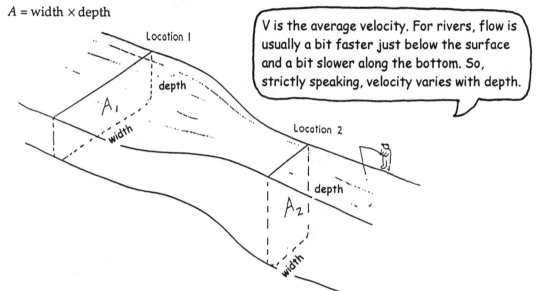

V is the average velocity. For rivers, flow is usually a bit faster just below the surface and a bit slower along the bottom. So, strictly speaking, velocity varies with depth.

1. The two locations shown have no inlets or outlets between them, so Q remains constant. Suppose the cross-sectional areas are also constant ($A_1 = A_2$), with Location 2 deeper but narrower than Location 1. What change, if any, occurs for the stream velocity?

_____

2. If Q remains constant, what happens to stream velocity at Location 2 if A_2 is less than A_1?

_____

3. If Q remains constant, what happens to stream velocity at Location 2 if A_2 is greater than A_1?

_____

4. What happens to stream velocity at Location 2 if area A_2 remains the same, but Q increases (perhaps by an inlet along the way?)

_____

5. What happens to stream velocity at Location 2 if both A_2 and Q increase?

_____

CONCEPTUAL **Physical Science** PRACTICE SHEET

Chapter 29: Surface Processes
Glacial Movement

From season to season the mass of a glacier changes. With each change in mass, the glacier moves. Glacier movement is measured by placing a line of markers across the ice and recording their changes in position over a period of time.

In the example below, we show the initial position of a line of markers and the glaciers terminus (the end of the glacier).

Draw the markers and glacier terminus at a later time for each of the following scenarios.

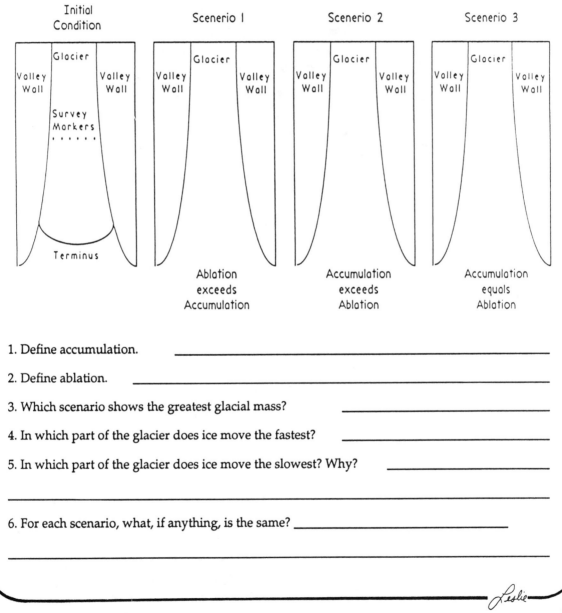

1. Define accumulation. _____

2. Define ablation. _____

3. Which scenario shows the greatest glacial mass? _____

4. In which part of the glacier does ice move the fastest? _____

5. In which part of the glacier does ice move the slowest? Why? _____

_____

6. For each scenario, what, if anything, is the same? _____

_____

CONCEPTUAL **Physical Science** PRACTICE SHEET

Chapter 30: A Brief History of the Earth
Relative Time—What Came First?

The cross section below depicts many geologic events. List to the right the sequences of geologic history starting with the oldest event to the youngest event — and where appropriate include tectonic events(such as folding, deposition of beds, subsidence, uplift, erosion, intrusion).

Youngest _____

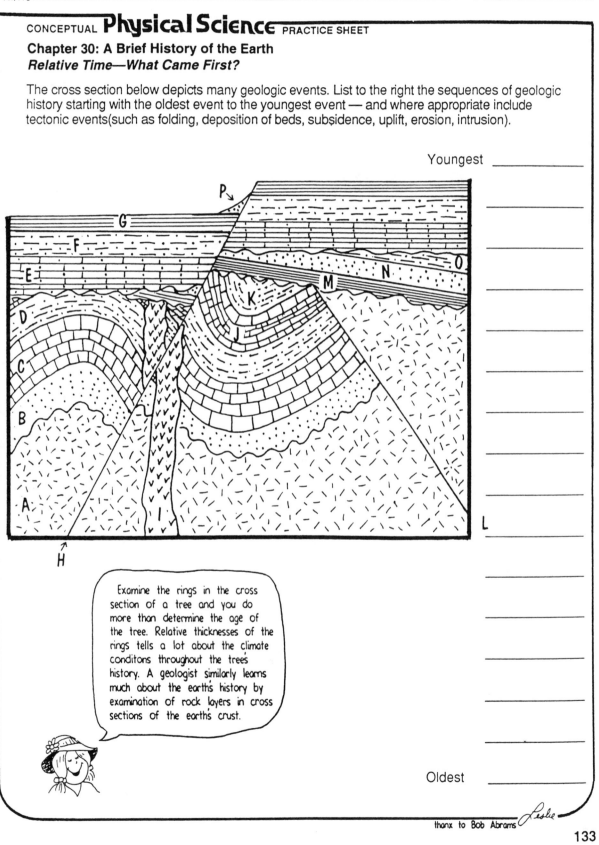

Examine the rings in the cross section of a tree and you do more than determine the age of the tree. Relative thicknesses of the rings tells a lot about the climate conditons throughout the trees history. A geologist similarly learns much about the earths history by examination of rock layers in cross sections of the earths crust.

Oldest _____

thanx to Bob Abrams

CONCEPTUAL **Physical Science** PRACTICE SHEET

Chapter 30: A Brief History of the Earth
Age Relationships

From your investigation of the 6 geologic regions shown, answer the questions below.
The number of each question refers to the same-numbered region.

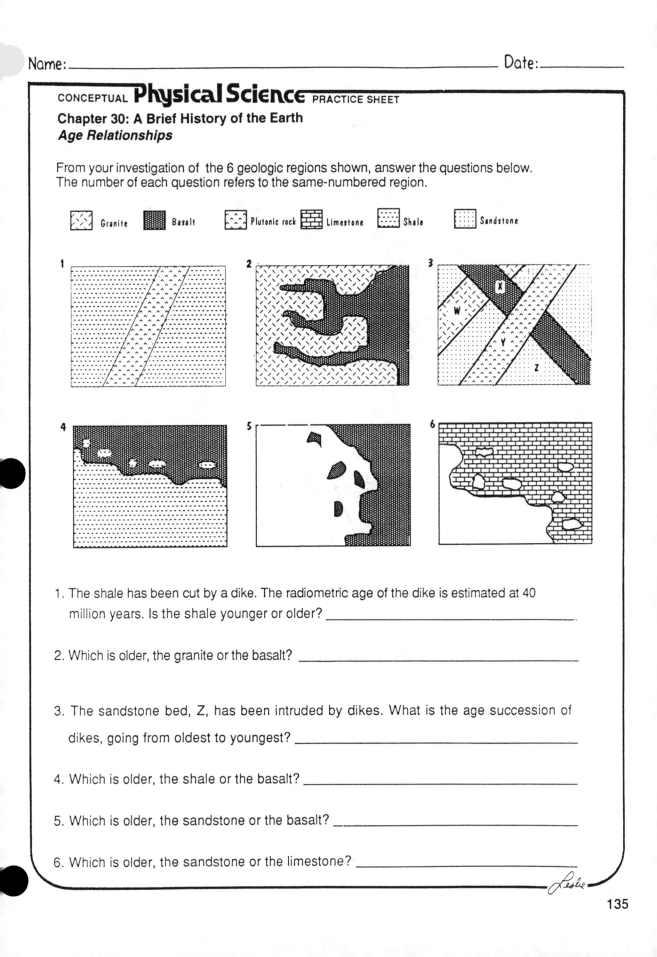

1. The shale has been cut by a dike. The radiometric age of the dike is estimated at 40 million years. Is the shale younger or older? _____.

2. Which is older, the granite or the basalt? _____

3. The sandstone bed, Z, has been intruded by dikes. What is the age succession of dikes, going from oldest to youngest? _____

4. Which is older, the shale or the basalt? _____

5. Which is older, the sandstone or the basalt? _____

6. Which is older, the sandstone or the limestone? _____

Leslie

Unconformities and Age Relationships

The wavy lines in the 4 regions below represent unconformities. Investigate the regions and answer corresponding questions 1 — 4 below.

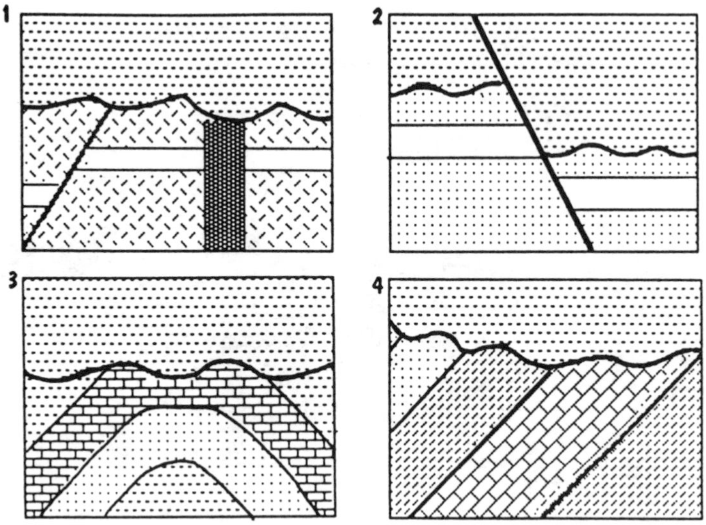

1. Did the faulting and dike occur before or after the unconformity? _____

   What kind of unconformity is it? _____

2. Did the faulting occur before or after the unconformity? _____

   What kind of unconformity is represented? _____

3. Did the folding occur before or after the unconformity? _____

   What kind of unconformity is it? _____

4. What kind of unconformity is represented? _____

5. Interestingly, the age of the earth is some 4.5 billion years old — yet the oldest rocks found are some 3.7 billion years old. Why do we find no 4.5-billion year old rocks?

   _____

6. What is the age of the innermost ring in a living redwood tree that is 2000 years old? What is the age of the outermost ring? How does this example relate to the previous question?

   _____

   _____

7. What is the approximate age of the atoms that make up a 3.7-billion year old rock?

   _____

Leslie

CONCEPTUAL **Physical Science** PRACTICE SHEET

Chapter 30: A Brief History of the Earth
Radiometric Dating

Isotopes Commonly Used for Radiometric Dating		
Radioactive Parent	Stable Daughter Product	Half-life Value
Uranium-238	lead-206	4.5 billion years
Uranium-235	lead-207	704 million years
Potassium-40	argon-40	1.3 billion years
Carbon-14	nitrogen-14	5730 years

1. Consider a radiometric lab experiment wherein 99.98791 % of a certain radioactive sample of material remains after one year. What is the decay rate of the sample?

_____

2. What is the rate constant?
(Assume that the decay rate is constant for the one year period.)

_____

3. What is the half-life?

_____

4. Identify the isotope.

_____

5. In a sample collected in the field, this isotope was found to be 1/16 of its original amount. What is the age of the sample?

_____

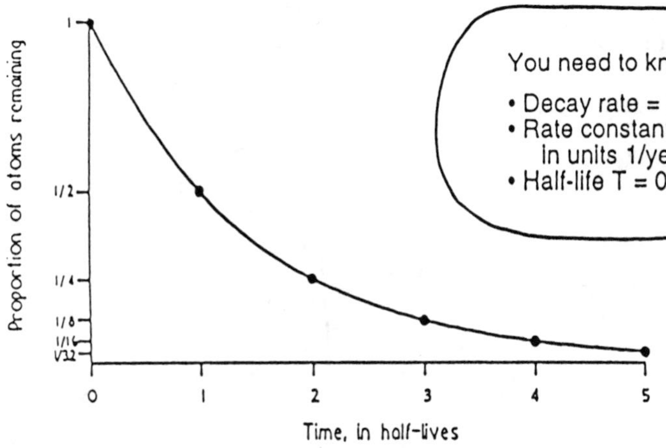

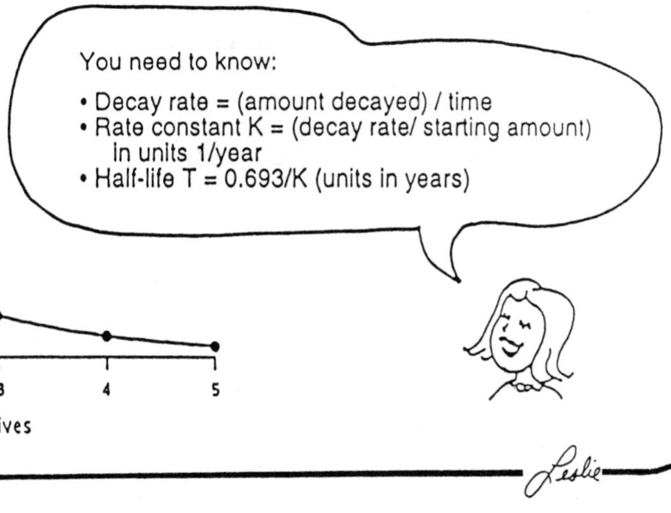

You need to know:

- Decay rate = (amount decayed) / time
- Rate constant K = (decay rate/ starting amount) in units 1/year
- Half-life T = 0.693/K (units in years)

Leslie

Chapter 30: A Brief History of the Earth
Our Earth's Hot Interior

A major puzzle faced scientist in the 19th century. Volcanoes showed
that the Earth's interior is semi-molten. Penetration into the crust by
bore-holes and mines showed that the Earth's temperature increases
with depth. Scientists knew that heat flows from the interior to the
surface. They assumed that the source of the Earth's internal heat
was primordial, the afterglow of its fiery birth. Measurements of the
Earth's rate of cooling indicated a relatively young Earth—some 25
to 30 million years in age. But geological evidence indicated an older
Earth. This puzzle wasn't solved until the discovery of radioactivity.
Then it was learned that the interior was kept hot by the energy of
radioactive decay. We now know the age of the Earth is some 4.5
billion years—a much older Earth.

All rock contains trace amounts of radioactive minerals. Radioactive minerals in common granite
release energy at the rate 0.03 J/kg·yr. Granite at the Earth's surface transfers this energy to the
surroundings practically as fast as it is generated, so we don't find granite any warmer than other
parts of our environment. But what if a sample of granite were thermally insulated? That is,
suppose all the increase of thermal energy due to radioactive decay were contained. Then it would
get hotter. How much hotter? Let's figure it out, using 790 J/kg·C° as the specific heat of granite.

Calculations to make:

1. How many joules are required to increase the
   temperature of 1 kg of granite by 500 C°?

_____

2. How many years would it take radioactivity in a
   kilogram of granite to produce this many joules?

_____

> Let's see now... back in Chapter 7 we
> learned that the relationship between
> quantity of heat, mass, specific heat
> and temperature difference is
>
> $Q = cm\Delta T$

Questions to answer:

1. How many years would it take a thermally insulated 1-kilogram chunk off granite to undergo
   a 500 C° increase in temperature?

_____

2. How many years would it take a thermally insulated one-million-kilogram chunk off granite
   to undergo a 500 C° increase in temperature?

_____

3. Why does the Earth's interior remain molten hot?

_____

4. Rock has a higher melting temperature deep in the interior. Why?

_____

5. Why doesn't the Earth just keep getting hotter until it all melts?

> An electric toaster stays hot
> while electric energy is
> supplied, and doesn't cool until
> switched off. Similarly, do you
> think the energy source now
> keeping the Earth hot will one
> day suddenly switch off like a
> disconnected toaster -
> gradually decrease over a long
> time?

_____

Leslie

CONCEPTUAL **Physical Science** PRACTICE SHEET

Chapter 31: The Atmosphere, the Oceans, and Their Interactions
The Earth's Seasons

1. The warmth of equatorial regions and coldness of polar regions on the Earth can be understood by considering light from a flashlight striking a surface. If it strikes perpendicularly, light energy is more concentrated as it covers a smaller area; if it strikes at an angle, the energy spreads over a larger area. So the energy per unit area is less.

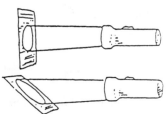

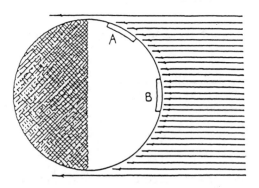

The arrows represent rays of light from the distant sun incident upon the Earth. Two areas of equal size are shown, Area A near the north pole and Area B near the equator. Count the rays that reach each area, and explain why region B is warmer than region A.

2. The Earth's seasons result from the 23.5-degree tilt of the Earth's daily spin axis as it orbits the sun. When the Earth is at the position shown on the right in the sketch below (not shown to scale), the Northern Hemisphere tilts toward the sun, and sunlight striking it is strong (more rays per area). Sunlight striking the Southern Hemisphere is weak (fewer rays per area). Days in the north are warmer, and daylight lasts longer. You can see this by imagining the Earth making its complete daily 24-hour spin.

Do two things on the sketch: (1) Shade the Earth in nighttime darkness for all positions, as is already done in the left position. (2) Label each position with the proper month — March, June, September, or December.

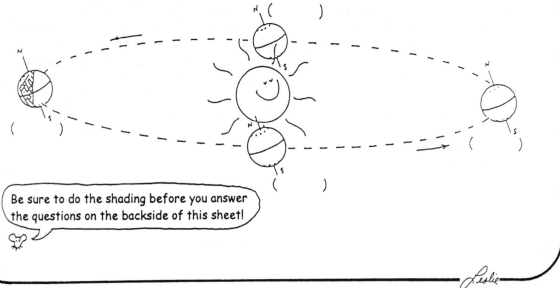

Be sure to do the shading before you answer the questions on the backside of this sheet!

Leslie

a. When the Earth is in any of the four positions shown, during one 24-hour spin a location at the equator receives sunlight half the time and is in darkness the other half of the time. This means that regions at the equator always get about _____ hours of sunlight and _____ hours of darkness.

b. Can you see that in the June position regions farther north have longer days and shorter nights? Locations north of the Arctic Circle (dotted in the Northern Hemisphere) are always illuminated by the sun as the Earth spins, so they get daylight _____ hours a day.

c. How many hours of light and darkness are there in June at regions south of the Antarctic Circle (dotted line in Southern Hemisphere)?

_____

d. Six months later, when the Earth is at the December position, is the situation in the Antarctic the same or is it the reverse?

_____

e. Why do South America and Australia enjoy warm weather in December instead of in June?

_____

3. The Earth spins about its polar axis once each 24 hours, which gives us day and night. If the Earth's spin was instead only one rotation per year, what difference would there be with day and night as we enjoy them now?

_____

_____

If the spin of the Earth was the same as its revolution rate around the sun, would we be like the moon — one side always facing the body it orbits?

In Section 33.2 read ahead about gravity lock and why the moon shows only one face to Earth.

CONCEPTUAL **Physical Science** PRACTICE SHEET

Chapter 31: The Atmosphere, the Oceans, and Their Interactions
Short and Long Wavelength

The sine curve is a pictorial representation of a wave—the high points being crests, and the low points troughs. The height of the wave is its *amplitude*. The wavelength is the distance between successive identical parts of the wave (like between crest to crest, or trough to trough). Wavelengths of water waves at the beach are measured in meters, wavelengths of ripples in a pond are measured in centimeters, and the wavelengths of light in billionths of a meter (nanometers).

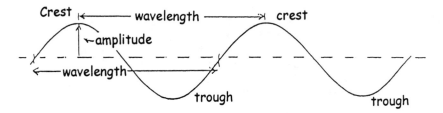

In the boxes below sketch three waves of the same amplitude—Wave A with half the wavelength of Wave B, and Wave C with wavelength twice as long as Wave B.

Wave A

Wave B

Wave C

1. If all three waves have the same speed, which has the highest frequency? _____

2. Compared with solar radiation, terrestrial radiation has a _____ wavelength.

3. In a florist's greenhouse, _____ waves are able to penetrate the greenhouse glass, but _____ waves cannot.

4. The Earth's atmosphere is similar to the glass in a greenhouse. If the atmosphere were to contain excess amounts of water vapor and carbon dioxide, the air would be opaque to _____ waves.

Chapter 31: The Atmosphere, the Oceans, and Their Interactions
Driving Forces of Air Motion

The primary driving force of the Earth's weather is _____. The unequal distribution of solar radiation on the Earth's surface creates temperature differences which in turn result in pressure differences in the atmosphere. These pressure differences generate horizontal winds as air moves from _____ pressure to _____ pressure. The weather patterns are not strictly horizontal though, there are other forces affecting the movement of air. Recall from Newton's second law that an object moves in the direction of the *net* force acting on it. The forces acting on the movement of air include:

  1) pressure gradient force 2) Coriolis force 3) centripetal force, and 4) friction.

The greater the pressure difference the greater the force, and the greater the wind. The "push" caused by the horizontal differences in pressure across a surface is called the *pressure gradient force*. This force is represented by isobars on a weather map. Isobars connect locations on a map that have equal atmospheric pressure. The pressure gradient force is perpendicular to the isobars and strongest where the isobars are closely spaced. So,

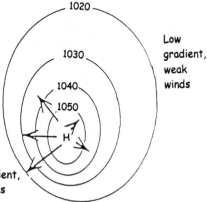

Low gradient, weak winds

Steep gradient, strong winds

the steeper the pressure gradient, the _____ the wind.

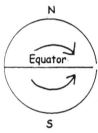

The *Coriolis force* is a result of the Earth's rotation. The Coriolis force is the deflection of the wind from a _____ path to a _____ path. The Coriolis force causes the wind to veer to the right of its path in the Northern Hemisphere and to the left of its path in the Southern Hemisphere.

As the wind blows around a low or high pressure center it constantly changes its direction. A change in speed or direction is acceleration. In order to keep the wind moving in a circular path the net force must be directed inward. This _____ force is called *centripetal force*.

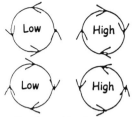

The forces described above greatly influence the flow of upper winds (winds not influenced by surface frictional forces). The interaction of these forces cause the winds in the Northern Hemisphere to rotate _____ around regions of high pressure and _____ around regions of low pressure. In the Southern Hemisphere the situation is reversed — winds rotate _____ around a high and _____ around a low.

Winds blowing near the Earth's surface are slowed by *frictional forces.* In the Northern Hemisphere surface winds blow in a direction _____ into the centers of a low pressure area and _____ out of the centers of a high pressure area. The spiral direction is reversed in the Southern Hemisphere. Draw arrows to show the direction of the pressure gradient force.

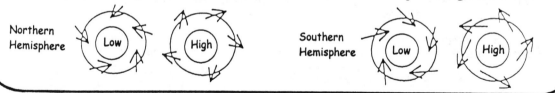

CONCEPTUAL **Physical Science** PRACTICE SHEET

Chapter 32: Weather
Air Temperature and Pressure Patterns

Temperature patterns on weather maps are depicted by isotherms—lines that connect all points having the same temperature. Each isotherm separates temperatures having higher values from temperatures having lower values.

The following weather map to the right shows temperatures in degrees Fahrenheit for various locations. Using 10 degree intervals, connect same value numbers to construct isotherms. Label the temperature value at each end of the isotherm.
One isotherm has been completed as an example.

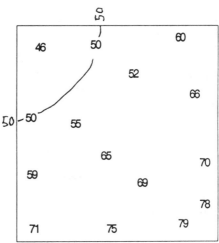

Tips for drawing Isotherms
- Isotherms can never be open ended.
- Isotherms are "closed" if they reach the boundary of plotted data, or make a loop.
- Isotherms can never touch, cross, or fork.
- Isotherms must always appear in sequence; for example, there must be a 60° isotherm between a 50- and 70-degree isotherm.
- Isotherms should be labeled with their values.

Pressure patterns on weather maps are depicted by isobars—lines which connect all points having equal pressure. Each isobar separates stations of higher pressure from stations of lower pressure.

The weather map below shows air pressure in millibar (mb) units at various locations. Using an interval of 4 (for example, 1008, 1012, 1016 etc.), connect equal pressure values to construct isobars. Label the pressure value at each end of the isobar. One isobar has been completed as an example.

- Tips for drawing isobars are similar to those for drawing isotherms.

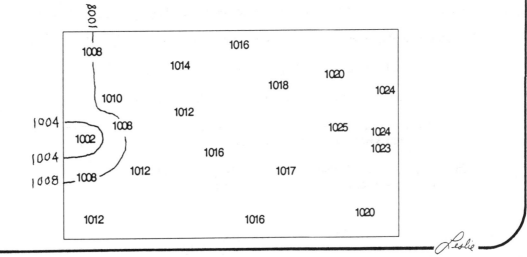

Air Temperature and Pressure Patterns continued:

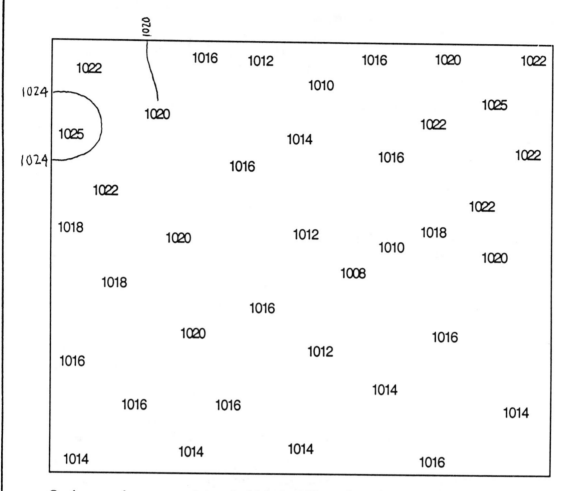

On the map above, use an interval of 4 to draw lines of equal pressure (isobars) to show the pattern of air pressure. Locate and mark regions of high pressure with an "H" and regions of low pressure with an "L". Use the map to answer the questions below.

1. On the map above, areas of high pressure are depicted by the _____ isobar.

2. On the map above, areas of low pressure are depicted by the _____ isobar.

Circle the correct answer

3. Highs are usually accompanied by (stormy weather) (fair weather).

4. In the Northern Hemisphere, surface winds surrounding a high pressure system blow in a (clockwise direction) (counterclockwise direction).

5. In the Northern Hemisphere, surface winds spiral inward into a (region of low pressure) (region of high pressure).

Name _____ Date _____

Chapter 32: Weather
Surface Weather Maps

Station models are used on weather maps to depict weather conditions for individual localities. Weather codes are plotted in, on, and around a central circle that describes the overall appearance of the sky. Jutting from the circle is a wind arrow, its tail in the direction from which the wind comes and its feathers indicating the wind speed. Other weather codes are in standard position around the circle.

Use the simplified station model and weather symbols to complete the statements below.

Total Sky Cover

◯	No clouds
◍	Less than one-tenth or one-tenth
◖	Two-tenths or three-tenths
◐	Four-tenths
◑	Five-tenths
◒	Six-tenths
◕	Seven-tenths or eight-tenths
◕	Nine-tenths or overcast with openings
●	Completely overcast
⊗	Sky obscured

Pressure Tendency

⟋	Rising, then falling	
⟋	Rising, then steady; or rising, then rising more slowly	Barometer no higher than 3 hours ago
⟋	Rising steadily, or unsteadily	
⟍	Falling or steady, then rising; or rising, then rising more quickly	
—	Steady, same as 3 hours ago	
⋁	Falling, then rising, same or lower than 3 hours ago	
⟍	Falling, then steady; or falling, then falling more slowly	Barometer no lower than 3 hours ago
⟍	Falling steadily, or unsteadily	
⟋	Steady or rising, then falling; or falling, then falling more quickly	

Wind Entries

	Miles (Statute) Per Hour	Knots	Kilometers Per Hour
◎	Calm	Calm	Calm
—	1-2	1-2	1-3
⌐	3-8	3-7	4-13
⌐	9-14	8-12	14-19
⌐	15-20	13-17	20-32
⌐	21-25	18-22	33-40
⌐	26-31	23-27	41-50
⌐	32-37	28-32	51-60
⌐	38-43	33-37	61-69
⌐	44-49	38-42	70-79
⌐	50-54	43-47	80-87
⌐	55-60	48-52	88-96
⌐	61-66	53-57	97-106
⌐	67-71	58-62	107-114
⌐	72-77	63-67	115-124
⌐	78-83	68-72	125-143

Common Weather Symbols

•	Light rain	▽	Rain shower
•ׁ•	Moderate rain	▽	Snow shower
•ׁ•ׁ•	Heavy rain	△	Showers of hail
* *	Light snow	⇥	Drifting or blowing snow
* * *	Moderate snow	S	Dust storm
* * *	Heavy snow	≡	Fog
9 9	Light drizzle	∞	Haze
⚠	Ice pellets (sleet)	∿	Smoke
⟋•⟍	Freezing rain	⚡	Thunderstorm
⟋9⟍	Freezing drizzle	⚡	Hurricane

Wind speed →

Wind direction →

Barometric pressure reduced to sea level

Temperature (F°) 31

250

Pressure higher or lower than 3 hours ago

Present Weather ★

+28 Barometric tendency in last 3 hours

Visibility 24

Amount of change during last 3 hours 4

Dew Point 30

45 ★ Time precipitation began or ended

Amount of precipitation during past 6 hours

Weather during past 6 hours

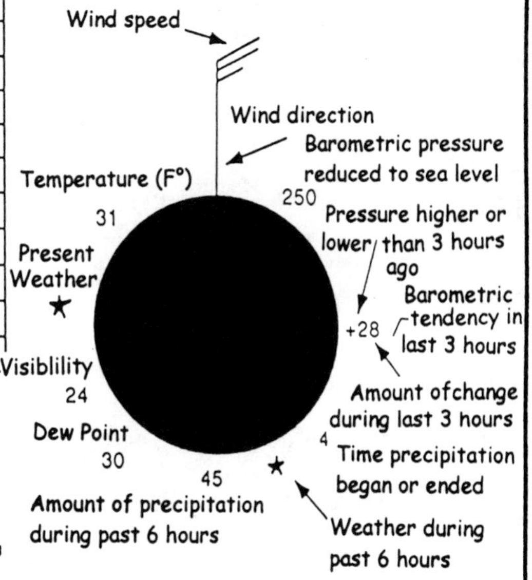

1. The overall appearance of the sky is _____

2. The wind speed is _____ kilometers per hour.

3. The wind direction is coming from the _____

4. The present weather conditions call for _____

5. The barometric tendency is _____

6. For the past 6 hours the weather conditions have been _____

Leslie

Use the unlabeled station model to answer the questions below.

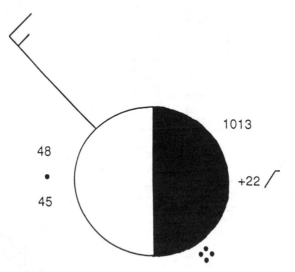

1. The overall appearance of the sky is _____ .

2. The wind speed is _____ kilometers per hour.

3. The wind direction is coming from the _____ .

4. The present weather conditions call for _____ .

5. The barometric tendency is _____ .

6. For the past 6 hours the weather conditions have been _____ .

7. The barometric pressure is _____ .

8. The dew point is _____ .

9. The current temperature is _____ .

10. Compared to the past few hours, barometric pressure is _____ .

Name _____ Date _____

Chapter 32: Weather
Chilly Winds

Often times it feels colder outside than a thermometer indicates. The
apparent difference is called *wind chill*. On November 1, 2001, the
National Weather Service implemented a new Wind Chill Temperature
index. The new formula uses advances in science, technology, and
computer modeling to provide a more accurate, understandable, and
useful formula for calculating the dangers from winter winds and
freezing temperatures.

For temperatures less than 50°F and wind speeds greater than 3 mph,
the new formula used to estimate the temperature we perceive when a cold wind blows is:

$$\text{Wind Chill Temperature (°F)} = 35.74 + 0.6215T - 35.75(V^{0.16}) + 0.4275T(V^{0.16})$$

where V is the wind speed in miles per hour and T is the temperature in degrees Fahrenheit.

Wind Chill Temperature Table

V (mph)	$V^{0.16}$	Temperature (°F)			
		5.00	10.00	15.00	32.00
5.00	1.2937	-4.64	1.24	7.11	
10.00	1.4454				
15.00	1.5423	-12.99	-6.59	-0.19	

1. Using the formula given for Wind Chill Temperature (WCT), complete the above table. The variable
   $V^{0.16}$ (wind speed raised to 0.16 power) is provided in the table to simplify your calculations.

2. Which has a stronger impact on WCT, changes in wind speed or changes in temperature? (Defend
   your answer with data from your completed table.)

   _____

   _____

   _____

3. How does WCT vary when wind speed remains fixed and only temperature changes? (Defend your answer.)

   _____

   _____

   _____

4. How does WCT vary when temperature stays fixed and only wind speed changes? (Defend your answer.)

   _____

   _____

   _____

More information can be found on the National Weather Service's Web site: http://www.nws.noaa.gov/om/windchill

Leslie

CONCEPTUAL **Physical Science** PRACTICE SHEET

Chapter 33: The Solar System
Earth-Moon-Sun Alignment

Here we see a shadow on a wall cast by an
apple. Note how the rays define the darkest
part of the shadow, the *umbra*, and the lighter
part of the shadow, the *penumbra*. The shadows
that comprise eclipses of planetary bodies are
similarly formed. Below is a diagram of the sun,

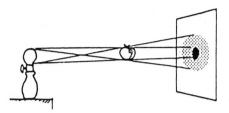

earth, and the orbital path of the moon (dashed circle). One position of the moon is shown.
Draw the moon in the appropriate positions on the dashed circle to represent (a) a quarter
moon; (b) a half moon; (c) a solar eclipse; (d) a lunar eclipse. Label your positions. For c and
d, extend rays from the top and bottom of the sun to show umbra and penumbra regions.

The diagram below is an extension of Figure 33.21, which shows 3 positions of the sun, A, B, C.
Sketch the appropriate positions of the moon in its orbit about the earth for (a) a solar eclipse;
(b) a lunar eclipse. Label your positions. Sketch solar rays similar to the above exercise.

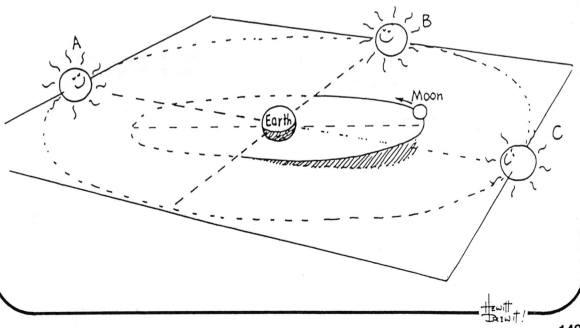

Pinhole Image Formation

Look carefully at the round spots of light on the shady ground beneath trees. These are *sunballs*, which are images of the sun. They are cast by openings between leaves in the trees that act as pinholes. (Did you make a pinhole "camera" back in middle school?) Large sunballs, several centimeters in diameter or so, are cast by openings that are relatively high above the ground, while small ones are produced by

closer "pinholes." The interesting point is that the ratio of the diameter of the sunball to its distance from the pinhole is the same as the ratio of the sun's diameter to its distance from the pinhole. We know the sun is approximately 150,000,000 km from the pinhole, so careful measurements of the ratio of diameter/distance for a sunball leads you to the diameter of the sun. That's what this page is about. Instead of measuring sunballs under the shade of trees on a sunny day, make your own easier-to-measure sunball.

150,000,000 km

1. Poke a small hole in a piece of card. Perhaps an index card will do, and poke the hole with a sharp pencil or pen. Hold the card in the sunlight and note the circular image that is cast. This is an image of the sun. Note that its size doesn't depend on the size of the hole in the card, but only on its distance. The image is a circle when cast on a surface perpendicular to the rays — otherwise it's "stretched out" as an ellipse.

2. Try holes of various shapes; say a square hole, or a triangular hole. What is the shape of the image when its distance from the card is large compared with the size of the hole? Does the shape of the pinhole make a difference?

_____

_____

3. Measure the diameter of a small coin. Then place the coin on a viewing area that is perpendicular to the sun's rays. Position the card so the image of the sunball exactly covers the coin. Carefully measure the distance between the coin and the small hole in the card. Complete the following:

$$\frac{\text{Diameter of sunball}}{\text{Distance to pinhole}} = \underline{\hspace{2cm}}$$

With this ratio, estimate the diameter of the sun. Show your work on a separate piece of paper.

4. If you did this on a day when the sun is partially eclipsed, what shape of image would you expect to see?

WHAT SHAPE DO SUNBALLS HAVE DURING A PARTIAL ECLIPSE OF THE SUN?

_____

CONCEPTUAL **Physical Science** PRACTICE SHEET

Chapter 34: The Stars and Beyond
Stellar Parallax

Finding distances to objects beyond the solar system is based on the simple phenomenon of
parallax. Hold a pencil at arm's length and view it against a distant background — each eye sees
a different view (try it and see). The displaced view indicates distance. Likewise, when the Earth
travels around the sun each year, the position of relatively nearby stars shifts slightly relative to
the background stars. By carefully measuring this shift, astronomer types can determine the
distance to nearby stars.

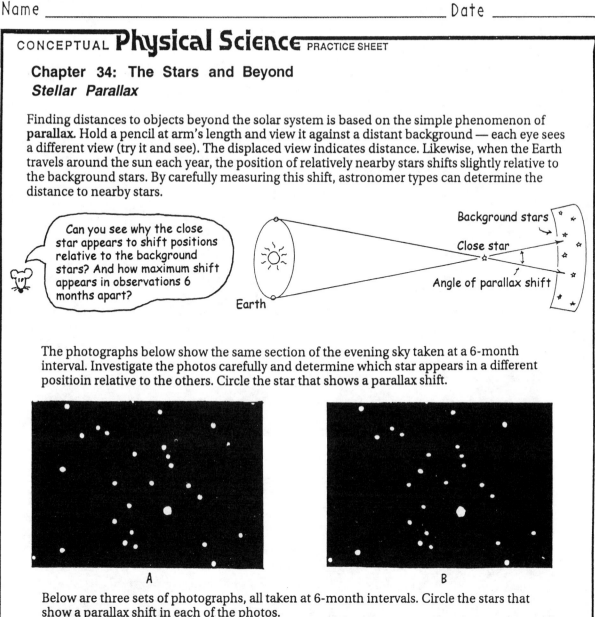

Can you see why the close
star appears to shift positions
relative to the background
stars? And how maximum shift
appears in observations 6
months apart?

Background stars

Close star

Angle of parallax shift

Earth

The photographs below show the same section of the evening sky taken at a 6-month
interval. Investigate the photos carefully and determine which star appears in a different
positioin relative to the others. Circle the star that shows a parallax shift.

A   B

Below are three sets of photographs, all taken at 6-month intervals. Circle the stars that
show a parallax shift in each of the photos.

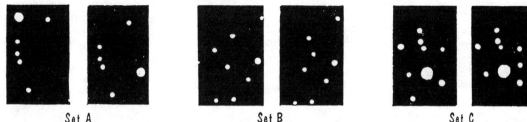

Set A   Set B   Set C

Use a fine ruler and measure the distance of shift in millimeters and place the values below:

Set A _____ mm   Set B _____   Set C _____ mm

Which set of photos indicate the closest star? The most distant "parallaxed" star?.

CONCEPTUAL **Physical Science** PRACTICE SHEET

Chapter 35: Special and General Relativity
Time Dilation and the Twin Trip

This is about identical twins, one an astronaut who takes a high-speed round-trip journey while the other twin stays home on earth. The traveling twin returns younger than the stay-at-home twin. How much younger depends on the relative speeds involved. If the traveler maintains a speed 0.5c for 1 year (according to clocks aboard the spaceship), 1.15 years elapse on earth. For a speed of 0.87c for a year, 2 years elapse on earth. At 0.995c, 10 earth years pass in one spaceship year; the traveling twin ages a single year while the stay-at-home twin ages 10 years.

This exercise will show that from the frames of reference of both twins, the earthbound twin ages more.

Case 1: No Motion First, consider a spaceship hovering at rest relative to a distant planet (Figure 1). Suppose the ship sends regularly-spaced brief flashes of light to the planet. The light flashes encounter a receiver on the planet a slight time later at speed c.

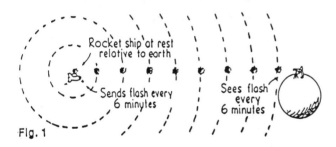

Rocket ship at rest relative to earth
Sends flash every 6 minutes
Sees flash every 6 minutes
Fig. 1

Since there is no relative motion between sender and receiver, successive flashes are received as frequently as they are sent. We'll suppose a flash is sent from the ship every 6 minutes; after slight delay, the receiver sees a flash every 6 minutes. Nothing unusual, because no motion is involved.

Case 2: Motion For motion the situation is quite different. Although the speed of the flashes are c, regardless of motion, how *frequently* the flashes are seen very much depends on relative motion. When the ship approaches the receiver, the receiver sees the flashes more frequently. This makes sense because each succeeding flash has less distance to travel as the ship gets closer to the receiver. Flashes are "crowded together" and are seen more frequently. Flashes sent at 6-min intervals are seen as less than 6 min apart. We'll suppose the ship is traveling fast enough for the flashes to be seen twice as frequently, at intervals of 3 min (Figure 2). This is the Doppler effect (Chapter 11) for light.

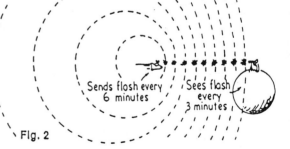

Sends flash every 6 minutes
Sees flash every 3 minutes
Fig. 2

Motion away from the receiver stretches the flashes apart and they are seen less frequently. If the ship recedes from the receiver at the same speed and still emits flashes at 6-min intervals, these flashes are seen stretched out to 12-min intervals by the receiver. Put another way, they will be seen half as frequently, that is, one flash each 12-

min interval (Figure 3). This makes sense because each succeeding flash has a longer distance to travel as the ship gets farther away from the receiver.

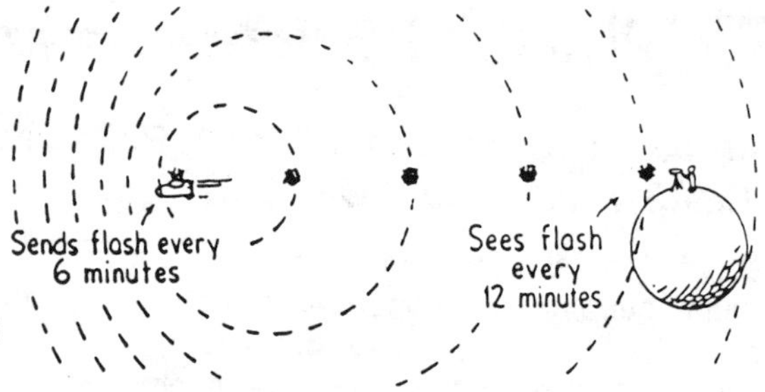

Fig. 3

Note the effect of moving away is just the opposite of moving closer to the receiver. Flashes are received twice as frequently when the spaceship is approaching (6-min flash intervals are seen every 3 min), and are received half as frequently when receding (6-min flash intervals are seen every 12 min).

The light flashes make up a light clock. Any reliable clock would show that in the receiver's frame of reference, events that take 6 min in the spaceship are seen to take 12 min when the spaceship recedes and only 3 min when the ship is approaching.

• •

1. If the spaceship travels for 1 h and emits a flash every 6 min, how many flashes will be emitted? _____

2. The ship sends equally spaced 6-min flashes while approaching the receiver at constant speed. Will these flashes be equally spaced when they encounter the receiver? _____ How about if the ship is accelerating when sending flashes? _____

3. If the receiver sees these flashes at 3-min intervals, how much time will occur between the first and the last flash (in the frame of reference of the receiver)?

_____

• •

Case 3 The Twins Let's apply all this to the twins. Suppose the traveling twin leaves the earthbound twin at the same high speed for 1 hour and then quickly turns around and returns in 1 hour. The traveling twin takes a round trip of 2 hours, according to all clocks aboard the spaceship. The time for the round trip will be something else from the earth frame of reference!

In Figure 4a we see the ship receding from earth, emitting a flash each 6 min. Due to motion, flashes are received on earth every 12 min. During the hour of going away from earth, a total of ten flashes are emitted. If the ship departs from the earth at noon, clocks aboard the ship read 1 PM when the tenth flash is emitted. What time will it be on earth when this tenth flash reaches the earth? The answer is 2 PM. Why? Because the time it takes the earth to receive 10 flashes at 12-min intervals is 10 x (12 min), or 120 min (= 2 hours).

Suppose the spaceship turns around suddenly in a negligibly short time and returns at the same high speed. During the hour of return it emits another ten flashes at 6-min intervals. These flashes are received every 3 min on earth, so all ten flashes come in 30 min. A clock on earth will read 2:30 PM when the spaceship completes its 2-hour trip. This means the earthbound twin has aged 1/2 hour more than the twin aboard the spaceship!

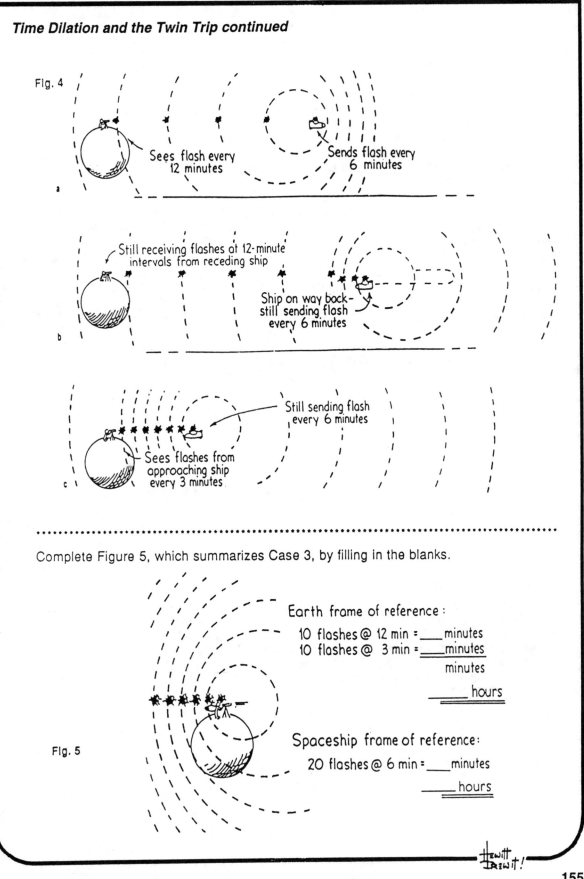

Fig. 4

Sees flash every
12 minutes

Sends flash every
6 minutes

a

Still receiving flashes at 12-minute
intervals from receding ship

Ship on way back—
still sending flash
every 6 minutes

b

Still sending flash
every 6 minutes

Sees flashes from
approaching ship
every 3 minutes

c

Complete Figure 5, which summarizes Case 3, by filling in the blanks.

Earth frame of reference:

10 flashes @ 12 min = ____ minutes
10 flashes @ 3 min = ____ minutes
____ minutes

____ hours

Fig. 5

Spaceship frame of reference:

20 flashes @ 6 min = ____ minutes

____ hours

Time Dilation and the Twin Trip continued

Case 4 Sending and Receiving Twins Interchanged Let's switch sender and receiver and see if the result is the same from either frame of reference. Flashes are emitted from the earth at regularly spaced 6-min intervals in earth time, but are seen from the frame of reference of the receding spaceship at 12-min intervals (Figure 6a). This means that a total of five flashes are seen by the spaceship during the hour of receding from earth. During the spaceship's hour of approaching, the light flashes are seen at 3-min intervals (Figure 6b), so 20 flashes will be seen.

    So the spaceship receives a total of 25 flashes during its 2-hour trip. According to clocks on the earth, however, the time it takes to emit the 25 flashes at 6-min intervals is 25 x (6 min), or 150 min (= 2.5 hour).

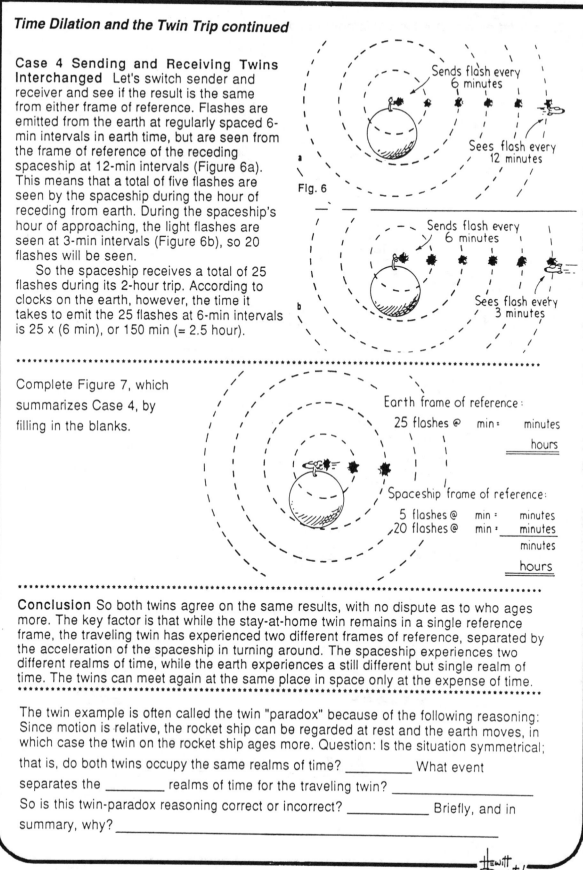

Fig. 6

Sends flash every 6 minutes

Sees flash every 12 minutes

Sends flash every 6 minutes

Sees flash every 3 minutes

Complete Figure 7, which summarizes Case 4, by filling in the blanks.

Earth frame of reference:
    25 flashes @ ____ min = ____ minutes
                                    ____ hours

Spaceship frame of reference:
    5 flashes @ ____ min = ____ minutes
    20 flashes @ ____ min = ____ minutes
                             ____ minutes
                             ____ hours

Conclusion So both twins agree on the same results, with no dispute as to who ages more. The key factor is that while the stay-at-home twin remains in a single reference frame, the traveling twin has experienced two different frames of reference, separated by the acceleration of the spaceship in turning around. The spaceship experiences two different realms of time, while the earth experiences a still different but single realm of time. The twins can meet again at the same place in space only at the expense of time.

The twin example is often called the twin "paradox" because of the following reasoning: Since motion is relative, the rocket ship can be regarded at rest and the earth moves, in which case the twin on the rocket ship ages more. Question: Is the situation symmetrical; that is, do both twins occupy the same realms of time? _____ What event separates the _____ realms of time for the traveling twin? _____
So is this twin-paradox reasoning correct or incorrect? _____ Briefly, and in summary, why? _____

Hewitt Drewit!

CONCEPTUAL **Physical Science** PRACTICE SHEET

Chapter 35: Special and General Relativity
Relativistic Time Dilation

This practice sheet recaps the *twin trip* of the previous practice sheets, where a traveling twin takes a 2-hour journey while a stay-at-home bother records the passage of 2 1/2 hours. Quite remarkable! Times in both frames of reference are marked by flashes of light, sent each 6 minutes from the spaceship, and received on earth at 12-min intervals for the ship going away, and 3-min intervals for the ship returning. Fill in the clock readings aboard the spaceship when each flash is emitted, and the clock reading on earth when each flash is received.

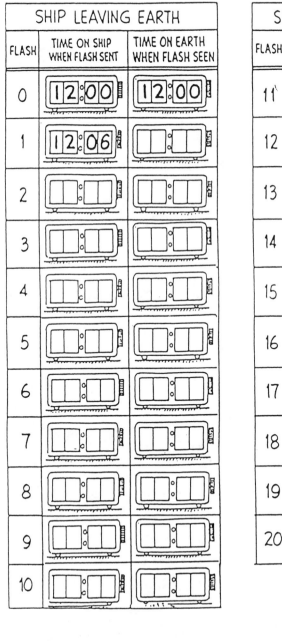

FLASH	SHIP LEAVING EARTH TIME ON SHIP WHEN FLASH SENT	TIME ON EARTH WHEN FLASH SEEN
0	12:00	12:00
1	12:06	
2		
3		
4		
5		
6		
7		
8		
9		
10		

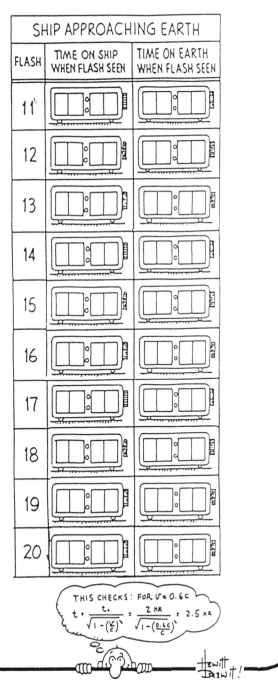

FLASH	SHIP APPROACHING EARTH TIME ON SHIP WHEN FLASH SEEN	TIME ON EARTH WHEN FLASH SEEN
11		
12		
13		
14		
15		
16		
17		
18		
19		
20		

THIS CHECKS: FOR $v = 0.6c$

$$t = \frac{t_v}{\sqrt{1-\left(\frac{v}{c}\right)^2}} = \frac{2 \text{ HR}}{\sqrt{1-\left(\frac{0.6c}{c}\right)^2}} = 2.5 \text{ HR}$$

CONCEPTUAL Physical Science PRACTICE SHEET

Appendix B: Rotational Mechanics
Mobile Torques

Apply what you know about torques by making a mobile. Shown below are five horizontal arms with fixed 1- and 2-kg masses attached, and four hangers with ends that fit in the loops of the arms, lettered A through R. You are to figure where the loops should be attached so that when the whole system is suspended from the spring scale at the top, it will hang as a proper mobile, with its arms suspended horizontally. This is best done by working from the bottom upward. Circle the loops where the hangers should be attached. When the mobile is complete, how many kilograms will be indicated on the scale? (Assume the horizontal struts and connecting hooks are practically massless compared to the 1- and 2-kg masses.) On a separate sheet of paper, make a sketch of your completed mobile.

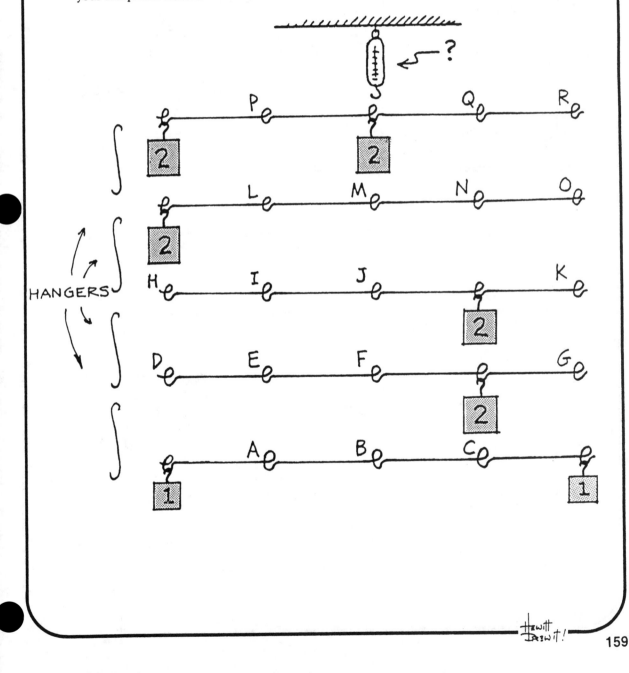

Torques and See-Saws

1. Complete the data for the three seesaws in equilibrium.

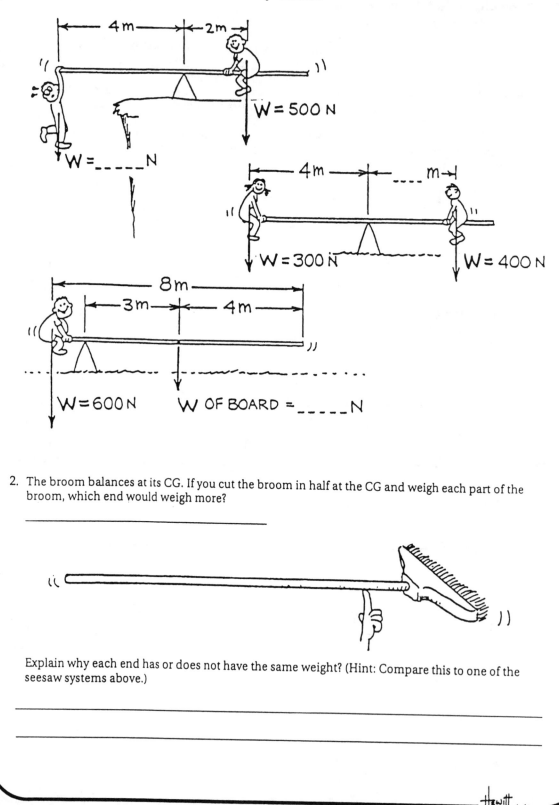

W = 500 N

W = _____ N

W = 300 N   W = 400 N

W = 600 N   W OF BOARD = _____ N

2. The broom balances at its CG. If you cut the broom in half at the CG and weigh each part of the broom, which end would weigh more?

_____

Explain why each end has or does not have the same weight? (Hint: Compare this to one of the seesaw systems above.)

_____

_____

Name _____ Date _____

Appendix C: Vectors
Vectors and Sailboats

(Do not attempt this until you have studied Appendix C!)

1. The sketch shows a top view of a small railroad car pulled by a rope. The force **F** that the rope exerts on the car has one component along the track, and another component perpendicular to the track.

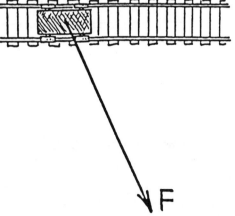

   a. Draw these components on the sketch. Which component is larger?

   _____

   b. Which component produces acceleration?

   _____

   c. What would be the effect of pulling on the rope if it were perpendicular to the track?

   _____

2. The sketches below represent simplified top views of sailboats in a cross-wind direction. The impact of the wind produces a FORCE vector on each as shown.
   (We do NOT consider *velocity* vectors here!)

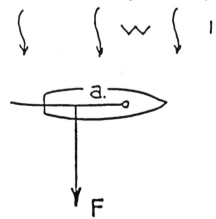

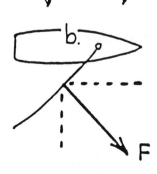

   a. Why is the position of the sail above useless for propelling the boat along its forward direction? (Relate this to Question 1c. above. Where the train is constrained by tracks to move in one direction, the boat is similarly constrained to move along one direction by its deep vertical fin — the *keel*.)

   _____

   _____

   b. Sketch the component of force parallel to the direction of the boat's motion (along its keel), and the component perpendicular to its motion. Will the boat move in a forward direction? (Relate this to Question 1b. above.)

   _____

   _____

Vectors and Sailboats continued

3. The boat to the right is oriented at an angle into the wind. Draw the force vector and its forward and perpendicular components.

   a. Will the boat move in a forward direction and tack into the wind? Why or why not?

   ___

   ___

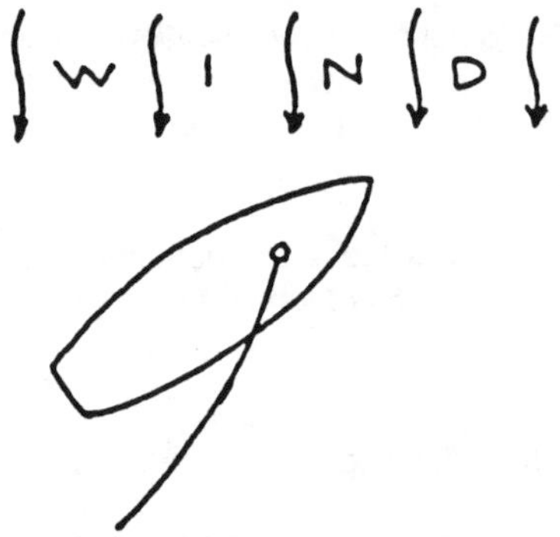

4. The sketch below is a top view of five identical sailboats. Where they exist, draw force vectors to represent wind impact on the sails. Then draw components parallel and perpendicular to the keels of each boat.

   a. Which boat will sail the fastest in a forward direction?

   ___

   b. Which will respond least to the wind?

   ___

   c. Which will move in a backward direction?

   ___

   d. Which will experience less and less wind impact with increasing speed?

   ___

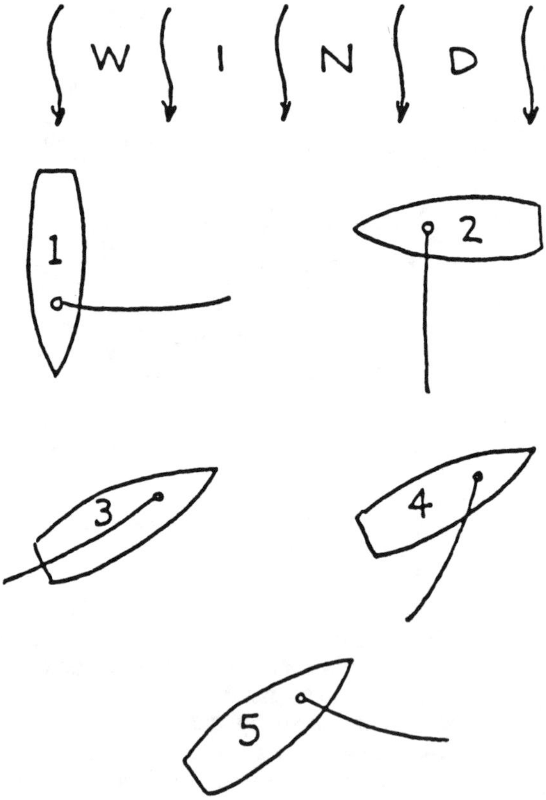

Answers to the Practice Sheets

Notice that the pages that follow are greatly reduced, with Practice-Sheet copy that is difficult to read. But the answers are legible, which you should look at *AFTER* you've made your own responses to the sheets. Then compare your responses with those of the authors.

CONCEPTUAL Physical Science PRACTICE SHEET

Chapter 1: Patterns of Motion and Equilibrium
The Equilibrium Rule: ΣF = 0

1. Gymnast Nellie Newton hangs from a variety of positions as shown. Since she is not accelerating, the net force on her is zero. This means the upward pull of the rope(s) equals the downward pull of gravity. She weighs 300 N. Show the scale reading for each case.

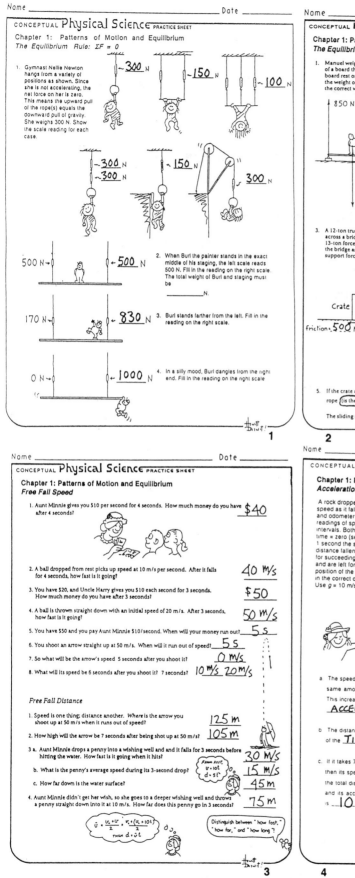

~300 N

~150 N

~100 N

~300 N
~300 N

~150 N

300 N

500 N → | ← 500 N

2. When Burl the painter stands in the exact middle of his staging, the left scale reads 500 N. Fill in the reading on the right scale. The total weight of Burl and staging must be _____ N.

170 N → | ← 830 N

3. Burl stands farther from the left. Fill in the reading on the right scale.

0 N → | ← 1000 N

4. In a silly mood, Burl dangles from the right end. Fill in the reading on the right scale.

1

CONCEPTUAL Physical Science PRACTICE SHEET

Chapter 1: Patterns of Motion and Equilibrium
The Equilibrium Rule: ΣF = 0

1. Manuel weighs 1000 N, and stands in the middle of a board that weighs 200 N. The ends of the board rest on bathroom scales. (We can assume the weight of the board acts at its center). Fill in the correct weight reading on each scale.

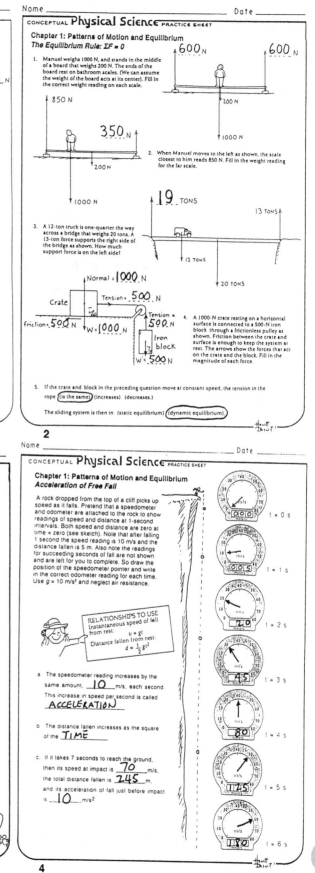

600 N   600 N

850 N

350 N ↑

200 N

200 N

1000 N

2. When Manuel moves to the left as shown, the scale closest to him reads 850 N. Fill in the weight reading for the far scale.

19 TONS

13 TONS ↑

12 TONS

20 TONS

3. A 12-ton truck is one-quarter the way across a bridge that weighs 20 tons. A 13-ton force supports the right side of the bridge as shown. How much support force is on the left side?

Normal = 1000 N

Crate

Tension = 500 N

friction = 500 N   W = 1000 N

Tension = 500 N

Iron block

W = 500 N

4. A 1000-N crate resting on a horizontal surface is connected to a 500-N iron block through a frictionless pulley as shown. Friction between the crate and surface is enough to keep the system at rest. The arrows show the forces that act on the crate and the block. Fill in the magnitude of each force.

5. If the crate and block in the preceding question move at constant speed, the tension in the rope (is the same) (increases) (decreases.)

The sliding system is then in (static equilibrium) (dynamic equilibrium).

2

CONCEPTUAL Physical Science PRACTICE SHEET

Chapter 1: Patterns of Motion and Equilibrium
Free Fall Speed

1. Aunt Minnie gives you $10 per second for 4 seconds. How much money do you have after 4 seconds?   **$40**

2. A ball dropped from rest picks up speed at 10 m/s per second. After it falls for 4 seconds, how fast is it going?   **40 m/s**

3. You have $20, and Uncle Harry gives you $10 each second for 3 seconds. How much money do you have after 3 seconds?   **$50**

4. A ball is thrown straight down with an initial speed of 20 m/s. After 3 seconds, how fast is it going?   **50 m/s**

5. You have $50 and you pay Aunt Minnie $10/second. When will your money run out?   **5 s**

6. You shoot an arrow straight up at 50 m/s. When will it run out of speed?   **5 s**

7. So what will be the arrow's speed 5 seconds after you shoot it?   **0 m/s**

8. What will its speed be 6 seconds after you shoot it? 7 seconds?   **10 m/s 20 m/s**

Free Fall Distance

1. Speed is one thing; distance another. *Where* is the arrow you shoot up at 50 m/s when it runs out of speed?   **125 m**

2. How high will the arrow be 7 seconds after being shot up at 50 m/s?   **105 m**

3 a. Aunt Minnie drops a penny into a wishing well and it falls for 3 seconds before hitting the water. How fast is it going when it hits?   **30 m/s**

   b. What is the penny's average speed during its 3-second drop?   **15 m/s**

   c. How far down is the water surface?   **45 m**

4. Aunt Minnie didn't get her wish, so she goes to a deeper wishing well and throws a penny straight down into it at 10 m/s. How far does this penny go in 3 seconds?   **75 m**

$$\bar{v} = \frac{v_i + v_f}{2}, \quad v_f = \frac{v_i + (v_i + 10t)}{2}$$ then d = \bar{v}t

Distinguish between " how fast," " how far," and " how long."

3

CONCEPTUAL Physical Science PRACTICE SHEET

Chapter 1: Patterns of Motion and Equilibrium
Acceleration of Free Fall

A rock dropped from the top of a cliff picks up speed as it falls. Pretend that a speedometer and odometer are attached to the rock to show readings of speed and distance at 1-second intervals. Both speed and distance are zero at time = zero (see sketch). Note that after falling 1 second the speed reading is 10 m/s and the distance fallen is 5 m. Also note the readings for succeeding seconds of fall are not shown and are left for you to complete. So draw the position of the speedometer pointer and write in the correct odometer reading for each time. Use $g = 10$ m/s² and neglect air resistance.

RELATIONSHIPS TO USE
Instantaneous speed of fall from rest:
$$v = gt$$
Distance fallen from rest:
$$d = \frac{1}{2}gt^2$$

a. The speedometer reading increases by the same amount, **10** m/s, each second. This increase in speed per second is called **ACCELERATION**

b. The distance fallen increases as the square of the **TIME**

c. If it takes 7 seconds to reach the ground, then its speed at impact is **70** m/s, the total distance fallen is **245** m, and its acceleration of fall just before impact is **10** m/s²

t = 0 s

t = 1 s

t = 2 s

t = 3 s

t = 4 s

t = 5 s

t = 6 s

4

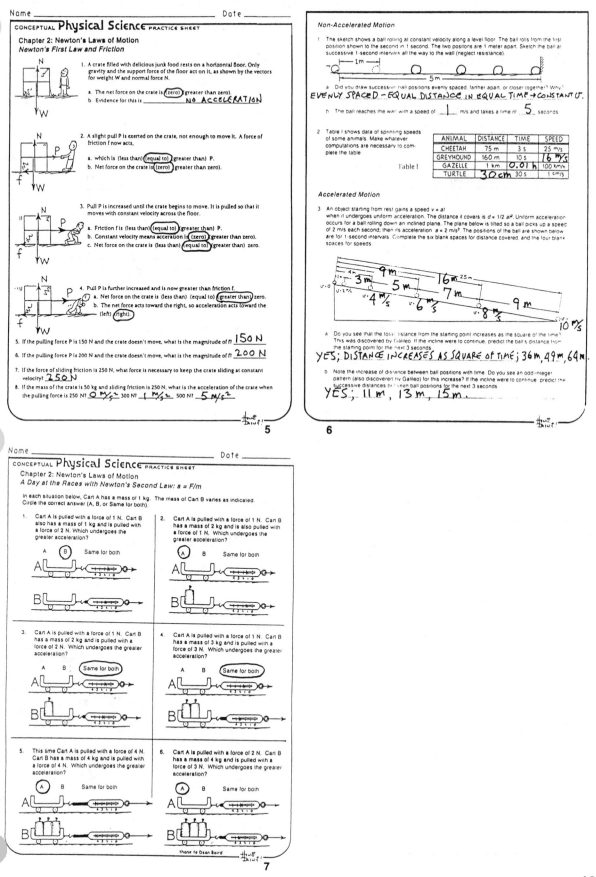

CONCEPTUAL **Physical Science** PRACTICE SHEET

Chapter 2: Newton's Laws of Motion
Newton's First Law and Friction

1. A crate filled with delicious junk food rests on a horizontal floor. Only gravity and the support force of the floor act on it, as shown by the vectors for weight W and normal force N.

   a. The net force on the crate is (zero) (greater than zero).
   b. Evidence for this is _____ **NO ACCELERATION**

2. A slight pull P is exerted on the crate, not enough to move it. A force of friction f now acts.

   a. which is (less than) (equal to) (greater than) P.
   b. Net force on the crate is (zero) (greater than zero).

3. Pull P is increased until the crate begins to move. It is pulled so that it moves with constant velocity across the floor.

   a. Friction f is (less than) (equal to) (greater than) P.
   b. Constant velocity means acceration is (zero) (greater than zero).
   c. Net force on the crate is (less than) (equal to) (greater than) zero.

4. Pull P is further increased and is now greater than friction f.
   a. Net force on the crate is (less than) (equal to) (greater than) zero.
   b. The net force acts toward the right, so acceleration acts toward the (left) (right).

5. If the pulling force P is 150 N and the crate doesn't move, what is the magnitude of f? **150 N**

6. If the pulling force P is 200 N and the crate doesn't move, what is the magnitude of f? **200 N**

7. If the force of sliding friction is 250 N, what force is necessary to keep the crate sliding at constant velocity? **250 N**

8. If the mass of the crate is 50 kg and sliding friction is 250 N, what is the acceleration of the crate when the pulling force is 250 N? **0 m/s²** 300 N? **1 m/s²** 500 N? **5 m/s²**

5

Non-Accelerated Motion

1. The sketch shows a ball rolling at constant velocity along a level floor. The ball rolls from the first position shown to the second in 1 second. The two positions are 1 meter apart. Sketch the ball at successive 1-second intervals all the way to the wall (neglect resistance).

   a. Did you draw successive ball positions evenly spaced, farther apart, or closer together? Why?
   EVENLY SPACED — EQUAL DISTANCE IN EQUAL TIME → CONSTANT V.

   b. The ball reaches the wall with a speed of **1** m/s and takes a time of **5** seconds.

2. Table I shows data of sprinting speeds of some animals. Make whatever computations are necessary to complete the table.

   Table I

ANIMAL	DISTANCE	TIME	SPEED
CHEETAH	75 m	3 s	25 m/s
GREYHOUND	160 m	10 s	16 m/s
GAZELLE	1 km	0.01 h	100 km/h
TURTLE	30 cm	30 s	1 cm/s

Accelerated Motion

3. An object starting from rest gains a speed $v = at$ when it undergoes uniform acceleration. The distance it covers is $d = 1/2\ at^2$. Uniform acceleration occurs for a ball rolling down an inclined plane. The plane below is tilted so a ball picks up a speed of 2 m/s each second; then its acceleration $a = 2$ m/s². The positions of the ball are shown below are for 1-second intervals. Complete the six blank spaces for distance covered, and the four blank spaces for speeds.

   a. Do you see that the total distance from the starting point increases as the square of the time? This was discovered by Galileo. If the incline were to continue, predict the ball's distance from the starting point for the next 3 seconds.
   YES; DISTANCE INCREASES AS SQUARE OF TIME; 36 m, 49 m, 64 m.

   b. Note the increase of distance between ball positions with time. Do you see an odd-integer pattern (also discovered by Galileo) for this increase? If the incline were to continue, predict the successive distances between ball positions for the next 3 seconds.
   YES; 11 m, 13 m, 15 m.

6

CONCEPTUAL **Physical Science** PRACTICE SHEET

Chapter 2: Newton's Laws of Motion
A Day at the Races with Newton's Second Law: a = F/m

In each situation below, Cart A has a mass of 1 kg. The mass of Cart B varies as indicated. Circle the correct answer (A, B, or Same for both).

1. Cart A is pulled with a force of 1 N. Cart B also has a mass of 1 kg and is pulled with a force of 2 N. Which undergoes the greater acceleration?
   A **(B)** Same for both

2. Cart A is pulled with a force of 1 N. Can B has a mass of 2 kg and is also pulled with a force of 1 N. Which undergoes the greater acceleration?
   (A) B Same for both

3. Cart A is pulled with a force of 1 N. Cart B has a mass of 2 kg and is pulled with a force of 2 N. Which undergoes the greater acceleration?
   A B **(Same for both)**

4. Cart A is pulled with a force of 1 N. Cart B has a mass of 3 kg and is pulled with a force of 3 N. Which undergoes the greater acceleration?
   A B **(Same for both)**

5. This time Cart A is pulled with a force of 4 N. Cart B has a mass of 4 kg and is pulled with a force of 4 N. Which undergoes the greater acceleration?
   (A) B Same for both

6. Cart A is pulled with a force of 2 N. Cart B has a mass of 4 kg and is pulled with a force of 3 N. Which undergoes the greater acceleration?
   (A) B Same for both

thanx to Dean Baird

7

CONCEPTUAL Physical Science PRACTICE SHEET

Chapter 2: Newton's Laws of Motion
Dropping Masses and Accelerating Cart

1. Consider the simple case of a 1-kg cart being pulled by a 10-N applied force. According to Newton's 2nd law, acceleration of the cart is

$$a = \frac{F}{m} = \frac{10\,N}{1\,kg} = 10\,m/s^2$$

> This is the same as the acceleration of free fall, *g*—because a force equal to the cart's weight accelerates it.

2. Now consider the acceleration of the cart when a second mass is also accelerated. This time the applied force is due to a 10-N iron weight attached to a string draped over a pulley. Will the cart accelerate as before, at 10 m/s²? The answer is no, because the mass being accelerated is the mass of the cart *plus* the mass of the piece of iron that pulls it. Both masses accelerate. The mass of the 10-N iron weight is 1 kg—so the total mass being accelerated (cart + iron) is 2 kg. Then,

> The pulley changes only the direction of the force.

$$a = \frac{F}{m} = \frac{10\,N}{2\,kg} = 5\,m/s^2.$$

> Don't forget: the total mass of a system includes the mass of the hanging iron.

> Note this is half the acceleration due to gravity alone, *g*. So the acceleration of 2 kg produced by the weight of 1 kg is *g*/2.

(a) Find the acceleration of the 1-kg cart when two identical 10-N weights are attached to the string.

$$a = \frac{F}{m} = \frac{unbalanced\ force}{total\ mass} = \frac{20\,N}{3\,Kg} = \underline{6.7}\ m/s^2.$$

> Note that the mass being accelerated is 1 kg for the cart + 1 kg each for the weights = 3 kg.

8

Chapter 2: Newton's Laws of Motion
Dropping Masses and Accelerating Cart—continued

(b) Find the acceleration of the 1-kg cart when three identical 10-N weights are attached to the string.

$$a = \frac{F}{m} = \frac{unbalanced\ force}{total\ mass} = \frac{30\,N}{4\,Kg} = \underline{7.5}\ m/s^2.$$

(c) Find the acceleration of the 1-kg cart when four identical 10-N weights (not shown) are attached to the string.

$$a = \frac{F}{m} = \frac{unbalanced\ force}{total\ mass} = \frac{40\,N}{5\,Kg} = \underline{8.0}\ m/s^2.$$

(d) This time 1 kg of iron is added to the cart, and only one iron piece dangles from the pulley. Find the acceleration of the cart.

$$a = \frac{F}{m} = \frac{unbalanced\ force}{total\ mass} = \frac{10\,N}{3\,Kg} = \underline{3.4}\ m/s^2.$$

> The force due to gravity on a mass *m* is *mg*. So gravitational force on 1 kg is (1 kg)(10 m/s²) = 10 N.

(e) Find the acceleration of the cart when it carries 2 pieces of iron and only one iron piece dangles from the pulley.

$$a = \frac{F}{m} = \frac{unbalanced\ force}{total\ mass} = \frac{10\,N}{4\,Kg} = \underline{2.5}\ m/s^2.$$

9

Chapter 2: Newton's Laws of Motion
Dropping Masses and Accelerating Cart—continued

(f) Find the acceleration of the cart when it carries 3 pieces of iron and only one iron piece dangles from the pulley.

$$a = \frac{F}{m} = \frac{unbalanced\ force}{total\ mass} = \frac{10\,N}{5\,Kg} = \underline{2.0}\ m/s^2.$$

(g) Find the acceleration of the cart when it carries 3 pieces of iron and 4 iron pieces dangle from the pulley.

$$a = \frac{F}{m} = \frac{unbalanced\ force}{total\ mass} = \frac{40\,N}{8\,Kg} = \underline{5.0}\ m/s^2.$$

How does this compare with the acceleration of (2) above, and why?

> Mass of cart is 1 kg. Mass of 10-N iron is also 1 kg.

(h) Draw your own combination of masses and find the acceleration.

> OPEN

$$a = \frac{F}{m} = \frac{unbalanced\ force}{total\ mass} = \frac{}{} = \underline{\quad}\ m/s^2.$$

10

CONCEPTUAL Physical Science PRACTICE SHEET

Chapter 2: Newton's Laws of Motion
Bronco and Newton's Second Law

Bronco skydives and parachutes from a stationary helicopter. Various stages of fall are shown in positions *a* through *f*. Using Newton's 2nd law,

$$a = \frac{F_{NET}}{m} = \frac{W - R}{m}$$

find Bronco's acceleration at each position (answer in the blanks to the right). You need to know that Bronco's mass *m* is 100 kg so his weight is a constant 1000 N. Air resistance *R* varies with speed and cross-sectional area as shown.

Circle the correct answers.

1. When Bronco's speed is least, his acceleration is
   (least) **(most)**

2. In which position(s) does Bronco experience a downward acceleration?
   (a) (b) (c) (d) (e) (f)

3. In which position(s) does Bronco experience an upward acceleration?
   (a) (b) (c) **(d) (e)** (f)

4. When Bronco experiences an upward acceleration, his velocity is
   (still downward) (upward also).

5. In which position(s) is Bronco's velocity constant?
   (a) (b) **(c)** (d) (e) **(f)**

6. In which position(s) does Bronco experience terminal velocity?
   (a) (b) **(c)** (d) (e) **(f)**

7. In which position(s) is terminal velocity greatest?
   (a) (b) **(c)** (d) (e) (f)

8. If Bronco were heavier, his terminal velocity would be
   (greater) (less) (the same).

a. R = 0   W = 1000 N $a = \underline{10\ m/s^2}$

b. R = 400 N   W = 1000 N $a = \underline{6\ m/s^2}$

c. R = 1000 N   W = 1000 N $a = \underline{0\ m/s^2}$

d. R = 1200 N   W = 1000 N $a = \underline{-2\ m/s^2}$

> NOTE WE TAKE ACC DOWN AS +. IF —, THEN — SIGNS BECOME +. EITHER WAY OKAY IF CONSISTENT

e. R = 2000 N   W = 1000 N $a = \underline{-10\ m/s^2}$

f. R = 1000 N   W = 1000 N $a = \underline{0\ m/s^2}$

11

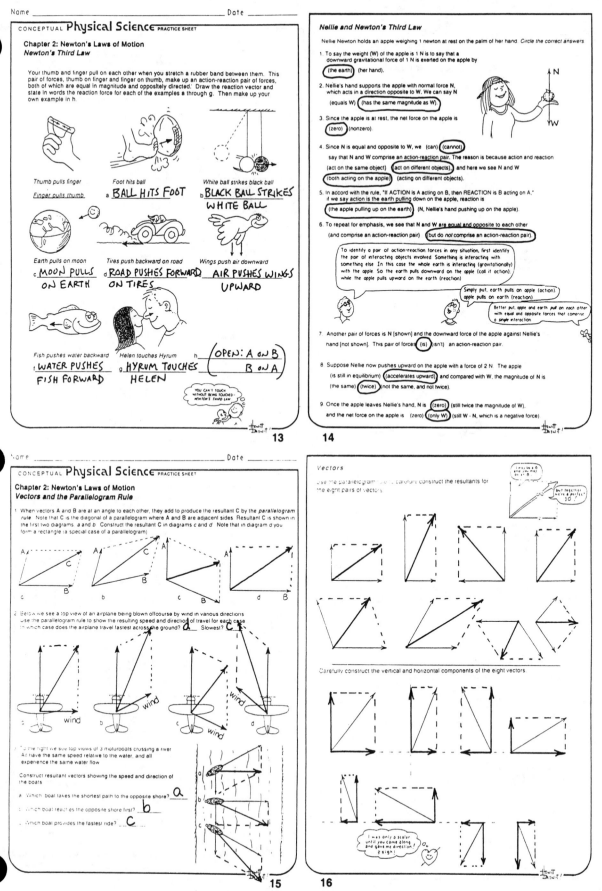

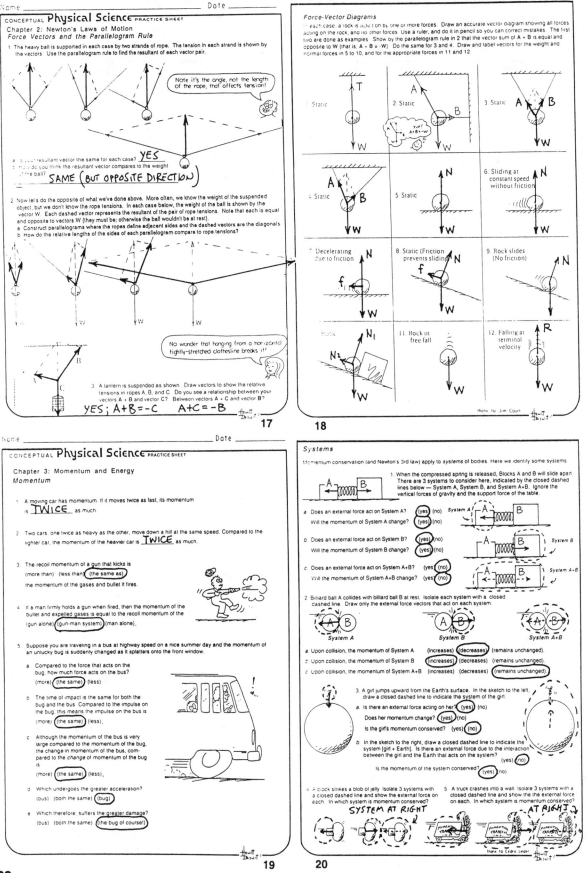

CONCEPTUAL **Physical Science** PRACTICE SHEET

Chapter 2: Newton's Laws of Motion
Force Vectors and the Parallelogram Rule

1. The heavy ball is supported in each case by two strands of rope. The tension in each strand is shown by the vectors. Use the parallelogram rule to find the resultant of each vector pair.

Note it's the angle, not the length of the rope, that affects tension!

a. Is your resultant vector the same for each case? **YES**
b. How do you think the resultant vector compares to the weight of the ball? **SAME (BUT OPPOSITE DIRECTION)**

2. Now let's do the opposite of what we've done above. More often, we know the weight of the suspended object, but we don't know the rope tensions. In each case below, the weight of the ball is shown by the vector W. Each dashed vector represents the resultant of the pair of rope tensions. Note that each is equal and opposite to vectors W (they must be; otherwise the ball wouldn't be at rest).
a. Construct parallelograms where the ropes define adjacent sides and the dashed vectors are the diagonals.
b. How do the relative lengths of the sides of each parallelogram compare to rope tensions?

No wonder that hanging from a horizontal tightly-stretched clothesline breaks it!

3. A lantern is suspended as shown. Draw vectors to show the relative tensions in ropes A, B, and C. Do you see a relationship between your vectors A + B and vector C? Between vectors A + C and vector B?
YES; A+B = -C   A+C = -B

17

Force-Vector Diagrams

In each case, a rock is acted on by one or more forces. Draw an accurate vector diagram showing all forces acting on the rock, and no other forces. Use a ruler, and do it in pencil so you can correct mistakes. The first two are done as examples. Show by the parallelogram rule in 2 that the vector sum of A + B is equal and opposite to W (that is, A + B = -W). Do the same for 3 and 4. Draw and label vectors for the weight and normal forces in 5 to 10, and for the appropriate forces in 11 and 12.

1. Static
2. Static
3. Static
4. Static
5. Static
6. Sliding at constant speed without friction
7. Decelerating due to friction
8. Static (Friction prevents sliding)
9. Rock slides (No friction)
10. Static
11. Rock in free fall
12. Falling at terminal velocity

Thanks to Jim Court.

18

CONCEPTUAL **Physical Science** PRACTICE SHEET

Chapter 3: Momentum and Energy
Momentum

1. A moving car has momentum. If it moves twice as fast, its momentum is **TWICE** as much.

2. Two cars, one twice as heavy as the other, move down a hill at the same speed. Compared to the lighter car, the momentum of the heavier car is **TWICE** as much.

3. The recoil momentum of a gun that kicks is (more than) (less than) (**the same as**) the momentum of the gases and bullet it fires.

4. If a man firmly holds a gun when fired, then the momentum of the bullet and expelled gases is equal to the recoil momentum of the (gun alone) (**gun-man system**) (man alone).

5. Suppose you are traveling in a bus at highway speed on a nice summer day and the momentum of an unlucky bug is suddenly changed as it splatters onto the front window.
   a. Compared to the force that acts on the bug, how much force acts on the bus? (more) (**the same**) (less)
   b. The time of impact is the same for both the bug and the bus. Compared to the impulse on the bug, this means the impulse on the bus is (more) (**the same**) (less).
   c. Although the momentum of the bus is very large compared to the momentum of the bug, the change in momentum of the bus, compared to the *change* of momentum of the bug is (more) (**the same**) (less).
   d. Which undergoes the greater acceleration? (bus) (both the same) (**bug**)
   e. Which therefore, suffers the greater damage? (bus) (both the same) (**the bug of course!**)

19

Systems

Momentum conservation (and Newton's 3rd law) apply to *systems* of bodies. Here we identify some systems.

1. When the compressed spring is released, Blocks A and B will slide apart. There are 3 systems to consider here, indicated by the closed dashed lines below — System A, System B, and System A+B. Ignore the vertical forces of gravity and the support force of the table.
   a. Does an external force act on System A? (yes) (**no**)   System A
      Will the momentum of System A change? (**yes**) (no)
   b. Does an external force act on System B? (**yes**) (no)   System B
      Will the momentum of System B change? (**yes**) (no)
   c. Does an external force act on System A+B? (yes) (**no**)
      Will the momentum of System A+B change? (yes) (**no**)   System A+B

2. Billiard ball A collides with billiard ball B at rest. Isolate each system with a closed dashed line. Draw only the external force vectors that act on each system.
   System A   System B   System A+B
   a. Upon collision, the momentum of System A (increases) (**decreases**) (remains unchanged).
   b. Upon collision, the momentum of System B (**increases**) (decreases) (remains unchanged).
   c. Upon collision, the momentum of System A+B (increases) (decreases) (**remains unchanged**).

3. A girl jumps upward from the Earth's surface. In the sketch to the left, draw a closed dashed line to indicate the system of the girl.
   a. Is there an external force acting on her? (**yes**) (no)
      Does her momentum change? (**yes**) (no)
      Is the girl's momentum conserved? (yes) (**no**)
   b. In the sketch to the right, draw a closed dashed line to indicate the system [girl + Earth]. Is there an external force due to the interaction between the girl and the Earth that acts on the system? (yes) (**no**)
      Is the momentum of the system conserved? (**yes**) (no)

4. A block strikes a blob of jelly. Isolate 3 systems with a closed dashed line and show the external force on each. In which system is momentum conserved? **SYSTEM AT RIGHT**

5. A truck crashes into a wall. Isolate 3 systems with a closed dashed line and show the the external force on each. In which system is momentum conserved? **AT RIGHT**

Thanks to Cedric Linder.

20

CONCEPTUAL **Physical Science** PRACTICE SHEET

Chapter 3: Momentum and Energy
Impulse—Momentum

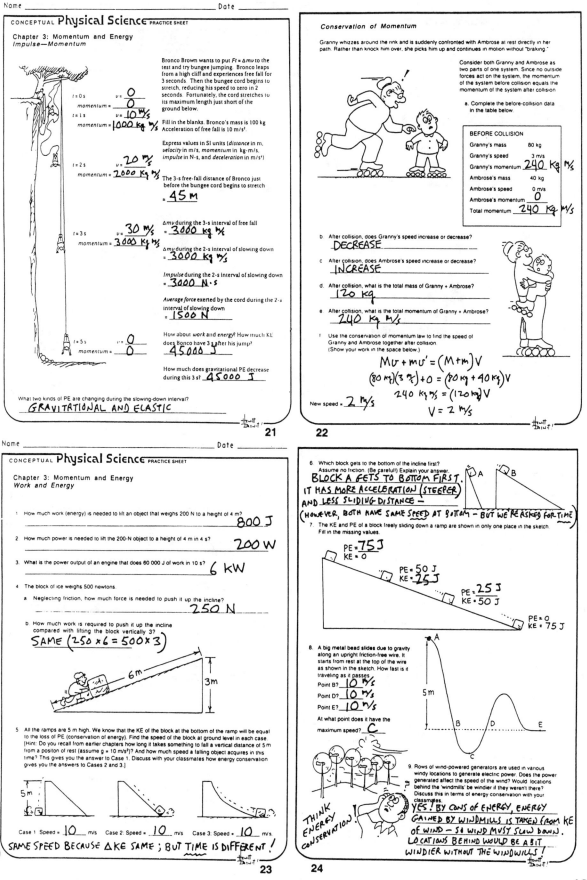

Bronco Brown wants to put $Ft = \Delta mv$ to the test and try bungee jumping. Bronco leaps from a high cliff and experiences free fall for 3 seconds. Then the bungee cord begins to stretch, reducing his speed to zero in 2 seconds. Fortunately, the cord stretches to its maximum length just short of the ground below.

Fill in the blanks. Bronco's mass is 100 kg. Acceleration of free fall is 10 m/s².

$t = 0$ s $v = $ **0**
momentum = **0**

$t = 1$ s $v = $ **10 m/s**
momentum = **1000 kg·m/s**

Express values in SI units (*distance* in m, *velocity* in m/s, *momentum* in kg·m/s, *impulse* in N·s, and *deceleration* in m/s²)

$t = 2$ s $v = $ **20 m/s**
momentum = **2000 kg·m/s**

The 3-s free-fall distance of Bronco just before the bungee cord begins to stretch
45 m

$t = 3$ s $v = $ **30 m/s**
momentum = **3000 kg·m/s**

Δmv during the 3-s interval of free fall
= **3000 kg·m/s**

Δmv during the 2-s interval of slowing down
= **3000 kg·m/s**

Impulse during the 2-s interval of slowing down
= **3000 N·s**

Average force exerted by the cord during the 2-s interval of slowing down
= **1500 N**

$t = 5$ s $v = $ **0**
momentum = **0**

How about *work* and *energy*? How much KE does Bronco have 3 s after his jump?
45000 J

How much does gravitational PE decrease during this 3 s? **45000 J**

What two kinds of PE are changing during the slowing-down interval?
GRAVITATIONAL AND ELASTIC

21

Conservation of Momentum

Granny whizzes around the rink and is suddenly confronted with Ambrose at rest directly in her path. Rather than knock him over, she picks him up and continues in motion without "braking."

Consider both Granny and Ambrose as two parts of one system. Since no outside forces act on the system, the momentum of the system before collision equals the momentum of the system after collision.

a. Complete the before-collision data in the table below.

BEFORE COLLISION	
Granny's mass	80 kg
Granny's speed	3 m/s
Granny's momentum	**240 kg·m/s**
Ambrose's mass	40 kg
Ambrose's speed	0 m/s
Ambrose's momentum	**0**
Total momentum	**240 kg·m/s**

b. After collision, does Granny's speed increase or decrease?
DECREASE

c. After collision, does Ambrose's speed increase or decrease?
INCREASE

d. After collision, what is the total mass of Granny + Ambrose?
120 kg

e. After collision, what is the total momentum of Granny + Ambrose?
240 kg·m/s

f. Use the conservation of momentum law to find the speed of Granny and Ambrose together after collision. (Show your work in the space below.)

$$Mv + mv' = (M + m)V$$
$$(80\ kg)(3\ m/s) + 0 = (80\ kg + 40\ kg)V$$
$$240\ kg·m/s = (120\ kg)V$$
$$V = 2\ m/s$$

New speed = **2 m/s**

22

CONCEPTUAL **Physical Science** PRACTICE SHEET

Chapter 3: Momentum and Energy
Work and Energy

1. How much work (energy) is needed to lift an object that weighs 200 N to a height of 4 m?
800 J

2. How much power is needed to lift the 200-N object to a height of 4 m in 4 s?
200 W

3. What is the power output of an engine that does 60 000 J of work in 10 s?
6 kW

4. The block of ice weighs 500 newtons.

a. Neglecting friction, how much force is needed to push it up the incline?
250 N

b. How much work is required to push it up the incline compared with lifting the block vertically 3?
SAME (250 × 6 = 500 × 3)

6 m   3m

5. All the ramps are 5 m high. We know that the KE of the block at the bottom of the ramp will be equal to the loss of PE (conservation of energy). Find the speed of the block at ground level in each case. [Hint: Do you recall from earlier chapters how long it takes something to fall a vertical distance of 5 m from a positon of rest (assume g = 10 m/s²)? And how much speed a falling object acquires in this time? This gives you the answer to Case 1. Discuss with your classmates how energy conservation gives you the answers to Cases 2 and 3.]

5 m

Case 1: Speed = **10** m/s   Case 2: Speed = **10** m/s   Case 3: Speed = **10** m/s

SAME SPEED BECAUSE ΔKE SAME; BUT TIME IS DIFFERENT!

23

---

6. Which block gets to the bottom of the incline first? Assume no friction. (Be careful!) Explain your answer.
BLOCK A GETS TO BOTTOM FIRST. IT HAS MORE ACCELERATION (STEEPER) AND LESS SLIDING DISTANCE — (HOWEVER, BOTH HAVE SAME SPEED AT BOTTOM - BUT WE'RE ASKED FOR TIME)

A   B

7. The KE and PE of a block freely sliding down a ramp are shown in only one place in the sketch. Fill in the missing values.

PE = **75 J**
KE = 0

PE = 50 J
KE = **25 J**

PE = 25 J
KE = **50 J**

PE = 0
KE = 75 J

8. A big metal bead slides due to gravity along an upright friction-free wire. It starts from rest at the top of the wire as shown in the sketch. How fast is it traveling as it passes

Point B? **10 m/s**
Point D? **10 m/s**
Point E? **10 m/s**

At what point does it have the maximum speed? **C**

5 m

A   B   C   D   E

9. Rows of wind-powered generators are used in various windy locations to generate electric power. Does the power generated affect the speed of the wind? Would locations behind the 'windmills' be windier if they weren't there? Discuss this in terms of energy conservation with your classmates.
YES! BY CONS OF ENERGY, ENERGY GAINED BY WINDMILLS IS TAKEN FROM KE OF WIND - SO WIND MUST SLOW DOWN. LOCATIONS BEHIND WOULD BE A BIT WINDIER WITHOUT THE WINDMILLS

THINK ENERGY CONSERVATION!

24

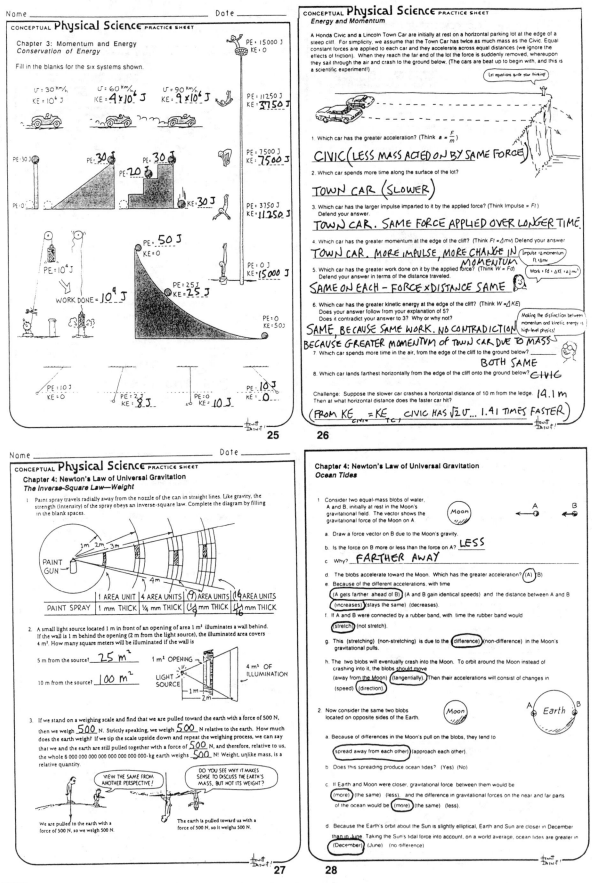

Name _____ **Date** _____

Chapter 3: Momentum and Energy
Conservation of Energy

Fill in the blanks for the six systems shown.

PE = 15000 J
KE = 0

$v = 30$ km/h
KE = 10^5 J

$v = 60$ km/h
KE = **4×10^5 J**

$v = 90$ km/h
KE = **9×10^5 J**

PE = 11250 J
KE = **3750 J**

PE = 30 J
PE = **30** J
PE = **30** J
PE = **20** J
PE = 0

PE = 7500 J
KE = **7500 J**

KE = **30 J**

PE = 3750 J
KE = **11250 J**

PE = **50 J**
KE = 0

PE = 10^4 J

WORK DONE = **10^4 J**

PE = **25 J**
KE = **25 J**

PE = 0 J
KE = **15,000**

PE = 0
KE = 50 J

PE = 10 J
KE = 0

PE = 2 J
KE = **8 J**

PE = **0** J
KE = **10 J**

PE = **10** J
KE = **0**

25

A Honda Civic and a Lincoln Town Car are initially at rest on a horizontal parking lot at the edge of a steep cliff. For simplicity, we assume that the Town Car has twice as much mass as the Civic. Equal constant forces are applied to each car and they accelerate across equal distances (we ignore the effects of friction). When they reach the far end of the lot the force is suddenly removed, whereupon they sail through the air and crash to the ground below. (The cars are beat up to begin with, and this is a scientific experiment!)

Let equations guide your thinking!

1. Which car has the greater acceleration? (Think $a = \frac{F}{m}$)

CIVIC (LESS MASS ACTED ON BY SAME FORCE)

2. Which car spends more time along the surface of the lot?

TOWN CAR (SLOWER)

3. Which car has the larger impulse imparted to it by the applied force? (Think Impulse = Ft)
Defend your answer.

TOWN CAR. SAME FORCE APPLIED OVER LONGER TIME.

4. Which car has the greater momentum at the edge of the cliff? (Think Ft = Δmv) Defend your answer

TOWN CAR. MORE IMPULSE, MORE CHANGE IN MOMENTUM

Impulse :Δ momentum Ft :Δmv

5. Which car has the greater work done on it by the applied force? (Think W = Fd)
Defend your answer in terms of the distance traveled.

SAME ON EACH - FORCE × DISTANCE SAME

Work : Fd : ΔKE (:Δ½mv²)

6. Which car has the greater kinetic energy at the edge of the cliff? (Think W = ΔKE)
Does your answer follow from your explanation of 5?
Does it contradict your answer to 3? Why or why not?

SAME, BECAUSE SAME WORK. NO CONTRADICTION BECAUSE GREATER MOMENTUM OF TOWN CAR DUE TO MASS

Making the distinction between momentum and kinetic energy is high-level physics!

7. Which car spends more time in the air, from the edge of the cliff to the ground below?

BOTH SAME

8. Which car lands farthest horizontally from the edge of the cliff onto the ground below? **CIVIC**

Challenge: Suppose the slower car crashes a horizontal distance of 10 m from the ledge. **14.1 m** Then at what horizontal distance does the faster car hit?

(FROM KE_CIVIC = KE_TC CIVIC HAS $\sqrt{2} v$... 1.41 TIMES FASTER)

26

Name _____ **Date** _____

Chapter 4: Newton's Law of Universal Gravitation
The Inverse-Square Law—Weight

1. Paint spray travels radially away from the nozzle of the can in straight lines. Like gravity, the strength (intensity) of the spray obeys an inverse-square law. Complete the diagram by filling in the blank spaces.

PAINT GUN

1m 2m 3m
4m

	1 AREA UNIT	4 AREA UNITS	**9** AREA UNITS	**16** AREA UNITS
PAINT SPRAY	1 mm THICK	¼ mm THICK	**⅑** mm THICK	**1/16** mm THICK

2. A small light source located 1 m in front of an opening of area 1 m² illuminates a wall behind. If the wall is 1 m behind the opening (2 m from the light source), the illuminated area covers 4 m². How many square meters will be illuminated if the wall is

5 m from the source? **25 m²**

10 m from the source? **100 m²**

1 m² OPENING
LIGHT SOURCE
4 m² OF ILLUMINATION
1 m
2 m

3. If we stand on a weighing scale and find that we are pulled toward the earth with a force of 500 N, then we weigh **500** N. Strictly speaking, we weigh **500** N relative to the earth. How much does the earth weigh? If we tip the scale upside down and repeat the weighing process, we can say that we and the earth are still pulled together with a force of **500** N, and therefore, relative to us, the whole 6 000 000 000 000 000 000 000 000-kg earth weighs **500** N! Weight, unlike mass, is a relative quantity.

VIEW THE SAME FROM ANOTHER PERSPECTIVE!

DO YOU SEE WHY IT MAKES SENSE TO DISCUSS THE EARTH'S MASS, BUT NOT ITS WEIGHT?

We are pulled to the earth with a force of 500 N, so we weigh 500 N.

The earth is pulled toward us with a force of 500 N, so it weighs 500 N.

27

---

1. Consider two equal-mass blobs of water, A and B, initially at rest in the Moon's gravitational field. The vector shows the gravitational force of the Moon on A.

Moon   A   B

a. Draw a force vector on B due to the Moon's gravity.

b. Is the force on B more or less than the force on A? **LESS**

c. Why? **FARTHER AWAY**

d. The blobs accelerate toward the Moon. Which has the greater acceleration? **(A)** B)

e. Because of the different accelerations, with time

(A gets farther ahead of B) (A and B gain identical speeds) and the distance between A and B

(increases) (stays the same) (decreases).

f. If A and B were connected by a rubber band, with time the rubber band would

(stretch) (not stretch).

g. This (stretching) (non-stretching) is due to the **(difference)** (non-difference) in the Moon's gravitational pulls.

h. The two blobs will eventually crash into the Moon. To orbit around the Moon instead of crashing into it, the blobs should move

(away from the Moon) **(tangentially)**. Then their accelerations will consist of changes in

(speed) **(direction)**.

2. Now consider the same two blobs located on opposite sides of the Earth.

Moon   A   Earth   B

a. Because of differences in the Moon's pull on the blobs, they tend to

(spread away from each other) (approach each other).

b. Does this spreading produce ocean tides? **(Yes)** (No)

c. If Earth and Moon were closer, gravitational force between them would be

(more) (the same) (less), and the difference in gravitational forces on the near and far parts of the ocean would be **(more)** (the same) (less).

d. Because the Earth's orbit about the Sun is slightly elliptical, Earth and Sun are closer in December than in June. Taking the Sun's tidal force into account, on a world average, ocean tides are greater in

(December) (June) (no difference).

28

170

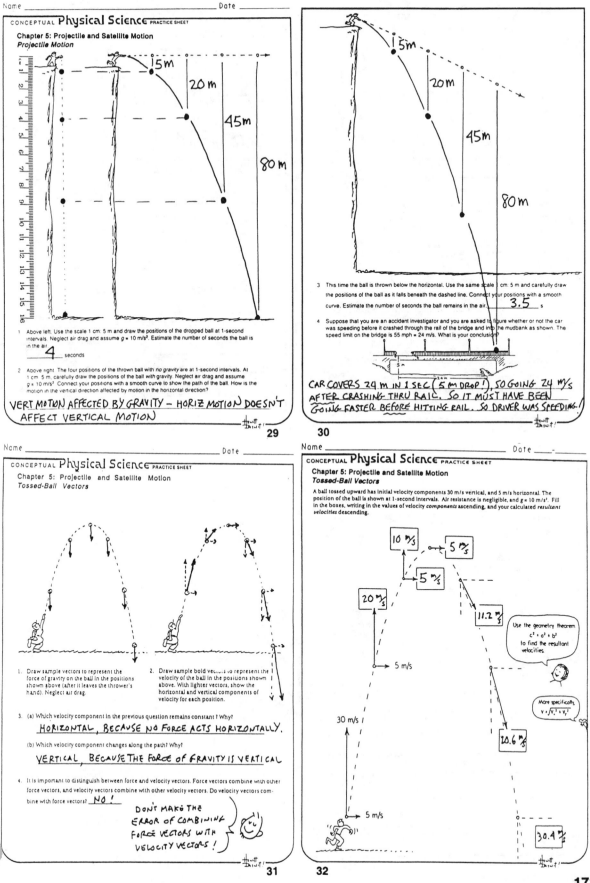

CONCEPTUAL **Physical Science** PRACTICE SHEET

Chapter 5: Projectile and Satellite Motion
Projectile Motion

15 m
20 m
45 m
80 m

1 Above left. Use the scale 1 cm: 5 m and draw the positions of the dropped ball at 1-second intervals. Neglect air drag and assume *g* = 10 m/s². Estimate the number of seconds the ball is in the air.

_____**4**_____ seconds

2 Above right. The four positions of the thrown ball with *no gravity* are at 1-second intervals. At 1 cm: 5 m, carefully draw the positions of the ball *with* gravity. Neglect air drag and assume *g* = 10 m/s? Connect your positions with a smooth curve to show the path of the ball. How is the motion in the vertical direction affected by motion in the horizontal direction?

VERT MOTION AFFECTED BY GRAVITY — HORIZ MOTION DOESN'T AFFECT VERTICAL MOTION

29

---

15 m
20 m
45 m
80 m

3 This time the ball is thrown below the horizontal. Use the same scale 1 cm: 5 m and carefully draw the positions of the ball as it falls beneath the dashed line. Connect your positions with a smooth curve. Estimate the number of seconds the ball remains in the air. **3.5** s

4 Suppose that you are an accident investigator and you are asked to figure whether or not the car was speeding before it crashed through the rail of the bridge and into the mudbank as shown. The speed limit on the bridge is 55 mph = 24 m/s. What is your conclusion?

CAR COVERS 24 m IN 1 SEC (5 m DROP!), SO GOING 24 M/s AFTER CRASHING THRU RAIL. SO IT MUST HAVE BEEN GOING FASTER BEFORE HITTING RAIL. SO DRIVER WAS SPEEDING!

30

CONCEPTUAL **Physical Science** PRACTICE SHEET

Chapter 5: Projectile and Satellite Motion
Tossed-Ball Vectors

1. Draw sample vectors to represent the force of gravity on the ball in the positions shown above (after it leaves the thrower's hand). Neglect air drag.

2. Draw sample bold vectors to represent the velocity of the ball in the positions shown above. With lighter vectors, show the horizontal and vertical components of velocity for each position.

3. (a) Which velocity component in the previous question remains constant? Why?

HORIZONTAL, BECAUSE NO FORCE ACTS HORIZONTALLY.

(b) Which velocity component changes along the path? Why?

VERTICAL, BECAUSE THE FORCE OF GRAVITY IS VERTICAL

4. It is important to distinguish between force and velocity vectors. Force vectors combine with other force vectors, and velocity vectors combine with other velocity vectors. Do velocity vectors combine with force vectors? NO !

DON'T MAKE THE ERROR OF COMBINING FORCE VECTORS WITH VELOCITY VECTORS !

31

CONCEPTUAL **Physical Science** PRACTICE SHEET

Chapter 5: Projectile and Satellite Motion
Tossed-Ball Vectors

A ball tossed upward has initial velocity components 30 m/s vertical, and 5 m/s horizontal. The position of the ball is shown at 1-second intervals. Air resistance is negligible, and *g* = 10 m/s². Fill in the boxes, writing in the values of velocity *components* ascending, and your calculated *resultant velocities* descending.

10 m/s
5 m/s
5 m/s
20 m/s
11.2 m/s
5 m/s
30 m/s
5 m/s
20.6 m/s
30.4 m/s

Use the geometry theorem $c^2 = a^2 + b^2$ to find the resultant velocities.

More specifically, $v = \sqrt{v_x^2 + v_y^2}$

32

CONCEPTUAL **Physical Science** PRACTICE SHEET

Chapter 5: Projectile and Satellite Motion
Circular Orbits

1. Figure A shows "Newton's Mountain," so high that its top is above the drag of the atmosphere. The cannonball is fired and hits the ground as shown.

   a. You draw the path the cannonball might take if it were fired a little bit faster.

   b. Repeat for a still greater speed, but still less than 8 km/s.

   c. Then draw the orbital path it would take if its speed were 8 km/s.

   d. What is the shape of the 8 km/s curve?
   __CIRCLE__

   e. What would be the shape of the orbital path if the cannonball were fired at a speed of about 9 km/s?
   __ELLIPSE__

2. Figure B shows a satellite in circular orbit.

   a. At each of the four positions draw a vector that represents the gravitational *force* exerted on the satellite.

   b. Label the force vectors *F*.

   c. Then draw at each position a vector to represent the *velocity* of the satellite at that position, and label it *V*.

   d. Are all four *F* vectors the same length? Why or why not?
   __YES; SAME DISTANCE, SAME FORCE__

   e. Are all four *V* vectors the same length? Why or why not?
   __YES – IN CIRCULAR ORBIT F ⊥ V SO NO COMPONENT OF F ALONG V__
   What is the angle between your *F* and *V* vectors? __90°__

   g. Is there any component of *F* along *V*? __NO, (F ⊥ V)__

   h. What does this tell you about the work the force of gravity does on the satellite?
   __NO WORK BECAUSE NO COMPONENT OF F ALONG PATH__

   i. Does the KE of the satellite in Figure B remain constant, or does it vary? __CONSTANT__

   j. Does the PE of the satellite remain constant, or does it vary?
   __CONSTANT__

Elliptical Orbits

3. Figure C shows a satellite in elliptical orbit.

   a. Repeat the procedure you used for the circular orbit, drawing vectors *F* and *V* for each position, including proper labeling. Show equal magnitudes with equal lengths, and greater magnitudes with greater lengths, but don't bother making the scale accurate.

   b. Are your vectors *F* all the same magnitude? Why or why not?
   __NO, FORCE DECREASES WHEN DISTANCE FROM EARTH INCREASES__

   c. Are your vectors *V* all the same magnitude? Why or why not?
   __NO. WHEN KE DECREASES, SPEED DECREASES. WHEN KE INCREASES (CLOSER TO EARTH) SPEED INCREASES.__

   d. Is the angle between vectors *F* and *V* everywhere the same, or does it vary?
   __IT VARIES__

   e. Are there places where there is a component of *F* along *V*?
   __YES (EVERYWHERE EXCEPT AT THE APOGEE AND PERIGEE)__

   f. Is work done on the satellite when there is a component of *F* along and in the same direction of *V* and if so, does this increase or decrease the KE of the satellite?
   __YES, THIS INCREASES KE OF SATELLITE__

   g. When there is a component of *F* along and opposite to the direction of *V*, does this increase or decrease the KE of the satellite?
   __THIS DECREASES KE OF SATELLITE__

   h. What can you say about the sum KE + PE along the orbit?
   __CONSTANT (IN ACCORD WITH CONSERVATION OF ENERGY)__

   Be very very careful when placing both velocity and force vectors on the same diagram. Not a good practice, for one may construct the resultant of the vectors -- ouch!

33   **34**

CONCEPTUAL **Physical Science** PRACTICE SHEET

Mechanics Overview

1. The sketch shows the elliptical path described by a satellite about the earth. In which of the marked positions, A - D, (put S for "same everywhere") does the satellite experience the maximum

   a. gravitational force? __A__

   b. speed? __A__

   c. velocity? __A__

   d. momentum? __A__

   e. kinetic energy? __A__

   f. gravitational potential energy? __C__

   g. total energy (KE + PE)? __S__

   h. acceleration? __A__
   $$a = \frac{F}{m}$$

2. Answer the above questions for a satellite in circular orbit.
   a. __S__ b. __S__ c. __S__ d. __S__ e. __S__ f. __S__ g. __S__ h. __S__

3. In which position(s) is there momentarily no work done on the satellite by the force of gravity? Why?
   __A AND C, BECAUSE NO FORCE COMPONENTS ALONG PATH__

4. Work changes energy. Let the equation for work, *W = Fd*, guide your thinking on these: Defend your answers in terms of *W = Fd*.

   a. In which position will a several-minutes thrust of rocket engines do the most work on the satellite and give it the greatest change in kinetic energy?
   __A, BECAUSE d GREATEST DURING THRUST - F × d IS MORE WORK__

   b. In which position will a several-minutes thrust of rocket engines do the most work on the *exhaust gases* and give the *exhaust gases* the greatest change in kinetic energy?
   __C, WHERE SATELLITE ROCKET IS SLOWEST__

   c. In which position will a several-minutes thrust of rocket engines give the satellite the least boost in kinetic energy?
   __C, BECAUSE RELATIVE TO PLANET, MOST ENERGY IS GIVEN TO THE EXHAUST GASES.__

35

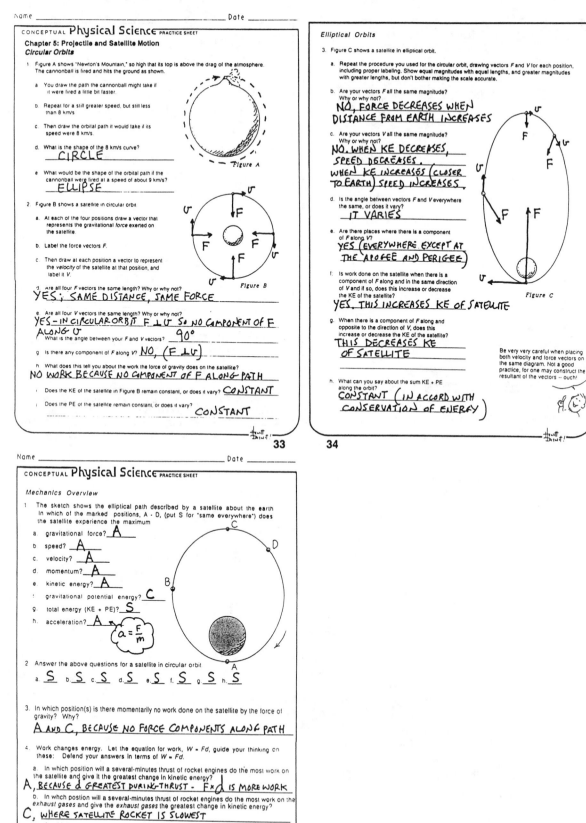

CONCEPTUAL Physical Science PRACTICE SHEET

Chapter 6: Fluid Mechanics
Archimedes' Principle

1. Consider a balloon filled with 1 liter of water (1000 cm³) in equilibrium in a container of water, as shown in Figure 1.

   a. What is the mass of the 1 liter of water?

   1 kg

   b. What is the weight of the 1 liter of water?

   9.8 N (OR 10 N)

   c. What is the weight of water displaced by the balloon?

   9.8 N (OR 10 N)

   d. What is the buoyant force on the balloon?

   9.8 N (OR 10 N)

   WATER DOES NOT SINK IN WATER!

   e. Sketch a pair of vectors in Figure 1: one for the weight of the balloon and the other for the buoyant force that acts on it. How do the size and directions of your vectors compare?

   SAME SIZE, OPPOSITE DIRECTIONS Figure 1

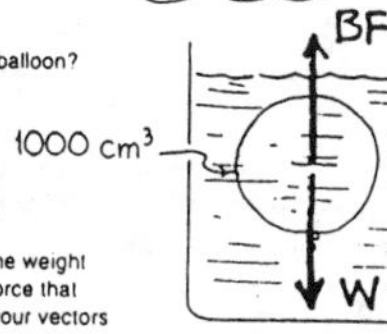

2. As a thought experiment, pretend we could remove the water from the balloon but still have it remain the same size of 1 liter. Then inside the balloon is a vacuum.

   a. What is the mass of the liter of nothing?

   0 kg

   b. What is the weight of the liter of nothing?

   0 N

   ANYTHING THAT DISPLACES 9.8 N OF WATER EXPERIENCES 9.8 N OF BUOYANT FORCE.

   c. What is the weight of water displaced by the massless balloon?

   9.8 N (OR 10 N)

   d. What is the buoyant force on the massless balloon?

   9.8 N (OR 10 N)

   CUZ IF YOU PUSH 9.8 N OF WATER ASIDE THE WATER PUSHES BACK ON YOU WITH 9.8 N!

   e. In which direction would the massless balloon be accelerated?

   UPWARD

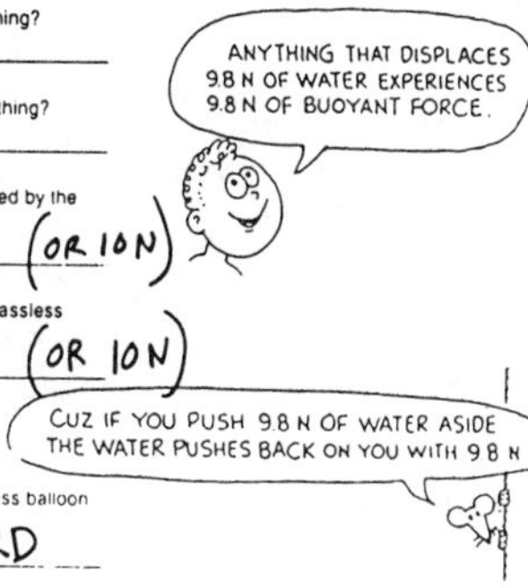

37

3. Assume the balloon is replaced by a 0.5-kilogram piece of wood that has exactly the same volume (1000 cm³), as shown in Figure 2. The wood is held in the same submerged position beneath the surface of the water.

   a. What volume of water is displaced by the wood?

   1000 cm³ = 1 L   1000 cm³

   b. What is the mass of the water displaced by the wood?

   1 kg

   c. What is the weight of the water displaced by the wood?

   9.8 N

   Figure 2

   d. How much buoyant force does the surrounding water exert on the wood?

   9.8 N

   e. When the hand is removed, what is the net force on the wood?

   NET FORCE = BF − W = 9.8 N − 4.9 N = 4.9 N UPWARD

   f. In which direction does the wood accelerate when released?   **UPWARD**

   THE BUOYANT FORCE ON A SUBMERGED OBJECT EQUALS THE WEIGHT OF WATER DISPLACED

   ... NOT THE WEIGHT OF THE OBJECT ITSELF!

   ...UNLESS IT IS FLOATING!

4. Repeat parts a through f in the previous question for a 5-kg rock that has the same volume (1000 cm³), as shown in Figure 3. Assume the rock is suspended by a string in the container of water.

   a. **1000 cm³ (SAME)**

   b. **1 kg (SAME)**

   c. **9.8 N (SAME)**

   d. **9.8 N (SAME)**

   e. **39 N DOWNWARD***

   f. **DOWNWARD**

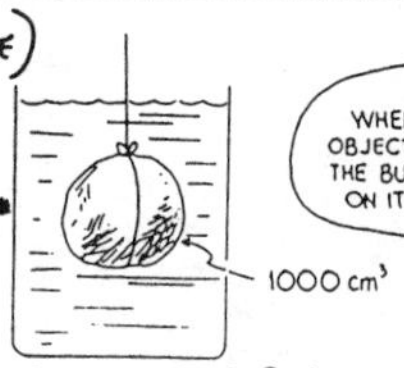

   Figure 3

   WHEN THE WEIGHT OF AN OBJECT IS GREATER THAN THE BUOYANT FORCE EXERTED ON IT, IT SINKS!

   1000 cm³

   * NET FORCE = W − BF = 49 N − 9.8 N ≈ 39 N

38

CONCEPTUAL Physical Science PRACTICE SHEET

Chapter 6: Fluid Mechanics
More Archimedes' Principle

1. The water lines for the first three cases are shown. Sketch in the appropriate water lines for cases d and e, and make up your own for case f.

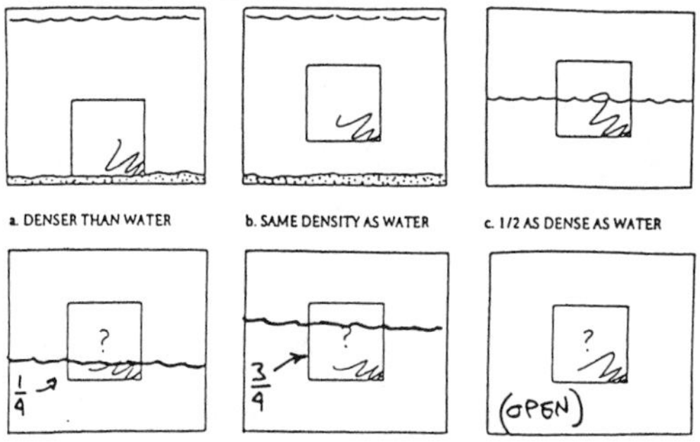

   a. DENSER THAN WATER
   b. SAME DENSITY AS WATER
   c. 1/2 AS DENSE AS WATER

   d. 1/4 AS DENSE AS WATER
   e. 3/4 AS DENSE AS WATER
   f. ____ AS DENSE AS WATER   (OPEN)

2. If the weight of a ship is 100 million N, then the water it displaces weighs **100 MILLION N**.
   If cargo weighing 1000 N is put on board then the ship will sink down until an extra **1000 N** of water is displaced.

3. The first two sketches below show the water line for an empty and a loaded ship. Draw in the appropriate water line for the third sketch.

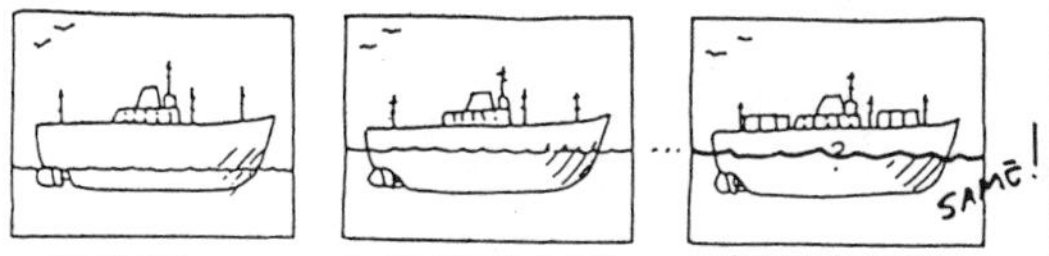

   a. SHIP EMPTY
   b. SHIP LOADED WITH 50 TONS OF IRON
   c. SHIP LOADED WITH 50 TONS OF STYROFOAM

   SAME!

39

4. Here is a glass of ice water with an ice cube floating in it. Draw the water line after the ice cube melts. (Will the water line rise, fall, or remain the same?)

   REMAINS SAME. VOL OF WATER WITH SAME WT OF ICE CUBE EQUALS VOL OF SUBMERGED PORTION OF ICE CUBE. THIS IS ALSO THE VOL OF WATER FROM MELTED ICE CUBE.

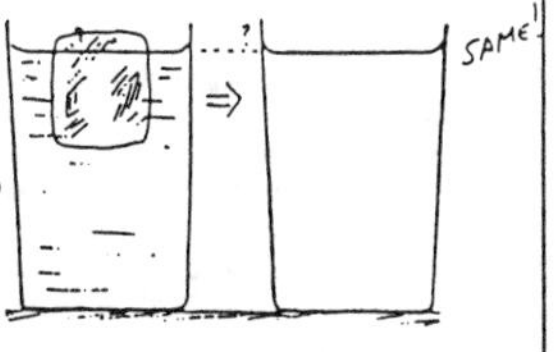

   SAME!

5. The air-filled balloon is weighted so it sinks in water. Near the surface, the balloon has a certain volume. Draw the balloon at the bottom (inside the dashed square) and show whether it is bigger, smaller, or the same size.

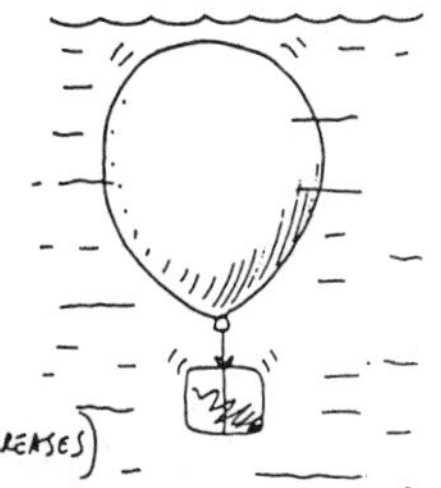

   a. Since the weighted balloon sinks, how does its overall density compare to the density of water?

   THE DENSITY OF BALLOON IS GREATER

   b. As the weighted balloon sinks, does its density increase, decrease, or remain the same?

   DENSITY INCREASES (BECAUSE VOL DECREASES)

   c. Since the weighted balloon sinks, how does the buoyant force on it compare to its weight?

   BF IS LESS THAN ITS WEIGHT

   d. As the weighted balloon sinks deeper, does the buoyant force on it increase, decrease, or remain the same?

   BF DECREASES (BECAUSE VOL DECREASES)

5. What would be your answers to Questions a, b, c and d for a rock instead of an air-filled balloon?

   a. **DENSITY OF ROCK IS GREATER**

   b. **DENSITY REMAINS SAME (SAME VOL)**

   c. **BF IS LESS THAN ITS WEIGHT**

   d. **BF STAYS SAME (VOL STAYS SAME)**

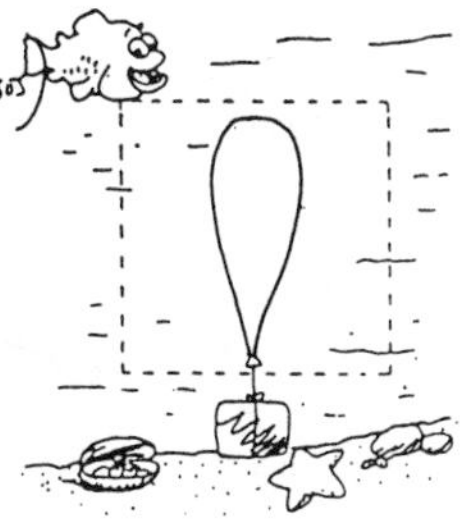

40

173

CONCEPTUAL **Physical Science** PRACTICE SHEET

Chapter 6: Fluid Mechanics
Gases

1. A principle difference between a liquid and a gas is that when a liquid is under pressure, its volume

   (increases) (decreases) (doesn't change noticeably)

   and its density

   (increases) (decreases) (doesn't change noticeably).

   When a gas is under pressure, its volume

   (increases) (decreases) (doesn't change noticeably)

   and its density

   (increases) (decreases) (doesn't change noticeably).

2. The sketch shows the launching of a weather balloon at sea level. Make a sketch of the same weather balloon when it is high in the atmosphere. In words, what is different about its size and why?

   BALLOON GROWS AS IT RISES. ATM PRESSURE TENDS TO COMPRESS THINGS—EVEN BALLOONS. MORE PRESSURE AT GROUND LEVEL, + MORE COMPRESSION. LESS COMPRESSION AT HIGH ALTITUDES + BIGGER BALLOON.

   HIGH-ALTITUDE SIZE

   GROUND-LEVEL SIZE

3. A hydrogen-filled balloon that weighs 10 N must displace 10 N of air in order to float in air.

   If it displaces less than 10 N it will be buoyed up with less than 10 N and sink.

   If it displaces more than 10 N of air it will move upward.

4. Why is the cartoon more humorous to physics types than to non-physics types? What physics has occurred?

   IN ACCORD WITH BERNOULLI'S PRINCIPLE, MOVEMENT OF AIR OVER CURVED TOP OF UMBRELLA CAUSES A REDUCTION OF AIR PRESSURE (LIKE AIRPLANE WING). THIS LIKELY PRODUCED A NET UPWARD FORCE THAT TURNED THE UMBRELLA INSIDE OUT.

   RATS TO YOU TOO, DANIEL BERNOULLI!

   41

CONCEPTUAL **Physical Science** PRACTICE SHEET

Chapter 7: Thermal Energy and Thermodynamics
Temperature Mix

1. You apply heat to 1 L of water and raise its temperature by 10°C. If you add the same quantity of heat to 2 L of water, how much will the temperature rise? To 3 L of water? Record your answers on the blanks in the drawing at the right.

   $\Delta T = 10°C$ $\Delta T = 5°C$ $\Delta T = 3.3°C$

2. A large bucket contains 1 L of 20°C water.

   a. What will be the temperature of the mixture when 1 L of 20°C water is added?

   STILL 20°C

   b. What will be the temperature of the mixture when 1 L of 40°C water is added?

   30°C

   c. If 2 L of 40°C water were added, would the temperature of the mixture be greater or less than 30°C?

   GREATER

   $Q = mc\Delta T$

   $Q_{LOST} = Q_{GAINED}$

   $1 \cdot 1(40-T) = 1 \cdot 1(T-20)$

   $2(40-T) = 1(T-20)$

   $T = 33.3°C$

3. A red-hot iron kilogram mass is put into 1 L of cool water. Mark each of the following statements true (T) or false (F). (Ignore heat transfer to the container.)

   a. The increase in the water temperature is equal to the decrease in the iron's temperature.
   F   NOTE DISTINCTION!

   b. The quantity of heat gained by the water is equal to the quantity of heat lost by the iron.
   T

   c. The iron and the water will both reach the same temperature. _____

   d. The final temperature of the iron and water is about halfway between the initial temperatures of each. **F**

   THERMAL EQUILIBRIUM

4. *True or False:* When Queen Elizabeth throws the last sip of her tea over Queen Mary's rail, the ocean gets a little warmer. **T** (UNLESS IT WAS ICE TEA.)

   43

Chapter 7: Thermal Energy and Thermodynamics
Absolute Zero

A mass of air is contained so that the volume can change but the pressure remains constant. Table I shows air volumes at various temperatures when the air is heated slowly.

1. Plot the data in Table I on the graph, and connect the points.

   T
   AIR
   HEAT

Table I

TEMP. (°C)	VOLUME (mL)
0	50
25	55
50	60
75	65
100	70

VOLUME (mL)

-273

TEMPERATURE (°C)

2. The graph shows how the volume of air varies with temperature at constant pressure. The straightness of the line means that the air expands uniformly with temperature. From your graph, you can predict what will happen to the volume of air when it is cooled.

   Extrapolate (extend) the straight line of your graph to find the temperature at which the volume of the air would become zero. Mark this point on your graph. Estimate this temperature: **-273 °C**

3. Although air would liquify before cooling to this temperature, the procedure suggests that there is a lower limit to how cold something can be. This is the absolute zero of temperature.

   Careful experiments show that absolute zero is **-273** °C.

4. Scientists measure temperature in *kelvins* instead of degrees Celsius, where the absolute zero of temperature is 0 kelvins. If you relabeled the temperature axis on the graph in Question 1 so that it shows temperature in kelvins, would your graph look like the one below? **YES**

   VOLUME (mL)

   273   373

   TEMPERATURE (K)

   44

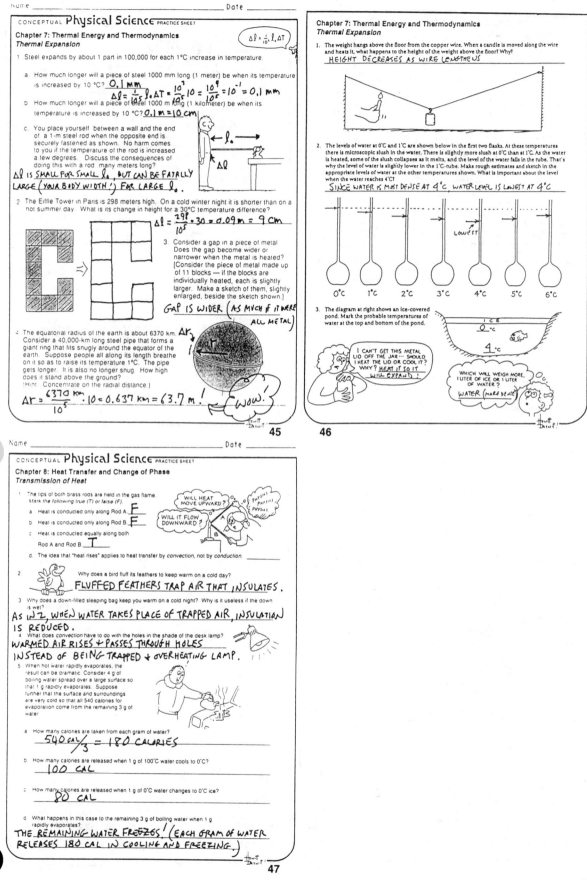

CONCEPTUAL Physical Science PRACTICE SHEET

Chapter 7: Thermal Energy and Thermodynamics
Thermal Expansion

$$\Delta \ell = \tfrac{1}{10^5}\,\ell\,\Delta T$$

1. Steel expands about 1 part in 100,000 for each 1°C increase in temperature.

a. How much longer will a piece of steel 1000 mm long (1 meter) be when its temperature is increased by 10 °C? **0.1 MM**
$$\Delta \ell = \tfrac{1}{10^5}\,\ell \cdot \Delta T = \tfrac{10^3}{10^5}\cdot 10 = \tfrac{10^4}{10^5} = 10^{-1} = 0.1\ \text{mm}$$

b. How much longer will a piece of steel 1000 m long (1 kilometer) be when its temperature is increased by 10 °C? **0.1 m = 10 cm**

c. You place yourself between a wall and the end of a 1-m steel rod when the opposite end is securely fastened as shown. No harm comes to you if the temperature of the rod is increased a few degrees. Discuss the consequences of doing this with a rod many meters long?

Δℓ IS SMALL FOR SMALL ℓ, BUT CAN BE FATALLY LARGE (YOUR BODY WIDTH!) FOR LARGE ℓ.

2. The Eiffel Tower in Paris is 298 meters high. On a cold winter night it is shorter than on a hot summer day. What is its change in height for a 30°C temperature difference?

$$\Delta \ell = \tfrac{298}{10^5}\cdot 30 = 0.09\,\text{m} = 9\ \text{cm}$$

3. Consider a gap in a piece of metal. Does the gap become wider or narrower when the metal is heated? [Consider the piece of metal made up of 11 blocks — if the blocks are individually heated, each is slightly larger. Make a sketch of them, slightly enlarged, beside the sketch shown.]

GAP IS WIDER (AS MUCH IF IT WERE ALL METAL)

4. The equatorial radius of the earth is about 6370 km. Consider a 40,000-km long steel pipe that forms a giant ring that fits snugly around the equator of the earth. Suppose people all along its length breathe on it so as to raise its temperature 1°C. The pipe gets longer. It is also no longer snug. How high does it stand above the ground? [Hint: Concentrate on the radial distance.]

$$\Delta r = \tfrac{6370\ \text{km}}{10^5}\cdot 10 = 0.637\ \text{km} = 63.7\ \text{m}!$$

WOW!

Chapter 7: Thermal Energy and Thermodynamics
Thermal Expansion

1. The weight hangs above the floor from the copper wire. When a candle is moved along the wire and heats it, what happens to the height of the weight above the floor? Why?

HEIGHT DECREASES AS WIRE LENGTHENS

2. The levels of water at 0°C and 1°C are shown below in the first two flasks. At these temperatures there is microscopic slush in the water. There is slightly more slush at 0°C than at 1°C. As the water is heated, some of the slush collapses as it melts, and the level of water falls in the tube. That's why the level of water is slightly lower in the 1°C-tube. Make rough estimates and sketch in the appropriate levels of water at the other temperatures shown. What is important about the level when the water reaches 4°C?

SINCE WATER IS MOST DENSE AT 4°C, WATER LEVEL IS LOWEST AT 4°C

0°C   1°C   2°C   3°C   4°C   5°C   6°C

(LOWEST)

3. The diagram at right shows an ice-covered pond. Mark the probable temperatures of water at the top and bottom of the pond.

ICE
0°C
4°C

I CAN'T GET THIS METAL LID OFF THE JAR — SHOULD I HEAT THE LID OR COOL IT? WHY? HEAT IT SO IT WILL EXPAND!

WHICH WILL WEIGH MORE, 1 LITER OF ICE OR 1 LITER OF WATER?
WATER (MORE DENSE)

CONCEPTUAL Physical Science PRACTICE SHEET

Chapter 8: Heat Transfer and Change of Phase
Transmission of Heat

1. The tips of both brass rods are held in the gas flame. Mark the following true (T) or false (F).

a. Heat is conducted only along Rod A. **F**

b. Heat is conducted only along Rod B. **F**

c. Heat is conducted equally along both Rod A and Rod B. **T**

d. The idea that "heat rises" applies to heat transfer by *convection*, not by *conduction*.

WILL HEAT MOVE UPWARD?
WILL IT FLOW DOWNWARD?
PHYSICS PHYSICS PHYSICS

2. Why does a bird fluff its feathers to keep warm on a cold day?

FLUFFED FEATHERS TRAP AIR THAT INSULATES.

3. Why does a down-filled sleeping bag keep you warm on a cold night? Why is it useless if the down is wet?

AS IN 2, WHEN WATER TAKES PLACE OF TRAPPED AIR, INSULATION IS REDUCED.

4. What does *convection* have to do with the holes in the shade of the desk lamp?

WARMED AIR RISES + PASSES THROUGH HOLES INSTEAD OF BEING TRAPPED + OVERHEATING LAMP.

5. When hot water rapidly evaporates, the result can be dramatic. Consider 4 g of boiling water spread over a large surface so that 1 g rapidly evaporates. Suppose further that the surface and surroundings are very cold so that all 540 calories for evaporation come from the remaining 3 g of water.

a. How many calories are taken from each gram of water?

540 cal/3 = 180 CALORIES

b. How many calories are released when 1 g of 100°C water cools to 0°C?

100 CAL

c. How many calories are released when 1 g of 0°C water changes to 0°C ice?

80 CAL

d. What happens in this case to the remaining 3 g of boiling water when 1 g rapidly evaporates?

THE REMAINING WATER FREEZES! (EACH GRAM OF WATER RELEASES 180 CAL IN COOLING AND FREEZING.)

Name _____ Date _____

CONCEPTUAL **Physical Science** PRACTICE SHEET

Chapter 8: Heat Transfer and Change of Phase
Change of Phase

All matter can exist in the solid, liquid, or gaseous phases. The solid phase exists at relatively low temperatures, the liquid phase at higher temperatures, and the gaseous phase at still higher temperatures. Water is the most common example, not only because of its abundance but also because the temperatures for all three phases are common. Study Section 8.10 in your textbook and then answer the following:

1. How many calories are needed to change 1 gram of 0°C ice to water?   **80**

2. How many calories are needed to change the temperature of 1 gram of water by 1°C?

3. How many calories are needed to melt 1 gram of 0°C ice and turn it to water at a room temperature of 23°C?
80 CAL + 23 CAL = 103 CAL

4. A 50-gram sample of ice at 0°C is placed in a glass beaker that contains 200 g of water at 20°C.

a. How much heat is needed to melt the ice? **4000 CAL**
SINCE THERE'S 50g OF ICE, AND 80 CAL REQUIRED PER GRAM
HEAT REQUIRED IS 50g(80 CAL) = 4000 CAL

b. By how much would the temperature of the water change if it gave up this much heat to the ice? **20°C**
200g OF WATER GIVES OFF 200 CAL FOR EACH 1°C DROP IN TEMPERATURE.
SO 4000 CAL/200 CAL = 20°C

c. What will be the final temperature of the mixture? (Disregard any heat absorbed by the glass or given off by the surrounding air.) **0°C**

5. How many calories are needed to change 1 gram of 100°C boiling water to 100°C steam?
540 CAL

6. Fill in the number of calories at each step below for changing the state of 1 gram of 0°C ice to 100°C steam.

HEAT NEEDED → **80** CAL + **100** CAL + **540** CAL = **720** CAL

48

---

7. One gram of steam at 100°C condenses, and the water cools to 22°C.

a. How much heat is released when the steam condenses?   **540 CALORIES**

b. How much heat is released when the water cools from 100°C to 22°C?
78 CALORIES (SINCE WATER COOLS BY 100° -22°, OR 78°C)

c. How much heat is released altogether?   **618 CALORIES**

8. In a household radiator 1000 g of steam at 100°C condenses, and the water cools to 90°C.

a. How much heat is released when the steam condenses?
540,000 CALORIES

b. How much heat is released when the water cools from 100°C to 90°C?
10,000 CAL

c. How much heat is released altogether?
550,000 CAL

9. Radioactive minerals in common granite release 0.01 cal/kg of energy per year. If a 1-kg chunk of 50°C granite is thermally insulated, so all this energy heats it, how many years does it take to reach its melting temperature of 700°C? (Assume the specific heat of granite is 200 cal/kg°C.)

Q = mcΔT = 1(200)(650) = 130,000 CAL; 130,000 CAL / 0.10 CAL/YR = 13 MILLION YEARS

10. How many years would be required if the chunk of granite had a mass of 1 million kg? Why?
SAME 13 MILLION YEARS (BECAUSE CORRESPONDINGLY MORE RADIATION)

11. To calculate the time it takes to melt the 700°C granite, what other information would you need?
AMOUNT OF ENERGY TO CHANGE PHASE OF GRANITE

12. So we see that radioactivity keeps the earth's interior hot. After energy due to radioactivity eventually migrates to the earth's surface, in what form does it leave the earth?
TERRESTRIAL RADIATION

13. To get water from the ground, even in the hot desert, dig a hole about a half meter wide and a half meter deep. Place a cup at the bottom. Spread a sheet of plastic wrap over the hole and place stones along the edge to hold it secure. Weight the center of the plastic with a stone so it forms a cone shape. Why will water collect in the cup? (Physics can save your life if you're ever stranded in a desert!)

EVAPORATED WATER FROM GROUND IS TRAPPED + CONDENSES ON THE UNDERSIDE OF PLASTIC, + RUNS INTO CUP. (AT NIGHT, CONDENSATION IN AIR COLLECTS ON TOP OF PLASTIC.

49

CONCEPTUAL **Physical Science** PRACTICE SHEET

Chapter 9: Static and Current Electricity
Electric Potential

Just as PE transforms to KE for a mass lifted against the gravitation field (left), the electric PE of an electric charge transforms to other forms of energy when it changes location in an electric field (right). In both cases, how does the KE acquired compare to the decrease in PE?

SAME

Complete the statements.

A force compresses the spring. The work done in compression is the product of the average force and the distance moved. W = Fd. This work increases the PE of the spring.

Similarly, a force pushes the charge (call it a test charge) closer to the charged sphere. The work done in moving the test charge is the product of the average **FORCE** and the **DISTANCE** moved. W = **Fd**. This work **INCREASES** the PE of the test charge.

If the test charge is released, it will be repelled and fly past the starting point. Its gain in KE at this point is **EQUAL** to its decrease in PE.

At any point, a greater amount of test charge means a greater amount of PE. But not a greater amount of PE *per amount* of charge. The quantities PE (measured in joules) and PE/charge (measured in volts) are different concepts.

By definition: Electric Potential = PE/charge. 1 volt = 1 joule/1 coulomb. So 1 C of charge with a PE of 1 J has an electric potential of 1 V. And 2 C of charge with a PE of 2 J has an electric potential of **1** V.

If a conductor connected to the terminal of a battery has an electric potential of 12 V, then each coulomb of charge on the conductor has a PE of **12** J.

You do very little work in rubbing a balloon on your hair to charge it. The PE of several thousand billion electrons (about one-millionth coulomb [10^{-6}C]) transferred may be a thousandth of a joule [10^{-3}J]. Impressively, however, the electric potential of the balloon is about **1000** V. ($\frac{10^{-3} J}{10^{-6} C} = 10^3 V$)

Why is contact with a balloon charged to thousands of volts not as dangerous as contact with household 110 V? **HOUSEHOLD CURRENT TRANSFERS MANY COULOMBS AND MUCH ENERGY. A BALLOON TRANSFERS VERY LITTLE OF BOTH.**

51

Chapter 9: Static and Current Electricity
Series Circuits

1. The simple circuit is a 6-V battery that pushes charge through a single lamp that has a resistance of 3 Ω. According to Ohm's law, the current in the lamp (and therefore the whole circuit) is **2** A.

2. If a second identical lamp is added, the 6-V battery must push charge through a total resistance of **6** Ω. The current in the circuit is then **1** A.

3. If a third identical lamp is added in series, the total resistance of the circuit (neglecting any internal resistance in the battery) is **9** Ω.

4. The current through all three lamps in series is **2/3** A. The current through each individual lamp is **2/3** A.

5. Does current in the lamps occur simultaneously, or does charge flow first through one lamp, then the other, and finally the last, in turn? **SIMULTANEOUSLY ~ SPEED OF LIGHT**

6. Does current flow *through* a resistor, or *across* a resistor? **THROUGH** Is voltage established *through* a resistor, or *across* a resistor? **ACROSS**

7. The voltage across all three lamps in series is 6 V. The voltage (or commonly, *voltage drop*) across each individual lamp is **2** V.

8. Suppose a wire connects points a and b in the circuit. The voltage drop across lamp 1 is now **3** V, across lamp 2 is **3** V, and across lamp 3 is **0** V. So the current through lamp 1 is now **1** A, through lamp 2 is **1** A, and through lamp 3 is **0** A. The current in the battery (neglecting internal battery resistance) is **2** A.

9. Which circuit dissipates more power, the 3-lamp circuit or the 2-lamp circuit? (Another way of asking this is which circuit would glow brightest; which would be best seen on a dark night from a great distance?) Defend your answer.
FOR 3 LAMPS: P = IV = 2/3 · 6 = 4W FOR 2 LAMPS P = IV = 1·6 = 6W ∴ THE 2-LAMP CIRCUIT IS BRIGHTEST (IT WOULD BE EVEN BRIGHTER, 12 W, IF THERE WERE 1 LAMP)

52

176

CONCEPTUAL Physical Science PRACTICE SHEET

Chapter 9: Static and Current Electricity
Parallel circuits

3 Ω
3 Ω
6V

THE SUM OF THE CURRENTS IN THE TWO BRANCH PATHS EQUALS THE CURRENT BOTH BEFORE AND AFTER IT DIVIDES!

1. In the circuit shown to the left there is a voltage drop of 6 V across each 3-Ω lamp. By Ohm's law, the current in each lamp is **2** A. The current through the battery is the sum of the currents in the lamps, **4** A.

2. Fill in the current in the eight blank spaces in the view of the same circuit shown again at the right.

2 A **2** A
2 A **2** A
2 A **2** A
4 A **4** A

3 Ω
3 Ω
3 Ω
6V

3. Suppose a third identical lamp is added in parallel to the circuit. Sketch a schematic diagram of the 3-lamp circuit in the space at the left.

4. For the three identical lamps in parallel, the voltage drop across each lamp is **6** V. The current through each lamp is **2** A. The current through the battery is now **6** A. Is the circuit resistance now greater or less than before the third lamp was added? Explain.

LESS, BECAUSE OF MORE PATHS, WHICH MEANS LESS RESISTANCE BETWEEN BATTERY TERMINALS

5. Which circuit dissipates more power, the 3-lamp circuit or the 2-lamp circuit? (Another way of asking this is which circuit would glow brightest; which would be best seen on a dark night from a great distance?) Defend your answer and compare this to the similar case for 2- and 3-lamp series circuits.

3 LAMPS: P = IV = 6·6 = 36 W   2 LAMPS: P = IV = 4·6 = 24 W

SO 3-LAMP CIRCUIT IS BRIGHTEST; MORE CURRENT FLOWS (BECAUSE OF REDUCED RESISTANCE) FOR THE SAME VOLTAGE. OPPOSITE FOR SERIES CIRCUIT.

53

Compound Circuits

The table beside circuit *a* below shows the current through each resistor, the voltage across each resistor, and the power dissipated as heat in each resistor. Find the similar correct values for circuits *b*, *c*, and *d*, and put your answers in the tables shown.

2 Ω   4 Ω
6 Ω
a   12 v

RESISTANCE	CURRENT ×	VOLTAGE =	POWER
2 Ω	2 A	4 V	8 W
4 Ω	2 A	8 V	16 W
6 Ω	2 A	12 V	24 W

1 Ω   2 Ω
b   6 v

RESISTANCE	CURRENT ×	VOLTAGE =	POWER
1 Ω	2 A	2 V	4 W
2 Ω	2 A	4 V	8 W

6 Ω
3 Ω
c   6 v

RESISTANCE	CURRENT ×	VOLTAGE =	POWER
6 Ω	1 A	6 V	6 W
3 Ω	2 A	6 V	12 W

2 Ω
1 Ω
2 Ω
d   6 v

RESISTANCE	CURRENT ×	VOLTAGE =	POWER
2 Ω	1.5 A	3 V	4.5 W
2 Ω	1.5 A	3 V	4.5 W
1 Ω	3 A	3 V	9 W

NOTE THAT TOTAL POWER DISSIPATED BY ALL RESISTORS IN A CIRCUIT EQUALS THE POWER SUPPLIED BY THE BATTERY: (VOLTAGE OF BATTERY × CURRENT THRU BATTERY)

A VOLT IS A UNIT OF POTENTIAL (OR "PRESSURE") AND AN AMPERE IS A UNIT OF CURRENT

DOES VOLTAGE CAUSE CURRENT, OR DOES CURRENT CAUSE VOLTAGE? WHICH IS THE CAUSE AND WHICH

54

CONCEPTUAL Physical Science PRACTICE SHEET

Chapter 10: Magnetism and Electromagnetic Induction
Magnetism

Fill in each blank with the appropriate word.

1. Attraction or repulsion of charges depends on their *signs*, positives or negatives. Attraction or repulsion of magnets depends on their magnetic **POLES** **NORTH** or **SOUTH**.

YOU HAVE A MAGNETIC PERSONALITY!

2. Opposite poles attract; like poles **REPEL**.

3. A magnetic field is produced by the **MOTION** of electric charge.

4. Clusters of magnetically aligned atoms are magnetic **DOMAINS**.

5. A magnetic **FIELD** surrounds a current-carrying wire.

6. When a current-carrying wire is made to form a coil around a piece of iron, the result is an **ELECTROMAGNET**.

7. A charged particle moving in a magnetic field experiences a deflecting **FORCE** that is maximum when the charge moves **PERPENDICULAR** to the field.

8. A current-carrying wire experiences a deflecting **FORCE** that is maximum when the wire and magnetic field are **PERPENDICULAR** to one another.

9. A simple instrument designed to detect electric current is the **GALVANOMETER**; when calibrated to measure current, it is an **AMMETER**; when calibrated to measure voltage, it is a **VOLTMETER**.

10. The largest size magnet in the world is the **WORLD** itself.

THEN TO REALLY MAKE THINGS "SIMPLE," THERE'S THE RIGHT-HAND RULE!

55

Field Patterns

1. The illustration below is similar to Figure 10.3 in your textbook. Iron filings trace out patterns of magnetic field lines about a bar magnet. In the field are some magnetic compasses. The compass needle in only one compass is shown. Draw in the needles with proper orientation in the other compasses.

2. The illustration below is similar to Figure 10.12b in your textbook. Iron filings trace out the magnetic field pattern abut the loop of current-carrying wire. Draw in the compass needle orientations for all the compasses.

56

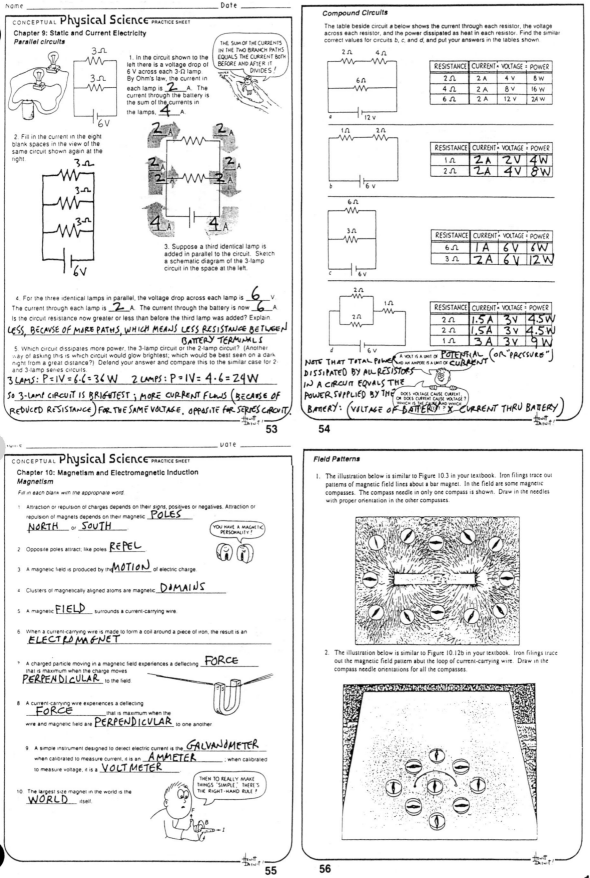

177

CONCEPTUAL **Physical Science** PRACTICE SHEET

Chapter 10: Magnetism and Electromagnetic Induction
Faraday's Law

1. Hans Christian Oersted discovered that magnetism and electricity are
   (**related**) (independent of each other).

   Magnetism is produced by
   (batteries) (**the motion of electric charges**).

   Faraday and Henry discovered that electric current can be produced by
   (batteries) (**motion of a magnet**).

   More specifically, voltage is induced in a loop of wire if there is a change in the
   (batteries) (**magnetic field in the loop**).

   This phenomenon is called
   (electromagnetism) (**electromagnetic induction**).

2. When a magnet is plunged in and out of a coil of wire, voltage is induced in the coil. If the rate of the in-and-out motion of the magnet is doubled, the induced voltage
   (**doubles**) (halves) (remains the same).

   If instead the number of loops in the coil is doubled, the induced voltage
   (**doubles**) (halves) (remains the same).

3. A rapidly changing magnetic field in any region of space induces a rapidly changing
   (**electric field**) (magnetic field) (gravitational field).

   which in turn induces a rapidly changing
   (**magnetic field**) (electric field) (baseball field).

   This generation and regeneration of electric and magnetic fields makes up
   (**electromagnetic waves**) (sound waves) (both of these).

PHYSICS
: SIGN :

Chapter 10: Magnetism and Electromagnetic Induction
E&M Induction—The Transformer

A changing magnetic field is produced in a coil of wire when a bar magnet is plunged in and out of the coil. This induces an electric pressure in the coil called **VOLTAGE**

If the number of loops in the coil are increased, the induced voltage is **INCREASES**

The physical movement of a bar magnet is one way to produce a changing magnetic field. Another is to use a stationary electromagnet powered with **ALTERNATING** current.

The square iron core (right) becomes an electromagnet when current flows through the primary loop. This magnetic field is enclosed by the secondary loop. If the current is ac, it induces an alternating magnetic field that induces voltage in the secondary loop. In (a) the voltage induced in the secondary equals the input voltage. (b) An extra secondary encloses the same changing magnetic field and voltage is induced in it also. (c) The induced voltages combine when the two secondaries are combined. Write in the induced voltage where indicated.

1 Volt ∝

Consider a more practical transformer with a 200 turn primary and a 1000-turn secondary (left). Suppose the primary is connected to a 120-volt alternating source, and the secondary is connected to an electrical device with a resistance of 600 ohms.

What will be the voltage output of the secondary? $5 \cdot 120 = 600$ V
What current will flow in the secondary circuit? $\frac{600}{600} = 1$ A
Knowing the voltage and current, what will be the power in the secondary? $P = IV = 600$ W
Neglecting small heat losses, and knowing that energy is conserved, what is the power in the primary? **SAME 600** W
What is the current drawn by the primary? $I = \frac{P}{V} = \frac{600}{120} = 5$ A
From this we see that the voltage is stepped up in the secondary, and compared to the current in the primary, is the current stepped up or down? **DOWN**
Can a transformer step up voltage? **YES**
Can a transformer step up current? **YES**
Can a transformer step up energy and or power? **NO!**

ENERGY CONSERVATION RULES!

CONCEPTUAL **Physical Science** PRACTICE SHEET

Chapter 11: Waves and Sound
Vibration and Wave Fundamentals

1. A sine curve that represents a transverse wave is drawn below. With a ruler, measure the wavelength and amplitude of the wave.

   a. Wavelength = **6 cm**   b. Amplitude = **1.4 cm**

2. A kid on a playground swing makes a complete to-and-fro swing each 2 seconds. The frequency of swing is
   (**0.5 hertz**) (1 hertz) (2 hertz)

   and the period is
   (0.5 second) (1 second) (**2 seconds**).

3. Complete the statements.

   THE PERIOD OF A 440-HERTZ SOUND WAVE IS **1/440 SECOND**.

   A MARINE WEATHER STATION REPORTS WAVES ALONG THE SHORE THAT ARE 8 SECONDS APART. THE FREQUENCY OF THE WAVES IS THEREFORE **1/8** HERTZ.

4. The annoying sound from a mosquito is produced when it beats its wings at the average rate of 600 wingbeats per second.

   a. What is the frequency of the soundwaves?
   600 Hz

   b. What is the wavelength? (Assume the speed of sound is 340 m/s.)
   0.57 m
   $\lambda = \frac{340 \text{ m}}{600 \text{ Hz}}$

---

5. A machine gun fires 10 rounds per second. The speed of the bullets is 300 m/s.

   a. What is the distance in the air between the flying bullets? **30 m**

   b. What happens to the distance between the bullets if the rate of fire is increased?
   DISTANCE BETWEEN BULLETS DECREASES

6. Consider a wave generator that produces 10 pulses per second. The speed of the waves is 300 cm/s.

   a. What is the wavelength of the waves? **30 cm**

   b. What happens to the wavelength if the frequency of pulses is increased?
   λ DECREASES, JUST AS DISTANCE BETWEEN BULLETS IN #5 DECREASES

7. The bird at the right watches the waves. If the portion of a wave between 2 crests passes the pole each second, what is the speed of the wave?
   $v = f\lambda = 2 \times 1 = 2$ m/s

   What is its period?
   $T = \frac{1}{f} = \frac{1}{2} = 0.5$ s

8. If the distance between crests in the above question were 1.5 meters apart, and 2 crests pass the pole each second, what would be the speed of the wave?
   $v = f\lambda = 2 \times 1.5 = 3$ m/s

   What would be its period?
   SAME (**0.5 s**)

9. When an automobile moves toward a listener, the sound of its horn seems relatively
   (low pitched) (normal)
   (**high pitched**)

   and when moving away from the listener, its horn seems
   (**low pitched**) (normal)
   (high pitched)

10. The changed pitch of the Doppler effect is due to changes in
    (wave speed) (**wave frequency**).

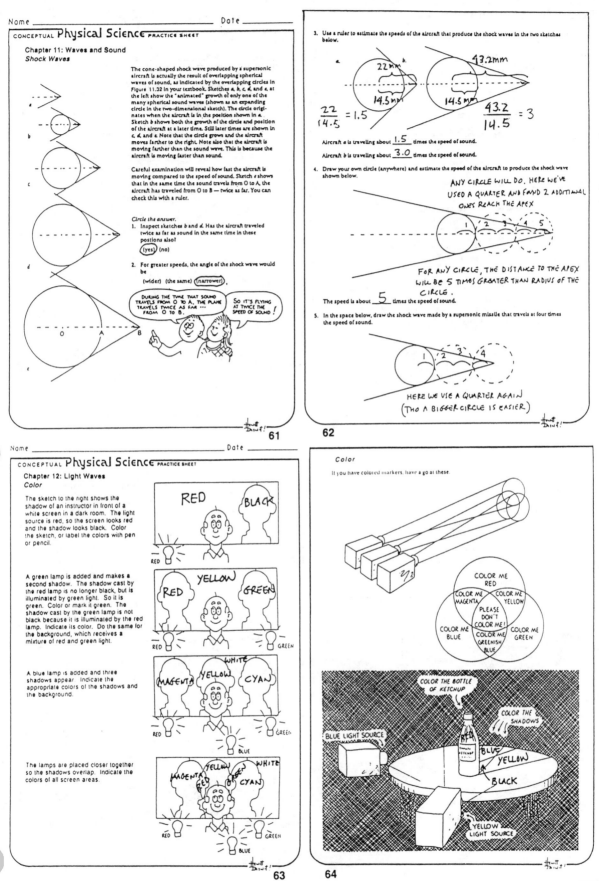

CONCEPTUAL **Physical Science** PRACTICE SHEET

Chapter 11: Waves and Sound
Shock Waves

The cone-shaped shock wave produced by a supersonic aircraft is actually the result of overlapping spherical waves of sound, as indicated by the overlapping circles in Figure 11.32 in your textbook. Sketches a, b, c, d, and e at the left show the "animated" growth of only one of the many spherical sound waves (shown as an expanding circle in the two-dimensional sketch). The circle originates when the aircraft is in the position shown in a. Sketch b shows both the growth of the circle and position of the aircraft at a later time. Still later times are shown in c, d, and e. Note that the circle grows and the aircraft moves farther to the right. Note also that the aircraft is moving farther than the sound wave. This is because the aircraft is moving faster than sound.

Careful examination will reveal how fast the aircraft is moving compared to the speed of sound. Sketch e shows that in the same time the sound travels from O to A, the aircraft has traveled from O to B—twice as far. You can check this with a ruler.

Circle the answer.

1. Inspect sketches b and d. Has the aircraft traveled twice as far as sound in the same time in these positions also?
   (yes) (no)

2. For greater speeds, the angle of the shock wave would be
   (wider) (the same) (narrower).

3. Use a ruler to estimate the speeds of the aircraft that produce the shock waves in the two sketches below.

a. 22 mm / 14.5 mm
   $\frac{22}{14.5} = 1.5$

b. 43.2 mm / 14.5 mm
   $\frac{43.2}{14.5} = 3$

Aircraft a is traveling about **1.5** times the speed of sound.

Aircraft b is traveling about **3.0** times the speed of sound.

4. Draw your own circle (anywhere) and estimate the speed of the aircraft to produce the shock wave shown below.

ANY CIRCLE WILL DO. HERE WE'VE USED A QUARTER AND FOUND 2 ADDITIONAL ONES REACH THE APEX

FOR ANY CIRCLE, THE DISTANCE TO THE APEX WILL BE 5 TIMES GREATER THAN RADIUS OF THE CIRCLE.

The speed is about **5** times the speed of sound.

5. In the space below, draw the shock wave made by a supersonic missile that travels at four times the speed of sound.

HERE WE USE A QUARTER AGAIN (THO A BIGGER CIRCLE IS EASIER)

61

62

CONCEPTUAL **Physical Science** PRACTICE SHEET

Chapter 12: Light Waves
Color

The sketch to the right shows the shadow of an instructor in front of a white screen in a dark room. The light source is red, so the screen looks red and the shadow looks black. Color the sketch, or label the colors with pen or pencil.

RED   BLACK
RED

A green lamp is added and makes a second shadow. The shadow cast by the red lamp is no longer black, but is illuminated by green light. So it is green. Color or mark it green. The shadow cast by the green lamp is not black because it is illuminated by the red lamp. Indicate its color. Do the same for the background, which receives a mixture of red and green light.

YELLOW
RED   GREEN
RED   GREEN

A blue lamp is added and three shadows appear. Indicate the appropriate colors of the shadows and the background.

WHITE
MAGENTA YELLOW CYAN
RED   GREEN
BLUE

The lamps are placed closer together so the shadows overlap. Indicate the colors of all screen areas.

WHITE
MAGENTA YELLOW GREEN CYAN
RED
RED   GREEN
BLUE

Color

If you have colored markers, have a go at these.

COLOR ME RED
COLOR ME MAGENTA   COLOR ME YELLOW
PLEASE DON'T COLOR ME!
COLOR ME BLUE   COLOR ME GREENISH BLUE   COLOR ME GREEN

COLOR THE BOTTLE OF KETCHUP

COLOR THE SHADOWS

BLUE LIGHT SOURCE

BLUE
YELLOW
BLACK

YELLOW LIGHT SOURCE

63

64

179

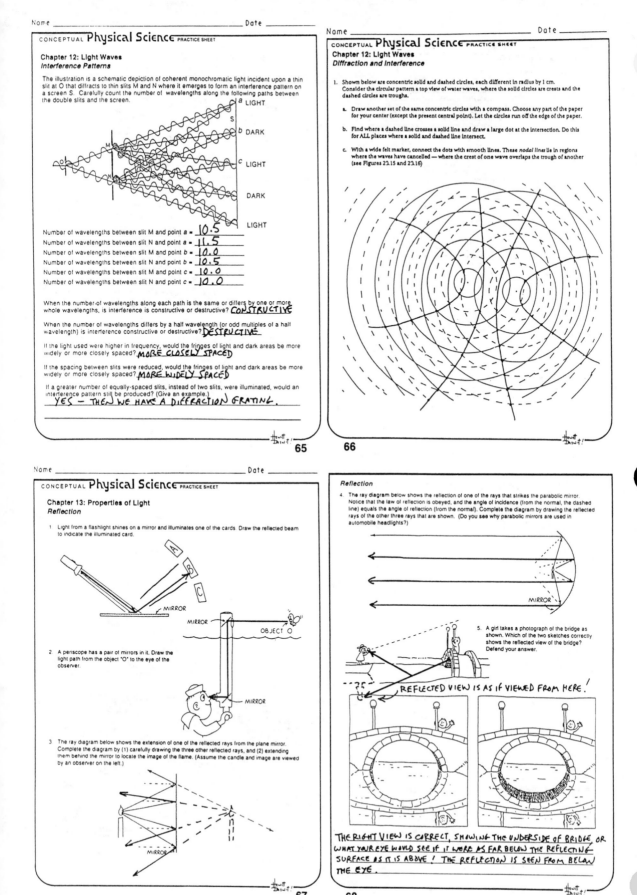

CONCEPTUAL **Physical Science** PRACTICE SHEET

Chapter 12: Light Waves
Interference Patterns

The illustration is a schematic depiction of coherent monochromatic light incident upon a thin slit at O that diffracts to thin slits M and N where it emerges to form an interference pattern on a screen S. Carefully count the number of wavelengths along the following paths between the double slits and the screen.

a LIGHT
b DARK
c LIGHT
DARK
LIGHT

Number of wavelengths between slit M and point a = **10.5**
Number of wavelengths between slit N and point a = **11.5**
Number of wavelengths between slit M and point b = **10.0**
Number of wavelengths between slit N and point b = **10.5**
Number of wavelengths between slit M and point c = **10.0**
Number of wavelengths between slit N and point c = **10.0**

When the number of wavelengths along each path is the same or differs by one or more whole wavelengths, is interference is constructive or destructive? **CONSTRUCTIVE**

When the number of wavelengths differs by a half wavelength (or odd multiples of a half wavelength) is interference constructive or destructive? **DESTRUCTIVE**

If the light used were higher in frequency, would the fringes of light and dark areas be more widely or more closely spaced? **MORE CLOSELY SPACED**

If the spacing between slits were reduced, would the fringes of light and dark areas be more widely or more closely spaced? **MORE WIDELY SPACED**

If a greater number of equally-spaced slits, instead of two slits, were illuminated, would an interference pattern still be produced? (Give an example.)
YES — THEN WE HAVE A DIFFRACTION GRATING.

65

CONCEPTUAL **Physical Science** PRACTICE SHEET

Chapter 12: Light Waves
Diffraction and Interference

1. Shown below are concentric solid and dashed circles, each different in radius by 1 cm. Consider the circular pattern a top view of water waves, where the solid circles are crests and the dashed circles are troughs.

   a. Draw another set of the same concentric circles with a compass. Choose any part of the paper for your center (except the present central point). Let the circles run off the edge of the paper.

   b. Find where a dashed line crosses a solid line and draw a large dot at the intersection. Do this for ALL places where a solid and dashed line intersect.

   c. With a wide felt marker, connect the dots with smooth lines. These *nodal lines* lie in regions where the waves have cancelled — where the crest of one wave overlaps the trough of another (see Figures 23.15 and 23.16)

66

CONCEPTUAL **Physical Science** PRACTICE SHEET

Chapter 13: Properties of Light
Reflection

1. Light from a flashlight shines on a mirror and illuminates one of the cards. Draw the reflected beam to indicate the illuminated card.

MIRROR

2. A periscope has a pair of mirrors in it. Draw the light path from the object "O" to the eye of the observer.

MIRROR
OBJECT O
MIRROR

3. The ray diagram below shows the extension of one of the reflected rays from the plane mirror. Complete the diagram by (1) carefully drawing the three other reflected rays, and (2) extending them behind the mirror to locate the image of the flame. (Assume the candle and image are viewed by an observer on the left.)

MIRROR

67

Reflection

4. The ray diagram below shows the reflection of one of the rays that strikes the parabolic mirror. Notice that the law of reflection is obeyed, and the angle of incidence (from the normal, the dashed line) equals the angle of reflection (from the normal). Complete the diagram by drawing the reflected rays of the other three rays that are shown. (Do you see why parabolic mirrors are used in automobile headlights?)

MIRROR

5. A girl takes a photograph of the bridge as shown. Which of the two sketches correctly shows the reflected view of the bridge? Defend your answer.

REFLECTED VIEW IS AS IF VIEWED FROM HERE!

THE RIGHT VIEW IS CORRECT, SHOWING THE UNDERSIDE OF BRIDGE, OR WHAT YOUR EYE WOULD SEE IF IT WERE AS FAR BELOW THE REFLECTING SURFACE AS IT IS ABOVE! THE REFLECTION IS SEEN FROM BELOW THE EYE.

68

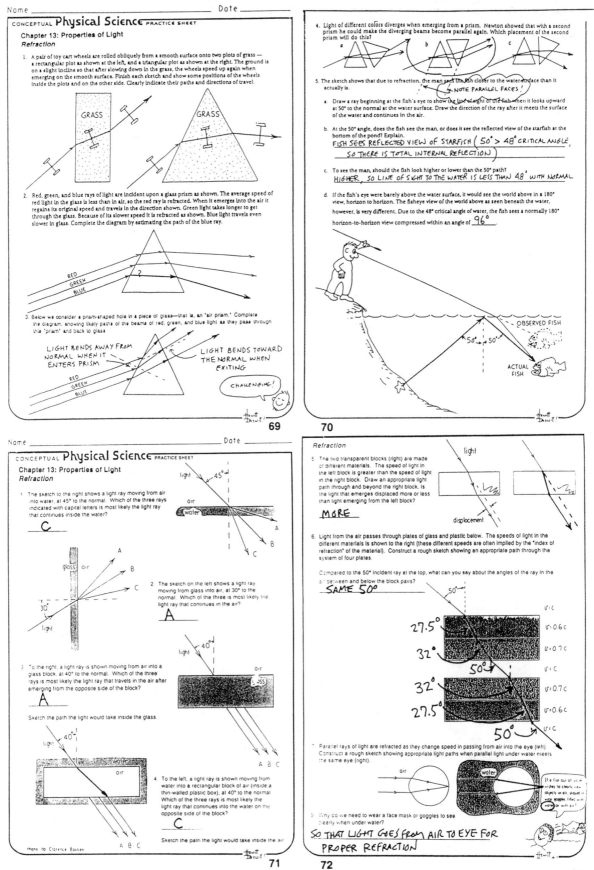

Chapter 13: Properties of Light
Refraction

1. A pair of toy cart wheels are rolled obliquely from a smooth surface onto two plots of grass — a rectangular plot as shown at the left, and a triangular plot as shown at the right. The ground is on a slight incline so that after slowing down in the grass, the wheels speed up again when emerging on the smooth surface. Finish each sketch and show some positions of the wheels inside the plots and on the other side. Clearly indicate their paths and directions of travel.

GRASS   GRASS

2. Red, green, and blue rays of light are incident upon a glass prism as shown. The average speed of red light in the glass is less than in air, so the red ray is refracted. When it emerges into the air it regains its original speed and travels in the direction shown. Green light takes longer to get through the glass. Because of its slower speed it is refracted as shown. Blue light travels even slower in glass. Complete the diagram by estimating the path of the blue ray.

RED
GREEN
BLUE
?

3. Below we consider a prism-shaped hole in a piece of glass—that is, an "air prism." Complete the diagram, showing likely paths of the beams of red, green, and blue light as they pass through this "prism" and back to glass

LIGHT BENDS AWAY FROM NORMAL WHEN IT ENTERS PRISM

LIGHT BENDS TOWARD THE NORMAL WHEN EXITING

CHALLENGING!

RED
GREEN
BLUE

69

4. Light of different colors diverges when emerging from a prism. Newton showed that with a second prism he could make the diverging beams become parallel again. Which placement of the second prism will do this?

a   b   c

5. The sketch shows that due to refraction, the man sees the fish closer to the water surface than it actually is.

← NOTE PARALLEL FACES!

a. Draw a ray beginning at the fish's eye to show the line of sight of the fish when it looks upward at 50° to the normal at the water surface. Draw the direction of the ray after it meets the surface of the water and continues in the air.

b. At the 50° angle, does the fish see the man, or does it see the reflected view of the starfish at the bottom of the pond? Explain.
FISH SEES REFLECTED VIEW OF STARFISH (50° > 48° CRITICAL ANGLE, SO THERE IS TOTAL INTERNAL REFLECTION)

c. To see the man, should the fish look higher or lower than the 50° path?
HIGHER, SO LINE OF SIGHT TO THE WATER IS LESS THAN 48° WITH NORMAL

d. If the fish's eye were barely above the water surface, it would see the world above in a 180° view, horizon to horizon. The fisheye view of the world above as seen beneath the water, however, is very different. Due to the 48° critical angle of water, the fish sees a normally 180° horizon-to-horizon view compressed within an angle of ___96°___.

OBSERVED FISH

50° | 50°

ACTUAL FISH

70

Chapter 13: Properties of Light
Refraction

1. The sketch to the right shows a light ray moving from air into water, at 45° to the normal. Which of the three rays indicated with capital letters is most likely the light ray that continues inside the water?
___C___

light   45°
air
water
A
B
C

A
B
glass air
C
30°
light

2. The sketch on the left shows a light ray moving from glass into air, at 30° to the normal. Which of the three is most likely the light ray that continues in the air?
___A___

3. To the right, a light ray is shown moving from air into a glass block, at 40° to the normal. Which of the three rays is most likely the light ray that travels in the air after emerging from the opposite side of the block?
___A___

Sketch the path the light would take inside the glass.

light 40°
air
glass
A B C

light 40°
water
air

4. To the left, a light ray is shown moving from water into a rectangular block of air (inside a thin-walled plastic box), at 40° to the normal. Which of the three rays is most likely the light ray that continues into the water on the opposite side of the block?
___C___

Sketch the path the light would take inside the air.

A B C

71

Refraction

5. The two transparent blocks (right) are made of different materials. The speed of light in the left block is greater than the speed of light in the right block. Draw an appropriate light path through and beyond the right block. Is the light that emerges displaced more or less than light emerging from the left block?

___MORE___

light

displacement

6. Light from the air passes through plates of glass and plastic below. The speeds of light in the different materials is shown to the right (these different speeds are often implied by the "index of refraction" of the material). Construct a rough sketch showing an appropriate path through the system of four plates.

Compared to the 50° incident ray at the top, what can you say about the angles of the ray in the air between and below the block pairs?
___SAME 50°___

50°
27.5°   v = c
32°   v = 0.6c
          v = 0.7c
50°
32°   v = c
27.5°   v = 0.7c
          v = 0.6c
50°   v = c

7. Parallel rays of light are refracted as they change speed in passing from air into the eye (left). Construct a rough sketch showing appropriate light paths when parallel light under water meets the same eye (right).

air   water

If a fish out of water wishes to clearly view objects in air, should it wear goggles filled with water or with air?

8. Why do we need to wear a face mask or goggles to see clearly when under water?
SO THAT LIGHT GOES FROM AIR TO EYE FOR PROPER REFRACTION

72

181

CONCEPTUAL **Physical Science** PRACTICE SHEET

Chapter 13: Properties of Light
Wave-Particle Duality

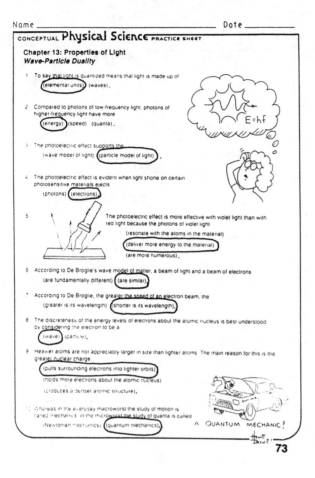

1. To say that light is quantized means that light is made up of
   (**elemental units**) (waves).

2. Compared to photons of low-frequency light, photons of higher-frequency light have more
   (**energy**) (speed) (quanta).

   $E = hf$

3. The photoelectric effect supports the
   (wave model of light) (**particle model of light**).

4. The photoelectric effect is evident when light shone on certain photosensitive materials ejects
   (photons) (**electrons**).

5. The photoelectric effect is more effective with violet light than with red light because the photons of violet light
   (resonate with the atoms in the material)
   (**deliver more energy to the material**)
   (are more numerous).

6. According to De Broglie's wave model of matter, a beam of light and a beam of electrons
   (are fundamentally different) (**are similar**).

7. According to De Broglie, the greater the speed of an electron beam, the
   (greater is its wavelength) (**shorter is its wavelength**).

8. The discreteness of the energy levels of electrons about the atomic nucleus is best understood by considering the electron to be a
   (**wave**) (particle).

9. Heavier atoms are not appreciably larger in size than lighter atoms. The main reason for this is the greater nuclear charge
   (**pulls surrounding electrons into tighter orbits**)
   (holds more electrons about the atomic nucleus)
   (produces a denser atomic structure).

10. Whereas in the everyday macroworld the study of motion is called mechanics, in the microworld the study of quanta is called
    (Newtonian mechanics) (**quantum mechanics**).

A QUANTUM MECHANIC!

73

CONCEPTUAL **Physical Science** PRACTICE SHEET

Chapter 14: Atoms and the Periodic Table
Subatomic Particles

Three fundamental particles of the atom are the **PROTON**, **NEUTRON** and **ELECTRON**. At the center of each atom lies the atomic **NUCLEUS**, which consists of **PROTONS** and **NEUTRONS**. The atomic number refers to the number of **PROTONS** in the nucleus. All atoms of the same element have the same number of **PROTONS**, hence, the same atomic number.

Isotopes are atoms that have the same number of **PROTONS** but a different number of **NEUTRONS**. An isotope is identified by its **atomic mass number**, which is the total number of **PROTONS** & **NEUTRONS** in the nucleus. A carbon isotope that has 6 **PROTONS** and 6 **NEUTRONS** is identified as carbon-12, where 12 is the atomic mass number. A carbon isotope having 6 **PROTONS** and 8 **NEUTRONS** on the other hand, is carbon-14.

1. Complete the following table:

Isotope	Number of...		
	Electrons	Protons	Neutrons
Hydrogen-1	1	1	0
Chlorine-36	17	17	19
Nitrogen-14	7	7	7
Potassium-40	19	19	21
Arsenic-75	33	33	42
Gold-197	79	79	118

2. Which results in a more valuable product — *adding* or *subtracting* protons from gold nuclei? **SUBTRACT FOR PLATINUM (MORE VALUABLE)**

3. Which has more mass, a helium atom or a neon atom? **NEON**

4. Which has a greater number of atoms, a gram of helium or a gram of neon? **HELIUM!**

75

CONCEPTUAL **Physical Science** PRACTICE SHEET

Chapter 14: Atoms and the Periodic Table
Melting Points of the Elements

There is a remarkable degree of organization in the periodic table. As discussed in your textbook, elements within the same atomic group (vertical column) share similar properties. Also, the chemical reactivity of an element can be deduced from its position in the periodic table. Two additional examples of the periodic table's organization are the melting points and densities of the elements.

The periodic table below shows the melting points of nearly all the elements. Note the melting points are not randomly oriented, but, with only a few exceptions, either gradually increase or decrease as you move in any particular direction. This can be clearly illustrated by color coding each element according to its melting point.

Use colored pencils to color in each element according to its melting point. Use the suggested color legend. Color lightly so that symbols and numbers are still visible.

Color	Temperature Range, °C	Color	Temperature Range, °C
Violet	-273 — -50	Yellow	1400 — 1900
Blue	-50 — 300	Orange	1900 — 2900
Cyan	300 — 700	Red	2900 — 3500
Green	700 — 1400		

Melting Points of the Elements (°C)

— TUNGSTEN

1. Which elements have the highest melting points?
THE ONES CLOSER TO TUNGSTEN

2. Which elements have the lowest melting points?
ELEMENTS TOWARD UPPER RIGHT

3. Which atomic groups tend to go from higher to lower melting points reading from top to bottom? (Identify each group by its group number).
1, 2, 3, 12, 13, 14

4. Which atomic groups tend to go from lower to higher melting points reading from top to bottom?
4 THROUGH 10 AND 15 THROUGH 18

77

Chapter 14: Atoms and the Periodic Table
Densities of the Elements

The periodic table below shows the densities of nearly all the elements. As with the melting points, the densities of the elements either gradually increase or decrease as you move in any particular direction. Use colored pencils to color in each element according to its density. Shown below is a suggested color legend. Color lightly so that symbols and numbers are still visible. (Note: All gaseous elements are marked with an asterisk and should be the same color. Their densities, which are given in units of g/L, are much less than the densities non-gaseous elements, which are given in units of g/mL.)

Color	Density (g/mL)	Color	Density (g/mL)
Violet	gaseous elements	Yellow	16 — 12
Blue	5 — 0	Orange	20 — 16
Cyan	8 — 5	Red.	23 — 20
Green	12 — 8		

Densities of the Elements (g/mL)

OSMIUM* density of gaseous phase is

1. Which elements are the most dense?
THE ONES CLOSER TO OSMIUM, Os

2. How variable are the densities of the lanthanides compared to the densities of the actinides?
THE ACTINIDES ARE MUCH MORE VARIABLE

3. Which atomic groups tend to go from higher to lower densities reading from top to bottom? (Identify each group by its group number).
NONE

4. Which atomic groups tend to go from lower to higher densities reading from top to bottom?
ALL

78

CONCEPTUAL **Physical Science** PRACTICE SHEET

Chapter 15: Visualizing the Atom
Losing Valence Electrons

The shell model described in Section 15.4 can be used to explain a wide variety of properties of atoms. Using the shell model, for example, we can explain how atoms within the same group tend to lose (or gain) the same number of electrons. Let's consider the case of three group 1 elements: lithium, sodium, and potassium. Look to a periodic table and find the nuclear charge of each of these atoms:

	Lithium, Li	Sodium, Na	Potassium, K
Nuclear charge:	+3	+11	+19
Number of inner shell electrons:	2 (that's a charge of -2)	10 (that's a charge of -10)	18 (that's a charge of -18)

How strongly the valence electron is held to the nucleus depends on the strength of the nuclear charge—the stronger the charge, the stronger the valence electron is held. There's more to it, however, because inner-shell electrons weaken the attraction outer-shell electrons have for the nucleus. The valence shell in lithium, for example, doesn't experience the full effect of three protons. Instead, it experiences a diminished nuclear charge of about +1. We get this by subtracting the number of inner-shell electrons from the actual nuclear charge. What do the valence electrons for sodium and potassium experience?

Diminished nuclear charge:	(+3 - 2 = +1) about +1	(+11 - 10 = +1) about +1	(+19 - 18 = +1) about +1

Question: Potassium has a nuclear charge many times greater than that of lithium. Why is it actually *easier* for a potassium atom to lose its valence electron than it is for a lithium atom to lose its valence electron?

Hint: Remember from Chapter 9 what happens to the electric force as distance is increased!

Potassium's valence electron is much farther from the nucleus. Because the electric force decreases with distance, the +1 charge for potassium's valence electron is not so effective at holding to the atom. Hence, it is easily lost.

79

183

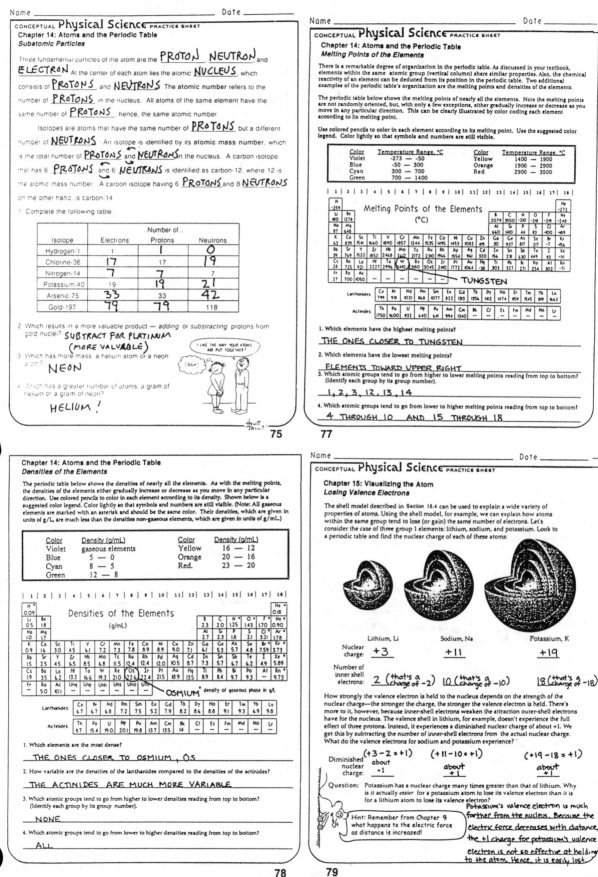

CONCEPTUAL **Physical Science** PRACTICE SHEET
Chapter 16: The Atomic Nucleus
Radioactivity

1. *Complete the following statements*

   a. A lone neutron spontaneously decays into a proton plus an
   ELECTRON

   b. Alpha and beta rays are made of streams of particles, whereas gamma rays are streams of **PHOTONS**

   c. An electrically charged atom is called an **ION**

   d. Different **ISOTOPES** of an element are chemically identical but differ in the number of neutrons in the nucleus.

   e. Transuranic elements are those beyond atomic number **92**

   f. If the amount of a certain radioactive sample decreases by half in four weeks, in four more weeks the amount remaining should be **¼** the original amount.

   g. Water from a natural hot spring is warmed by **RADIOACTIVITY** inside the earth.

2. The gas in the little girl's balloon is made up of former alpha and beta particles produced by radioactive decay.

   PHYSICS IS FUN!

   a. If the mixture is electrically neutral, how many more beta particles are in the balloon?
   TWICE AS MANY BETA PARTICLES AS ALPHA PARTICLES

   b. Why is your answer not "same"?
   ALPHA HAS DOUBLE CHARGE; THE CHARGE OF 2 BETAS = MAGNITUDE OF CHARGE OF 1 ALPHA

   c. Why are the alpha and beta particles no longer harmful to the child?
   THEY HAVE LOST THEIR HIGH KE, WHICH IS NOW REDUCED TO THERMAL ENERGY OF RANDOM MOLECULAR MOTION.

   d. What element does this mixture make?
   HELIUM

81

Radioactivity

Draw in a decay-scheme diagram below, similar to Figure 16.16 in your text. In this case you begin at the upper right with U-235 and end up with a different isotope of lead. Use the table at the left and identify each element in the series by its chemical symbol.

Step	Particle Emitted
1	Alpha
2	Beta
3	Alpha
4	Alpha
5	Beta
6	Alpha
7	Alpha
8	Alpha
9	Beta
10	Alpha
11	Beta
12	Stable

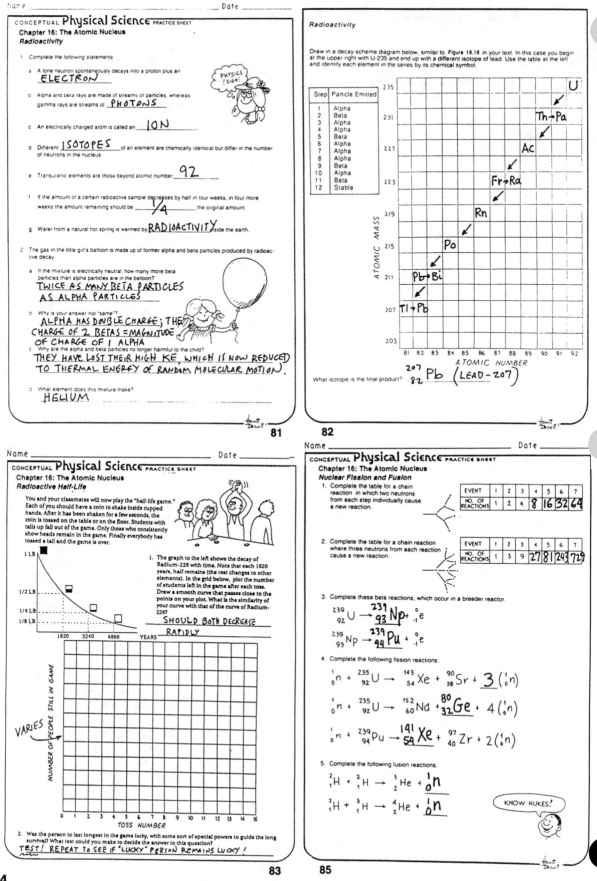

ATOMIC MASS (vertical axis): 235, 231, 227, 223, 219, 215, 211, 207, 203
ATOMIC NUMBER (horizontal axis): 81 82 83 84 85 86 87 88 89 90 91 92

Labels on diagram: U, Th→Pa, Ac, Fr→Ra, Rn, Po, Pb→Bi, Tl→Pb

What isotope is the final product? $^{207}_{82}Pb$ **(LEAD-207)**

82

CONCEPTUAL **Physical Science** PRACTICE SHEET
Chapter 16: The Atomic Nucleus
Radioactive Half-Life

You and your classmates will now play the "half-life game." Each of you should have a coin to shake inside cupped hands. After it has been shaken for a few seconds, the coin is tossed on the table or on the floor. Students with tails up fall out of the game. Only those who consistently show heads remain in the game. Finally everybody has tossed a tail and the game is over.

1. The graph to the left shows the decay of Radium-226 with time. Note that each 1620 years, half remains (the rest changes to other elements). In the grid below, plot the number of students left in the game after each toss. Draw a smooth curve that passes close to the points on your plot. What is the similarity of your curve with that of the curve of Radium-226?
SHOULD BOTH DECREASE RAPIDLY

(graph axes left: 1 LB, 1/2 LB, 1/4 LB, 1/8 LB vs YEARS 1620, 3240, 4860)

(lower graph: NUMBER OF PEOPLE STILL IN GAME vs TOSS NUMBER 0–15) **VARIES**

2. Was the person to last longest in the game *lucky*, with some sort of special powers to guide the long survival? What test could you make to decide the answer to this question?
TEST! REPEAT TO SEE IF "LUCKY" PERSON REMAINS LUCKY!

83

CONCEPTUAL **Physical Science** PRACTICE SHEET
Chapter 16: The Atomic Nucleus
Nuclear Fission and Fusion

1. Complete the table for a chain reaction in which two neutrons from each step individually cause a new reaction.

EVENT	1	2	3	4	5	6	7
NO. OF REACTIONS	1	2	4	**8**	**16**	**32**	**64**

2. Complete the table for a chain reaction where three neutrons from each reaction cause a new reaction.

EVENT	1	2	3	4	5	6	7
NO. OF REACTIONS	1	3	9	**27**	**81**	**243**	**729**

3. Complete these beta reactions, which occur in a breeder reactor.

$$^{239}_{92}U \rightarrow ^{239}_{93}Np + ^{0}_{-1}e$$

$$^{239}_{93}Np \rightarrow ^{239}_{94}Pu + ^{0}_{-1}e$$

4. Complete the following fission reactions.

$$^{1}_{0}n + ^{235}_{92}U \rightarrow ^{143}_{54}Xe + ^{90}_{38}Sr + 3(^{1}_{0}n)$$

$$^{1}_{0}n + ^{235}_{92}U \rightarrow ^{152}_{60}Nd + ^{80}_{32}Ge + 4(^{1}_{0}n)$$

$$^{1}_{0}n + ^{239}_{94}Pu \rightarrow ^{141}_{54}Xe + ^{97}_{40}Zr + 2(^{1}_{0}n)$$

5. Complete the following fusion reactions.

$$^{2}_{1}H + ^{2}_{1}H \rightarrow ^{3}_{2}He + ^{1}_{0}n$$

$$^{2}_{1}H + ^{3}_{1}H \rightarrow ^{4}_{2}He + ^{1}_{0}n$$

KNOW NUKES!

85

CONCEPTUAL **Physical Science** PRACTICE SHEET

Chapter 16: The Atomic Nucleus
Nuclear Reactions

Complete these nuclear reactions.

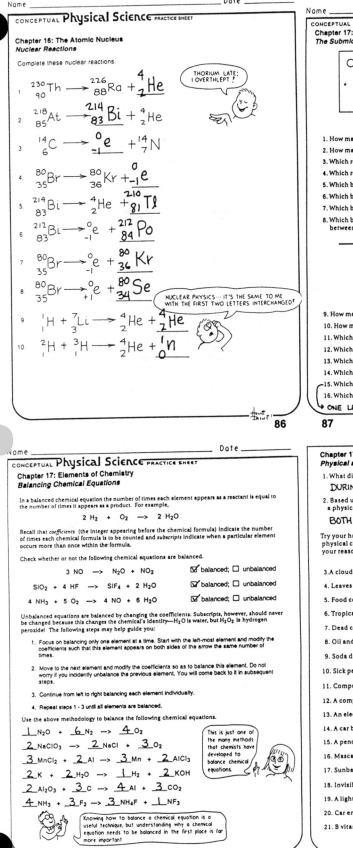

1. $^{230}_{90}Th \longrightarrow ^{226}_{88}Ra + ^{4}_{2}He$

THORIUM LATE; I OVERTHLEPT!

2. $^{218}_{85}At \longrightarrow ^{214}_{83}Bi + ^{4}_{2}He$

3. $^{14}_{6}C \longrightarrow ^{0}_{-1}e + ^{14}_{7}N$

4. $^{80}_{35}Br \longrightarrow ^{80}_{36}Kr + ^{0}_{-1}e$

5. $^{214}_{83}Bi \longrightarrow ^{4}_{2}He + ^{210}_{81}Tl$

6. $^{212}_{83}Bi \longrightarrow ^{0}_{-1}e + ^{212}_{84}Po$

7. $^{80}_{35}Br \longrightarrow ^{0}_{-1}e + ^{80}_{36}Kr$

8. $^{80}_{35}Br \longrightarrow ^{0}_{+1}e + ^{80}_{34}Se$

NUCLEAR PHYSICS ... IT'S THE SAME TO ME WITH THE FIRST TWO LETTERS INTERCHANGED!

9. $^{1}_{1}H + ^{7}_{3}Li \longrightarrow ^{4}_{2}He + ^{4}_{2}He$

10. $^{2}_{1}H + ^{3}_{1}H \longrightarrow ^{4}_{2}He + ^{1}_{0}n$

CONCEPTUAL **Physical Science** PRACTICE SHEET

Chapter 17: Elements of Chemistry
The Submicroscopic

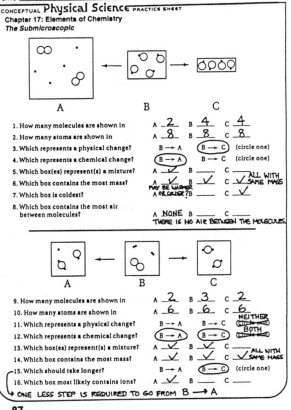

	A	B	C

1. How many molecules are shown in   A **2** B **4** C **4**
2. How many atoms are shown in   A **8** B **8** C **8**
3. Which represents a physical change?   B → A   **B → C**   (circle one)
4. Which represents a chemical change?   **B → A**   B → C   (circle one)
5. Which box(es) represent(s) a mixture?   A **✓** B ___ C ___
6. Which box contains the most mass?   A ___ B **✓** C **✓** _ALL WITH SAME MASS_
   MAY BE WARMER A OR COLDER? B
7. Which box is coldest?   A ___ B ___ C **✓**
8. Which box contains the most air between molecules?   A **NONE** B ___ C ___
   THERE IS NO AIR BETWEEN THE MOLECULES.

	A	B	C

9. How many molecules are shown in   A **2** B **3** C **2**
10. How many atoms are shown in   A **6** B **6** C **6**
11. Which represents a physical change?   B → A   B → C   *NEITHER* ~~(circle one)~~
12. Which represents a chemical change?   **B → A**   **B → C**   *BOTH* ~~(circle one)~~
13. Which box(es) represent(s) a mixture?   A **✓** B **✓** C ___
14. Which box contains the most mass?   A **✓** B **✓** C **✓** _ALL WITH SAME MASS_
15. Which should take longer?   B → A   **B → C**   (circle one)
16. Which box most likely contains ions?   A **✓** B ___ C ___

→ ONE LESS STEP IS REQUIRED TO GO FROM B → A

CONCEPTUAL **Physical Science** PRACTICE SHEET

Chapter 17: Elements of Chemistry
Balancing Chemical Equations

In a balanced chemical equation the number of times each element appears as a reactant is equal to the number of times it appears as a product. For example,

$$2 H_2 + O_2 \longrightarrow 2 H_2O$$

Recall that *coefficients* (the integer appearing before the chemical formula) indicate the number of times each chemical formula is to be counted and *subscripts* indicate when a particular element occurs more than once within the formula.

Check whether or not the following chemical equations are balanced.

$3 NO \longrightarrow N_2O + NO_2$ ☑ balanced; ☐ unbalanced

$SiO_2 + 4 HF \longrightarrow SiF_4 + 2 H_2O$ ☑ balanced; ☐ unbalanced

$4 NH_3 + 5 O_2 \longrightarrow 4 NO + 6 H_2O$ ☑ balanced; ☐ unbalanced

Unbalanced equations are balanced by changing the coefficients. Subscripts, however, should never be changed because this changes the chemical's identity—H_2O is water, but H_2O_2 is hydrogen peroxide! The following steps may help guide you:

1. Focus on balancing only one element at a time. Start with the left-most element and modify the coefficients such that this element appears on both sides of the arrow the same number of times.

2. Move to the next element and modify the coefficients so as to balance this element. Do not worry if you incidently unbalance the previous element. You will come back to it in subsequent steps.

3. Continue from left to right balancing each element individually.

4. Repeat steps 1 - 3 until all elements are balanced.

Use the above methodology to balance the following chemical equations.

$\underline{1} N_2O + \underline{6} N_2 \longrightarrow \underline{4} O_2$

$\underline{2} NaClO_3 \longrightarrow \underline{2} NaCl + \underline{3} O_2$

$\underline{3} MnCl_2 + \underline{2} Al \longrightarrow \underline{3} Mn + \underline{2} AlCl_3$

$\underline{2} K + \underline{2} H_2O \longrightarrow \underline{1} H_2 + \underline{2} KOH$

$\underline{2} Al_2O_3 + \underline{3} C \longrightarrow \underline{4} Al + \underline{3} CO_2$

$\underline{4} NH_3 + \underline{3} F_2 \longrightarrow \underline{3} NH_4F + \underline{1} NF_3$

This is just one of the many methods that chemists have developed to balance chemical equations.

Knowing how to balance a chemical equation is a useful technique, but understanding why a chemical equation needs to be balanced in the first place is far more important.

Chapter 17: Elements of Chemistry
Physical and Chemical Changes

Chemistry sigh!

1. What distinguishes a chemical change from a physical change?

   DURING A CHEMICAL CHANGE ATOM CHANGE PARTNERS

2. Based upon observations alone, why is distinguishing a chemical change from a physical change not always so straight-forward?

   BOTH INVOLVE A CHANGE IN PHYSICAL APPEARANCE

Try your hand at categorizing the following processes as either chemical or physical changes. Some of these examples are debatable! Be sure to discuss your reasoning with fellow classmates or your instructor.

(circle one)

3. A cloud grows dark - - - - - - - - - - - chemical **(physical)**
4. Leaves produce oxygen. - - - - - - - - **(chemical)** physical
5. Food coloring is added to water. - - - - - chemical **(physical)**
6. Tropical coral reef dies. - - - - - - - - **(chemical)** physical
7. Dead coral reef is pounded by waves into beach sand. - - - - chemical **(physical)**
8. Oil and vinegar separate. - - - - - - - - chemical **(physical)**
9. Soda drink goes flat. - - - - - - - - - - chemical **(physical)**
10. Sick person develops a fever. - - - - - - **(chemical)** physical
11. Compost pit turns into mulch - - - - - - **(chemical)** physical
12. A computer is turned on. *AT THE ELECTRIC POWER PLANT* **(chemical)** **(physical)**
13. An electrical short melts a computer's integrated circuits. - chemical **(physical)**
14. A car battery runs down. - - - - - - - - **(chemical)** physical
15. A pencil is sharpened. - - - - - - - - - chemical **(physical)**
16. Mascara is applied to eyelashes. - - - - - chemical **(physical)**
17. Sunbather gets tan lying in the sun. - - - - **(chemical)** physical
18. Invisible ink turns visible upon heating - - **(chemical)** physical
19. A light bulb burns out. - - - - - - - - - **(chemical)** physical
20. Car engine consumes a tank of gasoline. - - **(chemical)** physical
21. B vitamins turn urine yellow. *ASSUMING "XS" VITAMIN* chemical **(physical)**
    PASSES THROUGH BODY UNCHANGED

CONCEPTUAL **Physical Science** PRACTICE SHEET

Chapter 18: Mixtures
Solutions

1. Use these terms to complete the following sentences. Some terms may be used more than once.

solution	solvent	solute
dissolve	concentrated	dilute
saturated	concentration	mole
molarity	solubility	soluble
insoluble	precipitate	supersaturated

Sugar is __SOLUBLE__ in water for the two can be mixed homogeneously to form a __SOLUTION__.

The __SOLUBILITY__ of sugar in water is so great that __CONCENTRATED__ homogeneous mixtures are easily

prepared. Sugar, however, is not infinitely __SOLUBLE__ in water for when too much of this

__SOLUTE__ is added to water, which behaves as the __SOLVENT__, the solution becomes

__SATURATED__. At this point any additional sugar is __INSOLUBLE__ for it will not __DISSOLVE__. If

the temperature of a saturated sugar solution is lowered, the __SOLUBILITY__ of the sugar in water is also

lowered. If some of the sugar comes out of solution, it is said to form a __PRECIPITATE__. If, however, the

sugar remains in solution despite the decrease in solubility, then the solution is said to be

__SUPER-SATURATED__. Adding only a small amount of sugar to water results in a __DILUTE__ solution.

The __CONCENTRATION__ of this solution or any solution can be measure in terms of __MOLARITY__, which

tells us the number of solute molecules per liter of solution. If there are 6.022×10^{23} molecules in 1 liter

of solution, then the __CONCENTRATION__ of the solution is 1 __MOLE__ per liter.

2. Temperature has a variety of effects on the solubilities of various solutes. With some solutes, such as sugar, solubility increases with increasing temperature. With other solutes, such as sodium chloride (table salt), changing temperature has no significant effect. With some solutes, such as lithium sulfate, Li_2SO_4, the solubility actually decreases with increasing temperature.

a. Describe how you would prepare a supersaturated solution of lithium sulfate.

__FORM A SATURATED SOLUTION AND THEN SLOWLY RAISE THE TEMPERATURE.__

b. How might you cause a saturated solution of lithium sulfate to form a precipitate?

__INCREASE ITS TEMPERATURE__

CONCEPTUAL **Physical Science** PRACTICE SHEET

Chapter 18: Mixtures
Pure Mathematics

Using a scientist's definition of pure, identify whether each of the following is 100% pure:

	100% pure?	
Freshly squeezed orange juice	Yes	(No)
Country air	Yes	(No)
Ocean water	Yes	(No)
Fresh drinking water	Yes	(No)
Skim milk	Yes	(No)
Stainless steel	Yes	(No)
A single water molecule	(Yes)	No

A glass of water contains on the order of a trillion trillion (1×10^{24}) molecules. If the water in this were 99.9999% pure, you could calculate the percent of impurities by subtracting from 100.0000%

$$\begin{array}{r} 100.0000\% \text{ water + impurity molecules} \\ - \ 99.9999\% \text{ water molecules} \\ \hline 0.0001\% \text{ impurity molecules} \end{array}$$

Pull out your calculator and calculate the number of impurity molecules in the glass of water. Do this by finding 0.0001% of 1×10^{24}, which is the same as muliplying 1×10^{24} by 0.000001.

$$(1 \times 10^{24})(0.000001) = \underline{\quad 1 \times 10^{18} \quad}$$

How many impurity molecules are there in a glass of water that's 99.9999% pure?

a) 1,000 (one thousand: 10^3) b) 1,000,000 (one million: 10^6)
c) 1,000,000,000 (one billion: 10^9) ⓓ 1,000,000,000,000,000,000 (one million trillion: 10^{18}).

How does your answer make you feel about drinking water that is 99.9999 percent free of some poison, such as a pesticide?
__That there are a million trillion poison molecules in a glass of water might make one hesitate ... but read on!__

For every one impurity molecule, how many water molecules are there? (Divide the number of water molecules by the number of impurity molecules.)
$$10^{24}/10^{18} = 10^6 = 1,000,000 = \text{one million}$$

Would you describe these impurity molecules within water that's 99.9999% pure as "rare" or "common"? __For every one impurity molecule there are one million water molecules. One in a million is rare!__

A friend argues that he or she doesn't drink tap water because it contains thousands of molecules of some impurity in each glass. How would you respond in defense of the water's purity, if it indeed does contain thousands of molecules of some impurity per glass?

__Only a 1,000 impurity molecules in this glass of water would make this water incredibly pure... about 99.9999999999999999 % pure!__

CONCEPTUAL **Physical Science** PRACTICE SHEET

Chapter 19: How Atoms Bond
Chemical Bonds

1. Based upon their positions in the periodic table, predict whether each pair of elements will form an ionic, covalent, or neither (atomic number in parenthesis)

a. Gold (79) and Platinum (78) __N__   b. Rubidium (37) and Iodine (53) __I__

c. Sulfur (16) and Chlorine (17) __C__   d. Sulfur (16) and Magnesium (12) __I__

e. Calcium (20) and Chlorine (17) __I__   f. Germanium(32) and Arsenic (33) __C__

g. Iron (26) and Chromium (24) __N__   h. Chlorine (17) and Iodine (53) __C__

i. Carbon (6) and Bromine (35) __C__   j. Barium (56) and Astatine (85) __I__

2. The most common ions of lithium, magnesium, aluminum, chlorine, oxygen, and nitrogen and their respective charges are as follows:

Positively Charged Ions	Negatively Charged Ions
Lithium ion: Li^{1+}	Chloride ion: Cl^{1-}
Barium ion: Ba^{2+}	Oxide ion: O^{2-}
Aluminum ion: Al^{3+}	Nitride ion: N^{3-}

Use this information to predict the chemical formulas for the following ionic compounds:

a. Lithium Chloride: __LiCl__   b. Barium Chloride: __$BaCl_2$__   c. Aluminum Chloride: __$AlCl_2$__

d. Lithium Oxide: __Li_2O__   e. Barium Oxide: __BaO__   f. Aluminum Oxide: __Al_2O_3__

g. Lithium Nitride: __Li_3O__   h. Barium Nitride: __Ba_3N_2__   i. Aluminum Nitride: __AlN__

j. How are elements that form positive ions grouped in the periodic table relative to elements that form negative ions? __POSITIVE ION ELEMENTS TOWARD THE LEFT AND NEGATIVE IONS TOWARD THE RIGHT.__

3. Predict whether the following chemical structures are polar or nonpolar:

__POLAR__   __POLAR__   __NONPOLAR__

__NONPOLAR__   __NONPOLAR__   __POLAR__

__NONPOLAR__   __NONPOLAR__   __POLAR__

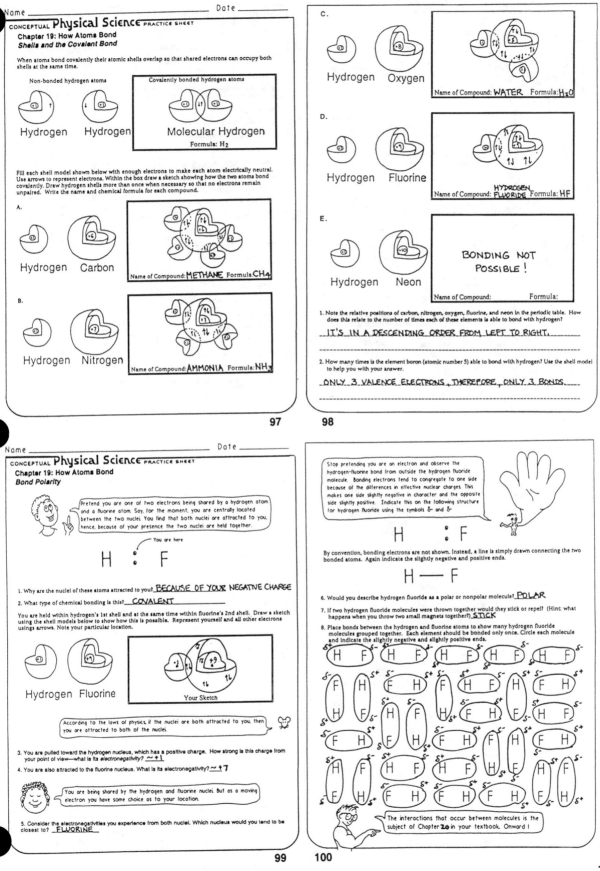

CONCEPTUAL **Physical Science** PRACTICE SHEET

Chapter 19: How Atoms Bond
Shells and the Covalent Bond

When atoms bond covalently their atomic shells overlap so that shared electrons can occupy both shells at the same time.

Non-bonded hydrogen atoms

Hydrogen   Hydrogen

Covalently bonded hydrogen atoms

Molecular Hydrogen
Formula: H_2

Fill each shell model shown below with enough electrons to make each atom electrically neutral. Use arrows to represent electrons. Within the box draw a sketch showing how the two atoms bond covalently. Draw hydrogen shells more than once when necessary so that no electrons remain unpaired. Write the name and chemical formula for each compound.

A.
Hydrogen   Carbon
Name of Compound: METHANE Formula: CH_4

B.
Hydrogen   Nitrogen
Name of Compound: AMMONIA Formula: NH_3

C.
Hydrogen   Oxygen
Name of Compound: WATER Formula: H_2O

D.
Hydrogen   Fluorine
Name of Compound: HYDROGEN FLUORIDE Formula: HF

E.
Hydrogen   Neon
BONDING NOT POSSIBLE !
Name of Compound: _____ Formula: _____

1. Note the relative positions of carbon, nitrogen, oxygen, fluorine, and neon in the periodic table. How does this relate to the number of times each of these elements is able to bond with hydrogen?

IT'S IN A DESCENDING ORDER FROM LEFT TO RIGHT.

2. How many times is the element boron (atomic number 5) able to bond with hydrogen? Use the shell model to help you with your answer.

ONLY 3 VALENCE ELECTRONS, THEREFORE, ONLY 3 BONDS.

97
98

CONCEPTUAL **Physical Science** PRACTICE SHEET

Chapter 19: How Atoms Bond
Bond Polarity

Pretend you are one of two electrons being shared by a hydrogen atom and a fluorine atom. Say, for the moment, you are centrally located between the two nuclei. You find that both nuclei are attracted to you, hence, because of your presence the two nuclei are held together.

You are here

H : F

1. Why are the nuclei of these atoms attracted to you? BECAUSE OF YOUR NEGATIVE CHARGE

2. What type of chemical bonding is this? COVALENT

You are held within hydrogen's 1st shell and at the same time within fluorine's 2nd shell. Draw a sketch using the shell models below to show how this is possible. Represent yourself and all other electrons using arrows. Note your particular location.

Hydrogen   Fluorine
Your Sketch

According to the laws of physics, if the nuclei are both attracted to you, then you are attracted to both of the nuclei.

3. You are pulled toward the hydrogen nucleus, which has a positive charge. How strong is this charge from your point of view—what is its *electronegativity*? ~ +1

4. You are also attracted to the fluorine nucleus. What is its electronegativity? ~ +7

You are being shared by the hydrogen and fluorine nuclei. But as a moving electron you have some choice as to your location.

5. Consider the electronegativities you experience from both nuclei. Which nucleus would you tend to be closest to? FLUORINE

Stop pretending you are an electron and observe the hydrogen-fluorine bond from outside the hydrogen fluoride molecule. Bonding electrons tend to congregate to one side because of the differences in effective nuclear charges. This makes one side slightly negative in character and the opposite side slightly positive. Indicate this on the following structure for hydrogen fluoride using the symbols δ- and δ-

H : F

By convention, bonding electrons are not shown. Instead, a line is simply drawn connecting the two bonded atoms. Again indicate the slightly negative and positive ends.

H — F

6. Would you describe hydrogen fluoride as a polar or nonpolar molecule? POLAR

7. If two hydrogen fluoride molecules were thrown together would they stick or repel? (Hint: what happens when you throw two small magnets together?) STICK

8. Place bonds between the hydrogen and fluorine atoms to show many hydrogen fluoride molecules grouped together. Each element should be bonded only once. Circle each molecule and indicate the slightly negative and slightly positive ends.

The interactions that occur between molecules is the subject of Chapter 20 in your textbook. Onward !

99
100

187

CONCEPTUAL **Physical Science** PRACTICE SHEET

Chapter 20: Molecular Attractions
Atoms to Molecules

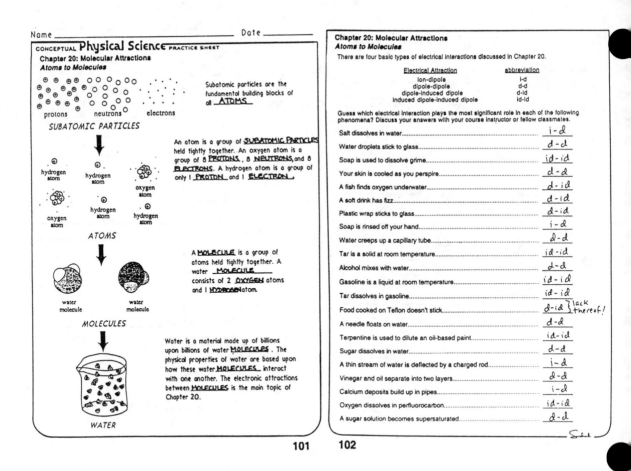

Subatomic particles are the fundamental building blocks of all __ATOMS__

protons   neutrons   electrons

SUBATOMIC PARTICLES

hydrogen atom   hydrogen atom   oxygen atom

oxygen atom   hydrogen atom   hydrogen atom

ATOMS

An atom is a group of **SUBATOMIC PARTICLES** held tightly together. An oxygen atom is a group of 8 **PROTONS**, 8 **NEUTRONS**, and 8 **ELECTRONS**. A hydrogen atom is a group of only 1 __PROTON__ and 1 __ELECTRON__.

water molecule   water molecule

MOLECULES

A **MOLECULE** is a group of atoms held tightly together. A water __MOLECULE__ consists of 2 **OXYGEN** atoms and 1 **HYDROGEN** atom.

WATER

Water is a material made up of billions upon billions of water **MOLECULES**. The physical properties of water are based upon how these water **MOLECULES** interact with one another. The electronic attractions between **MOLECULES** is the main topic of Chapter 20.

101

Chapter 20: Molecular Attractions
Atoms to Molecules

There are four basic types of electrical interactions discussed in Chapter 20.

Electrical Attraction	abbreviation
Ion-dipole	i-d
dipole-dipole	d-d
dipole-induced dipole	d-id
induced dipole-induced dipole	id-id

Guess which electrical interaction plays the most significant role in each of the following phenomena? Discuss your answers with your course instructor or fellow classmates.

Salt dissolves in water .... i-d

Water droplets stick to glass .... d-d

Soap is used to dissolve grime .... id-id

Your skin is cooled as you perspire .... d-d

A fish finds oxygen underwater .... d-id

A soft drink has fizz .... d-id

Plastic wrap sticks to glass .... d-id

Soap is rinsed off your hand .... i-d

Water creeps up a capillary tube .... d-d

Tar is a solid at room temperature .... id-id

Alcohol mixes with water .... d-d

Gasoline is a liquid at room temperature .... id-id

Tar dissolves in gasoline .... id-id

Food cooked on Teflon doesn't stick .... d-id {lack thereof!}

A needle floats on water .... d-d

Terpentine is used to dilute an oil-based paint .... id-id

Sugar dissolves in water .... d-d

A thin stream of water is deflected by a charged rod .... i-d

Vinegar and oil separate into two layers .... d-d

Calcium deposits build up in pipes .... i-d

Oxygen dissolves in perfluorocarbon .... id-id

A sugar solution becomes supersaturated .... d-d

102

CONCEPTUAL **Physical Science** PRACTICE SHEET

Chapter 21: Chemical Reactions
Relative Masses

In any chemical reaction, a specific number of atoms or molecules react to form a specific number of product atoms or molecules. Since we cannot count out atoms or molecules individually, we instead calculate the number of them in a given bulk using their relative masses.

Assume a baseball is 8 times more massive than a tennis ball.

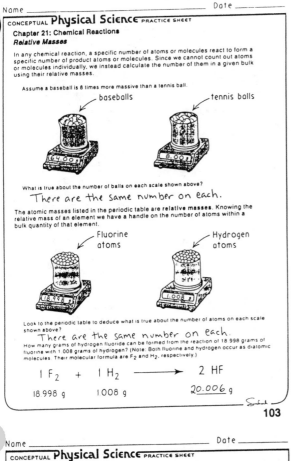

baseballs   tennis balls

What is true about the number of balls on each scale shown above?

There are the same number on each.

The atomic masses listed in the periodic table are relative masses. Knowing the relative mass of an element we have a handle on the number of atoms within a bulk quantity of that element.

Fluorine atoms   Hydrogen atoms

Look to the periodic table to deduce what is true about the number of atoms on each scale shown above?

There are the same number on each.

How many grams of hydrogen fluoride can be formed from the reaction of 18.998 grams of fluorine with 1.008 grams of hydrogen? (Note: Both fluorine and hydrogen occur as diatomic molecules. Their molecular formula are F_2 and H_2, respectively.)

$$1\,F_2 \; + \; 1\,H_2 \longrightarrow 2\,HF$$
18.998 g   1.008 g   **20.006** g

Just as we count shoes by pairs and eggs by dozens, we count atoms and molecules by moles. One mole equals 6.02×10^{23} (also known as Avogadro's number). Why is Avogadro's number so large when atoms and molecules are so small?

Atoms and molecules are so small that this many fit within a macroscopic sample.

For reasons discussed in your textbook, the atomic mass of an element when expressed in grams is equal to one mole. For example, there is one mole of carbon atoms in 12.011 grams of carbon (C, atomic mass = 12.011). Likewise, the formula mass of a compound when expressed in grams is equal to one mole. For example, there is one mole of water molecules in 18.00 grams of water (H_2O, formula mass = 18.00).

Assume the containers shown below hold fluorine in its diatomic molecular state. In moles, write down the number of atoms and molecules contained in each.

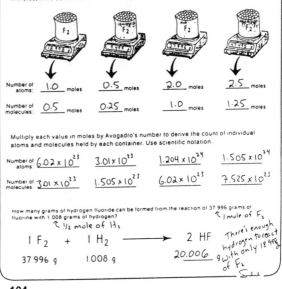

| Number of atoms: | 1.0 moles | 0.5 moles | 2.0 moles | 2.5 moles |
| Number of molecules: | 0.5 moles | 0.25 moles | 1.0 moles | 1.25 moles |

Multiply each value in moles by Avogadro's number to derive the count of individual atoms and molecules held by each container. Use scientific notation.

| Number of atoms: | 6.02×10^{23} | 3.01×10^{23} | 1.204×10^{24} | 1.505×10^{24} |
| Number of molecules: | 3.01×10^{23} | 1.505×10^{23} | 6.02×10^{23} | 7.525×10^{23} |

How many grams of hydrogen fluoride can be formed from the reaction of 37.996 grams of fluorine with 1.008 grams of hydrogen?

$\curvearrowright$ ½ mole of H_2 $\curvearrowright$ 1 mole of F_2

$$1\,F_2 \; + \; 1\,H_2 \longrightarrow 2\,HF$$
37.996 g   1.008 g   **20.006** g

There's enough hydrogen to react with only 18.998 g of F_2

CONCEPTUAL **Physical Science** PRACTICE SHEET

Chapter 21: Chemical Reactions
Relative Masses

On each line "a" indicate the mass of hydrogen fluoride, HF, that can form from the given masses of fluorine, F_2, and hydrogen, H_2. Below each mass on line "b" indicate the corresponding number of moles.

$$1\,F_2 \; + \; 1\,H_2 \longrightarrow 2\,HF$$

1.
a) 9.499 g + 0.504 g → **10.003** g
b) **0.25** mole F_2 **0.25** mole H_2 **0.50** mole HF

2.
a) 18.998 g + 1.008 g → **20.006** g
b) **0.50** mole F_2 **0.50** mole H_2 **1.00** mole

3.
a) 37.996 g + 2.016 g → **40.012** g
b) **1.0** mole F_2 **1.0** mole H_2 **2.0** mole

4.
a) 47.495 g + 2.520 g → **50.015** g
b) **1.25** mole   **1.25** mole   **2.5** mole

What do lines 1b, 2b, 3b, and 4b have in common with the coefficients of the chemical equation shown above? **They are all the same as a 1:1:2 ratio.**

How many grams of hydrogen fluoride can be formed from the reaction of 37.996 grams of fluorine, F_2, with 2.520 grams of hydrogen, H_2?

$$1\,F_2 \; + \; 1\,H_2 \longrightarrow 2\,HF$$
37.996 g   2.520 g   **40.012** g   + 0.504 g H_2 left-over

In the preceding reaction, which is too much: 37.996 grams of fluorine, F_2, or 2.520 grams of hydrogen, H_2? Explain. **37.996 g of F_2 (1 mole) will react with only 2.016 g of H_2 (1 mole). 2.520 g of H_2 is 0.504 grams too much! This 0.504 g H_2 remains left-over unreacted.**

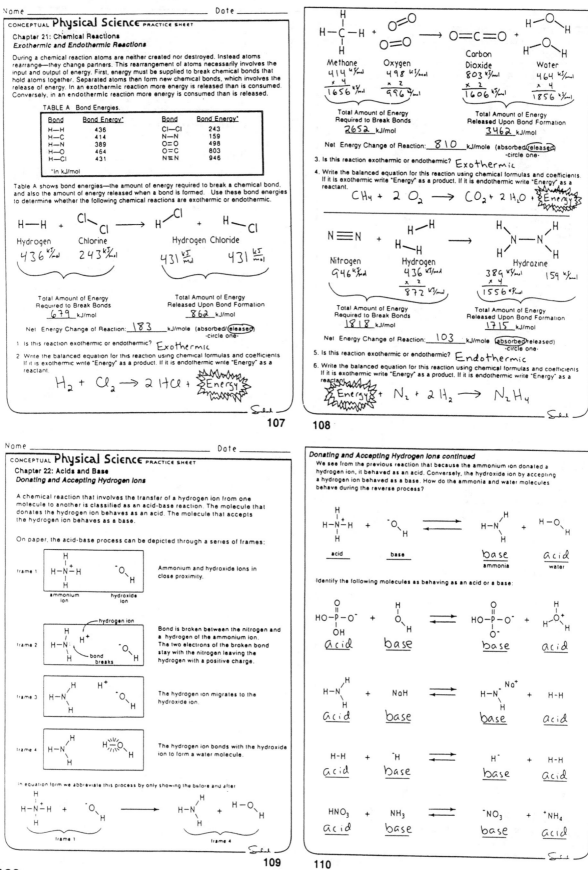

CONCEPTUAL **Physical Science** PRACTICE SHEET

Chapter 21: Chemical Reactions
Exothermic and Endothermic Reactions

During a chemical reaction atoms are neither created nor destroyed. Instead atoms rearrange—they change partners. This rearrangement of atoms necessarily involves the input and output of energy. First, energy must be supplied to break chemical bonds that hold atoms together. Separated atoms then form new chemical bonds, which involves the release of energy. In an exothermic reaction more energy is released than is consumed. Conversely, in an endothermic reaction more energy is consumed than is released.

TABLE A Bond Energies.

Bond	Bond Energy*	Bond	Bond Energy*
H—H	436	Cl—Cl	243
H—C	414	N—N	159
H—N	389	O=O	498
H—O	464	O=C	803
H—Cl	431	N≡N	946

*In kJ/mol

Table A shows bond energies—the amount of energy required to break a chemical bond, and also the amount of energy released when a bond is formed. Use these bond energies to determine whether the following chemical reactions are exothermic or endothermic.

Hydrogen Chlorine   Hydrogen Chloride
436 kJ/mol 243 kJ/mol   431 kJ/mol   431 kJ/mol

Total Amount of Energy
Required to Break Bonds
679 kJ/mol

Total Amount of Energy
Released Upon Bond Formation
862 kJ/mol

Net Energy Change of Reaction: 183 kJ/mole (absorbed / released)
-circle one-

1 Is this reaction exothermic or endothermic? Exothermic

2 Write the balanced equation for this reaction using chemical formulas and coefficients. If it is exothermic write "Energy" as a product. If it is endothermic write "Energy" as a reactant.

$H_2 + Cl_2 \rightarrow 2 HCl + Energy$

107

Methane Oxygen   Carbon Dioxide Water
414 kJ/mol 498 kJ/mol   803 kJ/mol   464 kJ/mol
× 4   × 2   × 2   × 4
1656 kJ/mol 996 kJ/mol   1606 kJ/mol 1856 kJ/mol

Total Amount of Energy
Required to Break Bonds
2652 kJ/mol

Total Amount of Energy
Released Upon Bond Formation
3462 kJ/mol

Net Energy Change of Reaction: 810 kJ/mole (absorbed / released)
-circle one-

3. Is this reaction exothermic or endothermic? Exothermic

4. Write the balanced equation for this reaction using chemical formulas and coefficients. If it is exothermic write "Energy" as a product. If it is endothermic write "Energy" as a reactant.

$CH_4 + 2 O_2 \rightarrow CO_2 + 2 H_2O + Energy$

Nitrogen Hydrogen   Hydrazine
946 kJ/mol 436 kJ/mol   389 kJ/mol   159 kJ/mol
          × 2   × 4
          872 kJ/mol   1556 kJ/mol

Total Amount of Energy
Required to Break Bonds
1818 kJ/mol

Total Amount of Energy
Released Upon Bond Formation
1715 kJ/mol

Net Energy Change of Reaction: 103 kJ/mole (absorbed / released)
-circle one-

5. Is this reaction exothermic or endothermic? Endothermic

6. Write the balanced equation for this reaction using chemical formulas and coefficients. If it is exothermic write "Energy" as a product. If it is endothermic write "Energy" as a reactant.

$Energy + N_2 + 2 H_2 \rightarrow N_2H_4$

108

CONCEPTUAL **Physical Science** PRACTICE SHEET

Chapter 22: Acids and Base
Donating and Accepting Hydrogen Ions

A chemical reaction that involves the transfer of a hydrogen ion from one molecule to another is classified as an acid-base reaction. The molecule that donates the hydrogen ion behaves as an acid. The molecule that accepts the hydrogen ion behaves as a base.

On paper, the acid-base process can be depicted through a series of frames:

frame 1   ammonium ion   hydroxide ion   Ammonium and hydroxide ions in close proximity.

frame 2   hydrogen ion   bond breaks   Bond is broken between the nitrogen and a hydrogen of the ammonium ion. The two electrons of the broken bond stay with the nitrogen leaving the hydrogen with a positive charge.

frame 3   The hydrogen ion migrates to the hydroxide ion.

frame 4   The hydrogen ion bonds with the hydroxide ion to form a water molecule.

In equation form we abbreviate this process by only showing the before and after.

frame 1   frame 4

109

Donating and Accepting Hydrogen Ions continued

We see from the previous reaction that because the ammonium ion donated a hydrogen ion, it behaved as an acid. Conversely, the hydroxide ion by accepting a hydrogen ion behaved as a base. How do the ammonia and water molecules behave during the reverse process?

acid   base   base   acid
                              ammonia   water

Identify the following molecules as behaving as an acid or a base:

Acid   base   base   acid

Acid   base   base   acid

acid   base   base   acid

HNO_3 NH_3 $^-NO_3$ $^+NH_4$
acid   base   base   acid

110

190

CONCEPTUAL Physical Science PRACTICE SHEET

Chapter 23: Oxidation and Reduction
Loss and Gain of Electrons

A chemical reaction that involves the transfer of an electron is classified as an oxidation-reduction reaction. Oxidation is the process of losing an electrons, while reduction is the process of gaining them. Any chemical that causes another chemical to lose electrons (become oxidized) is called an oxidizing agent. Conversely, any chemical that causes another chemical to gain electrons is called a reducing agent.

1. What is the relationship between an atom's ability to behave as an oxidizing agent and its electron affinity? **The greater the electron affinity, the greater its ability to behave as an oxidizing agent.**

2. Relative to the periodic table, which elements tend to behave as strong oxidizing agents? **Those to the upper left with the exception of the noble gases.**

3. Why don't the noble gases behave as oxidizing agents? **They have no space in their shells to accomodate additional electrons.**

4. How is it that an oxidizing agent is itself reduced? **Reduction is the gaining of electrons. In pulling an electron away from another atom an oxidizing agent necessarily gains an electron.**

5. Is it possible to have an endothermic oxidation-reduction reaction? If so, cite examples. **Yes... the electrolysis of water is an endothermic oxidation-reduction reaction.**

6. Specify whether each reactant is about to be oxidized or reduced.

$$2 K + H_2O \longrightarrow 2 K^+ + {}^-OH$$
ox   red

$$2 Mg + O_2 \longrightarrow 2 Mg^{2+}O^{2-}$$
ox   red

$$2 Na + Cl_2 \longrightarrow 2 Na^+Cl^-$$
ox   red

$$CH_4 + 2 O_2 \longrightarrow O=C=O + \overset{O-H}{\underset{H}{}}$$
ox   red

7. Which oxygen atom enjoys a greater negative charge?

this one   -or-   (that one)   (circle one)

$O=O$ $H-\overset{\delta -}{O}$ H $\delta +$

8. Relate your answer to question 7 to how it is that O_2 is reduced upon reacting with CH_4 to form carbon dioxide and water. **In transforming from O_2 to H_2O, an oxygen atom is gaining electrons as best as it can. With its greater negative charge it can be thought of as "reduced."** —Sd.

CONCEPTUAL Physical Science PRACTICE SHEET

Chapter 24: Organic Compounds
Structures of Organic Compounds

1. What are the chemical formulas for the following structures.

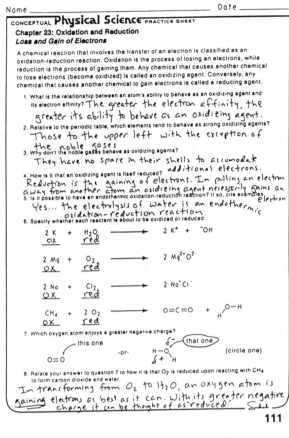

Formula: C_6H_{14} CH_6O C_8H_{18} $C_{10}H_{15}NO$

2. How many covalent bonds is carbon able to form? **4**

3. What is wrong with the structure shown in the box: **The carbon of the carbonyl is bonded 5 times**

4a. Draw a hydrocarbon that contains 4 carbon atoms.

4b. Redraw your structure and transform it into an amine.

4c. Transform your amine into an amide. You may need to relocate the nitrogen.

4d. Redraw your amide transforming it into a carboxylic acid.

4e. Redraw your carboxylic acid transforming it into an alcohol.

4f. Rearrange the carbons of your alcohol to make an ether.

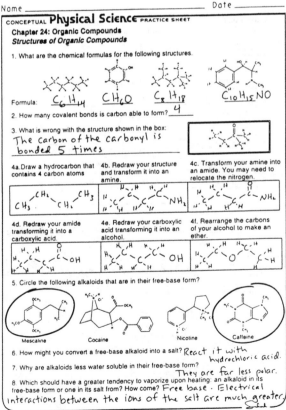

5. Circle the following alkaloids that are in their free-base form?

Mescaline   Cocaine   Nicotine   Caffeine

6. How might you convert a free-base alkaloid into a salt? **React it with hydrochloric acid.**

7. Why are alkaloids less water soluble in their free-base form? **They are far less polar.**

8. Which should have a greater tendency to vaporize upon heating: an alkaloid in its free-base form or one in its salt from? How come? **Free base. Electrical interactions between the ions of the salt are much greater.** —Sd.

CONCEPTUAL Physical Science PRACTICE SHEET

Chapter 24: Organic Compounds
Polymers

1. Circle the monomers that may be useful for forming an addition polymer and draw a box around the ones that may be useful for forming a condensation polymer.

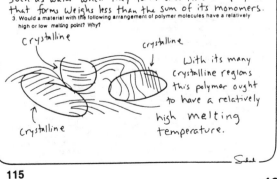

2. Which type of polymer always weighs less than the sum of its parts? Why? **The condensation polymers lose small molecules such as water when they form and thus the polymer that forms weighs less than the sum of its monomers.**

3. Would a material with the following arrangement of polymer molecules have a relatively high or low melting point? Why?

crystalline   crystalline   crystalline

With its many crystalline regions this polymer ought to have a relatively high melting temperature. —Sd.

CONCEPTUAL Physical Science PRACTICE SHEET

Chapter 25: Minerals and How We Use Them
Chemical Structure and Formulas of Minerals

Out of the more than 3400 types of minerals, only about two dozen are abundant and composed predominantly of eight elements. These eight elements combine to form six common mineral groups: *silicates, oxides, carbonates, sulfides, sulfates,* and *halides*.

For each mineral structure diagrammed below, look for a pattern in the structure, count the number of atoms (ions) in each, and fill in the blanks.

> The schematic diagrams are simple representations of small mineral structures. Actual mineral structures extend farther and comprise more atoms.

1. Circle pairs of Na and Cl ions in the structure and add any ion(s) needed to complete pairing. This mineral structure contains __14__ Na ions and __14__ Cl ions.
   The mineral's formula is __NaCl__
   This mineral belongs to the __Halide__ group.

   ⊖ Cl
   ⊙ Na

2. This mineral structure contains __8__ Ca atoms, __8__ C atoms, and __24__ O atoms.
   The mineral's formula is __CaCO₃__
   This mineral belongs to the __Carbonate__ group

   ○ Ca
   • C
   ○ ○ O

3. This mineral structure contains __6__ Ca atoms, __6__ S atoms, and __24__ O atoms.
   The mineral's formula is __CaSO₄__
   This mineral belongs to the __Sulfate__ group.

   ○ Ca
   ⊘ S
   ○ ○ O

4. This mineral structure contains __14__ Fe atoms and __26__ S atoms. Complete the structure by adding the needed atom(s).
   The mineral's formula is __FeS₂__
   This mineral belongs to the __Sulfite__ group.

   ⊛ Fe
   ⊘ S

5. Complete the mineral structure so that each Ca atom is linked to two F atoms (you will need to draw in extra atoms). Now the mineral structure contains __14__ Ca atoms and __28__ F atoms.
   The mineral's formula is __CaF₂__
   This mineral belongs to the __Halide__ group

   ○ Ca
   ⊘ F

117

118

CONCEPTUAL Physical Science PRACTICE SHEET

Chapter 26: Rocks
The Rock Cycle

Complete the illustration which depicts the different paths in the rock cycle. Insert arrows to show paths of direction.

Magma
crystallization
melting
Metamorphic Rock
heat and pressure
Igneous Rock
weathering, erosion, transportation, deposition
weathering, erosion, transportation, deposition
Sedimentary Rock
weathering, erosion, transportation, deposition
Sediment
Lithification

1. Can a rock that has undergone metamorphism turn into a sedimentary rock? If so, how? If not, how come?
Yes, metamorphic rock subjected to weathering breaks down into sediment. As the weathered material undergoes lithification it becomes sedimentary rock.

2. By what process does hot molten magma become rock?
Hot molten magma becomes igneous rock after it has cooled and solidified (the process of crystallization).

3. List three rocks generated from the different types of magma.
Basalt, Andesite, and Granite (others too!)

4. Carbonate rocks found in the Colorado Rocky Mountains imply what type of deposition environment?
A shallow sea environment, the remains of ancient sea floors.

5. In what section of the rock cycle are gemstones formed? Support your answer.
All sections. Gems form from the slow cooling of magma- peridot and topaz form in igneous environments. Pressure and heat result in the recrystallization of minerals - metamorphism. Garnet is a metamorphic gem. Only a few gems, such as turquoise and opal, are actually formed in a sedimentary environment.

6. The big island of Hawaii is 1 million years old. Yet rocks on the island never older than 1 thousand years old. Why?
The island of Hawaii is still in the process of formation. The Island is a large shield volcano formed from the accumulation of successive lava flows. With each new flow, rocks from previous flows are covered. So the rock we walk on is never more than a thousand years old.

119

Chapter 26: Rocks
Igneous Rock Differentiation: How to Make Granite

A mineral is called a *high temperature* mineral if its melting/freezing temperature is relatively high. A mineral is called a *low temperature* mineral if its melting/freezing temperature is relatively low.

Suppose we start with solid, basaltic rock. If it is heated, it will partially melt.

1) Is the type of mineral left behind (that doesn't liquefy) a high temperature or low temperature mineral?
High temperature mineral

2) Which type will melt to form a liquid? Low temperature

3) Will the resulting liquid be higher or lower in silica content than the original rock? Why?
Higher. Low temperature minerals have a higher silica content than high temperature minerals.

4) If this liquid is separated from the original rock and then cooled relatively quickly, what is the name of the rock that will most likely form? Andesite

5) Repeat steps 1 through 4 for the rock formed in question 4. What is the name of the resulting rock if the liquid is allowed to cool very slowly?
Granite

Now consider a magma chamber that contains completely molten basaltic magma. Let's allow this magma to cool very slowly.

6) Which type of minerals will be the first to form? High temperature minerals.

7) Will the remaining liquid be higher or lower in silica than the original liquid? Why?
Higher — high temperature minerals are lower in silica content so the liquid becomes enriched in silica.

Assume that the newly formed crystals settle to the bottom of the magma chamber so that there is no chemical interaction between the newly formed crystals and the remaining liquid.

8) If this process continues, will the low temperature minerals eventually crystallize?
Yes

If so, would a rock formed from these minerals be higher or lower in silica content than a basalt?
It will be higher

> Do you think granite could form in this manner?

120

192

CONCEPTUAL **Physical Science** PRACTICE SHEET

Chapter 27: The Dynamic Earth
Faults

Three block diagrams are illustrated below. Draw arrows on each diagram to show the direction of movement. Answer the questions next to each diagram.

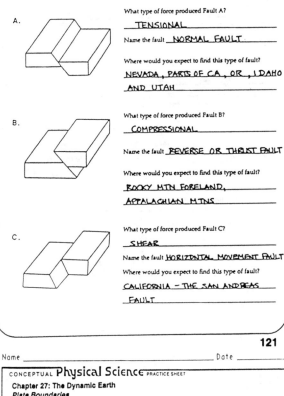

A.

What type of force produced Fault A?

TENSIONAL

Name the fault NORMAL FAULT

Where would you expect to find this type of fault?

NEVADA, PARTS OF CA, OR, IDAHO
AND UTAH

B.

What type of force produced Fault B?

COMPRESSIONAL

Name the fault REVERSE OR THRUST FAULT

Where would you expect to find this type of fault?

ROCKY MTN FORELAND,
APPALACHIAN MTNS

C.

What type of force produced Fault C?

SHEAR

Name the fault HORIZONTAL MOVEMENT FAULT

Where would you expect to find this type of fault?

CALIFORNIA - THE SAN ANDREAS
FAULT

121

Chapter 27: The Dynamic Earth
Structural Geology

Much subsurface information is learned by oil companies when wells are drilled. Some of this information leads to the discovery of oil, and some reveals subsurface structures such as folds and/or faults in the Earth's crust.

Four oil wells that have been drilled to the same depth are shown on the cross section below. Each well encounters contacts between different rock formations at the depths shown in the table below. Rock formations are labeled A—F, with youngest A and oldest F.

	Depth to Contact (in meters)			
Contact	Oil well #1	Oil well #2	Oil well #3	Oil well #4
A-B	200	not encountered	200	not encountered
B-C	400	100	400	100
C-D	600	300	600	300
D-E	800	500	800	500
E-F	1000	700	1000	700

1 In the cross section below, Contacts D-E and E-F are plotted for Oil Wells 1 and 2. Plot the remainder of the data for all four wells, labeling each point you plot.

2 Draw lines to connect the contacts between the rock formations (as is done for Contacts D-E and E-F for Oil Wells 1 and 2).

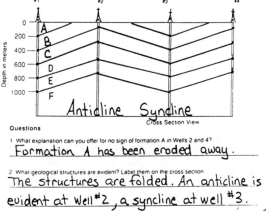

Anticline   Syncline

Cross Section View

Questions

1 What explanation can you offer for no sign of formation A in Wells 2 and 4?

Formation A has been eroded away.

2 What geological structures are evident? Label them on the cross section

The structures are folded. An anticline is evident at Well #2, a syncline at well #3.

122

CONCEPTUAL **Physical Science** PRACTICE SHEET

Chapter 27: The Dynamic Earth
Plate Boundaries

Draw arrows on the plate boundaries A, B, and C, to show the relative direction of movement

Type of plate boundary for A? Convergent

What type of force generates this type of boundary?

Compressional

Is this a site of crustal formation, destruction, or crustal transport?

Destruction

Type of plate boundary for B? Transform fault

What type of force generates this type of boundary?

Shear

Is this a site of crustal formation, destruction, or crustal transport?

Transport

Type of plate boundary for C? Divergent

What type of force generates this type of boundary?

Tensional

Is this a site of crustal formation, destruction, or crustal transport?

Formation

Draw arrows on the transform faults below to indicate relative motion.

Mid-ocean spreading ridge ——— Transform fault

Geology is a
down-to-earth science

123

CONCEPTUAL **Physical Science** PRACTICE SHEET

Chapter 27: The Dynamic Earth
Sea-Floor Spreading

The rate of sea floor spreading is from 1 to 10 centimeters per year. If we know the distance and age between two points on the ocean floor, we can determine the rate of spreading. Diagrams A, B, and C show stages of sea-floor spreading. Spreading begins at A, continues to B where rocks at location P begin to spread to the farther-apart positions we see in C. At C newer rock at the ocean crest S dated at 10 million years. Using the scale: 1 mm = 50 km, use a ruler on C to find the

1. separation rate of the two continental landmasses in the past 10 million years, in cm/yr **2.5**

2. age of the sea floor at P in Diagram C (1 cm/yr = 10 km/million years) **92 million years**

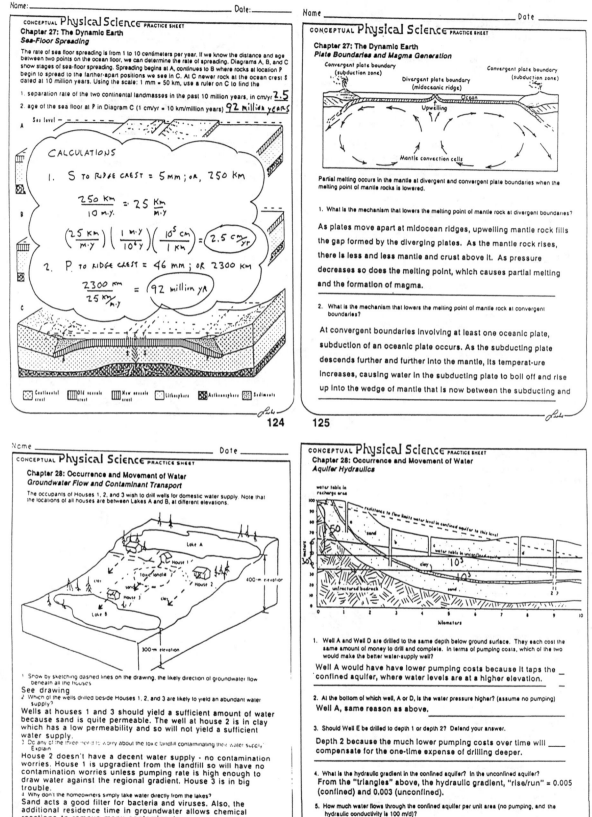

CALCULATIONS

1. S TO RIDGE CREST = 5 mm; OR, 250 Km

$$\frac{250 \text{ Km}}{10 \text{ m.y.}} = 25 \frac{\text{Km}}{\text{m·y}}$$

$$\left(25 \frac{\text{Km}}{\text{m·y}}\right)\left(\frac{1 \text{ m·y}}{10^6 \text{ y}}\right)\left(\frac{10^5 \text{ cm}}{1 \text{ Km}}\right) = 2.5 \frac{\text{cm}}{\text{yr}}$$

2. P TO RIDGE CREST = 46 mm; OR 2300 Km

$$\frac{2300 \text{ mm}}{25 \frac{\text{Km}}{\text{m·y}}} = 92 \text{ million YA}$$

Continental crust / Old oceanic crust / New oceanic crust / Lithosphere / Asthenosphere / Sediments

124

CONCEPTUAL **Physical Science** PRACTICE SHEET

Chapter 27: The Dynamic Earth
Plate Boundaries and Magma Generation

Partial melting occurs in the mantle at divergent and convergent plate boundaries when the melting point of mantle rocks is lowered.

1. What is the mechanism that lowers the melting point of mantle rock at divergent boundaries?

As plates move apart at midocean ridges, upwelling mantle rock fills the gap formed by the diverging plates. As the mantle rock rises, there is less and less mantle and crust above it. As pressure decreases so does the melting point, which causes partial melting and the formation of magma.

2. What is the mechanism that lowers the melting point of mantle rock at convergent boundaries?

At convergent boundaries involving at least one oceanic plate, subduction of an oceanic plate occurs. As the subducting plate descends further and further into the mantle, its temperature increases, causing water in the subducting plate to boil off and rise up into the wedge of mantle that is now between the subducting and

125

CONCEPTUAL **Physical Science** PRACTICE SHEET

Chapter 28: Occurrence and Movement of Water
Groundwater Flow and Contaminant Transport

The occupants of Houses 1, 2, and 3 wish to drill wells for domestic water supply. Note that the locations of all houses are between Lakes A and B, at different elevations.

1 Show by sketching dashed lines on the drawing, the likely direction of groundwater flow beneath all the houses.
See drawing

2 Which of the wells drilled beside Houses 1, 2, and 3 are likely to yield an abundant water supply?
Wells at houses 1 and 3 should yield a sufficient amount of water because sand is quite permeable. The well at house 2 is in clay which has a low permeability and so will not yield a sufficient water supply.

3 Do any of the three need to worry about the toxic landfill contaminating their water supply. Explain
House 2 doesn't have a decent water supply - no contamination worries. House 1 is upgradient from the landfill so will have no contamination worries unless pumping rate is high enough to draw water against the regional gradient. House 3 is in big trouble.

4 Why don't the homeowners simply take water directly from the lakes?
Sand acts a good filter for bacteria and viruses. Also, the additional residence time in groundwater allows chemical reactions to remove many contaminants.

5 Suggest a potentially better location for the landfill. Defend your choice
A better location would be in the clay. Clay's low permeability would hinder leaching of contaminants to the groundwater

127

CONCEPTUAL **Physical Science** PRACTICE SHEET

Chapter 28: Occurrence and Movement of Water
Aquifer Hydraulics

1. Well A and Well D are drilled to the same depth below ground surface. They each cost the same amount of money to drill and complete. In terms of pumping costs, which of the two would make the better water-supply well?
Well A would have have lower pumping costs because it taps the confined aquifer, where water levels are at a higher elevation.

2. At the bottom of which well, A or D, is the water pressure higher? (assume no pumping)
Well A, same reason as above.

3. Should Well E be drilled to depth 1 or depth 2? Defend your answer.
Depth 2 because the much lower pumping costs over time will compensate for the one-time expense of drilling deeper.

4. What is the hydraulic gradient in the confined aquifer? In the unconfined aquifer?
From the "triangles" above, the hydraulic gradient, "rise/run" = 0.005 (confined) and 0.003 (unconfined).

5. How much water flows through the confined aquifer per unit area (no pumping, and the hydraulic conductivity is 100 m/d)?
By Darcy's law, $q = kA\,\Delta h/\Delta l = (100 \text{ m/d})(1 \text{ m}^2)(0.005) = 0.5 \text{ m}^3/\text{d}$.

128

CONCEPTUAL **Physical Science** PRACTICE SHEET

Chapter 29: Surface Processes
Stream Flow

The diagram below illustrates a stream. Coarse sediment grains will be deposited primarily at one type of location, and finer sediment grains at another. On the diagram, mark the likely locations of each size of deposited grain.

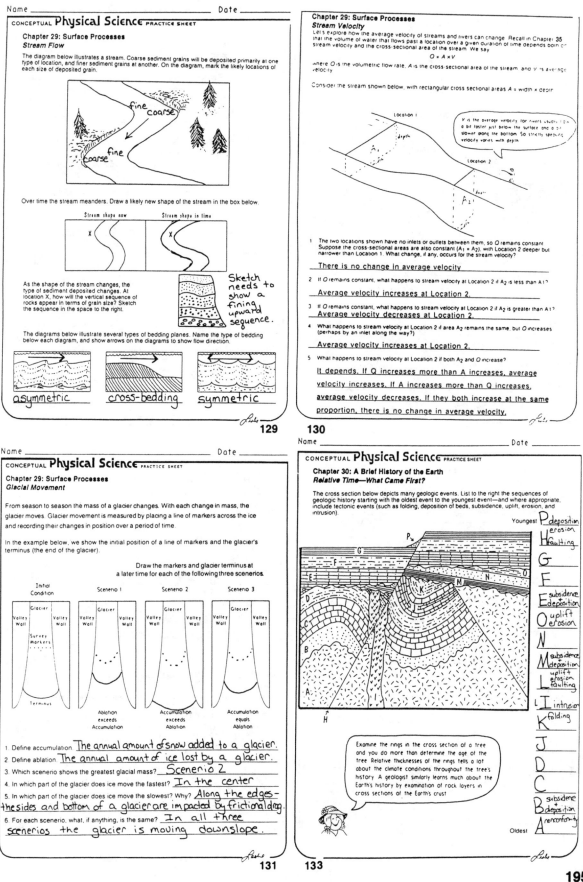

Over time the stream meanders. Draw a likely new shape of the stream in the box below.

Stream shape now   Stream shape in time

As the shape of the stream changes, the type of sediment deposited changes. At location X, how will the vertical sequence of rocks appear in terms of grain size? Sketch the sequence in the space to the right.

Sketch needs to show a fining upward sequence.

The diagrams below illustrate several types of bedding planes. Name the type of bedding below each diagram, and show arrows on the diagrams to show flow direction.

asymmetric   cross-bedding   symmetric

129

Chapter 29: Surface Processes
Stream Velocity

Let's explore how the average velocity of streams and rivers can change. Recall in Chapter 35 that the volume of water that flows past a location over a given duration of time depends both on stream velocity and the cross-sectional area of the stream. We say

$$Q = A \times V$$

where Q is the volumetric flow rate, A is the cross-sectional area of the stream, and V is average velocity.

Consider the stream shown below, with rectangular cross sectional areas A = width x depth.

V is the average velocity for rivers which is a bit faster just below the surface and a bit slower along the bottom. So strictly speaking, velocity varies with depth.

Location 1

Location 2

1. The two locations shown have no inlets or outlets between them, so Q remains constant. Suppose the cross-sectional areas are also constant ($A_1 = A_2$), with Location 2 deeper but narrower than Location 1. What change, if any, occurs for the stream velocity?

    There is no change in average velocity

2. If Q remains constant, what happens to stream velocity at Location 2 if A_2 is less than A_1?

    Average velocity increases at Location 2.

3. If Q remains constant, what happens to stream velocity at Location 2 if A_2 is greater than A_1?

    Average velocity decreases at Location 2.

4. What happens to stream velocity at Location 2 if area A_2 remains the same, but Q increases (perhaps by an inlet along the way)?

    Average velocity increases at Location 2.

5. What happens to stream velocity at Location 2 if both A_2 and Q increase?

    It depends. If Q increases more than A increases, average velocity increases. If A increases more than Q increases, average velocity decreases. If they both increase at the same proportion, there is no change in average velocity.

130

CONCEPTUAL **Physical Science** PRACTICE SHEET

Chapter 29: Surface Processes
Glacial Movement

From season to season the mass of a glacier changes. With each change in mass, the glacier moves. Glacier movement is measured by placing a line of markers across the ice and recording their changes in position over a period of time.

In the example below, we show the initial position of a line of markers and the glacier's terminus (the end of the glacier).

Draw the markers and glacier terminus at a later time for each of the following three scenarios.

Initial Condition   Scenario 1   Scenario 2   Scenario 3

Ablation exceeds Accumulation   Accumulation exceeds Ablation   Accumulation equals Ablation

1. Define accumulation. The annual amount of snow added to a glacier.
2. Define ablation. The annual amount of ice lost by a glacier.
3. Which scenario shows the greatest glacial mass? Scenario 2
4. In which part of the glacier does ice move the fastest? In the center
5. In which part of the glacier does ice move the slowest? Why? Along the edges— the sides and bottom of a glacier are impacted by frictional drag.
6. For each scenario, what, if anything, is the same? In all three scenarios the glacier is moving downslope.

131

CONCEPTUAL **Physical Science** PRACTICE SHEET

Chapter 30: A Brief History of the Earth
Relative Time—What Came First?

The cross section below depicts many geologic events. List to the right the sequences of geologic history starting with the oldest event to the youngest event—and where appropriate, include tectonic events (such as folding, deposition of beds, subsidence, uplift, erosion, and intrusion).

Youngest P deposition
erosion
H faulting
G
F
E subsidence
E deposition
O uplift
erosion
N
M subsidence
deposition
uplift
L erosion
faulting
L
I intrusion
K folding
J
D
C
B subsidence + deposition
A nonconformity
Oldest

Examine the rings in the cross section of a tree and you do more than determine the age of the tree. Relative thicknesses of the rings tells a lot about the climate conditions throughout the tree's history. A geologist similarly learns much about the Earth's history by examination of rock layers in cross sections of the Earth's crust.

133

195

CONCEPTUAL **Physical Science** PRACTICE SHEET

Chapter 30: A Brief History of the Earth
Age Relationships

From your investigation of the 6 geologic regions shown, answer the questions below. The number of each question refers to the same-numbered region.

▫️ Granite   ◼️ Basalt   ▨ Plutonic rock   ▦ Limestone   ▫️ Shale   ▫️ Sandstone

1. The shale has been cut by a dike. The radiometric age of the dike is estimated at 40 million years. Is the shale younger or older?   _older_

2. Which is older, the granite or the basalt?   _the granite_

3. The sandstone bed, **Z**, has been intruded by dikes. What is the age succession of dikes, going from oldest to youngest?   _w, x, y_

4. Which is older, the shale or the basalt?   _the shale_

5. Which is older, the sandstone or the basalt?   _the basalt_

6. Which is older, the sandstone or the limestone?   _the sandstone_

Unconformities and Age Relationships

The wavy lines in the 4 regions below represent unconformities. Investigate the regions and answer corresponding questions about the 4 regions below.

1. Did the faulting and dike occur before or after the unconformity?   _before_
   What kind of unconformity is it?   _nonconformity_

2. Did the faulting occur before or after the unconformity?   _after_
   What kind of unconformity is represented?   _erosional unconformity_

3. Did the folding occur before or after the unconformity?   _before_
   What kind of unconformity is it?   _angular unconformity_

4. What kind of unconformity is represented?   _angular unconformity_

5. Interestingly, the age of the Earth is some 4.5 billion years old—yet the oldest rocks found are some 3.7 billion years old. Why do we find no 4.5-billion year old rocks?
   The Earth's earliest crustal surface has been reworked. Rocks that formed 4.5 b.y.a. have been remelted into new rock.

6. What is the age of the innermost ring in a living redwood tree that is 2000 years old?
   What is the age of the outermost ring? How does this example relate to the previous question?
   The innermost ring is 2000 years old; the outermost ring is 1 year old. New layers cover older layers.

7. What is the approximate age of the atoms that make up a 3.7-billion year old rock?
   They are older than 3.7 billion years.

CONCEPTUAL **Physical Science** PRACTICE SHEET

Chapter 30: A Brief History of the Earth
Radiometric Dating

Isotopes Most Commonly Used for Radiometric Dating

Radioactive Parent	Stable Daughter Product	Currently Accepted Half-life Value
Uranium-238	lead-206	4.5 billion years
Uranium-235	lead-207	704 million years
Potassium-40	argon-40	1.3 billion years
Carbon-14	nitrogen-14	5730 years

1. Consider a radiometric lab experiment wherein 99.98791 % of a certain radioactive sample of material remains after one year. What is the decay rate of the sample?

$$1.000... - 0.9998791 = 0.0001209/yr$$

2. What is the rate constant?
   (Assume that the decay rate is constant for the one year period.)
   $$K = \frac{decay\ rate}{starting\ amount} = \frac{0.0001209/yr}{1.000...} = 0.0001209/yr$$

3. What is the half-life?
   $$T = \frac{0.693}{0.0001209/yr} = 5732\ yr$$

4. Identify the isotope.   _Carbon 14_

5. In a sample collected in the field, this isotope was found to be 1/16 of its original amount. What is the age of the sample?
   Note from graph that 1/16 is 4 half lives
   $$4 \times 5732 = 22,928\ yr$$

You need to know:
- Decay rate = (amount decayed) / time
- Rate constant K = (decay rate/ starting amount) in units 1/year
- Half-life T = 0.693/K (units in years)

Chapter 30: A Brief History of the Earth
Our Earth's Hot Interior

A major puzzle faced scientists in the 19th century. Volcanoes showed that the Earth is molten beneath its crust. Penetration into the crust by bore-holes and mines showed that the Earth's temperature increases with depth. Scientists knew that heat flows from the interior to the surface. They assumed that the source of the Earth's internal heat was primordial, the afterglow of its fiery birth. Measurements of the Earth's rate of cooling indicated a relatively young Earth—some 25 to 30 million years in age. But geological evidence indicated an older Earth. This puzzle wasn't solved until the discovery of radioactivity. Then it was learned that the interior was kept hot by the energy of radioactive decay. We now know the age of the Earth is some 4.5 billion years—a much older Earth.

All rock contains trace amounts of radioactive minerals. Radioactive minerals in common granite release energy at the rate 0.03 J/kg·yr. Granite at the Earth's surface transfers this energy to the surroundings practically as fast as it is generated, so we don't find granite any warmer than other parts of our environment. But what if a sample of granite were thermally insulated? That is, suppose all the increase of thermal energy due to radioactive decay were contained. Then it would get hotter. How much? Let's figure it out, using 790 J/kg·C° as the specific heat of granite.

Calculations to make:

1. How many joules are required to increase the temperature of 1 kg of granite by 500 C°?

$$Q = mc\Delta T = (1kg)\left(\frac{790}{kg\ C°}\right)500C° = 395,000J$$

Let's see now back in Chapter 7 we learned that the relationship between quantity of heat, mass, specific heat, and temperature difference was $Q \propto mc\Delta T$

2. How many years would it take radioactivity in a kilogram of granite to produce this many joules?

$$\frac{395,000\ J}{0.03\ J/kg·yr} \times 1kg \approx 13\ million\ years$$

Questions to answer:

1. How many years would it take a thermally insulated 1-kilogram chunk of granite to undergo a 500 C increase in temperature?
   Same   13 million years

2. How many years would it take a thermally insulated one-million-kilogram chunk of granite to undergo a 500 C° increase in temperature?
   Same (correspondingly more radiation!)

An electric toaster stays hot while electric energy is supplied and doesn't cool until switched off. Similarly do you think the energy source now keeping the Earth hot will one day suddenly switch off like a disconnected toaster—or gradually decrease over a long time?

3. Why does the Earth's interior remain molten hot?
   Because of radioactivity

4. Rock has a higher melting temperature deep in the interior. Why?   _(like water in a) (pressure cooker)_
   Greater pressure

5. Why doesn't the Earth just keep getting hotter until it all melts?
   Interior is not perfectly insulated - heat migrates to surface

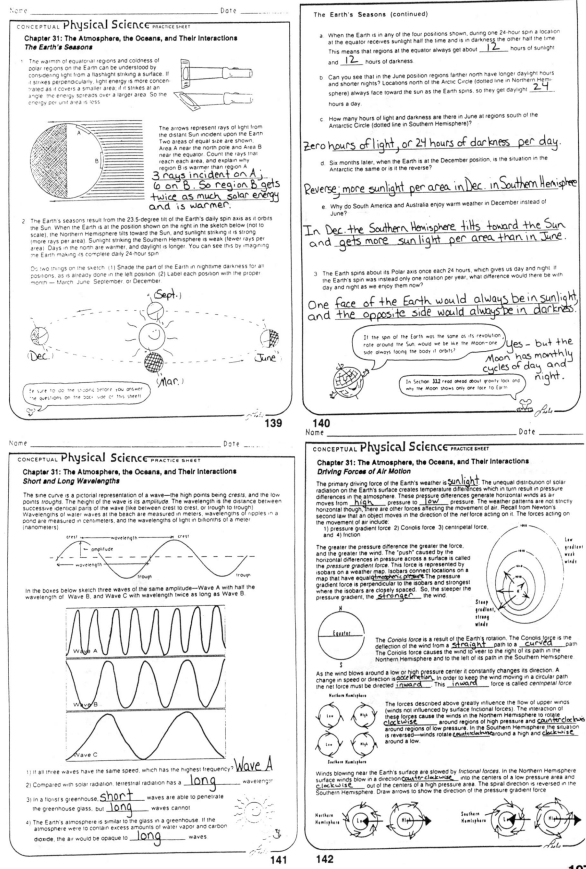

CONCEPTUAL **Physical Science** PRACTICE SHEET

Chapter 31: The Atmosphere, the Oceans, and Their Interactions
The Earth's Seasons

1. The warmth of equatorial regions and coldness of polar regions on the Earth can be understood by considering light from a flashlight striking a surface. If it strikes perpendicularly, light energy is more concentrated as it covers a smaller area; if it strikes at an angle the energy spreads over a larger area. So the energy per unit area is less.

The arrows represent rays of light from the distant Sun incident upon the Earth. Two areas of equal size are shown. Area A near the north pole and Area B near the equator. Count the rays that reach each area, and explain why region B is warmer than region A.

3 rays incident on A; 6 on B. So region B gets twice as much solar energy and is warmer.

2. The Earth's seasons result from the 23.5-degree tilt of the Earth's daily spin axis as it orbits the Sun. When the Earth is at the position shown on the right in the sketch below (not to scale), the Northern Hemisphere tilts toward the Sun, and sunlight striking it is strong (more rays per area). Sunlight striking the Southern Hemisphere is weak (fewer rays per area). Days in the north are warmer, and daylight is longer. You can see this by imagining the Earth making its complete daily 24-hour spin.

Do two things on the sketch. (1) Shade the part of the Earth in nighttime darkness for all positions, as is already done in the left sketch for each position. (2) Label each position with the proper month — March, June, September, or December.

(Sept.) *(Dec.)* *(Mar.)* *June*

Be sure to do the shading before you answer the questions on the back side of this sheet!

a. When the Earth is in any of the four positions shown, during one 24-hour spin a location at the equator receives sunlight half the time and is in darkness the other half the time. This means that regions at the equator always get about __12__ hours of sunlight and __12__ hours of darkness.

b. Can you see that in the June position regions farther north have longer daylight hours and shorter nights? Locations north of the Arctic Circle (dotted line in Northern Hemisphere) always face toward the sun as the Earth spins, so they get daylight __24__ hours a day.

c. How many hours of light and darkness are there in June at regions south of the Antarctic Circle (dotted line in Southern Hemisphere)?

Zero hours of light, or 24 hours of darkness per day.

d. Six months later, when the Earth is at the December position, is the situation in the Antarctic the same or is it the reverse?

Reverse; more sunlight per area in Dec. in Southern Hemisphere

e. Why do South America and Australia enjoy warm weather in December instead of June?

In Dec. the Southern Hemisphere tilts toward the Sun and gets more sunlight per area than in June.

3. The Earth spins about its Polar axis once each 24 hours, which gives us day and night. If the Earth's spin was instead only one rotation per year, what difference would there be with day and night as we enjoy them now?

One face of the Earth would always be in sunlight, and the opposite side would always be in darkness.

If the spin of the Earth was the same as its revolution rate around the Sun, would we be like the Moon—one side always facing the body it orbits?

Yes — but the Moon has monthly cycles of day and night.

In Section 31.2 read ahead about gravity lock and why the Moon shows only one face to Earth.

139 **140**

CONCEPTUAL **Physical Science** PRACTICE SHEET

Chapter 31: The Atmosphere, the Oceans, and Their Interactions
Short and Long Wavelengths

The sine curve is a pictorial representation of a wave—the high points being *crests*, and the low points *troughs*. The height of the wave is its *amplitude*. The wavelength is the distance between successive identical parts of the wave (like between crest to crest, or trough to trough). Wavelengths of water waves at the beach are measured in meters, wavelengths of ripples in a pond are measured in centimeters, and the wavelengths of light in billionths of a meter (nanometers).

crest — wavelength — crest
amplitude
wavelength
trough — trough

In the boxes below sketch three waves of the same amplitude—Wave A with half the wavelength of Wave B, and Wave C with wavelength twice as long as Wave B.

Wave A
Wave B
Wave C

1) If all three waves have the same speed, which has the highest frequency? *Wave A*

2) Compared with solar radiation, terrestrial radiation has a __long__ wavelength.

3) In a florist's greenhouse, __short__ waves are able to penetrate the greenhouse glass, but __long__ waves cannot.

4) The Earth's atmosphere is similar to the glass in a greenhouse. If the atmosphere were to contain excess amounts of water vapor and carbon dioxide, the air would be opaque to __long__ waves.

141

CONCEPTUAL **Physical Science** PRACTICE SHEET

Chapter 31: The Atmosphere, the Oceans, and Their Interactions
Driving Forces of Air Motion

The primary driving force of the Earth's weather is __sunlight__. The unequal distribution of solar radiation on the Earth's surface creates temperature differences which in turn result in pressure differences in the atmosphere. These pressure differences generate horizontal winds as air moves from __high__ pressure to __low__ pressure. The weather patterns are not strictly horizontal though, there are other forces affecting the movement of air. Recall from Newton's second law that an object moves in the direction of the *net* force acting on it. The forces acting on the movement of air include:
1) pressure gradient force 2) Coriolis force 3) centripetal force, and 4) friction

The greater the pressure difference the greater the force, and the greater the wind. The "push" caused by the horizontal differences in pressure across a surface is called the *pressure gradient force*. This force is represented by isobars on a weather map. Isobars connect locations on a map that have equal __atmospheric pressure__. The pressure gradient force is perpendicular to the isobars and strongest where the isobars are closely spaced. So, the steeper the pressure gradient, the __stronger__ the wind.

Low gradient weak winds

Steep gradient, strong winds

The *Coriolis force* is a result of the Earth's rotation. The Coriolis force is the deflection of the wind from a __straight__ path to a __curved__ path. The Coriolis force causes the wind to veer to the right of its path in the Northern Hemisphere and to the left of its path in the Southern Hemisphere.

As the wind blows around a low or high pressure center it constantly changes its direction. A change in speed or direction is __acceleration__. In order to keep the wind moving in a circular path the net force must be directed __inward__. This __inward__ force is called *centripetal force*.

Northern Hemisphere

The forces described above greatly influence the flow of upper winds (winds not influenced by surface frictional forces). The interaction of these forces cause the winds in the Northern Hemisphere to rotate __clockwise__ around regions of high pressure and __counterclockwise__ around regions of low pressure. In the Southern Hemisphere the situation is reversed—winds rotate __counterclockwise__ around a high and __clockwise__ around a low.

Southern Hemisphere

Winds blowing near the Earth's surface are slowed by *frictional forces*. In the Northern Hemisphere surface winds blow in a direction __counterclockwise__ into the centers of a low pressure area and __clockwise__ out of the centers of a high pressure area. The spiral direction is reversed in the Southern Hemisphere. Draw arrows to show the direction of the pressure gradient force.

Northern Hemisphere   Southern Hemisphere

142

CONCEPTUAL Physical Science PRACTICE SHEET
Chapter 32: Weather
Air Temperature and Pressure Patterns

Temperature patterns on weather maps are depicted by *isotherms*—lines which connect all points having the same temperature. Each isotherm separates temperatures of higher values from temperatures of lower values

The weather map to the right shows temperatures in degrees Fahrenheit for various locations Using 10 degree intervals, connect same-value numbers to construct isotherms. Label the temperature value at each end of the isotherm. One isotherm has been completed as an example

Tips for drawing Isotherms
- Isotherms can never be open ended.
- Isotherms are "closed" if they reach the boundary of plotted data, or make a loop.
- Isotherms can never touch, cross, or fork.
- Isotherms must always appear in sequence; for example, there must be a 60° isotherm between a 50° and 70° isotherm.
- Isotherms should be labeled with their values.

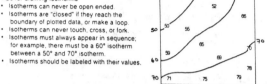

Pressure patterns on weather maps are depicted by *isobars*—lines which connect all points having equal pressure. Each isobar separates stations of higher pressure from stations of lower pressure

The weather map below shows air pressure in millibar (mb) units at various locations Using an interval of 4, (for example, 1008, 1012, 1016, etc.) connect equal pressure values to construct isobars. Label the pressure value at each end of the isobar. Two isobars have been completed for an example.

- Tips for drawing isobars are similar to those for drawing isotherms.

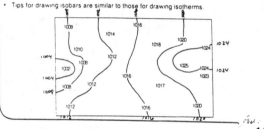

Air Temperature and Pressure Patterns

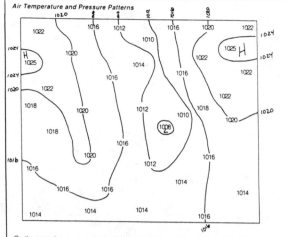

On the map above, use an interval of 4 to draw lines of equal pressure (isobars) to show the pattern of air pressure. Locate and mark regions of high pressure with an "H" and regions of low pressure with an "L".

1. On the map above, areas of high pressure are depicted by the __1024__ isobar.

2. On the map above, areas of low pressure are depicted by the __1008__ isobar.

Circle the correct answer

3. Highs are usually accompanied by (stormy weather) (fair weather)

4. In the Northern Hemisphere, surface winds surrounding a high pressure system blow in a (clockwise direction) (counterclockwise direction)

5. In the Northern Hemisphere, surface winds spiral inward into a (region of low pressure) (region of high pressure).

CONCEPTUAL Physical Science PRACTICE SHEET
Chapter 32: Weather
Surface Weather Maps

Station models are used on weather maps to depict weather conditions for individual localities. Weather codes are plotted in, on, and around a central circle that describes the overall appearance of the sky. Jutting from the circle is a wind arrow, its tail in the direction from which the wind comes and its feathers indicating the wind speed Other weather codes are in standard position around the circle.

Use the simplified station model and weather symbols to complete the statements below:

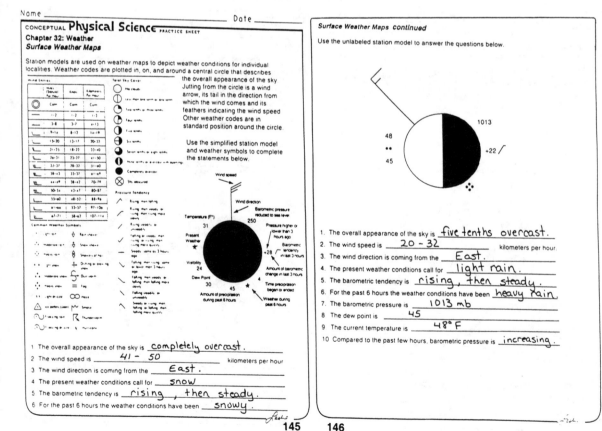

1. The overall appearance of the sky is __completely overcast.__
2. The wind speed is __41 - 50__ kilometers per hour
3. The wind direction is coming from the __East.__
4. The present weather conditions call for __snow__
5. The barometric tendency is __rising, then steady.__
6. For the past 6 hours the weather conditions have been __snowy.__

Surface Weather Maps *continued*

Use the unlabeled station model to answer the questions below.

1. The overall appearance of the sky is __five tenths overcast.__
2. The wind speed is __20 - 32__ kilometers per hour.
3. The wind direction is coming from the __East.__
4. The present weather conditions call for __light rain.__
5. The barometric tendency is __rising, then steady.__
6. For the past 6 hours the weather conditions have been __heavy rain.__
7. The barometric pressure is __1013 mb__
8. The dew point is __45__
9. The current temperature is __48° F__
10. Compared to the past few hours, barometric pressure is __increasing.__

CONCEPTUAL **Physical Science** PRACTICE SHEET

Chapter 32: Weather
Chilly Winds

Often times it feels colder outside than a thermometer indicates. The apparent difference is called *wind chill*. On November 1, 2001, the National Weather Service implemented a new Wind Chill Temperature index. The new formula uses advances in science, technology, and computer modeling to provide a more accurate, understandable, and useful formula for calculating the dangers from winter winds and freezing temperatures.

For temperatures less than 50°F and wind speeds greater than 3 mph, the new formula used to estimate the temperature we perceive when a cold wind blows is:

Wind Chill Temperature (°F) = 35.74 + 0.6215T - 35.75($V^{0.16}$) + 0.4275T($V^{0.16}$)

where V is the wind speed in miles per hour and T is the temperature in degrees Fahrenheit.

Wind Chill Temperature Table

V (mph)	$V^{0.16}$	Temperature (°F)			
		5.00	10.00	15.00	32.00
5.00	1.2937	-4.64	1.24	7.11	27.08
10.00	1.4454	-9.74	-3.54	2.66	23.73
15.00	1.5423	-12.99	-6.59	-0.19	21.59

1. Using the formula given for Wind Chill Temperature (WCT), complete the above table. The variable $V^{0.16}$ (wind speed raised to 0.16 power) is provided in the table to simplify your calculations.

2. Which has a stronger impact on WCT, changes in wind speed or changes in temperature? (Defend your answer with data from your completed table.)

From the table note that changes in temperature have a stronger impact than changes in wind speed. Each 5-degree change in temperature causes bigger changes in WCT than each 5-mph change in wind speed.

3. How does WCT vary when wind speed remains fixed and only temperature changes? (Defend your answer.)

Note the WCT equation is linear with respect to T. And as calculated differences in WCT across a given row in the table show, the WCT varies at even intervals as the true temperature changes.

4. How does WCT vary when temperature stays fixed and only wind speed changes? (Defend your answer.)

Note the WCT equation is non-linear with respect to V (because it varies as $V^{0.16}$). And as calculated differences in WCT down a given column of the table show, for a fixed temperature, WCT does not vary at even intervals as wind speed changes.

More information can be found on the National Weather Service's Web site: http://www.nws.noaa.gov/om/windchill

---

CONCEPTUAL **Physical Science** PRACTICE SHEET

Chapter 33: The Solar System
Earth-Moon-Sun Alignment

Here we see the shadow cast by an apple on the wall. Note how the rays define the darkest part of the shadow, the *umbra*, and the lighter part of the shadow, the *penumbra*. The shadows that comprise eclipses of planetary bodies are similarly formed. Below is a diagram of the sun, earth, and the orbital path of the moon (dashed circle). One position of the moon is shown. Draw the moon in the appropriate positions on the dashed circle to represent (a) a quarter moon; (b) a half moon; (c) a solar eclipse; (d) a lunar eclipse. Label your positions. For c and d, extend rays from the top and bottom of the sun to show umbra and penumbra regions.

The diagram below is an extension of Figure 33.21, which shows 3 positions of the sun, A, B, C. Sketch the appropriate positions of the moon in its orbit about the earth for (a) a solar eclipse; (b) a lunar eclipse. Label your positions. Sketch solar rays similar to the above exercise.

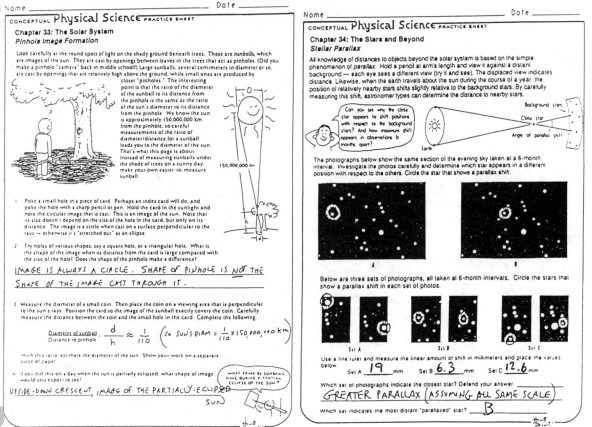

CONCEPTUAL **Physical Science** PRACTICE SHEET

Chapter 33: The Solar System
Pinhole Image Formation

Look carefully at the round spots of light on the shady ground beneath trees. These are *sunballs*, which are images of the sun. They are cast by openings between leaves in the trees that act as pinholes. (Did you make a pinhole "camera" back in middle school?) Large sunballs, several centimeters in diameter or so, are cast by openings that are relatively high above the ground, while small ones are produced by closer "pinholes." The interesting point is that the ratio of the diameter of the sunball to its distance from the pinhole is the same as the ratio of the sun's diameter to its distance from the pinhole. We know the sun is approximately 150,000,000 km from the pinhole, so careful measurements of the ratio of diameter/distance for a sunball leads you to the diameter of the sun. That's what this page is about. Instead of measuring sunballs under the shade of trees on a sunny day, make your own easier-to-measure sunball.

150,000,000 km

1. Poke a small hole in a piece of card. Perhaps an index card will do, and poke the hole with a sharp pencil or pen. Hold the card in the sunlight and note the circular image that is cast. This is an image of the sun. Note that its size doesn't depend on the size of the hole in the card, but only on its distance. The image is a circle when cast on a surface perpendicular to the rays — otherwise it's "stretched out" as an ellipse.

2. Try holes of various shapes; say a square hole, or a triangular hole. What is the shape of the image when its distance from the card is large compared with the size of the hole? Does the shape of the pinhole make a difference?

IMAGE IS ALWAYS A CIRCLE. SHAPE OF PINHOLE IS NOT THE SHAPE OF THE IMAGE CAST THROUGH IT.

3. Measure the diameter of a small coin. Then place the coin on a viewing area that is perpendicular to the sun's rays. Position the card so the image of the sunball exactly covers the coin. Carefully measure the distance between the coin and the small hole in the card. Complete the following:

$$\frac{\text{Diameter of sunball}}{\text{Distance to pinhole}} = \frac{d}{h} \approx \frac{1}{110} \quad \left(\text{so SUN'S DIAM} = \frac{1}{110} \times 150,000,000 \text{ km}\right)$$

With this ratio, estimate the diameter of the sun. Show your work on a separate piece of paper.

4. If you did this on a day when the sun was partially eclipsed, what shape of image would you expect to see?

WHAT SHAPE DO SUNBALLS HAVE DURING A PARTIAL ECLIPSE OF THE SUN?

UPSIDE-DOWN CRESCENT, IMAGE OF THE PARTIALLY-ECLIPSED SUN.

CONCEPTUAL **Physical Science** PRACTICE SHEET

Chapter 34: The Stars and Beyond
Stellar Parallax

All knowledge of distances to objects beyond the solar system is based on the simple phenomenon of *parallax*. Hold a pencil at arm's length and view it against a distant background — each eye sees a different view (try it and see). The displaced view indicates distance. Likewise, when the earth travels about the sun during the course of a year, the position of relatively nearby stars shifts slightly relative to the background stars. By carefully measuring this shift, astronomer types can determine the distance to nearby stars.

Can you see why the close star appears to shift positions with respect to the background stars? And how maximum shift appears in observations 6 months apart?

Background stars

Close star

Angle of parallax shift

earth

The photographs below show the same section of the evening sky taken at a 6-month interval. Investigate the photos carefully and determine which star appears in a different position with respect to the others. Circle the star that shows a parallax shift.

A

B

Below are three sets of photographs, all taken at 6-month intervals. Circle the stars that show a parallax shift in each set of photos.

Set A   Set B   Set C

Use a line ruler and measure the linear amount of shift in millimeters and place the values below   Set A **19** mm   Set B **6.3** mm   Set C **12.6** mm

Which set of photographs indicate the closest star? Defend your answer.

GREATER PARALLAX (ASSUMING ALL SAME SCALE)

Which set indicates the most distant "parallaxed" star?   **B**

CONCEPTUAL **Physical Science** PRACTICE SHEET

Chapter 35: Special and General Relativity
Time Dilation and the Twin Trip

This is about identical twins, one an astronaut who takes a high-speed round-trip journey while the other twin stays home on earth. The traveling twin returns younger than the stay-at-home twin. How much younger depends on the relative speeds involved. If the traveler maintains a speed 0.5c for 1 year (according to clocks aboard the spaceship), 1.15 years elapse on earth. For a speed of 0.87c for a year, 2 years elapse on earth. At 0.995c, 10 earth years pass in one spaceship year; the travelling twin ages a single year while the stay-at-home twin ages 10 years.

This exercise will show that from the frames of reference of both twins, the earthbound twin ages more.

Case 1: No Motion First, consider a spaceship hovering at rest relative to a distant planet (Figure 1). Suppose the ship sends regularly-spaced brief flashes of light to the planet. The light flashes encounter a receiver on the planet a slight time later at speed c.

Since there is no relative motion between sender and receiver, successive flashes are received as frequently as they are sent. We'll suppose a flash is sent from the ship every 6 minutes; after slight delay, the receiver sees a flash every 6 minutes. Nothing unusual, because no motion is involved.

Case 2: Motion For motion the situation is quite different. Although the speed of the flashes is c, regardless of motion, how *frequently* the flashes are seen very much depends on relative motion. When the ship approaches the receiver, the receiver sees the flashes more frequently. This makes sense because each succeeding flash has less distance to travel as the ship gets closer to the receiver. Flashes are "crowded together" and are seen more frequently. Flashes sent at 6-min intervals are seen as less than 6 min apart. We'll suppose the ship is traveling fast enough for the flashes to be seen twice as frequently, at intervals of 3 min (Figure 2). This is the Doppler effect (Chapter 11) for light.

Motion away from the receiver stretches the flashes apart and they are seen less frequently. If the ship recedes from the receiver at the same speed and still emits flashes at 6-min intervals, these flashes are seen stretched out to 12-min intervals by the receiver. Put another way, they will be seen half as frequently, that is, one flash each 12-

min interval (Figure 3). This makes sense because each succeeding flash has a longer distance to travel as the ship gets farther away from the receiver.

Note the effect of moving away is just the opposite of moving closer to the receiver. Flashes are received twice as frequently when the spaceship is approaching (6-min flash intervals are seen every 3 min), and are received half as frequently when receding (6-min flash intervals are seen every 12 min).

The light flashes make up a light clock. Any reliable clock would show that in the receiver's frame of reference, events that take 6 min in the spaceship are seen to take 12 min when the spaceship recedes and only 3 min when the ship is approaching.

....

1. If the spaceship travels for 1 h and emits a flash every 6 min, how many flashes will be emitted? **10**

2. The ship sends equally spaced 6-min flashes while approaching the receiver at constant speed. Will these flashes be equally spaced when they encounter the receiver? **YES** How about if the ship is accelerating when sending flashes? **NO (DIFFERENT DIST COVERED IN EQUAL TIMES IF ACCELERATING!)**

3. If the receiver sees these flashes at 3-min intervals, how much time will occur between the first and the last flash (in the frame of reference of the receiver)?

30 MIN (10 FLASHES, 3 MIN APART = 30 MIN)

....

Case 3 The Twins Let's apply all this to the twins. Suppose the traveling twin leaves the earthbound twin at the same high speed for 1 hour and then quickly turns around and returns in 1 hour. The traveling twin takes a round trip of 2 hours, according to all clocks aboard the spaceship. The time for the round trip will be something else from the earth frame of reference!

In Figure 4a we see the ship receding from earth, emitting a flash each 6 min. Due to motion, flashes are received on earth every 12 min. During the hour of going away from earth, a total of ten flashes are emitted. If the ship departs from the earth at noon, clocks aboard the ship read 1 PM when the tenth flash is emitted. What time will it be on earth when this tenth flash reaches the earth? The answer is 2 PM. Why? Because the time it takes the earth to receive 10 flashes at 12-min intervals is 10 x (12 min), or 120 min (= 2 hours).

Suppose the spaceship turns around suddenly in a negligibly short time and returns at the same high speed. During the hour of return it emits another ten flashes at 6-min intervals. These flashes are received every 3 min on earth, so all ten flashes come in 30 min. A clock on earth will read 2:30 PM when the spaceship completes its 2-hour trip. This means the earthbound twin has aged 1/2 hour more than the twin aboard the spaceship!

Time Dilation and the Twin Trip continued

Fig. 4

Sees flash every 12 minutes   Sends flash every 6 minutes

Still receiving flashes of 12-minute intervals from receding ship

Ship on way back - still sending flash every 6 minutes

Still sending flash every 6 minutes

Sees flashes from approaching ship every 3 minutes

....

Complete Figure 5, which summarizes Case 3, by filling in the blanks.

Earth frame of reference:
10 flashes @ 12 min = **120** minutes
10 flashes @ 3 min = **30** minutes
150 minutes
2.5 hours

Spaceship frame of reference:
20 flashes @ 6 min = **120** minutes
2 hours

Fig. 5

Time Dilation and the Twin Trip continued

Case 4 Sending and Receiving Twins Interchanged Let's switch sender and receiver and see if the result is the same from either frame of reference. Flashes are emitted from the earth at regularly spaced 6-min intervals in earth time, but are seen from the frame of reference of the receding spaceship at 12-min intervals (Figure 6a). This means that a total of five flashes are seen by the spaceship during the hour of receding from earth. During the spaceship's hour of approaching, the light flashes are seen at 3-min intervals (Figure 6b), so 20 flashes will be seen.

So the spaceship receives a total of 25 flashes during its 2-hour trip. According to clocks on the earth, however, the time it takes to emit the 25 flashes at 6-min intervals is 25 x (6 min), or 150 min (= 2.5 hour).

Fig. 6

Sends flash every 6 minutes   Sees flash every 12 minutes

Sends flash every 6 minutes   Sees flash every 3 minutes

....

Complete Figure 7, which summarizes Case 4, by filling in the blanks.

Earth frame of reference:
25 flashes @ 6 min = **150** minutes
2.5 hours

Spaceship frame of reference:
5 flashes @ 12 min = **60** minutes
20 flashes @ 3 min = **60** minutes
120 minutes
2 hours

....

Conclusion So both twins agree on the same results, with no dispute as to who ages more. The key factor is that while the stay-at-home twin remains in a single reference frame, the traveling twin has experienced two different frames of reference, separated by the acceleration of the spaceship in turning around. The spaceship experiences two different realms of time, while the earth experiences a still different but single realm of time. The twins can meet again at the same place in space only at the expense of time.

....

The twin example is often called the twin "paradox" because of the following reasoning: Since motion is relative, the rocket ship can be regarded at rest and the earth moves, in which case the twin on the rocket ship ages more. Question: Is the situation symmetrical; that is, do both twins occupy the same realms of time? **NO** What event separates the **2** realms of time for the traveling twin? **ACCELERATION OF TURN-AROUND** So is this twin-paradox reasoning correct or incorrect? _____ Briefly, and in summary, why? **NON-SYMMETRICAL; EARTH TWIN IN 1 REALM OF TIME; TRAVELING TWIN IN 2 REALMS OF TIME.**

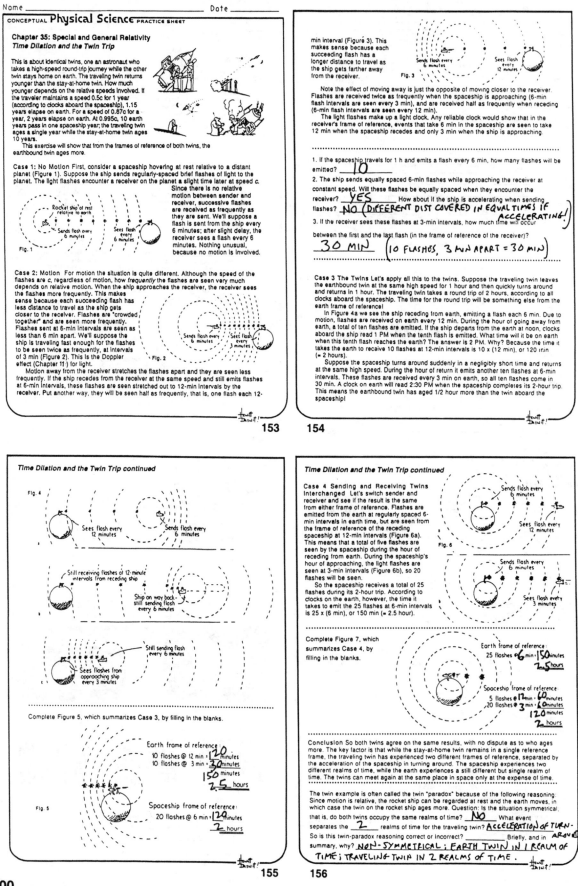

CONCEPTUAL **Physical Science** PRACTICE SHEET

Chapter 35: Special and General Relativity
Relativistic Time Dilation

This practice sheet recaps the *twin trip* of the previous practice sheets, where a traveling twin takes a 2-hour journey while a stay-at-home bother records the passage of 2 1/2 hours. Quite remarkable! Times in both frames of reference are marked by flashes of light, sent each 6 minutes from the spaceship, and received on earth at 12-min intervals for the ship going away, and 3-min intervals for the ship returning. Fill in the clock readings aboard the spaceship when each flash is emitted, and the clock reading on earth when each flash is received

SHIP LEAVING EARTH		
FLASH	TIME ON SHIP WHEN FLASH SENT	TIME ON EARTH WHEN FLASH SEEN
0	12:00	12:00
1	12:06	12:12
2	12:12	12:24
3	12:18	12:36
4	12:24	12:48
5	12:30	01:00
6	12:36	01:12
7	12:42	01:24
8	12:48	01:36
9	12:54	01:48
10	01:00	02:00

SHIP APPROACHING EARTH		
FLASH	TIME ON SHIP WHEN FLASH SEEN	TIME ON EARTH WHEN FLASH SEEN
11	01:06	02:03
12	01:12	02:06
13	01:18	02:09
14	01:24	02:12
15	01:30	02:15
16	01:36	02:18
17	01:42	02:21
18	01:48	02:24
19	01:54	02:27
20	02:00	02:30

THIS CHECKS FOR V = 0.6c

$$t = \frac{t_0}{\sqrt{1-(\frac{v}{c})^2}} = \frac{2h}{\sqrt{1-(0.6)^2}} = 2.5 h$$

157

CONCEPTUAL Physical Science PRACTICE SHEET

Appendix B: Rotational Mechanics
Mobile Torques

1. Apply what you know about torques by making a mobile. Shown below are five horizontal arms with fixed 1- and 2-kg masses attached, and four hangers with ends that fit in the loops of the arms, lettered A through R. You are to figure where the loops should be attached so that when the whole system is suspended from the spring scale at the top, it will hang as a proper mobile, with its arms suspended horizontally. This is best done by working from the bottom upward. Circle the loops where the hangers should be attached. When the mobile is complete, how many kilograms will be indicated on the scale? (Assume the horizontal struts and connecting hooks are practically massless compared to the 1- and 2-kg masses.) On a separate sheet of paper, make a sketch of your completed mobile.

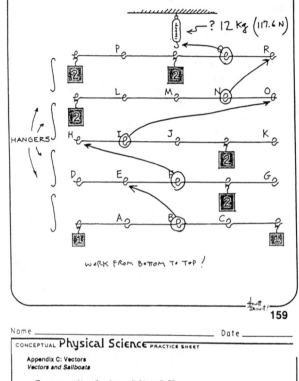

HANGERS

WORK FROM BOTTOM TO TOP !

? 12 Kg (117.6 N)

159

Torques and See-Saws

1. Complete the data for the three seesaws in equilibrium.

W = 500 N

W = 250 N

W = 300 N   W = 400 N

$600 N \times 1m = W \times 3m$
$W = \dfrac{600 N \times 1m}{3m} = 200 N$

W = 600 N   W OF BOARD = 200 N

2. The broom balances at its CG. If you cut the broom in half at the CG and weigh each part of the broom, which end would weigh more?

   PIECE WITH BRUSH WEIGHS MORE

   Explain why each end has or does not have the same weight? (Hint: Compare this to one of the seesaw systems above.)

   WEIGHT ON EITHER SIDE ISN'T SAME, BUT TORQUE IS !
   LIKE SEESAWS ABOVE, SHORTER LEVER ARM HAS MORE WEIGHT

160

CONCEPTUAL Physical Science PRACTICE SHEET

Appendix C: Vectors
Vectors and Sailboats

(Do not attempt this until you have studied Appendix D!)

1. The sketch shows a top view of a small railroad car pulled by a rope. The force *F* that the rope exerts on the car has one component along the track, and another component perpendicular to the track.

   a. Draw these components on the sketch. Which component is larger?
      PERPENDICULAR COMP.

   b. Which component produces acceleration?
      COMP PARALLEL TO TRACK

   c. What would be the effect of pulling on the rope if it were perpendicular to the track?
      NO ACCELERATION

2. The sketches below represent simplified top views of sailboats in a cross-wind direction. The impact of the wind produces a FORCE vector on each as shown. (We do NOT consider *velocity* vectors here!)

   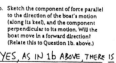

   a. Why is the position of the sail above useless for propelling the boat along its forward direction? (Relate this to Question 1c. above. Where the train is constrained by tracks to move in one direction, the boat is similarly constrained to move along one direction by its deep vertical fin — the *keel*.)
      AS IN 1C ABOVE, THERE'S NO COMP PARALLEL TO DIRECTION OF MOTION.

   b. Sketch the component of force parallel to the direction of the boat's motion (along its keel), and the component perpendicular to its motion. Will the boat move in a forward direction? (Relate this to Question 1b. above.)
      YES, AS IN 1b ABOVE, THERE IS A COMP PARALLEL TO DIRECTION of MOTION.

161

Vectors and Sailboats continued

3. The boat to the right is oriented at an angle into the wind. Draw the force vector and its forward and perpendicular components.

   a. Will the boat move in a forward direction and tack into the wind? Why or why not?
      YES BECAUSE THERE IS A COMPONENT OF FORCE PARALLEL TO THE DIRECTION OF MOTION.

4. The sketch below is a top view of five identical sailboats. Where they exist, draw force vectors to represent wind impact on the sails. Then draw components parallel and perpendicular to the keels of each boat.

   a. Which boat will sail the fastest in a forward direction?
      BOAT 4 (WILL USUALLY EXCEED BOAT 1)

   b. Which will respond least to the wind?
      BOAT 2 (OR BOAT 3) *

   c. Which will move in a backward direction?
      BOAT 5

   d. Which will experience less and less wind impact with increasing speed?
      BOAT 1 (NO IMPACT AT WIND SPEED)

   * THE WIND MISSES THE SAIL OF BOAT 2, AND THERE'S NO COMPONENT PARALLEL TO THE KEEL FOR BOAT 3.

162

202

Answers and Solutions to Odd-Numbered Exercises and Problems from *Conceptual Physical Science—Third Edition*

Chapter 1: Patterns of Motion and Equilibrium
Answers to Exercises

1. Aristotle would likely say the ball slows to reach its natural state. Galileo would say the ball is encountering friction, an unbalanced force that slows it.

3. When rolling down it is going with gravity. Going up, against. (There are force components in the direction of motion, as we shall see later.) When moving horizontally, gravity is perpendicular, neither speeding or slowing the ball.

5. The piece of iron has more mass, but less volume. The answers are different because they address completely different concepts.

7. Like the massive ball that resists motion when pulled by the string, the massive anvil resists moving against Paul when hit with the hammer. Inertia in action.

9. The weight of a 10-kg object on the earth is 98 N, and on the moon 1/6 of this, or 16.3 N. The mass would be 10 kg in any location.

11. From $\Sigma F = 0$, the upward forces are 400 N, and the downward forces are 250 N + weight of the staging. So the staging must weigh 150 N.

13. No, not unless the force is zero. A net force will accelerate the object.

15. In the left figure, Harry is supported by two strands of rope that share his weight (like the little girl in the previous exercise). So each strand supports only 250 N, below the breaking point. Total force up supplied by ropes equals weight acting downward, giving a net force of zero and no acceleration. In the right figure, Harry is now supported by one strand, which for Harry's well-being requires that the tension be 500 N. Since this is above the breaking point of the rope, it breaks. The net force on Harry is then only his weight, giving him a downward acceleration of g. The sudden return to zero velocity changes his vacation plans.

17. Yes, for it doesn't change its state of motion (accelerate). Strictly speaking, some friction does act so it is close to being in equilibrium.

19. No, for the force of gravity acts on the object. It's motion undergoing change, as a moment later should be evident.

21. The friction force is opposite the velocity. Acceleration will be in the opposite direction to velocity, and therefore in the same direction as friction.

23. Constant velocity means constant direction, so your friend should say "…at a constant *speed* of 100 km/h."

25. Not very, for his speed will be zero relative to the land.

27. 10 m/s.

29. As water falls it picks up speed. Since the same amount of water issues from the faucet each second, it stretches out as distance increases. It becomes thinner just as taffy that is stretched gets thinner the more it is stretched. When the water is stretched too far, it breaks up into droplets.

31. Both hit the ground with the same speed (but not in the same time).

33. Acceleration is 10 m/s², constant, all the way down. (Velocity, however, is 50 m/s at 5 seconds, and 100 m/s at 10 seconds.)

35. (a) Average speed is greater for the ball on track B.
(b) The instantaneous speed at the ends of the tracks is the same because the speed gained on the down-ramp for B is equal to the speed lost on the up-ramp side. (Many people get the wrong answer for Exercise 35 because they assume that because the balls end up with the same speed that they roll for the same time. Not so.)

Solutions to Odd-Numbered Problems

1. (a) 30 N + 20 N = 50 N. (b) 30 N – 20 N = 10 N.

3. From $\Sigma F = 0$, friction equals weight, mg,
= (100 kg)(9.8 m/s²) = 980 N.

5. $a = \dfrac{change\ in\ velocity}{time\ interval} = \dfrac{-100\ km/h}{10s} = $ -10 km/h·s.
(The vehicle decelerates at 10 km/h·s.)

7. Since it starts going up at 40 m/s and loses 10 m/s each second, its time going up is 4 seconds. Its time returning is also 4 seconds, so it's in the air for a total of 8 seconds. Distance up (or down) is $1/2\ gt^2 = 5 \times 4^2 = 80$ m. Or from $d = vt$, where average velocity is $(40 + 0)/2 = 20$ m/s, and time is 4 seconds, we also get $d = 20$ m/s $\times 4$ s $= 80$ m.

9. Airborne for one second means 0.5 seconds up (and 0.5 s down). So $d = 1/2\ gt^2 = 1/2\ 10\ (0.5)^2 = 5(0.25) = 1.25$ m. Airborne for one second means 0.5 seconds up (and 0.5 s down). $V = at = 10$ m/s$^2(0.5$ s$) = 0.5$ m/s.

Chapter 2: Newton's Laws of Motion
Answers to Exercises

1. Poke or kick the boxes. The one that more greatly resists a change in motion is the one with the greater mass—the one filled with sand.

3. The massive cleaver tends to keep moving when it encounters the vegetables, cutting them more effectively.

5. Newton's first law again—when the stone is released it is already moving as fast as the ship, and this horizontal motion continues as the stone falls. Much more about this in Chapter 6.

7. You exert a force to overcome the force of friction. This makes the net force zero, which is why the wagon moves without acceleration. If you pull harder, then net force will be greater than zero and acceleration will occur.

9. Let Newton's second law guide the answer to this; $a = F/m$. As m gets less (much the mass of the fuel), acceleration a increases for a constant force.

11. The sudden stop involves a large acceleration. So in accord with $a = F/m$, a large a means a large F. Ouch!

13. When air resistance affects motion, the ball thrown upward returns to its starting level with less speed than its initial speed; and also less speed than the ball tossed downward. So the downward thrown ball hits the ground below with a greater speed.

15. The scale will read 100 N, the same that it would read if one of the ends were tied to a wall instead of tied to the 100-N hanging weight. Although the net force on the system is zero, the tension in the rope within the system is 100 N, as shown on the scale reading.

17. Held at rest the net force on the apple is zero. When released the net force is mg.

19. Neither a stick of dynamite nor anything else "contains" force. We will see later that a stick of dynamite contains *energy*, which is capable of producing forces when an interaction of some kind occurs.

21. When the barbell is accelerated upward, the force exerted by the athlete is greater than the weight of the barbell (the barbell, simultaneously, pushes with greater force against the athlete). When acceleration is downward, the force supplied by the athlete is less.

23. 1000 N.

25. As in the preceding exercise, the force on each cart will be the same. But since the masses are different, the accelerations will differ. The twice-as-massive cart will undergo only half the acceleration of the less massive cart and will gain only half the speed.

27. In accord with Newton's 3rd law, the force on each will be of the same magnitude. But the effect of the force (acceleration) will be different for each because of the different mass. The more massive truck undergoes less change in motion than the motorcycle.

29. The person with twice the mass slides half as far as the twice-as-massive person. That means the lighter one slides 4 feet and the heavier one slides 8 feet (for a total of 12 feet).

31. In accord with Newton's third law, Steve and Gretchen are touching each other. One may initiate the touch, but the physical interaction can't occur without contact between both Steve and Gretchen. Indeed, you cannot touch without being touched!

33. The terminal speed attained by the falling cat is the same whether it falls from 50 stories or 20 stories. Once terminal speed is reached, falling extra distance does not affect the speed. (The low terminal velocities of small creatures enables them to fall without harm from heights that would kill larger creatures.)

35. Before reaching terminal velocity, weight is greater than air resistance. After reaching terminal velocity both weight and air resistance are of the same magnitude. Then the net force and acceleration are both zero.

37. Air resistance is not really negligible for so high a drop, so the heavier ball does strike the ground first. (This idea is shown in Figure 2.15.) But although a twice-as-heavy ball strikes first, it falls only a little faster, and not twice as fast, which is what followers of Aristotle believed. Galileo recognized that the small difference is due to friction and would not be present if there were no friction.

39. A hammock stretched tightly has more tension in the supporting ropes than one that sags. The tightly stretched ropes are more likely to break.

41. No, for the component of your velocity in a direction perpendicular to the water flow (directly across the river) does not depend on stream speed. The total distance you travel while swimming across, however, *does* depend on stream speed. For a swift current you'll be swept farther downstream, but the crossing time will remain the same.

43. (a) The other vector is upward as shown. (b) It is called the normal force.

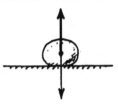

45. a) As shown. (b) Upward tension force is greater to result in upward net force.

47. The acceleration of the stone at the top of its path, or anywhere where the net force on the stone is mg, is g.

49. (a) As shown.
(b) Note the resultant of both normals is equal and opposite to the stone's weight.

Solutions to Chapter 2 Problems

1. Constant velocity means zero acceleration, and therefore zero net force. So the friction force must be equal to the bear's weight, mg.

3. Acceleration $a = F_{net}/m = (20\ N - 12\ N)/2\ kg = 8\ N/2\ kg = 4\ m/s^2$.

5. Acceleration $a = F_{net}/m = 2N/2\ kg = 1\ m/s^2$, the same.

7. $F = ma = (100{,}000\ kg)(2\ m/s^2) = 200{,}000\ N.$

9. $F_{net} = (mg - f) = (800\ N - f) = ma = 80\ kg \times 4\ m/s^2 = 320\ N.$
So $f = 800\ N - 320\ N = 480\ N.$

11. The wall pushes with equal magnitude on you, 30 N. Acceleration $a = F_{net}/m = 30\ N/60\ kg = 0.5\ m/s^2.$

13. Acceleration $a = F_{net}/m = \sqrt{[(3.0\ N)^2 + (4.0\ N)^2]}/5\ kg = 1.0\ m/s^2.$

15. By the Pythagorean theorem,
$V = \sqrt{[(120\ m/s)^2 + (90\ m/s)^2]} = 150\ m/s.$

Chapter 3: Momentum and Energy
Answers to Exercises

1. A steady collapse in a crash extends the time that the seat belt and air bags slow the passengers less violently.

3. The time during which momentum decreases is lengthened, thereby decreasing the jolting force of the rope. Note that in all of these examples, bringing a person to a stop more gently does *not* reduce the impulse. It only reduces the force.

5. When the moving egg makes contact with a sagging sheet, the time it takes to stop it is extended. More time means less force, and a less-likely broken egg.

7. Impact with a boxing glove extends the time during which momentum of the fist is reduced, and lessens the force. A punch with a bare fist involves less time and therefore more force.

9. Without this slack, a locomotive might simply sit still and spin its wheels. The loose coupling enables a longer time for the entire train to gain momentum, requiring less force of the locomotive wheels against the track. In this way, the overall required impulse is broken into a series of smaller impulses. (This loose coupling can be very important for braking as well.)

11. The momentum of both bug and bus change by the same amount because both the amount of force and the time, and therefore the amount of impulse, is the same on each. Momentum is conserved. Speed is another story. Because of the huge mass of the bus, its reduction of speed is very tiny—too small for the passengers to notice.

13. Oops, the conservation of momentum was overlooked. Your momentum forward equals (approximately) the momentum of the recoiling raft.

15. The magnitude of force, impulse, and change in momentum will be the same for each. The Civic undergoes the greater acceleration because its mass is less.

17. If the rocket and its exhaust gases are treated as a single system, the forces between rocket and exhaust gases are internal, and momentum in the rocket-gases system is conserved. So any momentum given to the gases is equal and opposite to momentum given to the rocket. A rocket attains momentum by giving momentum to the exhaust gases.

19. We assume the equal strengths of the astronauts means that each throws with the same speed. Since the masses are equal, when the first throws the second, both the first and second move away from each other at equal speeds. Say the thrown astronaut moves to the right with velocity V, and the first recoils with velocity $-V$. When the third makes the catch, both she and the second move to the right at velocity $V/2$ (twice the mass moving at half the speed, like the freight cars in Figure 3.13). When the third makes her throw, she recoils at velocity V (the same speed she imparts to the thrown astronaut) which is added to the $V/2$ she acquired in the catch. So her velocity is $V + V/2 = 3V/2$, to the right—too fast to stay in the game. Why? Because the velocity of the second astronaut is $V/2 - V = -V/2$, to the left—too slow to catch up with the first astronaut who is still moving at $-V$. the game is over. Both the first and the third got to throw the second astronaut only once!

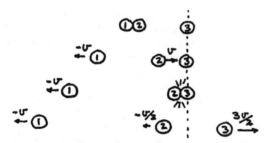

21. They may fly in opposite directions wherein the momenta cancel to zero. But if moving, there is no way kinetic energy can cancel. Hence the difference between a vector quantity (momentum) and a scalar quantity (kinetic energy).

23. When a cannon with a long barrel is fired, more work is done as the cannonball is pushed through the longer distance. A greater KE is the result of the greater work, so of course, the cannonball emerges with a greater velocity. (It might be mentioned that the force acting on the bullet is not constant, but decreases with increasing distance inside the barrel.)

25. If an object has KE, then it must have momentum—for it is moving. But it can have potential energy without being in motion, and therefore without having momentum. And every object has "energy of being"—stated in the celebrated equation $E = mc^2$. So whether an object moves or not, it has some form of energy. If it has KE, then with respect to the frame of reference in which its KE is measured, it also has momentum.

27. Energy is dissipated into non-useful forms in an inefficient machine, and is "lost" only in the loose sense of the word. In the strict sense, it can be accounted for and is therefore not lost.

29. Twenty-five times as much energy (as speed is squared for kinetic energy).

31. The KE of a pendulum bob is maximum where it moves fastest, at the lowest point; PE is maximum at the uppermost points; When the pendulum bob swings by the point that marks half its maximum height, it has half its maximum KE, and its PE is halfway between its minimum and maximum values. If we define PE = 0 at the bottom of the swing, the place where KE is half its maximum value is also the place where PE is half its maximum value, and KE = PE at this point. (In accordance with energy conservation: total energy = KE + PE).

33. No work is done on the bob by the string because the string tension is everywhere perpendicular to the path of the bob. There is no component of this string tension along the bob's path. But gravity is another story. The force of gravity acts downward, producing a component that does lie along the bob's path. It is this component of force that is responsible for the changing speed of the bob. Interestingly, the only place where there is no component of gravitational force on the bob is at the very bottom of its path. If it is moving, it overshoots this point. If the bob is at rest, it remains at rest here.

35. Both will have the same speed because both have the same PE at the ends of the track—and therefore same KEs. This is a relatively easy question to answer because *speed* is asked for, whereas the similar question in Chapter 1 asked for which ball got to the end sooner. The question asked for *time*—which meant first establishing which ball had the greater average speed.

37. Your friend may not realize that mass itself is congealed energy, so you tell your friend that much more energy in its congealed form is put into the reactor than is taken out from the reactor. Almost 1% of the mass of fission fuel is converted to energy of other forms.

39. An engine that is 100% efficient would not be warm to the touch, nor would its exhaust heat the air, nor would it make any noise, nor would it vibrate. This is because all these are transfers of energy, which cannot happen if all the energy given to the engine is transformed to useful work.

Solutions to Chapter 3 Problems

1. From $Ft = \Delta mv$, $F = \Delta mv/t = (1000 \text{ kg})(20 \text{ m/s})/10 \text{ s} = 2000 \text{ N}$.
   (Can you see this could also be solved by Newton's second law:
   $F = ma = (1000 \text{ kg})(20 \text{ m/s}/10 \text{ s}) = 2000 \text{ N}$.)

3. a. Momentum before lunch = momentum after lunch
   $(5 \text{ kg})(1 \text{ m/s}) + 0 = (5 \text{ kg} + 1 \text{ kg})v$
   $5 \text{ kg·m/s} = (6 \text{ kg}) \, v$
   $v = 5/6 \text{ m/s}$.
   b. Momentum before lunch = momentum after lunch
   $(5 \text{ kg})(1 \text{ m/s}) + 1 \text{ kg } (-4 \text{ m/s}) = (5 \text{ kg} + 1 \text{ kg}) \, 3v$
   $5 \text{ kg·m/s} - 4 \text{ kg·m/s} = (6 \text{ kg}) \, v$
   $v = 1/6 \text{ m/s}$

5. The freight cars have only half the KE possessed by the single car before collision. Here's how to figure it:
   $KE_{before} = 1/2 \, mv^2$.
   $KE_{after} = 1/2 \, (2m)(v/2)^2 = 1/2 \, (2m) \, v^2/4 = 1/4 \, mv^2$.
   What becomes of this energy? Most of it goes into nature's graveyard—thermal energy.

7. $(Fd)_{input} = (Fd)_{output}$
   $(100 \text{ N} \times 10 \text{ cm})_{input} = (? \times 1 \text{ cm})_{output}$
   So we see that the output force is 1000 N (or less if the efficiency is less than 100%).

9. Efficiency = (mechanical power output)/(power input) = $(2000 \text{ N} \times 1 \text{ m})/3000 \text{ J} = 0.66$, or 66%.

11. $v = \sqrt{2gh}$. As an object falls though a distance h, its loss of PE is mgh. This converted to KE ($1/2 \, mv^2$). From $mgh = 1/2 \, mv^2$, we see after canceling m and rearranging terms that $v = \sqrt{2gh}$.

Chapter 4: Newton's Law of Universal Gravitation
Answers to Exercises

1. Nothing to be concerned about on this consumer label. It simply states the universal law of gravitation, which applies to *all* products. It looks like the manufacturer knows some physics and has a sense of humor.

3. In accord with the law of inertia, the moon would move in a straight-line path instead of circling both the sun and earth.

5. The force of gravity is the same on each because the masses are the same, as Newton's equation for gravitational force verifies. When dropped the crumpled paper falls faster only because it encounters less air drag than the sheet.

7. If gravity between the moon and its rocks vanished, the rocks, like the moon, would continue in their orbital path around the earth. The assumption ignores the law of inertia.

9. Nearer the moon.

11. Your weight would decrease if the earth expanded with no change in its mass and would increase if the earth contracted with no change in its mass. Your mass and the earth's mass don't change, but the distance between you and the earth's center does change. Force is proportional to the inverse square of this distance.

13. By the geometry of Figure 4.5 on page 98, tripling the distance from the small source spreads the light over 9 times the area, or 9 m². Five times the distance spreads the light over 25 times the area, or 25 m², and for 10 times as far, 100 m².

15. The high-flying jet plane is not in free fall. It moves at approximately constant velocity so a passenger experiences no net force. The upward support force of the seat matches the downward pull of gravity, providing the sensation of weight. The orbiting space vehicle, on the other hand, is in a state of free fall. No support force is offered by a seat, for it falls at the same rate as the passenger. With no support force, the force of gravity on the passenger is not sensed as weight.

17. Gravitational force is indeed acting on a person who falls off a cliff, and on a person in a space shuttle. Both are falling under the influence of gravity.

19. If the station spins like a giant wheel, occupants inside the outer rim will experience a support force that acts like gravity.

21. The direction of the force is radial, toward the center of rotation.

23. Your weight decreases as you ascend, and is zero at the axis.

25. The gravitational pull of the sun on the earth is greater than the gravitational pull of the moon (page 105). The tides, however, are caused by the *differences* in gravitational forces by the moon on opposite sides of the earth. The difference in gravitational forces by the

moon on opposite sides of the earth is greater than the corresponding difference in forces by the stronger pulling but much more distant sun.

27. No. Tides are caused by differences in gravitational pulls. If there are no differences in pulls, there are no tides.

29. Lowest tides occur along with highest tides—spring tides. So the spring tide cycle consists of higher-than-average high tides followed by lower-than-average low tides (best for digging clams!).

31. Because of its relatively small size, different parts of the Mediterranean Sea are essentially equidistant from the moon (or from the sun). As a result, one part is not pulled with any appreciably different force than any other part. This results in extremely tiny tides. The same argument applies, with even more force, to smaller bodies of water, such as lakes, ponds, and puddles. In a glass of water under a full moon you'll detect no tides because no part of the water surface is closer to the moon than any other part of the surface. Tides are caused by appreciable differences in pulls.

33. Yes, the earth's tides would be due only to the sun. They'd occur twice per day (every 12 hours instead of every 12.5 hours) due to the earth's daily rotation.

35. From the nearest body, the earth.

37. More fuel is required for a rocket that leaves the earth to go to the moon than the other way around. This is because a rocket must move against the greater gravitational field of the earth most of the way. (If launched from the moon to the earth, then it would be traveling with the earth's field most of the way.)

39. You weigh a tiny bit less in the lower part of a massive building because the mass of the building above pulls upward on you.

Solutions to Chapter 4 Problems

1. From $F = GmM/d^2$, five times d squared is $1/25$ d, which means the force is 25 times greater.

3. $g = \dfrac{GM}{d^2}$ $= \dfrac{(6.67 \times 10^{-11})(6.0 \times 10^{24})}{[(6380 + 200) \times 10^3]^2}$ $=$

9.24 N/kg, or 9.24 m/s^2; 9.24/9.8 = 0.94 or

94%.

Chapter 5: Projectile and Satellite Motion
Answers to Exercises

1. When air resistance is negligible, the vertical component of motion for a projectile is identical to that of free fall.

3. Minimum speed occurs at the top, which is the same as the horizontal component of velocity anywhere along the path.

5. The path of the falling object will be a parabola as seen by an observer off to the side on the ground. You, however, will see the object fall straight down along a vertical path beneath you. You'll be directly above the point of impact. In the case of air resistance, where the airplane maintains constant velocity via its engines while air resistance decreases the horizontal component of velocity for the falling object, impact will be somewhere behind the airplane.

7. Kicking the ball at angles greater than 45° sacrifices some distance to gain extra time. A 45° kick doesn't go as far, but stays in the air longer, giving players on the kicker's team a chance to run down field and be close to the player on the other team who catches the ball.

9. The bullet falls beneath the projected line of the barrel. To compensate for the bullet's fall, the barrel is elevated. How much elevation depends on the velocity and distance to the target. Correspondingly, the gunsight is raised so the line of sight from the gunsight to the end of the barrel extends to the target. If a scope is used, it is tilted downward to accomplish the same line of sight

11. Hang time depends only on the vertical component of your lift-off velocity. If you can increase this vertical component from a running position rather than from a dead stop, perhaps by bounding harder against the ground, then hang time is also increased. In any case, hang time depends *only* on the vertical component of your lift-off velocity.

13. Gravity changes the speed of a cannonball when the cannonball moves in the direction of earth gravity. At low speeds, the cannonball curves downward and gains speed because there is a component of the force of gravity along its direction of motion. Fired fast enough, however, the curvature matches the curvature of the earth so the cannonball moves at right angles to the force of gravity. With no component of force along its direction of motion, its speed remains constant.

15. Yes, the shuttle is accelerating, as evidenced by its continual change of direction. It accelerates due to the gravitational force between it and the earth. The acceleration is toward the earth's center.

17. Neither the speed of a falling object (without air resistance) nor the speed of a satellite in orbit depends on its mass. In both cases, a greater mass (greater inertia) is balanced by a correspondingly greater gravitational force, so the acceleration remains the same ($a = F/m$, Newton's 2nd law).

19. The moon has no atmosphere (because escape velocity at the moon's surface is less than the speeds of any atmospheric gases). A satellite 5 km above the earth's surface is still in considerable atmosphere, as well as in range of some mountain peaks. Atmospheric drag is the factor that most determines orbiting altitude.

21. Rockets for launching satellites into orbit are fired easterly to take advantage of the spin of the earth. Any point on the equator of the earth moves at nearly 0.5 km/s with respect to the center of the earth or the earth's polar axis. This extra speed does not have to be provided by the rocket engines. At higher latitudes, this "extra free ride" is less.

23. Hawaii is closer to the equator, and therefore has a greater tangential speed about the polar axis. This speed could be added to the launch speed of a satellite and thereby save fuel.

25. The component along the direction of motion does work on the satellite to change its speed. The component perpendicular to the direction of motion changes its direction of motion.

27. The period of any satellite at the same distance from earth as the moon would be the same as the moon's, 28 days.

29. The plane of a satellite coasting in orbit intersects the earth's center. If its orbit were tilted relative to the equator, it would be sometimes over the northern hemisphere, sometimes over the southern hemisphere. To stay over a fixed point off the equator, it would have to be following a circle whose center is not at the center of the earth.

31. No, for an orbit in the plane of the Arctic Circle does not intersect the earth's center. All earth satellites orbit in a plane that intersects the center of the earth. A satellite may pass over the Arctic Circle, but cannot remain above it indefinitely, as a satellite can over the equator.

33. When a capsule is projected rearward at 7 km/s with respect to the spaceship, which is itself moving forward at 7 km/s with respect to the earth, the speed of the capsule with respect to the earth will be zero. It will have no tangential speed for orbit. What will happen? It will simply drop vertically to earth and crash.

35. This is similar to Exercises 33 and 34. The tangential velocity of the earth about the sun is 30 km/s. If a rocket carrying the radioactive wastes were fired at 30 km/s from the earth in the direction opposite to the earth's orbital motion about the sun, the wastes would have no tangential velocity with respect to the sun. They would simply fall into the sun.

37. The half brought to rest will fall vertically to earth. The other half, in accord with the conservation of linear momentum will have twice the initial velocity, overshoot the circular orbit, and enter an elliptical orbit.

39. The satellite experiences the greatest gravitational force at A, where it is closest to the earth; and the greatest speed and the greatest velocity at A, and by the same token the greatest momentum and greatest kinetic energy at A, and the greatest gravitational potential energy at the farthest point C. It would have the same total energy (KE + PE) at all parts of its orbit because it's conserved. It would have the greatest acceleration at A, where F/m is greatest.

Solutions to Chapter 5 Problems

1. One second after being thrown, its horizontal component of velocity is 10 m/s, and its vertical component is also 10 m/s. By the Pythagorean theorem, $V = \sqrt{(10^2 + 10^2)} = 14.1$ m/s. (It is moving at a 45° angle.)

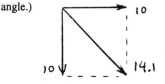

3. 100 m/s. At the top of its trajectory, the vertical component of velocity is zero, leaving only the horizontal component. The horizontal component at the top or anywhere along the path is the same as the initial horizontal component, 100 m/s (the side of a square where the diagonal is 141).

5. John and Tracy's horizontal jumping velocity will be the horizontal distance traveled divided by the time of the jump. The horizontal distance will be a minimum of 20 m, but what will be the time? Aha, the same time it would take John and Tracy to fall straight down!

$$d = 5\, t^2, \text{ where rearrangement gives } t = \sqrt{\frac{d}{5}}$$

$$= \sqrt{\frac{80}{5}} \qquad = 4 \text{ s.}$$

So to travel 20 m horizontally in this time means John and Tracy should jump horizontally with a velocity of 20 m/4 s = 5 m/s. But this would put them at the edge of the pool, so they should jump a little faster. If we knew the length of the pool, we could calculate how much faster without hitting the far end of the pool. (John and Tracy would be better advised to take the elevator.)

7. Hang time depends only on the vertical component of initial velocity and the corresponding vertical distance attained. From $d = 5t^2$ a vertical 1.25 m drop corresponds to 0.5 s ($t = \sqrt{2d/g} = \sqrt{2(1.25)/10} = 0.5$ s). Double this (time up + time down) and we get a hang time of 1 s. Hang time is the same whatever the horizontal distance traveled.

Chapter 6: Fluid Mechanics
Answers to Exercises

1. The scale measures force, not pressure, and is calibrated to read your weight. That's why your weight on the scale is the same whether you stand on one foot or both.

3. Like the loaf of bread in Figure 6.1, its volume is decreased. Its mass stays the same so the density increases. A whale is denser when it swims deeper in the ocean.

5. A person lying on a waterbed experiences less bodyweight pressure because more of the body is in contact with the supporting surface. The greater area reduces the support pressure.

7. A woman with spike heels exerts considerably more pressure on the ground than an elephant! Example: A 500-N woman with 1-cm^2 spike heels puts half her weight on each foot, distributed (let's say) half on her heel and half on her sole. So the pressure exerted by each heel will be (125 N/1 cm^2) = 125 N/cm^2. A 20,000-N elephant with 1000 cm^2 feet exerting 1/4 its weight on each foot produces (5000N/1000 cm^2) = 5N/cm^2; about 25 times less pressure. (So a woman with spike heels will make greater dents in a new linoleum floor than an elephant will.)

9. In deep water, you are buoyed up by the water displaced and as a result, you don't exert as much pressure against the stones on the bottom. When you are up to your neck in water, you hardly feel the bottom at all.

11. As per the Link to Geology box in the chapter, mountain ranges are very similar to icebergs: both float in a denser medium, and extend farther down into that medium than they extend above it.

13. Heavy objects may or may not sink, depending on their densities (a heavy log floats while a small rock sinks, or a boat floats while a paper clip sinks, for example). People who say that heavy objects sink really mean that

dense objects sink. Be careful to distinguish between how heavy an object is and how dense it is.

15. The water level will fall. This is because the iron will displace a greater amount of water while being supported than when submerged. A floating object displaces its weight of water, which is more than its own volume, while a submerged object displaces only its volume. (This may be illustrated in the kitchen sink with a dish floating in a dishpan full of water. Silverware in the dish takes the place of the scrap iron. Note the level of water at the side of the dishpan, and then throw the silverware overboard. The floating dish will float higher and the water level at the side of the dishpan will fall. Will the volume of the silverware displace enough water to bring the level to its starting point? No, not as long as it is denser than water.)

17. The balloon will sink to the bottom because its density increases with depth. The balloon is compressible, so the increase in water pressure beneath the surface compresses it and reduces its volume, thereby increasing its density. Density is further increased as it sinks to regions of greater pressure and compression. This sinking is understood also from a buoyant force point of view. As its volume is reduced by increasing pressure as it descends, the amount of water it displaces becomes less. The result is a decrease in the buoyant force that initially was sufficient to barely keep it afloat.

19. Since both preservers are the same size, they will displace the same amount of water when submerged and be buoyed up with equal forces. Effectiveness is another story. The amount of buoyant force exerted on the heavy lead-filled preserver is much less than its weight. If you wear it, you'll sink. The same amount of buoyant force exerted on the lighter Styrofoam preserver is greater than its weight and it will keep you afloat. The *amount* of the force and the *effectiveness* of the force are two different things.

21. When the ice cube melts the water level at the side of the glass is unchanged (neglecting temperature effects). To see this, suppose the ice cube to be a 5 gram cube; then while floating it will displace 5 grams of water. But when melted it becomes the same 5 grams of water. Hence the water level is unchanged. The same occurs when the ice cube with the air bubbles melts. Whether the ice cube is hollow or solid, it will displace as much water floating as it will melted. If the ice cube contains grains of heavy sand, however, upon melting, the water level at the edge of the glass will drop. This is similar to the case of the scrap iron of Exercise 15.

23. Because of surface tension, which tends to minimize the surface of a blob of water, its shape without gravity and other distorting forces will be a *sphere*—the shape with the least surface area for a given volume.

25. Some molecules in the earth 's atmosphere *do* go off into outer space—those like helium with speeds greater than escape speed. But the average speeds of most molecules in the atmosphere are well below escape speed, so the atmosphere is held to earth by earth gravity.

27. The density of air in a deep mine is greater than at the surface. The air filling up the mine adds weight and pressure at the bottom of the mine, and according to Boyle's law, greater pressure in a gas means greater density.

29. If the item is sealed in an air-tight package at sea level, then the pressure in the package is about 1 atmosphere. Cabin pressure is reduced somewhat for high altitude flying, so the pressure in the package is greater than the surrounding pressure so the package puffs outwards.

31. The can collapses under the weight of the atmosphere. When water was boiling in the can, much of the air inside was driven out and replaced by steam. Then, with the cap tightly fastened, the steam inside cooled and condensed back to the liquid state, creating a partial vacuum in the can which could not withstand the crushing force of the atmosphere outside.

33. A vacuum cleaner wouldn't work on the moon. A vacuum cleaner operates on Earth because the atmospheric pressure pushes dust into the machine's region of reduced pressure. On the moon there is no atmospheric pressure to push the dust anywhere.

35. Drinking through a straw is slightly more difficult atop a mountain. This is because the reduced atmospheric pressure is less effective in pushing soda up into the straw.

37. One's lungs, like an inflated balloon, are compressed when submerged in water, and the air within is compressed. Air will not of itself flow from a region of low pressure into a region of higher pressure. The diaphragm in one's body reduces lung pressure to permit breathing, but this limit is strained when nearly 1 m below the water surface. It is exceeded at more than 1 m.

39. An object rises in air only when buoyant force exceeds its weight. A steel tank of anything weighing more than the air it displaces won't rise. A helium-filled balloon weighs less than the air it displaces and rises.

41. The rotating habitat is a centrifuge, and denser air is "thrown to" the outer wall. Just as on Earth, the maximum air density is at "ground level," and becomes less with increasing altitude (distance toward the center). Air density in the rotating habitat is least at the zero-g region, the hub.

43. The force of the atmosphere is on both sides of the window; the net force is zero, so windows don't normally break under the weight of the atmosphere. In a strong wind, however, pressure will be reduced on the windward side (Bernoulli's Principle) and the forces no longer cancel to zero. Many windows are blown *outward* in strong winds.

45. (a) Speed increases (so that the same quantity of gas can move through the pipe in the same time). (b) Pressure decreases (Bernoulli's principle). (c) The spacing between the streamlines decreases, because the same number of streamlines fit in a smaller area.

47. The air density and pressure are less at higher altitude, so the wings (and, with them, the whole airplane) are tilted to a greater angle to produce the needed pressure difference between the upper and lower surfaces of the wing. In terms of force and air deflection, the greater angle of attack is needed to deflect a greater volume of lower-density air downward to give the same upward force.

49. The troughs are partially shielded from the wind, so the air moves faster over the crests than in the troughs. Pressure is therefore lower at the top of the crests than down below in the troughs. The greater pressure in the troughs pushes the water into even higher crests.

Solutions to Chapter 6 Problems

1. A 5-kg ball weighs 49 N, so the pressure is 49 N/cm^2 = 490 kPa.

3. Pressure = weight density × depth = 9800 $N/m3$ × 220 m = 2,160,000 $N/m2$ = 2160 kPa.

5. From Table 6.1 the density of gold is 19.3 $g/cm3$. Your gold has a mass of 1000 grams, so 1000 g/V = 19.3 $g/cm3$. Solving for V, V = (1000 g)/(19.3 g/cm^3) = 51.8 cm3.

7. 10% of ice extends above water. So 10% of the 9-cm thick ice would float above the water line; 0.9 cm. So the ice pops up. Interestingly, when mountains erode they become lighter and similarly pop up! Hence it takes a long time for mountains to wear away.

9. According to Boyle's law, the product of pressure and volume is constant (at constant temperature), so one-tenth the volume means ten times the pressure.

11. To find the buoyant force that the air exerts on you, find your volume and multiply by the weight density of air (From Table 6.1 we see that the mass of 1 m^3 of air is about 1.25 kg. Multiply this by 9.8 N/kg and you get 12.25 N/m^3). You can estimate your volume by your weight and by assuming your density is approximately

equal to that of water (a little less if you can float). The weight density of water is 104 N/m³, which we'll assume is your density. By ratio and proportion:
10^4 N/m³ = (your weight in newtons)/(your vol in m³)
If your weight is a heavy 1000 N, for example (about 220 lb), your volume is 0.1 m³.
So buoyant force = 12.25 N/m³ × 0.1 m³ = about 1.2 N, the weight of a big apple). (A useful conversion factor is 4.45 N = 1 pound.) Another way to do this is to say that the ratio of the buoyant force to your weight is the same as the ratio of air density to water density (which is your density). This ratio is 1.25/1000 = 0.00125. Multiply this ratio by your weight to get the buoyant force.

13. To effectively lift (0.25)(80 kg) = 20 kg the mass of displaced air would be 20 kg. Density of air is about 1.2 kg/m³. From density = mass/volume, the volume of 20 kg of air, also the volume of the balloon (neglecting the weight of the hydrogen) would be vol = mass/density = (20 kg)/(1.2 kg/m³) = 16.6 m3, slightly more than 3 m in diameter for a spherical balloon.

15. Lift will equal the difference in force below and above the wing surface. The difference in force will equal the difference in air pressure × wing area. Lift = 0.04 PA = (0.04)(105 N/m²)(100 m²) = 4 × 105 N. (That's about 44 tons.)

Chapter 7: Thermal Energy and Thermodynamics
Answers to Exercises

1. Gas molecules move haphazardly at random speeds. They continually run into one another, sometimes giving kinetic energy to neighbors, sometimes receiving kinetic energy. In this continual interaction, it would be statistically impossible for any large number of molecules to have the same speed. Temperature has to do with average speeds.

3. You cannot establish by your own touch whether or not you are running a fever because there would be no temperature difference between your hand and fore-head. If your forehead is a couple of degrees higher in temperature than normal, your hand is also a couple of degrees higher.

5. The hot coffee has a higher temperature, but not a greater internal energy. Although the iceberg has less internal energy per mass, its enormously greater mass gives it a greater total energy than that in the small cup of coffee. (For a smaller volume of ice, the fewer number of more energetic molecules in the hot cup of coffee may constitute a greater total amount of internal energy—but not compared to an iceberg.)

7. No, for a difference of 273 in 10,000,000 is insignificant.

9. Work is done in compressing the air, which in accord with the first law of thermodynamics, increases its thermal energy. This is evident by its increased temperature.

11. You do work on the liquid when you vigorously shake it, which increases its thermal energy. The temperature change should be noticeable.

13. The tires heat up, which heats the air within. The molecules in the heated air move faster, which increases air pressure in the tires.

15. The brick will cool off too fast and you'll be cold in the middle of the night. Bring a jug of hot water with its higher specific heat to bed and you'll make it through the night.

17. Different substances have different thermal properties due to differences in the way energy is stored internally in the substances. When the same amount of heat produces different changes in temperatures in two substances of the same mass, we say they have different specific heat capacities. Each substance has its own characteristic specific heat capacity. Temperature measures the average kinetic energy of random motion, but not other kinds of energy.

19. The climate of Bermuda, like that of all islands, is moderated by the high specific heat of water. What moderates the climates are the large amounts of energy given off and absorbed by water for small changes in temperature. When the air is cooler than the water, the water warms the air; when the air is warmer than the water, the water cools the air.

21. In winter months when the water is warmer than the air, the air is warmed by the water to produce a seacoast climate warmer than inland. In summer months when the air is warmer than the water, the air is cooled by the water to produce a seacoast climate cooler than inland. This is why seacoast communities and especially islands do not experience the high and low temperature extremes that characterize inland locations.

23. Water is an exception. Below 4 degrees Celsius, it expands when cooled.

25. When the rivets cool they contract. This tightens the plates being attached.

27. Cool the inner glass and heat the outer glass. If it's done the other way around, the glasses will stick even tighter (if not break).

29. Every part of a metal ring expands when it is heated—not only the thickness, but the outer and inner circumference as well. Hence the ball that normally passes through the hole when the temperatures are equal will more easily pass through the expanded hole when the ring is heated. (Interestingly enough, the hole will expand as much as a disk of the same metal undergoing the same increase in temperature. Blacksmiths mounted metal rims in wooden wagon wheels by first heating the rims. Upon cooling, the contraction resulted in a snug fit.)

31. The gap in the ring will become wider when the ring is heated. Try this: draw a couple of lines on a ring where you pretend a gap to be. When you heat the ring, the lines will be farther apart—the same amount as if a real gap were there. Every part of the ring expands proportionally when heated uniformly—thickness, length, gap and all.

33. Water has the greatest density at 4°C; therefore, either cooling or heating at this temperature will result in an expansion of the water. A small rise in water level would be ambiguous and make a water thermometer impractical in this temperature region.

35. At 0°C it will contract when warmed a little; at 4°C it will expand, and at 6°C it will expand.

37. If cooling occurred at the bottom of a pond instead of at the surface, ice would still form at the surface, but it would take much longer for ponds to freeze. This is because all the water in the pond would have to be reduced to a temperature of 0°C rather than 4°C before the first ice would form. Ice that forms at the bottom where the cooling process is occurring would be less dense and would float to the surface (except for ice that may form on material anchored to the bottom of the pond).

Solutions to Chapter 7 Problems

1. (a) The amount of heat absorbed by the water is $Q = cm\Delta T = (1.0 \text{ cal/g C°})(50.0 \text{ g})(50°C - 22°C) = 1400$ cal. At 40% efficiency only 0.4 the energy from the peanut raises the water temperature, so the calorie content of the peanut is 1400/0.4 = 3500 cal. (b) The food value of a peanut is 3500 cal/0.6 g = 5.8 kilocalories per gram.

3. Each kilogram requires 1 kilocalorie for each degree change, so 100 kg needs 100 kilocalories for each degree change. Twenty degrees means twenty times this, which is 2,000 kcal.

By formula, $Q = mc\Delta T = (100,000 \text{ g})(1 \text{ cal/g°C})(20°C) = 2000$ kcal. We can convert this to joules knowing that 4.18 J = 1 cal. In joules this quantity of heat is 8360 kJ.

5. Heat gained by water = heat lost by nails
$(cm \, \Delta T)_{water} = (cm \, \Delta T)_{nails}$
$(1)(100) \, (T - 20) = (0.12)(100)(40 - T)$, giving
$T = 22.1°C$.

7. By formula: $\Delta L = L_0 \alpha \Delta T =$
$(1300 \text{ m})(11 \times 10^{-6}/°C)(15°C) = 0.21$ m.

Chapter 8: Heat Transfer and Change of Phase
Answers to Exercises

1. No, the coat is not a source of heat, but merely keeps the thermal energy of the wearer from leaving rapidly.

3. Copper and aluminum are better conductors than stainless steel, and therefore more quickly transfer heat to the cookware's interior.

5. In touching the tongue to very cold metal, enough heat can be quickly conducted away from the tongue to bring the saliva to sub-zero temperature where it freezes, locking the tongue to the metal. In the case of relatively non-conducting wood, much less heat is conducted from the tongue and freezing does not take place fast enough for sudden sticking to occur.

7. Heat from the relatively warm ground is conducted by the gravestone to melt the snow in contact with the gravestone. Likewise for trees or any materials that are better conductors of heat than snow, and that extend into the ground.

9. Air is a poor conductor, whatever the temperature. So holding your hand in hot air for a short time is not harmful because very little heat is conducted by the air to your hand. But if you touch the hot conducting surface of the oven, heat readily conducts to you—ouch!

11. Agree, for your friend is correct.

13. The smoke, like hot air, is less dense than the surroundings and is buoyed upward. It cools with contact with the surrounding air and becomes more dense. When its density matches that of the surrounding air, its buoyancy and weight balance and rising ceases.

15. If they have the same temperature, then by definition, they have the same kinetic energies per molecule.

17. As in the explanation of the previous exercise, the molecules of gas with the lesser mass will have the higher average speeds. A look at the periodic table will show that argon (A = 18) has less massive atoms than krypton (A = 36). The faster atoms are those of argon. This is the case whether or not the gases are in separate containers.

19. When we warm a volume of air, we add energy to it. When we expand a volume of air, we normally take energy out of it (because the expanding air does work on its surroundings). So the conditions are quite different and the results will be different. Expanding a volume of air actually lowers its temperature.

21. The heat you received was from radiation.

23. A good reflector is a poor radiator of heat, and a poor reflector is a good radiator of heat.

25. Put the cream in right away for at least three reasons. Since black coffee radiates more heat than white coffee, make it whiter right away so it won't radiate and cool so quickly while you are waiting. Also, by Newton's law of cooling, the higher the temperature of the coffee above the surroundings, the greater will be the rate of cooling—so again add cream right away and lower the temperature to that of a reduced cooling rate, rather than allowing it to cool fast and then bring the temperature down still further by adding the cream later. Also—by adding the cream, you increase the total amount of liquid, which for the same surface area, cools more slowly.

27. Under open skies, the ground radiates upward but the sky radiates almost nothing back down. Under the benches, downward radiation of the benches decreases the net radiation from the ground, resulting in warmer ground and, likely, no frost.

29. Kelvins and Celsius degrees are the same size, and although ratios of these two scales will produce very different results, *differences* in Kelvins and *differences* in Celsius degrees will be the same. Since Newton's law of cooling involves temperature differences, either scale may be used.

31. Turn the air conditioner off altogether to keep ΔT small, as in the preceding answer. Heat leaks at a greater rate into a cold house than into a not-so-cold house. The greater the rate at which heat leaks into the house, the greater the amount of fuel consumed by the air conditioner.

33. In this hypothetical case evaporation would not cool the remaining liquid because the energy of exiting molecules would be no different than the energy of molecules left behind. Although internal energy of the liquid would decrease with evaporation, energy per

molecule would not change. No temperature change of the liquid would occur. (The surrounding air, on the other hand, would be cooled in this hypothetical case. Molecules flying away from the liquid surface would be slowed by the attractive force of the liquid acting on them.)

35. A bottle wrapped in wet cloth will cool by the evaporation of liquid from the cloth. As evaporation progresses, the average temperature of the liquid left behind in the cloth can easily drop below the temperature of the cool water that wet it in the first place. So to cool a bottle of beer, soda, or whatever at a picnic, wet a piece of cloth in a bucket of cool water. Wrap the wet cloth around the bottle to be cooled. As evaporation progresses, the temperature of the water in the cloth drops, and cools the bottle to a temperature below that of the bucket of water.

37. As the bubbles rise, less pressure is exerted on them.

39. When the jar reaches the boiling temperature, further heat does not enter it because it is in thermal equilibrium with the surrounding 100°C water. This is the principle of the "double boiler."

41. As in the answer to the previous exercise, high temperature and the resulting internal energy given to the food are responsible for cooking—if the water boils at a low temperature (presumably under reduced pressure), the food isn't hot enough to cook.

43. The lid on the pot traps heat which quickens boiling; the lid also slightly increases pressure on the boiling water which raises its boiling temperature. The hotter water correspondingly cooks food in a shorter time, although the effect is not significant unless the lid is held down as on a pressure cooker.

45. The wood, because its greater specific heat capacity means it will release more energy in cooling.

47. The answer to this is similar to the previous answer, and also the fact that the coating of ice acts as an insulating blanket. Every gram of water that freezes releases 80 calories, much of it to the fruit; the thin layer of ice then acts as an insulating blanket against further loss of heat.

Solutions to Chapter 8 Problems

1. $0.5\ mgh = cm\Delta T$
$\Delta T = 0.5\ mgh/cm = 0.5\ gh/c = $
$(0.5)(9.8\ \text{m/s}^2)(100\ \text{m})/450\ \text{J/kg} = 1.1°\text{C}.$
Again, note that the mass cancels, so the same temperature would hold for any mass ball, assuming half the heat generated goes into warming the ball. As in the previous problem, the units check because $1\ \text{J/kg} = 1\ \text{m}^2/\text{s}^2.$

3. From -273°C "ice" to 0°C ice requires (273)(0.5) = 140 calories.
From 0°C ice to 0°C water requires 80 calories.
From 0°C water to 100°C water requires 100 calories. The total is 320 calories.
Boiling this water at 100°C takes 540 calories, considerably more energy than it took to bring the water all the way from absolute zero to the boiling point! (In fact, at very low temperature, the specific heat capacity of ice is less than 0.5 cal/g°C, so the true difference is even greater than calculated here.)

5. The final temperature of the water will be the same as that of the ice, 0°C. The quantity of heat given to the ice by the water is $Q = cm\Delta T = (1 \text{ cal/g°C})(50 \text{ g})(80°C) = 4000$ cal. This heat melts ice. How much? From $Q = mL$, $m = Q/L = (4000 \text{ cal})/(80 \text{ cal/g}) = 50$ grams. So water at 80°C will melt an equal mass of ice at 0°C.

Note that the heat of vaporization of ethyl alcohol (200 cal/g) is 2.5 times more than the heat of fusion of water (80 cal/g), so in a change of phase for both, 2.5 times as much ice will change phase; $2.5 \times 2 \text{ kg} = 5$ kg.

Or via formula, the refrigerant would draw away $Q = mL = (2000 \text{ g})(200 \text{ cal/g}) = 4 \times 10^5$ calories.

The mass of ice formed is then $(4 \times 10^5 \text{ cal})/(80 \text{ cal/g}) = 5000$ g, or 5 kg.

Chapter 9: Static and Current Electricity
Answers to Exercises

1. There are no positives and negatives in gravitation—the interactions between masses are only attractive, whereas electrical interactions may be attractive as well as repulsive. The mass of one particle cannot "cancel" the mass of another, whereas the charge of one particle can cancel the effect of the opposite charge of another particle.

3. Excess electrons rubbed from your hair leave it with a positive charge; excess electrons on the comb give it a negative charge.

5. Cosmic rays produce ions in air, which offer a conducting path for the discharge of charged objects. Cosmic-ray particles streaming downward through the atmosphere are attenuated by radioactive decay and by absorption, so the radiation and the ionization are stronger at high altitude than at low altitude. Charged objects more quickly lose their charge at higher altitudes.

7. Electrons are easily dislodged from the outer regions of atoms, but protons are held tightly within the nucleus.

9. The electrons don't fly out of the penny because they are attracted to the five thousand billion billion

positively charged protons in the atomic nuclei of atoms in the penny.

11. The inverse-square law is at play here. At half the distance the electric force field is four times as strong; at 1/4 the distance, 16 times stronger. At four times the distance, one-sixteenth as strong.

13. For both electricity and heat, the conduction is via electrons, which in a metal are loosely bound, easy flowing, and easy to get moving. (Many fewer electrons in metals take part in heat conduction than in electric conduction, however.)

15. The forces on the electron and proton will be equal in magnitude, but opposite in direction. Because of the greater mass of the proton, its acceleration will be less than that of the electron, and be in the direction of the electric field. How much less? Since the mass of the proton is nearly 2000 times that of the electron, its acceleration will be about 1/2000 that of the electron. The greater acceleration of the electron will be in the direction opposite to the electric field. The electron and proton accelerate in opposite directions.

17. Yes, in both cases we have a ratio of energy per something. In the case of temperature, the ratio is energy/molecule. In the case of voltage it is energy/charge. Even with a small numerator, the ratio can be large if the denominator is small enough. Such is the case with the small energies involved to produce high-temperature sparklers and high-voltage metal balls.

19. As the current in the filament of a light bulb increases, the bulb glows brighter.

21. No. The net charge in a wire, whether carrying current or not, is normally zero. The number of electrons is ordinarily offset by an equal number of protons in the atomic lattice. Thus current and charge are not the same thing: Many people think that saying a wire carries current is the same thing as saying a wire is charged. But a wire that is charged carries no current at all unless the charge moves in some uniform direction. And a wire that carries a current is typically not electrically charged and won't affect an electroscope. (If the current consists of a beam of electrons in a vacuum, then the beam would be charged. Current is not charge itself: Current is the *flow* of charge.)

23. Only circuit number 5 is complete and will light the bulb. (Circuits 1 and 2 are "short-circuits" and will quickly drain the cell of its energy. In circuit 3 both ends of the lamp filament are connected to the same terminal and are therefore at the same potential. Only one end of the lamp filament is connected to the cell in circuit 4.)

25. An electric device does not "use up" electricity, but rather *energy*. And strictly speaking, it doesn't "use up" energy, but transforms it from one form to another. It is common to say that energy is used up when it is transformed to less concentrated forms—when it is degraded. Electrical energy ultimately becomes heat energy. In this sense it is used up.

27. Most of the energy, typically 95%, of the electrical energy in an incandescent lamp goes directly to heat. Thermal energy is the graveyard of electrical energy.

29. (a) The resistance will be half, 5 ohms, when cut in half. (b) The resistance will be half again when the cross-sectional area is doubled, so it will be 2.5 ohms.

31. Damage generally occurs by excess heating when too much current is driven through an appliance. For an appliance that converts electrical energy directly to thermal energy this happens when excess voltage is applied. So don't connect a 110-volt iron, toaster, or electric stove to a 220-volt circuit. Interestingly enough, if the appliance is an electric motor, then applying too *little* voltage can result in overheating and burn up the motor windings. (This is because the motor will spin at a low speed and the reverse "generator effect" will be small and allow too great a current to flow in the motor.) So don't hook up a 220-volt power saw or any 220-volt motor-driven appliance to 110 volts. To be safe use the recommended voltages with appliances of any kind.

33. Electric power in your home is likely supplied at 60 hertz and 110-120 volts via electrical outlets. This is ac (and delivered to your home via transformers between the power source and your home. We will see in Chapter 24 that transformers require ac power for operation.) Electric power in your car must be able to be supplied by the battery. Since the + and - terminals of the battery do not alternate, the current they produce does not alternate either. It flows in one direction and is dc.

35. Auto headlights are wired in parallel. Then when one burns out, the other remains lit. If you've ever seen an automobile with one burned out headlight, you have evidence they're wired in parallel.

37. (a) volt, (b) ampere, (c) joule.

39. The equivalent resistance of resistors in parallel is less than the smaller resistance of the two. So connect a pair of resistors in parallel for less resistance.

41. Zero. Power companies do not sell electrons; they sell energy. Whatever number of electrons flow into a home, the same number flows out.

43. Bulbs will glow brighter when connected in parallel, for the voltage of the battery is impressed across each bulb. When two identical bulbs are connected in series, half the voltage of the battery is impressed across each bulb. The battery will run down faster when the bulbs are in parallel.

45. Bulb C is the brightest because the voltage across it equals that of the battery. Bulbs A and B share the voltage of the parallel branch of the circuit and have half the current of bulb C (assuming resistances are independent of voltages). If bulb A is unscrewed, the top branch is no longer part of the circuit and current ceases in both A and B. They no longer give light, while bulb C glows as before. If bulb C is instead unscrewed, then it goes out and bulbs A and B glow as before.

47. What affects the other branches is the voltage impressed across them, and their own resistance—period. Opening or closing a branch doesn't alter either of these.

49. Household appliances are not connected in series for at least two reasons. First, the voltage, current, and power for each appliance would vary with the introduction of other appliances. Second, if one device burns out, the current in the whole circuit ceases. Only if each appliance is connected in parallel to the voltage source can the voltage and current through each appliance be independent of the others.

Solutions to Chapter 9 Problems

1. By the inverse-square law, twice as far is 1/4 the force; 5 N.
   The solution involves relative distance only, so the magnitude of charges is irrelevant.

3. From Coulomb's law, $F = k\dfrac{q_1 q_2}{d^2}$ =

   $(9 \times 10^9)\dfrac{(1.0 \times 10^{-6})^2}{(0.03)^2}$ = 10 N.

   This is the same as the weight of a 1-kg mass.

5. a. $\Delta V = \dfrac{\text{energy}}{\text{charge}}$ = $\dfrac{12 \text{ J}}{0.0001 \text{ C}}$ = 120,000 volts.

   b. ΔV for twice the charge is $\dfrac{24 \text{ J}}{0.0002}$ = same 120 kV.

7. From current = $\dfrac{\text{voltage}}{\text{resistance}}$, resistance = $\dfrac{\text{voltage}}{\text{current}}$ =

   $\dfrac{120 \text{V}}{20 \text{A}}$ = 6 Ω.

9. Two headlights draw 6 amps, so the 60 ampere-hour battery will last for about 10 hours.

11. a. From power = current × voltage, current = power/voltage = 4W/120V = 1/30 A.

b. From current = voltage/resistance (Ohm's law), resistance = voltage/current = 120 V/(1/30 A) = 3600 Ω.

c. First, 4 watts = 0.004 kilowatt. Second, there are 8760 hours in a year (24 hours/day × 365 days = 8760 hours). So 8760 hours × 0.004 kilowatt = 35.0 kWh.

d. At the rate of 20 cents per kWh, the annual cost is 35.0 kWh × $0.20/kWh = $7.00.

31. Since current is charge per unit time, charge is current × time: $q = It$ = (9 A)(60 s) = (9 C/s)(60 s) = 540 C. (Charges of this magnitude on the move are commonplace, but this quantity of charge accumulated in one place would be incredibly large.)

15. The resistance of the toaster is $R = V/I$ = (120 V)/(10 A) = 12 Ω. So when 108 V is applied, the current is $I = V/R$ = (108 V)/(12 W) = 9.0 A and the power is $P = IV$ = (9.0 A)(108 V) = 972 W, only 81 % of the normal power. (Can you see the reason for 81 %? Current and voltage are both decreased by 10 %, and 0.9 × 0.9 = 0.81.)

Chapter 10: Magnetism and Electromagnetic Induction

Answers to Exercises

1. All iron materials are not magnetized because the tiny magnetic domains are most often oriented in random directions and cancel one another's effects.

3. Refrigerator magnets have narrow strips of alternating north and south poles. These magnets are strong enough to hold sheets of paper against a refrigerator door, but have a very short range because the north and south poles cancel a short distance from the magnetic surface.

5. An electron always experiences a force in an electric field because that force depends on nothing more than the field strength and the charge. But the force an electron experiences in a magnetic field depends on an added factor: velocity. If there is no motion of the electron through the magnetic field in which it is located, no magnetic force acts. Furthermore, if motion is along the magnetic field direction, and not at some angle to it, then no magnetic force acts also. Magnetic force, unlike electric force, depends on the velocity of the charge relative to the magnetic field.

7. Apply a small magnet to the door. If it sticks, your friend is wrong because aluminum is not magnetic. If it doesn't stick, your friend might be right (but not necessarily; there are lots of nonmagnetic materials).

9. The net force on a compass needle is zero because its north and south poles are pulled in opposite directions with equal forces in the earth's magnetic field. When the needle is not aligned with the magnetic field of the earth, then a pair of torques (relative to the center of the compass) is produced (Figure 10.4). This pair of equal torques, called a "couple," rotates the needle into alignment with the earth's magnetic field.

11. Yes, for the compass aligns with the earth's magnetic field, which extends from the magnetic pole in the southern hemisphere to the magnetic pole in the northern hemisphere.

13. Back to Newton's 3rd law! Both A and B are equally pulling on each other. If A pulls on B with 50 newtons, then B also pulls on A with 50 newtons. Period!

15. Newton's 3rd law again: Yes, the paper clip, as part of the interaction, certainly does exert a force on the magnet — just as much as the magnet pulls on it. The magnet and paper clip pull equally on each other to comprise the single interaction between them.

17. An electron has to be moving across lines of magnetic field in order to feel a magnetic force. So an electron at rest in a stationary magnetic field will feel no force to set it in motion. In an electric field, however, an electron will be accelerated whether or not it is already moving. (A combination of magnetic and electric fields is used in particle accelerators such as cyclotrons. The electric field accelerates the charged particle in its direction, and the magnetic field accelerates it perpendicular to its direction, causing it to follow a nearly circular path.)

19. When we write *work = force × distance*, we really mean the component of force in the direction of motion multiplied by the distance moved (Chapter 3). Since the magnetic force that acts on a beam of electrons is always perpendicular to the beam, there is no component of magnetic force along the instantaneous direction of motion. Therefore a magnetic field can do no work on a charged particle. (Indirectly, however, a *time-varying magnetic field* can induce an electric field that *can* do work on a charged particle.)

21. Associated with every moving charged particle, electrons, protons, or whatever, is a magnetic field. Since a magnetic field is not unique to moving electrons, there is a magnetic field about moving protons as well. However, it differs in direction. The field lines about the proton beam circle in one direction, whereas the field lines about an electron beam circle in

the opposite direction. (Physicists use a "right-hand rule." If the right thumb points in the direction of motion of a positive particle, the curved fingers of that hand show the direction of the magnetic field. For negative particles, the left hand can be used.)

23. Cosmic ray intensity at the earth's surface would be greater when the earth's magnetic field passed through a zero phase. Fossil evidence suggests the periods of no protective magnetic field may have been as effective in changing life forms as X rays have been in the famous heredity studies of fruit flies.

25. Magnetic levitation will reduce surface friction to near zero. Then only air friction will remain. It can be made relatively small by aerodynamic design, but there is no way to eliminate it (short of sending vehicles through evacuated tunnels). Air friction gets rapidly larger as speed increases.

27. The magnetic domains that become aligned in the iron core contribute to the overall magnetic field of the coil and therefore increase its magnetic induction.

29. A cyclist will coast farther if the lamp is disconnected from the generator. The energy that goes into lighting the lamp is taken from the bike's kinetic energy, so the bike slows down. The work saved by not lighting the lamp will be the extra "force × distance" that allows the bike to coast farther.

31. As in the previous answer, eddy currents induced in the metal change the magnetic field, which in turn changes the ac current in the coils and sets off an alarm.

33. There is no fundamental difference between an electric motor and electric generator. When mechanical energy is put into the device and electricity is produced, we call it a generator. When electrical energy is put in and it spins and does mechanical work, we call it a motor. (While there are usually some practical differences in the designs of motors and generators, some devices are designed to operate either as motors or generators, depending only on whether the input is mechanical or electrical.)

35. In accord with electromagnetic induction, if the magnetic field alternates in the hole of the ring, an alternating voltage will be induced in the ring. Because the ring is metal, its relatively low resistance will result in a correspondingly high alternating current. This current is evident in the heating of the ring.

37. If the light bulb is connected to a wire loop that intercepts changing magnetic field lines from an electromagnet, voltage will be induced which can illuminate the bulb. Change is the key, so the electromagnet should be powered with ac.

39. The iron core increases the magnetic field of the primary coil, as stated in the answer to Exercise 2. The greater field means a greater magnetic field change in the primary, and a greater voltage induced in the secondary. The iron core in the secondary further increases the changing magnetic field through the secondary and further increases the secondary voltage. Furthermore, the core guides more magnetic field lines from the primary to the secondary. The effect of an iron core in the coils is the induction of appreciably more voltage in the secondary.

41. When the secondary voltage is twice the primary voltage and the secondary acts as a source of voltage for a resistive "load," the secondary current is half the value of current in the primary. This is in accord with energy conservation, or since the time intervals for each are the same, "power conservation." Power input = power output; or
(current × voltage)$_{primary}$ = (current × voltage)$_{secondary}$: with numerical values,
$(1 \times V)_{primary} = (1/2 \times 2V)_{secondary}$. (The simple rule power = current × voltage is strictly valid only for dc circuits and ac circuits where current and voltage oscillate in phase. When voltage and current are out of phase, which can occur in a transformer, the net power is less than the product current × voltage. Voltage and current are then not "working together." When the secondary of a transformer is open, for example, connected to nothing, current and voltage in both the primary and the secondary are completely out of phase—that is, one is maximum when the other is zero—and no net power is delivered even though neither voltage nor current is zero.)

43. The voltage impressed across the lamp is 120 V and the current through it is 0.1 A. We see that the first transformer steps the voltage down to 12 V and the second one steps it back up to 120 V. The current in the secondary of the second transformer, which is the same as the current in the bulb, is one-tenth of the current in the primary, or 0.1 A.

45. By symmetry, the voltage and current for both primary and secondary are the same. Hence we see that 12 V is impressed on the meter, with a current of 1 A ac.

47. The bar magnet induces current loops in the surrounding copper as it falls. The current loops produce magnetic fields that tend to repel the magnet as it approaches and attract it as it leaves, exerting a vertical upward force on it, opposite to gravity. The faster the magnet falls, the stronger is this upward force. At some speed, it will match gravity and the magnet will be at terminal speed. From an energy point of view, some of the gravitational potential energy is being transformed to heat in the copper pipe. The

current and therefore no magnetic field are induced to oppose the motion of the falling magnet.

49. Agree with your friend, for light is electromagnetic radiation having a frequency that matches the frequency to which our eyes are sensitive.

Solutions to Chapter 10 Problems

1. If power losses can be ignored, in accord with energy conservation, the power provided by the secondary is also 100W.

3. From the transformer relationship,
$$\frac{\text{primary voltage}}{\text{primary turns}} = \frac{\text{secondary voltage}}{\text{secondary turns}},$$

$$\frac{120\text{V}}{240 \text{ turns}} = \frac{6\text{V}}{\text{x turns}}$$

Solve for x: x = (6 V)(240 turns)/(120 V) = 12 turns

5. (a) Since power is voltage × current, the current supplied to the users is
$$\text{current} = \frac{\text{power}}{\text{voltage}} = \frac{100000 \text{ W}}{12000 \text{ V}} = 8.3 \text{ A.}$$

(b) Voltage in each wire = current × resistance of the wire = (8.3 A)(10 Ω) = 83 V.

(c) In each line, power = current × voltage = (8.3 A)(83 V) = 689 W. The total power wasted as heat is twice this, 1.38 kW. This is a small and tolerable loss. If the transmission voltage were ten times less, the losses to heat in the wires would be 100 times more! Then more energy would go into heat in the wires than into useful applications for the customers. That would not be tolerable. That's why high-voltage transmission is so important.

Chapter 11: Waves and Sound
Answers to Exercises

1. Something that vibrates.

3. As you dip your fingers more frequently into still water, the waves you produce will be of a higher frequency (we see the relationship between "how frequently" and "frequency"). The crests of the higher-frequency waves will be closer together—their wavelengths will be shorter.

5. Think of a period as one cycle in time, and a wavelength as one cycle in space, and a little thought will show that in a time of one period, a wave travels a full wavelength. Formally, we can see this as follows:
distance = speed × time
where speed = frequency × wavelength, which when substituted for speed above, gives
distance = frequency × wavelength × time
distance = 1/period × wavelength × period = wavelength.

7. To produce a transverse wave with a Slinky, shake it to and fro in a direction that is perpendicular to the length of the Slinky itself (as with the garden hose in the previous exercise). To produce a longitudinal wave, shake it to and fro along the direction of its length, so that a series of compressions and rarefactions is produced.

9. The shorter wavelengths are heard by bats (higher frequencies have shorter wavelengths).

11. The wavelength of sound from Source A is half the wavelength of sound from Source B.

13. Light travels about a million times faster than sound in air, so you see a distant event a million times sooner than you hear it.

15. At the instant that a high pressure region is created just outside the prongs of a tuning fork, a low pressure region is created between the prongs. This is because each prong acts like a Ping-Pong paddle in a region full of Ping-Pong balls. Forward motion of the paddle crowds Ping-Pong balls in front of it, leaving more space between balls in back of it. A half-cycle later when the prongs swing in toward the center, a high pressure region is produced between the prongs and a low-pressure region is produced just outside the prongs.

17. The fact that we can see a ringing bell but can't hear it indicates that light is a distinctly different phenomenon than sound. When we see the vibrations of the "ringing" bell in a vacuum, we know that light can pass through a vacuum. The fact that we can't hear the bell indicates that sound does not pass through a vacuum. Sound needs a material medium for its transmission; light does not.

19. The pitch of the tapped glass decreases as the glass is filled. As the mass of the system (glass plus water) increases, its natural frequency decreases. For systems of a given size, more mass usually means lower frequency. This can be seen on a guitar, where the most massive string has the lowest natural pitch. (If you've answered this exercise without actually trying it, shame on you!

21. If the frequency of sound is doubled, its speed will not change at all, but its wavelength will be "compressed" to half size. The speed of sound depends only on the medium through which it travels, not on its frequency, wavelength, or intensity (until the intensity gets so great that a shock wave results).

23. Sound travels faster in moist air because the less massive water vapor molecules, H_2O, travel faster than the more massive N_2 and O_2 molecules at the same temperature. This faster speed results in sound traveling faster, as covered in Exercise 34.

25. First, in outer space there is no air or other material to carry sound. Second, if there were, the faster-moving light would reach you before the sound.

27. If a single disturbance at some unknown distance sends longitudinal waves at one known speed, and transverse waves at a lesser known speed, and you measure the difference in time of the waves as they arrive, you can calculate the distance. The wider the gap in time, the greater the distance—which could be in any direction. If you use this distance as the radius of a circle on a map, you know the disturbance occurred somewhere on that circle. If you telephone two friends who have made similar measurements of the same event from different locations, you can transfer their circles to your map, and the point where the three circles intersect is the location of the disturbance.

29. The rhythm may match the resonant frequency of the balcony, which could result in its collapse. (This mishap has happened before.)

31. The sound is louder when a struck tuning fork is held against a table because a greater surface is set into vibration. In keeping with the conservation of energy, this reduces the length of time the fork keeps vibrating. Loud sound over a short time spends the same energy as weak sound for a long time.

32. These noise-canceling devices use interference to cancel the sound of the jackhammer in the ears of its operator. Because of the resulting low jackhammer noise in the ears of the operator, he can hear your voice clearly. But you, however, without the earphones experience no such cancellation of sound, so the voice of the operator is drowned out by the loud jackhammer noise.

35. The "beat frequency" is 2 per minute, so you and your friend will be in step twice per minute, or every 30 seconds. You can see this also from the fact that your friend's stride length is a little shorter than yours, 24/25 as long to be exact, so when you have taken exactly 24 strides—which is after half a minute—your friend will have taken exactly 25 and you will be back in step.

37. a) The frequency increases. (b) The wavelength decreases. (c) The speed is unchanged (because the air remains motionless relative to you).

39. There is no appreciable Doppler effect when motion of the sound source is at right angles to the listener. In this case, the source is neither approaching and crowding waves, nor receding and spreading waves. (For the record, however, there is a small "quadratic" transverse Doppler effect.)

41. The Doppler shifts show that one side approaches while the other side recedes, evidence that the sun is spinning.

43. The conical angle of a shock wave becomes narrower with greater speeds, as indicated in Figure11.33.

45. A shock wave and the resulting sonic boom are produced whenever an aircraft is supersonic, whether or not the aircraft has just become supersonic or has been supersonic for hours. It is a popular misconception that sonic booms are principally produced at the moment an aircraft becomes supersonic. This is akin to saying that a boat produces a bow wave at the moment it exceeds the wave-speed of water. It begins to produce a bow wave at this crucial moment, but if it moved no faster, the overlapping pattern of waves would not extend very far from the bow. Likewise with an aircraft. Both the boat and the aircraft must appreciably exceed wave speed to produce an ample bow and shock wave.

47. Resonance

Solutions to Chapter 11 Problems

1. (a) f = 1/T = 1/0.10 s = 10 Hz; (b) f = 1/5 = 0.2 Hz; (c) f = 1/(1/60) s = 60 Hz.

3. a. Frequency = 2 bobs/second = 2 hertz;
b. Period = 1/f = 1/2 second;
c. and the amplitude is the distance from the equilibrium position to maximum displacement, one-half the 20-cm peak-to-peak distance, or 10 cm.

5. To say that the frequency of radio waves is 100 MHz and that they travel at 300,000 km/s, is to say that there are 100 million wavelengths packed into 300,000 kilometers of space. Or expressed in meters, 300 million m of space. Now 300 million m divided by 100 million waves gives a wavelength of 3 meters per wave. Or

$$\text{Wavelength} = \frac{\text{speed}}{\text{frequency}} = \frac{(300 \text{ megameters/s})}{(100 \text{ megahertz})}$$
$$= 3 \text{ m.}$$

7. (a) Period = 1/frequency = 1/(256 Hz) = 0.00391 s, or 3.91 ms. (b) Speed = wavelength × frequency, so wavelength = speed/frequency = (340 m/s)/(256 Hz) = 1.33 m.

9. $v = f\lambda$ so $\lambda = v/f = (1530 \text{ m/s})/7 \text{ Hz} = 219$ m.

11. Assuming the speed of sound to be 340 m/s, the cave wall is 17 meters away. This is because the sound took 1/20 second to reach the wall (and 1/20 second to return).

    Distance = speed × time = 340 m/s × 1/20 s = 17 m.

13. Sound goes from the sleeper to the mountain in 4 hours and back in another 4 hours to wake him. The distance from the trapper to the mountain = speed of sound × time = 340 m/s × 3600 s/h × 4 h = 4.9×10^6 m = 4900 km (about the distance from New York to San Francisco)! (Very far, and due to the inverse-square law, also very weak!)

15. Speed of plane = 1.41 × speed of sound (Mach 1.41). In the time it takes sound to go from A to C, the plane goes from A to B. Since the triangle A-B-C is a 45-45-90 triangle, the distance AB is $\sqrt{2}$ = 1.41 times as long as the distance AC.

Chapter 12: Light Waves
Answers to Exercises

1. The fundamental source of electromagnetic radiation is oscillating electric charges, which emit oscillating electric and magnetic fields.

3. Ultraviolet has shorter waves than infrared. Correspondingly, ultraviolet also has the higher frequencies.

5. Sound requires a physical medium in which to travel. Light does not.

7. Radio waves and light are both electromagnetic, transverse, move at the speed of light, and are created and absorbed by oscillating charge. They differ in their frequency and wavelength and in the type of oscillating charge that creates and absorbs them.

9. The greater number of interactions per distance tends to slow the light and result is a smaller average speed.

11. Clouds are transparent to ultraviolet light, which is why clouds offer no protection from sunburn. Glass, however, is opaque to ultraviolet light, and will therefore shield you from sunburn.

13. The customer is being reasonable in requesting to see the colors in the daylight. Under fluorescent lighting, with its predominant higher frequencies, the bluer colors rather than the redder colors will be accented. Colors will appear quite different in sunlight.

15. We see not only yellow green, but also red and blue. All together, they mix to produce the white light we see.

17. If the yellow clothes of stage performers are illuminated with a complementary blue light, they will appear black.

19. Red and green produce yellow; red and blue produce magenta; red, blue, and green produce white.

21. The red shirt in the photo is seen as cyan in the negative, and the green shirt appears magenta—the complementary colors. When white light shines through the negative, red is transmitted where cyan is absorbed. Likewise, green is transmitted where magenta is absorbed.

23. Blue illumination produces black. A yellow banana reflects yellow and the adjacent colors, orange and green, so when illuminated with any of these colors it reflects that color and appears that color. A banana does not reflect blue, which is too far from yellow in the spectrum, so when illuminated with blue it appears black.

25. You see the complimentary colors due to retina fatigue. The blue will appear yellow, the red cyan, and the white black. Try it and see!

27. At higher altitudes, there are fewer molecules above you and therefore less scattering of sunlight. This results in a darker sky. The extreme, no molecules at all, results in a black sky, as on the moon.

29. Clouds are composed of atoms, molecules, and particles of a variety of sizes. So not only are high-frequency colors scattered from clouds, but middle and low frequencies as well. A combination of all the scattered colors produces white.

31. If we assume that Jupiter has an atmosphere which is similar to that of the earth in terms of transparency, then the sun would appear to be a deep reddish orange, just as it would when sunlight grazes 1000 kilometers of the earth's atmosphere for a sunset from an elevated position. Interestingly enough, there is a thick cloud cover in Jupiter's atmosphere that blocks all sunlight from reaching its "surface." And it doesn't even have a solid surface! Your grandchildren may visit one of Jupiter's moons, but will not "land" on Jupiter itself—not intentionally, anyway. (Incidentally, there are only 4 1/3 planets with "solid" surfaces: Mercury, Venus, Mars, Pluto, and 1/3 of Earth!)

33. The wavelengths of AM radio waves are hundreds of meters, much larger than the size of buildings, so they are easily diffracted around buildings. FM wavelengths are a few meters, borderline for diffraction around buildings. Light, with wavelengths a tiny fraction of a

centimeter, show no appreciable diffraction around buildings.

35. Young's interference experiment produces a clearer fringe pattern with slits than with pinholes because the pattern is of parallel straight-line-shaped fringes rather than the fringes of overlapping circles. Circles overlap in relatively smaller segments than the broader overlap of parallel straight lines. Also, the slits allow more light to get through; the pattern with pinholes is dimmer.

37. Diffraction is the principle by which peacocks and hummingbirds display their colors. The ridges in the surface layers of the feathers act as diffraction gratings.

39. The optical paths of light from upper and lower reflecting surfaces change with different viewing positions. Thus, different colors can be seen by holding the shell at different angles.

41. Blue, the complementary color. The blue is white minus the yellow light that is seen above.

43. Polarization tells you they are transverse.

45. To say that a Polaroid is ideal is to say that it will transmit 100% of the components of light that are parallel to its polarization axis, and absorb 100% of all components perpendicular to its polarization axis. Nonpolarized light has as many components along the polarization axis as it has perpendicular to that axis. That's 50% along the axis, and 50% perpendicular to the axis. A perfect Polaroid transmits the 50% that is parallel to its polarization axis.

47. With polarization axes aligned, a pair of Polaroids will transmit all components of light along the axes. That's 50%, as explained in the preceding answer. Half of the light gets through the first Polaroid, and all of that gets through the second. With axes at right angles, no light will be transmitted.

49. You can determine that the sky is partially polarized by rotating a single sheet of Polaroid in front of your eye while viewing the sky. You'll notice the sky darken when the axis of the Polaroid is perpendicular to the polarization axis of the skylight. (Although we humans don't naturally sense the polarization of the sky, creatures such as bees do, which provides them a sense of navigation.)

Solutions to Chapter 12 Problems

1. Earth-moon distance is 3.8×10^8 m, so the round-trip distance is 7.6×10^8 m. As in the previous problem,

$$t = \frac{d}{v} = \frac{7.6 \times 10^8 \text{ m}}{3 \times 10^8 \text{ m/s}} = 2.5 \text{ s}.$$

(In 1969, when TV showed astronauts first landing on the moon, people in their living rooms could listen in on conversations between the astronauts and "earthlings" and directly perceive the time delay. In 1675 Roemer saw the effect of light's finite speed "with his own eyes." Nearly 300 years later, millions of people heard the effect of the finite speed of electromagnetic waves "with their own ears.")

3. From $c = f\lambda$, $\lambda = \dfrac{c}{f} = \dfrac{3 \times 10^8 \text{m/s}}{6 \times 10^{14} \text{Hz}} = 5 \times 10^{-7} \text{m}$, or 500 nanometers. This is 5000 times larger than the size of an atom, which is 0.1 nanometer. (The nanometer is a common unit of length in atomic and optical physics.)

5. (a) Frequency = speed/wavelength = $(3 \times 10^8 \text{ m/s})/(0.03 \text{ m}) = 1.0 \times 10^{10}$ Hz = 10 GHz.

(b) Distance = speed × time, so time = distance/speed = $(10,000 \text{ m})/(3 \times 10^8 \text{ m/s}) = 3.3 \times 10^{-5}$ s. (Note the importance of consistent SI units to get the right numerical answers.)

Chapter 13: Properties of Light
Answers to Exercises

1. Only light from card number 2 reaches her eye.

3. Light that takes a path from point A to point B will take the same reverse path in going from point B to point A, even if reflection or refraction is involved. So if you can't see the driver, the driver can't see you. (This independence of direction along light's path is the "principle of reciprocity.")

5. When you wave your right hand, image of the waving hand is still on your right, just as your head is still up and your feet still down. Neither left and right nor up and down are inverted by the mirror—but *front and back* are, as the author's sister Marjorie illustrates in Figure 13.3. (Consider three axes at right angles to each other, the standard coordinate system; horizontal *x*, vertical *y*, and perpendicular-to-the-mirror *z*. The only axis to be inverted is *z*, where the image is -*z*.)

7. When the source of glare is somewhat above the horizon, a vertical window will reflect it to people in front of the window. By tipping the window inward at the bottom, glare is reflected downward rather than into the eyes of passersby. (Note the similarity of this exercise and the previous one.)

9. The pebbly uneven surface is easier to see. Light reflected back from your headlights is what lets you see the road. The mirror-smooth surface might reflect more light, but it would reflect it forward, not backward, so it wouldn't help you see.

11. First of all, the reflected view of a scene is different than an inverted view of the scene, for the reflected view is seen from lower down. Just as a view of a bridge may not show its underside where the reflection does, so it is with the bird. The view reflected in water is the inverted view you would see if your eye were positioned as far beneath the water level as your eye is above it (and there were no refraction). Then your line of sight would intersect the water surface where reflection occurs. Put a mirror on the floor between you and a distant table. If you are standing, your view of the

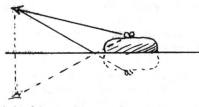

table is of the top. But the reflected view shows the table's bottom. Clearly, the two views are not simply inversions of each other. Take notice of this whenever you look at reflections (and of paintings of reflections — it's surprising how many artists are not aware of this).

13. The half-height mirror works at any distance, as shown in the sketch above. This is because if you move closer, your image moves closer as well. If you move farther away, your image does the same. Many people must actually try this before they believe it. The confusion arises because people know that they can see whole distant buildings or even mountain ranges in a hand-held pocket mirror. Even then, the distance the object is from the mirror is the same as the distance of the virtual image on the other side of the mirror. You can see all of a distant person in your mirror, but the distant person cannot see all of herself in your mirror.

15. The wiped area will be half as tall as your face.

17. If the water were perfectly smooth, you would see a mirror image of the round sun or moon, an ellipse on the surface of the water. If the water were slightly rough, the image would be wavy. If the water were a bit more rough, little glimmers of portions of the sun or moon would be seen above and below the main image. This is because the water waves act like tiny parallel mirrors. For small waves only light near the main image reaches you. But as the water becomes choppier, there is a greater variety of mirror facets that are oriented to reflect sunlight or moonlight into your eye. The facets do not radically depart from an average flatness with the otherwise smooth water surface, so the reflected sun

or moon is smeared into a long vertical streak. For still rougher water there are facets off to the side of the vertical streak that are tilted enough for sun or moon light to be reflected to you, and the vertical streak is wider.

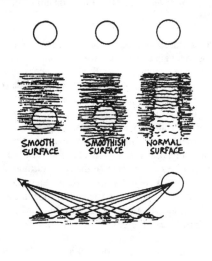

19.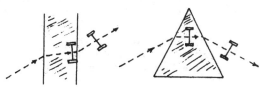

21. During a lunar eclipse the moon is not totally dark, even though it is in the earth's shadow. This is because the atmosphere of the earth acts as a converging lens that refracts light into the earth's shadow. It is the low frequencies that pass more easily through the long grazing path through the earth's atmosphere to be refracted finally onto the moon. Hence its reddish color—the refraction of the whole world's sunups and sunsets.

23. You would throw the spear below the apparent position of the fish, because the effect of refraction is to make the fish appear closer to the surface than it really is. But in zapping a fish with a laser, make no corrections and simply aim directly at the fish. This is because the light from the fish you see has been refracted in getting to you, and the laser light will refract along the same path in getting to the fish. A slight correction may be necessary, depending on the colors of the laser beam and the fish—see the next exercise.

25. A fish sees the sky (as well as some reflection from the bottom) when it looks upward at 45°, for the critical angle is 48° for water. If it looks at and beyond 48° it sees only a reflection of the bottom.

27. Total internal reflection occurs only for light rays that would gain speed in crossing the boundary they encounter. For light in air encountering a water surface, there is no total reflection. You can see this by sketching rays that go from water to air, and noting that light can travel in the other direction along all of these rays.

29. We cannot see a rainbow "off to the side," for a rainbow is not a tangible thing "out there." Colors are refracted in infinite directions and fill the sky. The only colors we see that aren't washed out by others are those that are along the conical angles between 40° and 42° to the sun-antisun axis. To understand this, consider a paper-cone cup with a hole cut at the bottom. You can view the circular rim of the cone as an ellipse when you look at it from a near side view. But if you view the rim only with your eye at the apex of the cone, through the hole, you can see it only as a circle. Hence viewing a rainbow. Our eye is at the apex of a cone, the axis of which is the sun-antisun axis, and the "rim" of which is the bow. Hence the bow forms part (or all) of a circle.

31. When the sun is high in the sky and people on the airplane are looking down toward a cloud opposite to the direction of the sun, they may see a rainbow that makes a complete circle. The shadow of the airplane will appear in the center of the circular bow. This is because the airplane is directly between the sun and the drops or rain cloud producing the bow.

33. A projecting lens with chromatic aberration casts a rainbow-colored fringe around a spot of white light. The reason these colors don't appear inside the spot is because they overlap to form white. Only at the edges, which act as a circular prism, do they not overlap.

35. The average intensity of sunlight at the bottom is the same whether the water is moving or is still. Light that misses one part of the bottom of the pool reaches another part. Every dark region is balanced by a bright region—"conservation of light."

37. Normal sight depends on the amount of refraction occurring for light traveling from air to the eye. The speed change ensures normal vision. But if the speed change is from water to eye, then light is refracted less and an unclear image results. A swimmer uses goggles to ensure that light travels from air to eye, even underwater.

39. If light had the same average speed in glass lenses that it has in air, no refraction of light would occur in lenses, and no magnification would occur. Magnification depends on refraction, that is, on speed changes.

41. Your image is twice as far from the camera as the mirror frame. So although you can adjust the focus of your camera to clearly photograph your image in a mirror, and you can readjust the focus to clearly photograph the mirror frame, you cannot in the same photograph focus on both your image and the mirror frame. This is because they are at different distances from the camera.

43. Moon maps are upside-down views of the moon to coincide with the upside-down image that moon watchers see in a telescope.

45. Since red light carries less energy per photon, and both beams have the same energy, there must be more photons in the beam of red light.

47. When a photon of UV encounters a living cell, it transfers to the cell energy that can damage it. When a photon of visible light encounters a living cell, the amount of energy it transfers to the cell is less, and less likely to be damaging. Hence skin exposure to UV can be damaging to the skin while exposure to visible light is appreciably less.

49. *Electric eye:* A beam of light is directed to a photosensitive surface that completes the path of an electric circuit. When the beam is interrupted, the circuit is broken, compromising a switch for another circuit. *Light meter:* the variation of photoelectric current with variations in light intensity activates a meter calibrated to show light intensity. *Sound track:* An optical sound track on motion picture film is a strip of emulsion of variable density that transmits light onto a photoelectric surface, which in turn produces a variable current. This current is amplified and activates a speaker.

Solutions to Chapter 13 Problems

1. When a mirror is rotated, its normal rotates also. Note how in the sample diagram, when the mirror is rotated by 10°, then the normal is rotated by 10° also, which results in a 20° total deviation of the reflected ray. This is one reason that mirrors are used to detect delicate movements in instruments such as galvanometers. Great amplification of displacement occurs by having the beam arrive at a scale some distance away.

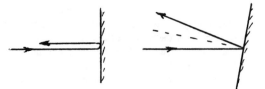

3. Set your focus for 6 m, for your image will be as far in back of the mirror as you are in front.

5. If 96% is transmitted through the first face, and 96% of 96% is transmitted through the second face, 92% is transmitted through both faces of the glass.

Chapter 14: Atoms and the Periodic Table
Answers to Exercises

1. The cat leaves a trail of molecules on the grass. These in turn leave the grass and mix with the air, where they enter the dog's nose, activating its sense of smell.

3. A body would have no odor if all its molecules remained intact. A body has odor only if some of its molecules enter a nose.

5. You really are a part of every person around you in the sense that you are composed of atoms not only from every person around you, but from every person who ever lived on earth!

7. With every breath of air you take, it is highly likely that you inhale one of the atoms exhaled during your very first breath. This is because the number of atoms of air in your lungs is about the same as the number of breaths of air in the atmosphere of the world.

9. Helium is placed over to the far right-hand side of the periodic table in group 18 because it has physical and chemical properties most similar to those of the other elements of group 18.

11. Calcium is readily absorbed by the body for the building of bones. Since calcium and strontium are in the same atomic group they have similar physical and chemical properties. The body, therefore, has a hard time distinguishing between the two and strontium is absorbed just as though it were calcium.

13. The one on the far right where the nucleus is not visible.

15. The remaining nucleus is that of Carbon-12.

17. Removing a proton from each gold nucleus would create the element platinum, which is more valued than is gold. Adding a proton would create the element mercury, which is less valued than either gold or platinum.

19. Lead, Pb.

21. The outsides of the atoms of the chair are made of negatively charged electrons, as are the outsides of the atoms that make up your body. Atoms don't pass through one another because of the repulsive forces that occur between these electrons. When you sit on the chair these repulsive forces hold you up against the force of gravity, which is pulling you downward.

23. The properties of elements across any period of the periodic table change gradually. For example, the size of the atoms of elements gradually decreases in moving from left to right.

25. The iron atom is electrically neutral when it has 26 electrons to balance its 26 protons.

27. Carbon-13 atoms are heavier than carbon-12 atoms. Because of this, any sample of carbon-13 will have a fewer number of atoms than any sample of carbon-12 of the same mass. Look at it this way—golf balls have more mass than Ping-Pong balls. So, which contains more balls: a kilogram of golf balls or a kilogram of Ping-Pong balls? Because Ping-Pong balls are so much lighter, you need many more of them to get to that kilogram amount.

29. The carbon atoms that make up Leslie's hair or anything else in this world originated in the explosions of ancient stars.

Solution to Chapter 14 Problem 1

1. Mass of Li-6: $6.0151 \times 0.0742 = 0.446$
   Mass of Li-7: $7.0160 \times 0.9258 = 6.495$
   Which gives a total of 6.941 amu.

Chapter 15: Visualizing the Atom
Answers to Exercises

1. Atoms are smaller than the wavelengths of visible light and hence they are not visible in the true sense of the word. We can, however, measure the topography of a collection of atoms by scanning an electric current back and forth across the topography. The data from such scanning can be assembled by a computer into an image that reveals how individual atoms are organized on the surface. It would be more appropriate to say that with the scanning tunneling microscope that we "feel" atoms, rather than "see" them.

3. Many objects or systems may be described just as well by a physical model as by a conceptual model. In general, the physical model is used to replicate an object or system of objects on a different scale. The conceptual model, by contrast, is used to represent abstract ideas or to demonstrate the behavior of a system. Of the examples given in the exercise the following might be adequately described using a physical model: the brain, the solar system, a stranger, a gold coin, a car engine, and a virus. The following might be adequately described using a conceptual model: the mind, the birth of the universe, your best friend (whose complex behavior you have some understanding of), and a dollar bill (which represents wealth but is really only a piece of paper), and the spread of a contagious disease, such as a cold.

5. The one electron can be boosted to many energy levels, and therefore make many combinations of transitions to lower levels. Each transition is of a specific energy and accompanied by the emission of a photon of a specific frequency. Thus the variety of spectal lines.

7. Six transitions are possible. The transition from the 4th to the lst level corresponds to the greatest ΔE and therefore highest frequency of light. The transition from the 4th to the 3rd level corresponds to the lowest ΔE and therefore lowest frequency of light.

9. The first visible color will be red because this is the visible frequency with the lowest amount of energy per photon.

11. The drop from $n = 3$ to $n = 2$ would be the same energy difference as the drop from $n = 2$ to $n = 1$. The frequencies emitted from these transitions, therefore, would be the same and would overlap each other in the atomic spectrum. The effect would be that two otherwise separate lines would converge into a single more intense line.

13. The spectral patterns emanating from the sun indicate the spectral patterns of heated iron atoms.

15. Twice the frequency means twice the energy.

17. The emission of blue light corresponds to a greater change of energy than the emission of green light.

19. An electron not restricted to particular energy levels would release light continuously as it spiraled closer into the nucleus. A broad spectrum of colors would be observed rather than the distinct lines.

21. It takes no time at all for this transition to occur. It is instantaneous. At no point is the electron found in between these two orbitals.

23.

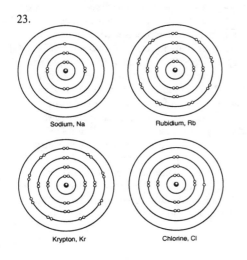

Sodium, Na   Rubidium, Rb

Krypton, Kr   Chlorine, Cl

25. A shell is just a region of space in which an electron may reside. This region of space exists with or without the electron.

27. Both the potassium and sodium atoms are in group 1 of the periodic table. The potassium atom, however, is larger than the sodium atoms because it contains an additional shell of electrons.

29. No. Light truly does behave as a particle just as it truly behaves as a wave. What we need to understand is that it's okay to use different models to describe different behaviors. The utility of one model doesn't negate the utility of another.

Chapter 16: The Atomic Nucleus
Answers to Exercises

1. Radioactivity is a part of nature, going back to the beginning of time.

3. A radioactive sample is always a little warmer than its surroundings because the radiating alpha or beta particles impart internal energy to the atoms of the sample. (Interestingly enough, the heat energy of the earth originates with radioactive decay of the earth's interior.)

5. Alpha and beta rays are deflected in opposite directions in a magnetic field because they are oppositely charged—alpha are positive and beta negative. Gamma rays have no electric charge and are therefore undeflected.

7. The alpha particle has twice the charge, but almost 8000 times the inertia (since each of the four nucleons has nearly 2000 times the mass of an electron). Hence it bends very little compared to the much less massive beta particles (electrons). Gamma rays carry no electric charge and so are not affected by an electric field.

9. Gamma radiation produces not only the least change in mass and atomic numbers, but produces no change in mass number, atomic number, or electric charge. Both alpha and beta radiation do produce these changes, as discussed in the previous answer.

11. The proton "bullets" need enough momentum to overcome the electric force of repulsion they experience once they get close to the atomic nucleus.

13. The strong nuclear force holds the nucleons of the nucleus together while the electric force pushes these nucleons apart.

15. No, it will not be entirely gone. Rather, after 1 day one-half of the sample will remain while after 2 days, one-fourth of the original sample will remain.

17. When radium (A = 88) emits an alpha particle, its atomic number reduces by 2 and becomes the new element radon (A = 86). The resulting atomic mass is reduced by 4. If the radium was of the most common isotope 226, then the radon isotope would have atomic mass number 222.

19. Deuterium has 1 proton and 1 neutron; carbon has 6 protons and 6 neutrons; iron has 26 protons and 30 neutrons; gold has 79 protons and 118 neutrons; strontium has 38 protons and 52 neutrons; uranium has 92 protons and 146 neutrons.

21. The elements below uranium in atomic number with short half-lives exist as the product of the radioactive decay of uranium. As long as uranium is decaying, their existence is assured.

23. Although there is significantly more radioactivity in a nuclear power plant than in a coal-fired power plant, the absence of shielding for coal plants results in more radioactivity in the environment of a typical coal plant than in the environment of a typical nuclear plant. All nukes are shielded; coal plants are not.

25. Film badges monitor gamma radiation, which after all, is very high frequency X rays. Like photographic film, the greater the exposure, the darker the film upon photoprocessing.

27. There are no fast-flying subatomic particles in gamma rays that might collide with the nuclei of the atoms within the food. Transformations within the nuclei of the atoms of the food, therefore, are not possible. Rather, the gamma rays are lethal to any living tissues within the food, such as those of pathogens. The gamma rays kill these pathogens, which helps to protect us from diseases, such as botulism, which are very dangerous.

29. Stone tablets cannot be dated by the carbon dating technique. Nonliving stone does not ingest carbon and transform that carbon by radioactive decay. Carbon dating pertains to organic material.

31. A neutron makes a better "bullet" for penetrating atomic nuclei because it has no electric charge and is therefore not deflected from its path by electrical interactions, nor is it electrically repelled by an atomic nucleus.

33. Because plutonium triggers more reactions per atom, a smaller mass will produce the same neutron flux as a somewhat larger mass of uranium. So plutonium has a smaller critical mass than a similar shape of uranium.

35. Plutonium has a short half-life (24,360 years), so any plutonium initially in the earth's crust has long since decayed. The same is true for any heavier elements with even shorter half lives from which plutonium

might originate. Trace amounts of plutonium can occur naturally in U-238 concentrations, however, as a result of neutron capture, where U-238 becomes U-239 and after beta emission becomes Np-239, and further beta emission to Pu-239. (There are elements in the earth's crust with half-lives even shorter than plutonium's, but these are the products of uranium decay; between uranium and lead in the periodic table of elements.)

37. A nucleus undergoes fission because the electric force of repulsion overcomes the strong nuclear force of attraction. This electric force of repulsion is of the very same nature as static electricity. So, in a way, your friend's claim that the explosive power of a nuclear bomb is due to static electricity is valid.

39. If the difference in mass for changes in the atomic nucleus increased tenfold (from 0.1% to 1.0%), the energy release from such reactions would increase tenfold as well.

41. Both convert mass to energy.

43. Energy would be released by the fissioning of gold and from the fusion of carbon, but by neither fission nor fusion for iron. Neither fission nor fusion will result in a decrease of mass for iron nucleons.

45. The radioactive decay of radioactive elements found under the earth's surface warms the insides of the earth and responsible for the molten lava that spews from volcanoes. The thermo-nuclear fusion of our sun is responsible for warming everything on our planet's suface exposed to the sun.

47. Such speculation could fill volumes. The energy and material abundance that is the expected outcome of a fusion age will likely prompt several fundamental changes. Obvious changes would occur in the fields of economics and commerce, which would be geared to relative abundance rather than scarcity. Already our present price system, which is geared to and in many ways dependent upon scarcity, often malfunctions in an environment of abundance. Hence we see instances where scarcity is created to keep the economic system functioning. Changes at the international level will likely be worldwide economic reform, and at the personal level in a reevaluation of the idea that scarcity ought to be the basis of value. A fusion age will likely see changes that will touch every facet of our way of life.

49. To create an abundant supply of molecular hydrogen will require an abundant source of energy, such as fusion power.

227

Solutions to Chapter 16 Problems

1. In accord with the inverse-square law, at 2 m, double the distance, the count rate will be 1/4 of 360, or 90 counts/minute. At 3 m, the count rate will be 1/9 of 360, or 40 counts/min.

3. At 3:00 PM (after 3 half-lives) there will be 1/8 of the original remaining, 0.125 grams. At 6:00 PM, after 3 more half-lives, there are 1/8 of 1/8 left, 0.016 grams. At 10:00 PM the amount remaining has halved ten times, which leaves $(1/2)10$, or about 1/1000 of the original. So the remaining amount will be 0.001 g, or 1 mg.

5. It will take four half-lives to decrease to one-sixteenth the original amount. Four half-lives of cesium-137 corresponds to 120 years.

7. Your count is 10/5000 for the gallon you remove. That's a ratio of 1/500, which means the tank must hold 500 gallons of gasoline.

Chapter 17: Elements of Chemistry
Answers to Exercises

1. When looked at macroscopically, matter appears continuous. On the submicroscopic level, however, we find that matter is made of extremely small particles, such as atoms or molecules. Similarly, a TV screen looked at from a distance appears as a smooth continuous flow of images. Up close, however, we see this is an illusion. What really exists are a series of tiny dots (pixels) that change color in a coordinated way to produce the series of images.

3. Chemistry is the careful study of matter and can take place at a number of different levels including the submicroscopic, microscopic, or macroscopic levels.

5. At 25°C there is a certain amount of thermal energy available to all the submicroscopic particles of a material. If the attractions between the particles are not strong enough, the particles may separate from each other to form a gaseous phase. If the attractions are strong, however, the particles may be held together in the solid phase. We can assume, therefore, that the attractions among the submicroscopic particles of a material in its solid phase at 25°C are stronger than they are within a material that is a gas at this temperature.

7. If each one of these particles represented a water molecule, the box on the left would be indicative of ice melting, which occurs at 0°C.

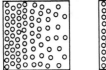

9. They are all examples of physical properties.

11. All of these changes involve the formation of new materials.

13. Density is the ratio of a material's mass to volume. As the mass stays the same and the volume decreases, the density of the material increases.

15. That this process is so reversible suggests a physical change. As you sleep in a reclined position, pressure is taken off of the discs within your spinal column, which allows them to expand so that you are significantly taller in the morning. Astronauts returning from extended space visits may be up to two inches taller upon their return.

17. a) chemical. b) chemical. c) chemical. d) physical.

19. Box B appears to contain a liquid as evidenced by the randomly oriented molecules condensed at the bottom of the box. These molecules in the liquid phase of Box B represent a compound because they consist of different types of atoms joined together. You cannot assume, however, that box B contains a liquid because the illustration is "still-frame". It might be that the molecules at the bottom of Box B are in a solid phase in which the molecules are just about as far apart from one another as they are in the liquid phase. To indicate either liquid or solid phase the box would need to be animated. If liquid, the molecules would be seen tumbling over one another. If solid, the molecules would be vibrating about fixed positions.

21. The change from A to B represents a physical change because no new types of molecules are formed. The collection of blue/yellow molecules on the bottom of B represents these molecules in the liquid or solid phase after having been in the gaseous phase in A. This must occur with a decrease in temperature. At this lower temperature the purely yellow molecules are still in the gaseous phase which means that they have a lower boiling point, while the blue/yellow molecules have a higher boiling point.

23. The ones that have atomic symbols that don't match their modern atomic names. Examples include iron, Fe, gold, Au, and copper, Cu.

25. This oxygen is bound to hydrogen within water molecules, H_2O. The oxygen we breathe is molecular oxygen, O_2, and there is very little of this in water.

27. Answer: d

29. H_2S

31. Ozone, O_3.

33. This equation is balanced.

35. a) 2,3,1   b) 1,6,4   c) 2,1,2   d) 1,2,1,2

Chapter 18: Mixtures
Answers to Exercises

1. A percentage is transformed into a fraction by dividing by 100. To find 50% of something, for example, you multiply that something by $50/100 = 0.50$. The percentage 0.0001% transforms into the fraction 0.000001, which when mulitplied by 1×10^{24} equals 1×10^{18}. This is certainly a lot of pesticides molecules in your glass of water.

3. According to Exercise 1, there are a trillion trillion water molecules in a glass of water. If this water is 99.9999% pure, then it also contains a million trillion impurity molecules. A trillion trillion is a million times more than a million trillion, therefore, there are a million times more water molecules than there are impurity molecules. In other words, for every million water molecules, there is only one impurity molecule. Thus, in a sample of water that is 99.9999% pure, the number of water molecules far exceeds the number of impurity molecules, even though there are trillions of each.

5. Chicken noodle soup and soil both consist of many different component all mixed together. In both of these materials one can visually distinguish many of these components.

7. Maple syrup, natural product; classification: mixture. Pepper, natural product; classification: mixture. Aluminum, metal; classification: in pure form—element (Sold commercially as a mixture of mostly aluminum with trace metals, such as magnesium.) Ice, dihydrogen oxide; classification: in pure form—compound; when made from impure tap water—mixture. Milk, natural product; classification: mixture. Cherry flavored cough drops, pharmaceutical; classification: mixture.

9. The atoms within a compound are chemically bonded together and do not come apart through the course of a physical change. The components of a mixture, however, may be separated from each other by physical means.

11. For a mixture of iron and sand, take advantage of the fact that only iron is attracted to a magnet.

13. The transformation of elements into a compound is necessarily a chemical change. To go backwards—from the compound back into the elements—would also be an example of a chemical change. The only way to separate an element from a compound, therefore, would be by chemical means.

15. A shaft of strong light, such as sunlight, passing through the air of your house reveals the presence of many floating dust particles. Because of these dust particles, we can say that the air inside your house is an example of a heterogeneous mixture. Fortunately, our nasal passage ways serve to filter out much of this dust.

17. Fruit punch is a mixture and mixtures can be separated into their components by differences in physical properties. Initially, freezing water molecules selectively bind to themselves to form ice crystals. This excludes the sugar molecules. The effect is that the liquid phase loses water molecules to the ice crystals. The proportion of sugar molecules in the liquid phase, therefore, increases, which makes the liquid phase tastes sweeter. Upon complete freezing, the sugar become trapped within the ice crystals and the frozen juice can be used as a popsicle. Suck hard on a frozen popsicle, however, and you'll find that only the concentrated sugar solution pulls into your mouth.

19. To tell whether a sugar solution is saturated or not, add more sugar and see if it will dissolve. If the sugar dissolves, the solution was not saturated. Alternatively, cool the solution and see if any sugar precipitates. If it precipitates then the solution was saturated. Because sugar forms supersaturated solutions so easily, however, neither of these methods are always successful.

21. A big advantage to using chlorine is that it provides protection from pathogens for several days after it has been applied. A drawback to this is that the residual chlorine can adversely affect the taste of the water.

23. Reverse osmosis can be applied to any solution for the generation of fresh water. The only prerequisite is that the solute particles be larger than the water molecules. This way, as pressure is applied to the solution, only the water molecules are able to pass through the semipermeable membrane from the solution side to the fresh water side.

25. Our mouths are pretty good at discerning the tastes of residual components of drinking water so much so that many of us are willing to pay the 1000% markup price that water bottlers charge for their products, which are only a fraction of a percentage more pure than the water we can obtain from a local water utility. Because their

purities are actually quite comparable, flushing toilets with municipal drinking water is about as wasteful as flushing it with bottled water. If water must be used, let it be a low-flush toilet or one that uses "gray water" from an upstairs bathtub.

27. The concentration of water inside the red blood cell is less than that of concentration of water outside the red blood cell when the cell is placed in fresh water. As a result, the water migrates into the cell (from a region of high concentration outside to low concentration inside) to the point that so much water collects within the cell that the cell bursts.

29. During the process of freezing, dissolved salts are naturally excluded during the formation of ice crystals. Sea water, therefore, can be desalinated by cooling the water to form crystals, which can then be melted to produce fresh water.

31. At the wastewater treatment facility, human waste is extracted from the water and typically ends up in a landfill. So why not use a composting toilet and skip the waste of water altogether and send our wastes directly to farmlands rather than to landfills?

33. Advanced integrated pond systems to date are best suited for small communities that have access to wide areas of land and lots of sunshine. But even if the conditions are right for a particular community, there is still the social inertia to overcome for doing something different.

35. Pros: This particular region of the world is arid and there is a great need for plentiful fresh water. Cons: It would be costly to pump the fresh water out of the Dead Sea basin to populated areas where it is needed. Also, the Dead Sea would fill with the discarded salt water, which would upset the local ecosystem. Eventually, the level of the Dead Sea would rise to a point where the reverse osmosis would no longer be possible.

Solutions to Chapter 18 Problems

1. Multiply concentration by volume:
   $(0.5 \text{ g/L})(5 \text{ L}) = 2.5 \text{ g}.$

3. a) $\dfrac{1 \text{ mole}}{1 \text{ Liter}} = 1$ Molar (1 M)

   b) $\dfrac{2 \text{ moles}}{0.5 \text{ Liters}} = 4$ Molar (4 M)

Chapter 19: How Atoms Bond
Answers to Exercises

1. This is an example of a chemical change involving the formation of ions, which are uniquely different from the neutral atoms from which they are made.

3. The nuclear charge experienced by an electron in sodium's third shell is not strong enough to hold this many electrons. As was discussed in Chapter 15, this is because there are 10 inner shell electrons shielding any third shell electron from the +11 nucleus. The effective nuclear charge in this shell, therefore, is about +1, which means that it is able to hold at most one electron.

5. Ba_3N_2

7. Because there is no more room available in its outermost occupied shell.

9. The hydrogen atom has only one electron to share.

11. There is a gradual change. We get this change by noting the relative positions of the bonding elements across the periodic table. If they are close together toward the upper right hand corner, then the bond is more covalent. When the elements are on opposite sides of the periodic table, the chemical bond between them is more ionic. For the bonding of atoms between these two extremes, the bonding tends to be a blend of both, which is also referred to as *polar covalent*.

13. When bonded to an atom with low electronegativity, such as any group 1 element, the nonmetal atom will pull the bonding electrons so closely to itself so as to form an ion.

15. The chemical formula for phosphine is PH_3, which is most similar to that of ammonia, NH_3. Note how phosphorus is directly below nitrogen in the periodic table.

17. O-H (The greatest difference in electro-negativity is between oxygen and hydrogen.)

19. The atoms found closer to the lower left-hand corner of the periodic table are those that will bare the positive charge: a) hydrogen b) bromine c) carbon d) neither!

21. A selenium-chlorine bond should be more polar. Observe their relative positions in the periodic table. Sulfur and bromine are more equidistant from the upper right hand corner.

23. The two oxygen atoms in carbon dioxide are 180° apart from each another such that their electron-pulls on the central carbon atom are equal and opposite. The two dipoles, therefore, balance each other out making carbon dioxide a nonpolar compound.

25. Borane, BH_3, has three hydrogen atoms bonded to a central atom (boron). The hydrogen atoms are distributed evenly around the boron atom within a single plane, much like that seen for BF_3 in Figure 19.25. The resulting symmetry gives rise to a nonpolarity. Ammonia, NH_3, also has three hydrogen atoms bonded to a central atom (nitrogen). Unlike boron in BH_3, however, the nitrogen in NH_3 also has a pair of nonbonded electrons. These nonbonded electrons repel the hydrogen atoms causing them to pucker so that the ammonia molecule is not flat. Instead, it forms a pyramid type structure and so appears bent much like a water molecule. This shape makes it so that the hydrogens are not exactly opposite one another, which means that there is some resultant polarity. This idea of nonbonding electrons affecting the shape of a molecule was not fully explained in the textbook so don't get too concerned if you feel a little lost. If you have the opportunity to work with molecular models under the guidance of your course instructor, however, this idea will become quite evident.

27. Definitely not! Metal halides are by no means restricted to group 1 metals. In fact, most metals are able to form halides. Iron chloride, $FeCl_3$, and copper chloride, $CuCl_2$, are examples. Figure 19.34 shows only the most common forms of metal compounds. In nature, iron is most commonly found as an oxide, while copper is most commonly found as a sulfide.

29. The problem is not whether or not we have the metal atoms on this planet we do! The problem is in the expense of collecting those metal atoms. This expense would be too great if the metal atoms were evenly distributed around the planet. We are fortunate, therefore, that there are geological formations where metal ores have been concentrated by natural processes. Bare in mind that they are only the metal atoms that we produce ourselves that we are able to recycle. If we don't recycle these metal atoms, then down the road we'll find substantial shortages of new metal ores from which to feed our ever growing appetite for metal-based consumer goods and building materials.

Chapter 20: Molecular Attractions
Answers to Exercises

1. Because the magnitude of the electric charge associated with an ion is much greater.

3. By way of induced dipole-induced dipole molecular attractions.

5.

	$CH_3-O^{\diagup H}$	$CH_3CH_2CH_2CH_2-O^{\diagup H}$	$CH_3CH_2CH_2CH_2CH_2-O^{\diagup H}$
Boiling point:	65 °C	117 °C	138 °C
Solubility:	infinite	8g/100mL	2.3g/100mL

The boiling points go up because of an increase in the number of molecular interactions between molecules. Remember, when we talk about the "boiling point" of a substance we are referring to a pure sample of that substance. We see the boiling point of 1-pentanol (the molecule on the far right) is relatively high because 1-pentanol molecules are so attracted to one another (by induced dipole-induced dipole as well as by dipole-dipole and dipole-induced dipole attractions). When we refer to the "solubility" of a substance we are referring to how well that substance interacts with a second substance—in this case water. Note that water is much less attracted to 1-pentanol because most of 1-pentanol is nonpolar (its only polar portion is the OH group). For this reason 1-pentanol is not very soluble in water. Put yourself in the point of view of a water molecule and ask yourself how attracted you might be to a methanol molecule (the one on the far left) compared to the pentanol molecule (the one on the far right).

7. The induced dipole-induced dipole forces of attraction between I_2 molecules must be overcome in order for the I_2 to dissolve.

9. Dipole-induced dipole forces of attraction exist between I_2 and CH_3OH molecules in solution.

11. The greater the pressure, the greater the solubility. Recall that the solubility of a gas in a liquid increases with increasing pressure. This principle is used in the manufacture of carbonated beverages.

13. Two substances that can be mixed homogeneously in any proportion are said to be infinitely soluble. By this definition noble gases are infinitely soluble in noble gases.

15. At 10°C a saturated solution of sodium nitrate, $NaNO_3$, is more concentrated than a saturated solution of sodium chloride, NaCl.

17. Salt is composed of ions that are too attracted to themselves. Gasoline is nonpolar so salt and gasoline will not interact very well.

19. The aluminum oxide has a higher melting point because of the greater charges of the ions, and hence the greater force of attractions between them.

21. No, because of the warmer temperatures. The solubility of oxygen in water *decreases* with increasing temperature.

23. Boiling involves the separation of many molecules (plural). With only one molecule, the concept of boiling is meaningless.

25. When an ionic compound melts, the ionic bonds between the ions are overcome. When a covalent compound melts, the molecular attractions between molecules are overcome. Because ionic bonds are so much stronger than molecular attractions, the melting points of ionic compounds are typically much higher.

27. Soap is not at all necessary for removing salt from your hands. The strong ion-dipole interactions between fresh water and salt are most sufficient to lift the salt away from your hands.

29. The boiling process removes the air that was dissolved in the water. Upon cooling the water is void of its usual air content, hence, the fish drowns.

Chapter 21 Chemical Reactions
Answers to Exercises

1. The carbon dioxide reactions occurring as the yeast digests the sugar take place faster at warmer temperatures for a variety of reasons, but especially in that the warmer temperatures favor a greater number of effective collisions among reacting molecules.

3. In pure oxygen there is a greater concentration of one of the reactants (the oxygen) for the chemical reaction (combustion). As discussed in this chapter, the greater the concentration of reactants, the greater the rate of the reaction.

5. The bubbling occurs as the result of a reaction between the Alka-Seltzer tablet and the water. In the alcoholic beverage there is a lower proportion of water molecules, which leads to a slow rate of reaction. In terms of molecular collisions, with fewer water molecules around, the probability of collisions between the molecules of the Alka-Seltzer and the water is less in the alcoholic beverage.

7. The final result of this reaction is the transformation of three oxygen molecules, O_2, into two ozone molecules, O_3. While there is no net consumption or production of the nitrogen monoxide, NO, nitrogen dioxide, NO_2, and the atomic oxygen, O, species, only the nitrogen monoxide, NO, appears to be required for this reaction to begin. The nitrogen monoxide, NO, therefore, is best described as the catalyst.

9. Putting more ozone into the atmosphere to replace that which has been destroyed is a bit like throwing more fish into a pool of sharks to replace those fish that have been eaten. The solution is to remove the CFC's that destroy the ozone. Unfortunately, CFC only degrade slowly and the ones up there now will remain there for many years to come. Our best bet is to stop the present production of CFC's and hope that we haven't already caused too much damage.

11.
Energy to break bonds:	Formation energy out:
N-N = 159 kJ	H-H = 436 kJ
N-H = 389 kJ	H-H = 436 kJ
N-H = 389 kJ	H-H = 436 kJ
N-H = 389 kJ	H-H = 436 kJ
N-H = 389 kJ	N͠N = 946 kJ
Total = 1715 kJ	Total = 2690 kJ
absorbed	released

NET = 1715 kJ absorbed - 2690kJ released = -975 kJ released (exothermic)

Energy to break bonds:	Formation energy out:
O-O = 138 kJ	
H-O = 464 kJ	O=O = 498 kJ
H-O = 464 kJ	H-O = 464 kJ
O-O = 138 kJ	H-O = 464 kJ
H-O = 464 kJ	O-H = 464 kJ
H-O = 464 kJ	O-H = 464 kJ
Total = 2132	Total = 2354 kJ
absorbed	released

NET = 2132 kJ absorbed - 2354 kJ released = -222 kJ released (exothermic)

13. Exothermic reaction because of the energy that batteries provide.

15. Because this reaction is indicated to need the input of ultraviolet energy in order to occur, it should be viewed as an endothermic reaction.

17. Energy is absorbed by this process and so it is endothermic. The process itself is a physical change in which the ammonium nitrate dissolves in the water.

19. 64.058 amu

21. There are four moles of atoms in 72.922 g of hydrogen chloride, which is more than the three moles of atoms found in 64.058 g of sulfur dioxide.

23. There are two moles of nitrogen atoms in 28 grams of N_2, and two moles of oxygen atoms in 32 g of O_2. There are five moles of atoms in 16 grams of methane, CH_4, and two moles of fluorine atoms in F_2. The greatest number of atoms are in c, 16 grams of methane, CH_4.

25. 3.322×10^{-24} gram

27. A single water molecule has a very small mass of 18 amu.

29. $(18)(1.661 \times 10^{-24}$ grams$) = 29.898 \times 10^{-24}$ grams or 2.9898×10^{-23} grams.

31. The mass of a single hydrogen atom is 1.01 amu, which is far less than the mass of all the hydrogen atoms in a 1.01 gram sample of hydrogen.

33. They likely contain the same material.

35. A mole of eggs equals 6.02×10^{23} eggs. To find how many dozen this is divide by 12, which gives 5.02×10^{22} dozens.

Solutions to Chapter 21 Problems

1. $(0.250$ g aspirin$)(\frac{1 \text{ mole aspirin}}{180 \text{ g aspirin}})$

   $(\frac{6.02 \times 10^{23}}{1 \text{ mole}}) = 8.38 \times 10^{20}$ molecules

3. From their formula masses we find that 60 grams of 2-propanol (60 amu) will form 42 grams of propene (42 amu) and 18 grams of water (18 amu). Six grams of 2-propanol, therefore, should yield 4.2 grams of propene and 1.8 grams of water.

5. The formula mass of sulfur dioxide is 64.058 g/mole, and in 64.058 g there is one mole of SO_2 molecules. According to the balanced equation, one mole of SO_2 reacts with 1 mole of CaO. One mole of CaO has a mass of 56.079 g, and so this is the amount of CaO that reacts with 64.058 g of SO_2. The balanced equation tells us one mole of $CaSO_3$ forms in this case, which is 120.137 g.

Chapter 22: Acids and Bases
Answers to Chapter 22 Exercises

1. The potassium carbonate found in ashes acts as a base and reacts with skin oils to produce slippery solutions of soap.

3. The base accepted the hydrogen ion, H^+, and thus gained a positive charge. The base thus forms the positively charged ion. Conversely, the acid donated a hydrogen ion and thus lost a positive charge. The acid thus forms the negatively charged ion.

5. For (a) note that the H_3O^+ transforms into a water molecule. This means that the H_3O^+ loses a hydrogen ion, which is donated to the Cl^-. The H_3O^+, therefore, is behaving as an acid while the Cl- is behaving as a base. In the reverse direction we see the H_2O gaining a hydrogen ion (behaving as a base) to become H_3O^+. It gets this hydrogen ion from the HCl, which in donating is behaving as an acid. You should be able make similar arguments for (b) and (c) to arrive at the following answers:
   a) acid, base, base, acid
   b) acid, base, acid, base
   c) acid, base, acid, base.

7. PH_3 accepts a proton so it is a base; NH_3 donates the proton so it is the acid.

9. Water behaves as an acid in that it donates a hydrogen ion to the ammonia.

11. The corrosive properties are no longer present because the acid and base no longer exist. Instead they have chemically reacted with each other to form completely new substances—salt and water—that are not so corrosive.

13. Both the hydronium and hydroxide ions are always present in an aqueous solution.

15. As more hydronium and hydroxide ions form, the concentration of these ions increases. This means that the product of their concentrations, which is K_w, also increases. Thus, K_w is constant only so long as the temperature is constant. Interestingly, K_w equals 1.0×10^{-14} only at 24°C. At a warmer 40°C K_w equals a larger value of 2.92×10^{-14}.

17. As water warms up, the hydronium ion concentration increases, but so does the hydroxide concentration—and by the same amount (See the previous two exercises). Thus, the pH decreases and yet the solution remains neutral because the hydronium and hydroxide ion concentrations are still equal. At 40°C, for example, the hydronium and hydroxide ion concentrations of pure water are both equal to 1.71×10^{-7} moles per liter (the square root of K_w). The pH of this solution is the minus log of this number, which is 6.77. This is why most pH meters need to be adjusted for the temperature of the solution being measured. Except for this exercise, which probes your powers of analytical thinking, this textbook ignores the slight role that temperature plays in pH. Unless noted otherwise, please continue to assume that K_w is a constant 1.0×10^{-14}; in other words, assume that the solution being measured is at 24°C.

19. The sum of the pH and pOH of a solution is always equal to the negative log of K_w, which is 14.

21. A solution with a pH of zero, as per previous exercise, is very acidic because the concentration of hydronium ions far exceeds that of the hydroxide ions.

23. A solution with a negative pH, as per previous exercise, is very, very acidic because the concentration of hydronium ions far, far exceeds that of the hydroxide ions.

25. As pure water is added to an acidic solution, the hydronium ions (and anything else that is dissolved in this acidic solution) become more dilute, that is, less concentrated. Thus, the pH increases.

27. As the soda water loses carbon dioxide molecules it is losing the carbonic acid that these carbon dioxide molecules form when in solution. Thus, the pH of a flat soda is typically higher than the pH of the same soda when carbonated.

29. Add it to some vinegar. If the toothpaste starts to bubble, there's a good chance it contains calcium carbonate.

31. Add a neutralizing substance such as limestone.

33. A buffer solution is one that serves to neutralize any incoming acids or bases. This is typically achieved by mixing two separate chemicals into a single solution. One chemical serves to neutralize the incoming acid, while the second serves to neutralize the incoming base. Note how the sodium end of the sodium bicarbonate structure is similar to the sodium end of sodium acetate, which, as shown in Figure 22.21, behaves as a weak base. The hydrogen end of sodium bicarbonate, meanwhile, is similar in structure to acetic acid, which is a weak acid. Thus, sodium bicarbonate is like two buffer components combined into one molecule.

35. The sodium hydroxide, which behaves as a base, reacts with the ammonium chloride, which behaves as an acid, to form sodium chloride and ammonia. The concentration of ammonia in this system, therefore, increases while the concentration of ammonium chloride decreases.

37. The buffer contains an acid that neutralizes the strong base. Likewise, it contains a base that neutralizes any strong acid.

39. Generally speaking, salts form from the neutralization of an acid and a base. So if a salt is the *product* of an acid/base reaction how can the salt itself be neutralized? The answer is that some salts are themselves slightly acidic or basic. As such, they can react with a base or an

acid to be neutralized a second time. This doesn't mean that the chemical simply disappears. Rather, as the acidic or basic salt is neutralized it forms another type of salt, which may have increased solubility in water and is therefore easier to mop up.

Solutions to Chapter 22 Problems

1. The concentration of hydroxide ions is 1×10^{-4} moles per liter.

3. The pH is of this solution is 4 and it is acidic.

5. The concentration of hydronium ions in the pH = 1 solution is 0.1M. Doubling the volume of solution with pure water means that its concentration is cut in half. The new concentration of hydronium ions after the addition of 500 mL of water, therefore, is 0.05 M. To calculate for pH:
$$pH = -\log[H_3O^+] = -\log(0.05) = -(-1.3) = 1.3$$

Chapter 23: Oxidation and Reduction
Answers to Exercises

1. The atom that loses an electron and thus gains a positive charge (the red one) is the one that was oxidized.

3. An oxidizing agent causes other materials to lose electrons. It does so by its tendency to gain electrons. Atoms with great electronegativity tend to have a strong attraction for electrons and, therefore, also behave as strong oxidizing agents.

5. To behave as an oxidizing agent, a chemical must have a tendency to gain electrons. Such atoms that have strong tendency to gain electrons also have a high ionization energy. In other words, once they grab onto an electron, they are less likely to let go.

7. Fluorine should behave as a stronger oxidizing agent because it has a greater effective nuclear charge in its outermost shell.

9. The electrons flow from the submerged nail to the copper ions in solution.

11. The anode is where oxidation takes place and free roaming electrons are generated. The negative sign at the anode of a battery indicates that this electrode is the source of negatively charged electrons. They run from the anode, through an external circuit, to the cathode, which bares a positive charge to which the electrons are attracted. (When a battery is recharged energy is used to

force the electrons to go in the opposite direction. In other words, during recharging, the electrons move from the positive electrode to the negative electrode—a place where they would not ever go without the input of energy. Electrons are thus gained at the negative electrode, which is now classified as the cathode because the cathode is where reduction occurs and the gain of electrons is reduction. Look carefully to Figure 23.10b to see how this is so.

13. According to the chemical formula for iron hydroxide, there are two hydroxide groups for every one iron atom. Each hydroxide group has a single negative charge. This means that the iron of iron hydroxide must carry a double positive charge, which is no different from the free Fe^{2+} ion from which it is formed. This reaction is merely the coming together of oppositely-charged ions.

15. The Cu^{2+} ion is reduced as it gains electrons to form copper metal, Cu. The magnesium metal, Mg, is oxidized as it loses electrons to form Mg^{2+}.

17. How much power a battery can deliver is a function of the number of ions in contact with the electrodes—the more ions, the greater the power. Assuming the lead electrodes (seen as a grid within the battery) are completely submerged both before and after the water has been added, then diluting the ionic solution of the car battery will decrease the number of ions in contact with the electrode and thus decrease the power of the battery. This effect is only temporary because more ions are soon generated as the battery is recharged by the generator. If the water level inside the battery, however, is so low that the internal lead electrodes are no longer completely submerged, then adding water increases the surface area of the electrode in contact with the solution. This counter-balances the weakening effect of diluting the ionic solution.

19. Aluminum oxide is insoluble in water and thus forms a protective coating that prevents continued oxidation of the aluminum.

21. Rusting is a surface phenomenon, and there is more surface area in steel wool than in a block of the same mass.

23. Combustion reactions are generally exothermic because they involve the transfer of electrons to oxygen, which of all atoms in the periodic table has one of the greatest tendencies for gaining electrons.

25. The oxygen is chemically bound to hydrogen atoms to make water, which is completely different from oxygen, O_2, which is what is required for combustion.
Another way to phrase an answer to this question would be to say that the oxygen in water is already "reduced" in the sense that it has gained electrons from the

hydrogen atoms to which it is attached. Being already reduced, this oxygen atom no longer has a great attraction for additional electrons.

27. This is very bad news to have iron and copper pipes in contact with each other. The iron atoms will lose electrons to the copper atoms, which will pass those electrons onto oxygen atoms that are in contact with the surface, much like that indicated in Figure 23.17.

29. This water is in the gaseous phase and merely floats away from the fire.

31. The other product formed is hydrogen gas, H_2, as per the following equation:
electricity + 2 NaCl + 2 H$_2$O --->
2 NaOH + Cl$_2$ + H$_2$

33. Water is needed in order for iron to rust. If the iron is coated with grease, this prevents the iron from being exposed to the water.

Chapter 24: Organic Compounds
Answers to Exercises

1. A saturated hydrocarbon with 5 carbon atoms will have 12 hydrogen atoms. An unsaturated hydrocarbon with 5 carbon atoms will have 10 or fewer hydrogen atoms.

3.

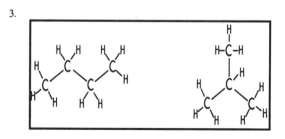

5. There are only two structural isomers drawn. The one in the middle and the one on the right are actually two conformations of the same isomer.

7. The pressure is greater at the bottom of the fractionation tower because of a higher temperature and because of a greater number of vaporized molecules.

9. If the bulk of the "large" alcohol is a nonpolar hydrocarbon chain, then the alcohol may be insoluble in water.

11. Ingesting methanol is indirectly harmful to one's eyes because in the body it is metabolized to formaldehyde—a chemical most toxic to living tissue. Methanol, just like ethanol, however, also has inherent toxicity and is thus also directly harmful.

13.

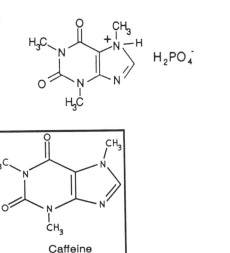

$H_2PO_4^-$

Caffeine
(free base) $+ H_2O + Na^+H_2PO_4^-$

15. The HCl would react with the free base to form the water-soluble, but diethyl ether-insoluble hydrochloric acid salt of caffeine. With no water available to dissolve this material, it precipitates out of the diethyl ether as a solid that may be collected by filtration.

17. The caprylic acid reacts with the sodium hydroxide to form a water soluble salt, which dissolves in the water. The aldehyde, on the other hand, is not acidic so it will not form a water soluble salt.

19. No! This label indicates that it contains the hydrogen chloride salt of phenylephrine, but no acidic hydrogen chloride. This organic salt is as different from hydrogen chloride as is sodium chloride (table salt), which may also go by the name of "the hydrogen chloride salt of sodium." Think of it this way: Assume you have a cousin named George. Now, you may be George's cousin, but in no way are you George. In a similar fashion, the hydrogen chloride salt of phenylephrine is made using hydrogen chloride, but it is in no way hydrogen chloride. A chemical substance is uniquely different from the elements or compounds from which it is made.

21.

(a)   (b)

At acidic pHs, the nitrogen atom of this molecule would accept hydrogen ions from solution to form a positive charge ion as shown in (b). The carboxylic acid, however, would remain unchanged and appear as it does in (a). Conversely, at alkaline pHs, the carboxylic

acid would react with hydroxide ions in solution to form the negatively charged ion as shown in (b). The nitrogen atom, however, would have no hydrogen ions to gain and so would remain as it is shown in (a). At neutral pH, the concentrations of hydronium and hydroxide ions are both quite low. This allows for the acidic carboxylic acid and the basic amine groups to react with each other to form the positively and negatively charged ion shown in (b).

23.   1. ether
       2. amide
       3. ester
       4. amide
       5. alcohol
       6. aldehyde
       7. amine
       8. ether
       9. ketone

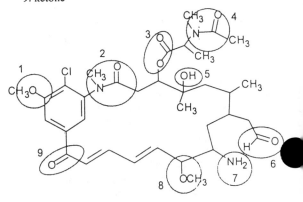

25. The combustion of polyacrylonitrile produces hydrogen cyanide. Any of the chlorine containing polymers will produce hydrogen chloride upon combustion. This would include polyvinyl chloride and polyvinylidene chloride.

27. A polymer made of long chains is likely to be more viscous because of the tendency of longer chains to get tangled among themselves.

29. A fluorine containing polymer such as Teflon.

Chapter 25: Minerals and How We Use Them
Answers to Exercises

1. An element is a material consisting of only one type of atom. Although a few minerals are composed of single elements, the majority of minerals are composed of a combination of elements. As such, they are composed of more than one type of atom.

3. Rock-type minerals are defined as naturally formed, inorganic, crystalline solids, composed of an ordered arrangement of atoms with a specific chemical composition. Minerals found in dietary supplements are human-made inorganic compounds that contain elements (calcium, potassium, magnesium, and iron) necessary for life functions. The sources of the elements used to make dietary supplements come from the naturally occurring minerals of the Earth's crust.

5. In a direct sense no. In an indirect sense, yes. Remember, the tendency of silicon to bond with oxygen is so strong that silicon is never found in nature as a pure element; it is always combined with oxygen. Because quartz is composed only of oxygen and silicon, it is the primary source of silicon for making microchips.

7. The sulfides make up the majority of ore minerals.

9. Anglesite is a sulfate.

11. The abundant form of asbestos, chrysotile, is generally not harmful to humans. Left undisturbed, chrysotile fibers typically occur in air at concentrations of 0.001 fibers per cubic centimeter. After a removal process, however, chrysotile fiber content in the air increases to about 40 fibers per cubic centimeter—a 40,000 times increase!

13. The first minerals to crystallize from a cooling magma have the highest melting point and the lowest percentage of silica, so mineral B would crystallize first.

15. Mineral B because minerals with low percentages silica are the last to melt.

17. Minerals that have the highest melting points (those that have the lowest percentage of silica) are the last to melt and the first to crystallize. Minerals with lower melting points (those containing larger percentages of silica) are the first to melt and the last to crystallize.

19. Yes, limestone is formed predominantly from the accumulation of dead marine organisms.

21. A polymorph is when two or more minerals contain the same elements in the same proportions but their atoms are arranged differently. As such, their crystalline structure and properties are different. Examples of polymorphs are graphite and diamond.

23. You could use the hardness test by scratching the mineral onto a common piece of glass. If it scratches the glass, the mineral has a hardness greater than or equal to 7. So you proved that it could be a diamond and you have ruled out every mineral with a hardness of 7 or less. Although quartz, the hardest of the common

minerals, will scratch glass, you're not yet positive it's diamond. To continue with the hardness test, you'd need a set of reference minerals.

25. The quartz, specific gravity of 2.65, will float. The chromite, specific gravity of 4.6, will sink.

27. No, the planar surfaces we see in cleavage are where a mineral breaks due to a weakness in crystal structure or bond strength. The planar surfaces in a crystal form are the external shape from the crystal's internal arrangement of atoms.

29. Galena (PbS) is an ore of lead; Hematite (Fe_2O_3) and Magnetite (Fe_3O_4) are iron ores; and Covelite (CuS) and Chalcocite (Cu_2S) are copper ores.

Solutions to Chapter 25 Problems

1. Looking at the periodic table, we calculate that the formula masses for MgO, FeO, and SiO_2 are 40 amu, 72 amu, and 60 amu, respectively. Therefore the formula mass of pyroxene is:

1 MgO + 1 FeO + 2 SiO_2 = 232 amu

and the mass percentages are:

(40 amu)/(232 amu) × 100% = 17% MgO

(72 amu)/(232 amu) × 100% = 31% FeO

(60 amu)/(232 amu) × 100% = 52% SiO_2.

3. Total silica removed from magma:

114 kg from olivine (from Figuring Physical Science box) + 117 from pyroxene = 231 kg silica

500 kg silica in original magma – 231 kg silica removed = 269 silica in remaining liquid

Mass of remaining liquid is 1000 kg – 325 kg – 225 kg = 450 kg

Mass percentage of silica:

(269 kg silica)/(450 kg magma) × 100% = 60%

Chapter 26: Rocks
Answers to Exercises

1. <u>Volcanic activity</u>: Hawaii Volcanoes National Park,
    Hawaii; Haleakuala National Park, Hawaii; Crater Lake
    National Park, Oregon; Katmai National Park, Alaska;
    Lassen National Park, California; Mount Rainier
    National Park, Washington; Craters of the Moon
    National Monument, Idaho; Yellowstone National Park,
    Wyoming.
    <u>Plutonic activity</u>: Yosemite National Park,
    California; Mount Rushmore National Park,
    South Dakota; Acadia National Park, Maine.

3. Volcanic rocks are extrusive—they form at the Earth's
    surface. Plutonic rocks are intrusive—they form
    beneath the Earth's surface. Because volcanic rock is
    extruded at the surface, it cools faster than plutonic
    rock. The shorter the cooling time, the smaller the
    crystals.

5. The amount of pressure placed on a rock and the
    amount of water that the rock is exposed to. Inside the
    Earth, pressure increases with depth as a result of the
    increased load of rock above. As pressure increases,
    melting point increases. The water content of a rock
    also affects its melting point. Rocks with a high water
    content have a lower melting point. Rocks with a low
    water content have a higher melting point.

7. Yes. In order for rock to become metamorphosed it
    needs to be subjected to heat and/or pressure. The heat
    source on a volcanic island lends itself to produce either
    contact metamorphism (rocks surrounding magmas are
    changed by the heat of the igneous body) or
    hydrothermal metamorphism (hot fluids that percolate
    through the rock, changing the rock).

9. Silica content. The internal resistance to flow is directly
    related to a magma's silica content. Basaltic magmas,
    with their low silica contents tend to be quite fluid,
    while granitic magmas, with their high silica contents
    have a high viscosity and flow so slowly that movement
    can be difficult to detect.

11. Clastic sedimentary rocks are composed primarily of
    quartz, feldspar, and clay minerals.

13. Clastic sedimentary rock's connected pore spaces
    between individual sediment particles permits the
    movement of oil.

15. Granite, predominantly composed of quartz and
    feldspar minerals, is resistant to chemical weathering.
    Marble, on the other hand, is metamorphosed limestone
    that succumbs more easily to chemical weathering.
    With time, marble may dissolve from the conglomerate.
    So we find more granite than marble in conglomerates.

17. Shale—extremely fine particle size suggests that
    deposition occurred in relatively quiet waters. The color
    indicates its environment of formation. For example,
    gray to black shale indicates buried organic matter,
    which can be preserved only in an oxygen-deficient,
    swampy environment.
    Conglomerates—large gravels and rock fragments
    provide useful information about the areas from which
    the sediments were eroded. Currents strong enough to
    carry them must have transported larger rock fragments.
    The roundness of their edges and corners are good
    guides to the distance they traveled. Conglomerates are
    often found in river channels and in rapidly eroding
    coastlines.

19. Sedimentary rock when the previously existing rock is
    subjected to forces of weathering and erosion.

21. The micas—muscovite and biotite.

23. Yes, by burial metamorphism. As rocks are buried they
    slowly heat up due to the geothermal gradient until they
    are in equilibrium with the temperatures surrounding
    them. This process alters the mineralogy and
    appearance of the rock. So although metamorphism,
    both contact and regional, usually involves magma,
    burial metamorphism can also occur without the
    presence of magma. If buried deep enough, the
    mineralogy and appearance will also be affected by
    pressure.

25. Foliation. Sheet structured minerals such as the micas
    orient themselves perpendicular to the direction of
    maximum pressure. These parallel flakes give schist
    and gneiss a layered look called foliation. Foliation
    does not develop if the rock doesn't have the right
    chemical composition for micas to form. The chemical
    compositions found in marble and quartzite do not
    favor the formation of micas.

27. No. Most of the Earth is actually solid, and the magma
    is derived from rocks that have melted. Although
    temperature increases with depth in the Earth's interior,
    the increasing temperature is not enough to cause all the
    rocks to melt. Rocks do not melt because water loss and
    increased pressure increases the melting point of the
    rock. Increased melting point counters the effect of the
    increased temperature.

29. The quartz because quartz is pure silica and minerals
    with high percentages of silica are the first to melt.

Solutions to Chapter 26 Problems

1. Using the formula for the volume of a cone, the height is:

$$h = \frac{3V}{\pi r^2} = \frac{3 \times 15000 \text{ km}^3}{3.14 \times 60 \text{ km} \times 60 \text{ km}} = \frac{45000 \text{ km}^3}{11304 \text{ km}^2}$$

$$= 3.98 \text{ km} \cong 4 \text{ km}$$

3. The height of the cone is 0.477 km and the radius of the base is 1 km. Plugging and chugging we have:

$$V = \frac{3.14 \times 1 \text{ km} \times 1 \text{ km} \times 0.477 \text{ km}}{3} = 0.499 \text{ km}^3$$

$$\cong 5 \text{ km}^3$$

Chapter 27: The Dynamic Earth
Answers to Exercises

1. The speed of a wave depends on the type of material it travels through. P-waves (primary waves) are the fastest seismic waves and travel through all mediums—solids and fluids. The less elastic (which usually correlates to denser) the material, the faster the movement. S-waves (secondary waves) are slower and can only travel through solids.

3. When a seismic wave encounters a boundary between layers with different properties, reflection and refraction of the wave occur. The reflected part of the wave tells us the location of the boundary, and as it continues into the layer and is once again reflected it reveals the boundary between the next layer. The relative reflections and refractions reveal a solid inner core, a liquid outer core, a rocky plastic-like mantle, and a rigid and brittle crust.

5. The lithosphere contains the crustal surface—continental and oceanic. The lithosphere is rigid because it is composed of material that has cooled and solidified. The deeper asthenosphere, however, is hotter. It flows as a plastic solid. Hence, the lithosphere rides above and "floats" on the asthenosphere.

7. The mountain requires a large "root" to support the large mass of rock that makes up the mountain. This is somewhat analogous to a floating iceberg. The more ice above the water line, the deeper the iceberg goes underwater.

9. Just as shaving off the top of an iceberg would lighten the iceberg, and cause it to float higher, the erosion and wearing away of mountains lightens them and causes them to buoyantly float higher on the mantle. Whether the elevation of the mountain increases or decreases depends on the rate of erosion compared to the rate of buoyant adjustment.

11. Most of the stress that builds up in the lithospheric plates does so where two (or three) plates are touching. They touch at their boundaries. When the stress reaches a critical threshold, rocks break, slide past each other, and earthquakes are generated.

13. One could find metamorphic rock at all three types of plate boundaries. At convergent boundaries, we expect regional metamorphism involving mechanical deformation and elevated temperatures. At divergent boundaries we might expect to find thermally metamorphosed rocks. At transform boundaries, we might find mechanically deformed rocks. By far the majority of metamorphic rocks are associated with convergent boundaries. Metamorphic rocks at the other two types of boundaries represent a small fraction of the total.

15. Possible answers include: (1) The granitic Sierra Nevada range, which are the batholiths left over from subduction-derived partial melting and magma crystallization. (2) The occurrence of trench deposits along the coastal areas of Northern California. (3) The occurrence of metamorphic rocks both in the Sierra Nevada and near the trench deposits.

17. The oceans on our planet have been around since very early in Earth's history. The present ocean basins, however, are not a permanent feature. The present day Atlantic Ocean did not exist when Pangaea was in existence. It began as a tiny rift area within continental lands. With a spreading center in the middle of the Atlantic, the floor of the Atlantic Ocean is constantly growing.

19. Ocean floors are subducted at convergent plate boundaries, while continental crust is not.

21. There are two supporting theories: Apparent polar wandering and magnetic surveys of the ocean floor. Studies during the 1950s used paleomagnetism to show that the position of the magnetic poles had gradually wandered around the globe. Since the geographic poles do not wander, it is hard to conceive that the related magnetic poles had wandered. To explain the apparent movement of the magnetic poles it was suggested that the continents had moved and not the poles. This idea was supported by magnetic surveys of the ocean floors. The surveys showed alternating strips of normal and reversed polarity, paralleling either side of the spreading rift areas. This showed that the seafloor had been growing when magnetic pole reversals had occurred.

23. Magnetic pole reversals have to do with the fact that the polarity of the Earth's magnetic field periodically reverses—the north magnetic pole becomes the south magnetic pole and vice versa. Because certain minerals align themselves with the magnetic field, rocks have a

preserved record of the Earth's magnetism. Pole reversals and paleomagnetism provide strong evidence for the concept of seafloor spreading. As new basalt is extruded at the oceanic ridge, it is magnetized according to the existing magnetic field. Magnetic surveys of the ocean's floor show alternating strips of normal and reversed polarity, paralleling either side of the rift area. Thus, the magnetic history of the Earth is recorded in spreading ocean floors as in a very slow magnetic tape. The dates of pole reversal can be determined by dating rocks that come from the ocean floor. Thus the rate of seafloor spreading can also be determined.

25. Horizontal movement occurs when two plates slide past one another with little upward or downward movement. This typically occurs along transform faults, which connect offset spreading ridge segments. The most famous fault zone with horizontal movement is the San Andreas Fault in California.

27. Lithosphere is created at spreading centers (divergent plate boundaries) and destroyed at subduction zones (convergent plate boundaries). They are considered to be in equilibrium because the theory of plate tectonics holds that the Earth is neither expanding nor contracting. Thus the rate of production of new lithosphere must equal the rate of destruction of old lithosphere.

29. Mountain ranges, volcanoes, plutonic rocks, metamorphic rocks, folded and faulted rocks are all explained by plate tectonics. Virtually all geologic processes can be tied back to plate tectonics, although sometimes the link is quite indirect. For example, consider the formation of a stream valley. As a mountain is growing, the stream gradient increases, which affects the development of the stream valley. The growth of mountains is a result of plate tectonics. There are many interesting examples!

31. The Himalayan Mountains are the result of continent-continent collision between the India Plate and the Eurasian Plate. The Andes Mountains are the result of volcanic eruptions and uplift related to the subduction of the Nazca Plate beneath the South American Plate.

33. Faults and folds are the strain that result from stress. Stress builds up in the lithosphere because it is rigid, broken into plates, and is in motion. Just as two cars in a crash become crumpled, colliding plates become crumpled.

35. Virtually the entire state of Nevada, and eastern California, southern Oregon, southern Idaho, and western Utah are greatly affected by normal faulting.

37. You would need to know the ages of the different rock layers. If the rocks at the center, or core, of a fold are the youngest, and as you move horizontally away from the axis, they get older, the fold is a syncline. If the rocks in the fold are oldest at the core, and as you move horizontally away from the axis, they get younger, the fold is an anticline.

39. At divergent boundaries, we find basaltic magma generated by partial melting of rising mantle rock. The melting occurs because the pressure on the rock decreases as the rock rises, which lowers the melting point enough for melting to occur. At convergent boundaries, andesitic magma dominates. Water migrating upward from the descending lithospheric plate lowers the melting point of mantle rock above the sinking slab, causing partial melting. As the magma rises and/or is impeded by overlying lithosphere, crystallization occurs. Crystallization increases the silica content of the magma, producing andesitic magma, and, given enough time, granitic magma.

Solutions to Chapter 27 Problems

1. The comparison is the weight of ocean 3 km deep (the number 3) with the weight of 10 km of crust 3 times as dense (the number 30). How big is 3 compared with 30? One tenth as much. The ocean contributes 10% of the crust's weight.

3. The form of the equation we need is:

$$time = \frac{distance}{rate}$$

Converting km to cm simultaneously we have:

$$time = \frac{600 \text{ km x } 1000 \text{ m/km x } 100 \text{ cm/m}}{3.5 \text{ cm/yr}} = 17142857$$

$\cong 17$ million years.

Chapter 28: Occurrence and Movement of Water Answers to Exercises

1. Fresh water provides the sustenance of life. This includes drinking water, agricultural uses, sanitation, and transportation.

3. Less than 3% of the earth's water is fresh water. Most of it is locked up on the polar ice caps and in glaciers.

5. Groundwater flows from areas where the water table is high to areas where the water table is low. So, groundwater would flow from Y to X.

7. An artesian system.

9. The overall mass balance is not affected much. The only possible effect is evaporation. Water quality is certainly effected, however.

11. Metals occur naturally in the ground. In most cases heavy metals that enter the water supply naturally, do so in limited quantities. When the quantities increase it is usually because of human interaction with the environment. Heavy metals and minerals in mining wastes can enter the water supply.

13. If the water supply is robbed of dissolved oxygen the life forms dependent on oxygen will cease to survive. Pollution of the water supply affects the food chain — plankton, fishes, birds, on up to mammals. Some likely sources of this type of pollution are from sewage and agricultural waste.

15. Discharge is the volume of water flowing past a certain point in a given amount of time. Discharge will increase in proportion to the amount of rain that falls. By knowing the area of the drainage basin and the amount of rainfall the change in discharge of a stream can be estimated. The rain that enters the subsurface must be accounted for.

17. The residence time of groundwater varies from a few hundred years up to thousands of years. The residence time of a lake varies from tens to hundreds of years. The difference in these residence times should give a clue as to the problem of groundwater pollution. Because groundwater contamination is in the subsurface it is very difficult to detect. In fact, most cases of aquifer contamination are discovered only after a water-supply well has been affected. The long residence time means that the water is moving at a very slow rate. Therefore long periods of time are required to flush out the contaminant. By the time subsurface water contamination is detected it may be too late for remediation.

19. As water enters a reservoir it abruptly slows down and drops its load of sediment. In time the reservoir may fill up with sediment making the dam useless.

21. If the cross-sectional area of the stream remains constant, discharge and stream speed increase as runoff into the stream increases. If the cross-sectional area of the stream changes, then stream discharge will increase but stream speed may or may not increase. (Speed increase depends on how big the increase in area is compared to the increased discharge.)

23. Stream speed will also double.

25. Stream gradient, stream discharge, and channel geometry.

27. Frictional drag slows down a glacier's external movement. The glacier experiences this drag as it encounters the bedrock. So, movement is slowest at the base and at the sides of the glacier.

29. To reduce the chances of groundwater contamination, the landfill can be capped with layers of compacted clay soil or a synthetic membrane to prevent generation of leachate. It can also be lined with the same material. Collection systems are often used to catch draining leachate and prevent its distribution.

Solutions to Chapter 28 Problems

1. Look at the percentage figures in Figure 28.1, calculate freshwater supplies to be equal to 100%.
   $2.14 + 0.61 + 0.009 + 0.005 = 2.76$

2) Ice caps and glaciers	$2.14/2.76 = 0.77$ or 77%
Groundwater	$0.61/2.76 = 0.22$ or 22%
Streams, lakes and rivers	$0.009/2.76 = 3.25 \times 10^{-3}$
or 0.32%	

3. Calculations are not necessary. The flow rate is equal to the hydraulic conductivity times the cross-sectional area times the hydraulic gradient. If the gradient increases 10 times and all else stays the same, the flow rate increases by 10 times as well.

5. The first step is to calculate the hydraulic gradient:

   $$\text{hydraulic gradient} = \frac{\text{head change}}{\text{distance}} = \frac{210 \text{ m} - 209 \text{ m}}{300 \text{ m}} = 0.0033333$$

   (keep the extra "significant" figures for an accurate solution.)
   then:

   specific discharge = hydraulic conductivity × hydraulic gradient

   specific discharge = 150 m/d × 0.0033333 = 0.5 m/d

Chapter 29: Surface Processes
Answers to Exercises

1. Large particles are deposited first because they are heavier. While slowing down, the river can transport smaller particles further into the standing body of water.

3. A sinkhole is a large cavity open to the sky. It can form indirectly from a cave with a collapsed roof or directly from the dissolution of limestone by acidic rain or groundwater. So, the factors that contribute to a sinkhole formation include: acidic rain or groundwater,

an existing cave or any type of opening that allows the seepage of water.

5. Ice has the greatest ability to transport sediment particles and thus can carry the largest loads. Glaciers moving across a landscape loosen and lift up blocks of rock and incorporate them into the ice. They literally pick up everything in their path. As the ice melts the rock debris is deposited.

7. At times in Earth's history, shallow seas covered continental land, allowing deposition of carbonate rocks. The shallow seas are now gone, so the carbonate rocks are exposed.

9. Yes. Underground rivers are often found where groundwater flows through limestone. In most other sediments and rocks, there are no underground rivers; groundwater usually flows through pores.

11. Yes, because the speed of a stream can increase without increasing the volume of water in the stream. As we learned in Chapter 28 and in this chapter, stream speed can increase in many ways. If stream speed increases, a laminar flow can become turbulent.

13. Sand-sized fragments from coral reefs and carbonate platforms make up the white-sand beaches in many island areas, such as Hawaii. Look carefully at the sand in such tropical beaches, and you'll see it is predominantly composed of shell fragments. The shell fragments come from the erosion of the nearby reefs and carbonate platforms.

15. Surface water erodes rocks and sediments and transports them from their original locations. Surface water also deposits sediments as a stream's ability to carry sediments declines with speed.

17. Modern-day and ancient evaporites are found in desert basins, tidal flats, and restricted sea basins. They all are environments where the evaporation of water dominates over the accumulation of water.

19. Roche moutonées are an erosional feature in which the steep side points in the direction of glacial advance. Drumlins are depositional features in which the steep side points in the direction of glacial retreat.

21. Because a glacier abrades and picks up everything in its path, glacial deposits are characteristically composed of unsorted rock fragments in a variety of shapes and sizes. River deposited sediments tend to be more sorted. Also, river deposited sediments tend to be more rounded.

23. The most dominant feature is the way the particles of sediment are laid down, layer upon layer. These layers are referred to as beds. Varying in both thickness and area, each bed represents one episode of deposition.

25. The breakwater will intercept sand that is being transported by the longshore current. The near-shore currents will also be disrupted, potentially heightening beach erosion on the downstream side of the breakwater.

27. Basically, because headlands stick out from the rest of the shoreline. Thus, they receive the full impact of waves.

29. Landscape evolution is progressive changes to the Earth's surface. It is mostly driven by flow of surface water, but groundwater, air, and ice also play roles in shaping the landscape.

Chapter 30: A Brief History of the Earth
Answers to Exercises

1. The fault is older than the basalt and younger than the sedimentary rock. The sedimentary rock had to be there before the fault in order for the fault to displace it. The reverse argument holds for the basalt.

3. From oldest to youngest the sequence is:
   G, A, B, C, D, I, H, F, E

5. Uranium has decreased and lead increased (via radioactive decay).

7. Geologists used (and still use) the principles of original horizontality, cross-cutting relationships, inclusions, and faunal succession.

9. The half-life of carbon-14 is only 5730 years. When a material is older than about 50,000 years the amount of carbon-14 that is left is too small to measure, so all we can tell is that the material is older than about 50,000 years.

11. The fossil leaves must be older than the shale, but the shale is at the top of the formation. Most of the rocks in the sequence are older than the fossil leaves. So we can say that the *average* age of the formation is younger than the trilobite and older than the fossil leaves. By average we mean that the formation was deposited over some finite time period, and the age we get from the fossils brackets the beginning and end of deposition of that formation.

13. A nonconformity is a gap in the rock record represented by sedimentary rocks overlying the eroded surface of intrusive igneous or metamorphic rocks. This type of unconformity represents large amounts of uplift and an enormous amount of "missing" time. An angular unconformity is tilted or folded sedimentary rocks

overlain by younger, relatively horizontal rock layers. This represents a deformational event, such as mountain building, followed by a period of subsidence and deposition.

15. Stromatolites and certain algae evolved photosynthesis, which uses sunlight and carbon dioxide and produces oxygen as a byproduct. With the release of free oxygen, a primitive ozone layer began to develop above the Earth's surface. The ozone layer reduced the amount of harmful ultraviolet radiation reaching the Earth. This protection and the accumulation of free oxygen in the Earth's atmosphere permitted the emergence of new life.

17. Several times during the Paleozoic the continents were flooded by shallow seas.

19. If found in granite, the date signifies the age of the granite (when the mineral crystallized from magma). If found in schist, it signifies the age of the metamorphic event, not the age of the original (precursor) rock.

21. Precambrian — first life; stromatolites, bacteria, algae; soft-bodied animals.
Paleozoic — trilobites, shelled animals, first life on land, first fish, first amphibians, first reptiles; major extinctions in the Ordovician and Permian.
Mesozoic — age of the reptiles, dominance and diversification of dinosaurs, first mammals, first bird, first flowering plants; major extinction at the end of the Cretaceous (bye-bye dinosaurs!!)
Cenozoic — age of mammals, diversification of mammals, expansion of flora, emergence of humans; extinction of many large mammals.

23. Melting of the polar ice caps. This could easily happen if the grim predictions of global warming were to occur. An increase in seafloor spreading rates could also cause sea level to rise. It is likely that sea level will rise in the future, as it has done in the past.

25. 100 million years.

27. The lowest elevations, like coastal regions, would be affected first. If the level continued to increase, higher elevations would also be affected, say, major river valleys like the Mississippi valley, etc. It is likely that the habitat destruction caused by rising sea level would cause some extinctions of land-based organisms.

29. A likely cause of glacial-interglacial cycles is the Milankovitch effect. By definition, we are currently in an ice age because there are continental-scale glaciers present on the Earth.

Chapter 31: The Atmosphere, the Oceans, and Their Interactions
Answers to Exercises

1. It does! The atmosphere is mostly concentrated near the surface because of gravity. Gravity is what holds most of the atmosphere from going off into space. It does, however, thin out as you move away from the Earth's surface until it becomes indistinguishable from the background gas in space. This is why there is no upper limit placed on the atmosphere.

3. The air density would be greater because there is a greater mass of air over a deep mine than at sea level. This greater mass causes the air pressure to be higher, which in turn creates denser air (Pressure is directly proportional to density).

5. The total hours of sunlight (and solar energy) are dependent on the incidence of the sun's rays on the Earth's surface. In tropical regions the sun's rays are concentrated as they strike perpendicular to the Earth's surface. As such, tropical regions receive twice as much solar energy as in polar regions. In polar regions, the sun's rays are at an angle and solar energy is spread out and dispersed. As such, polar regions are cool. The tilt of the Earth allows polar regions to receive nearly 24 hours of sunlight (albeit, dispersed sunlight) for half the year, and nearly 24 hours of darkness the other half of the year.

7. The Earth absorbs short-wavelength radiation from the sun and reradiates it as long-wavelength terrestrial radiation. Incoming short wavelength solar radiation easily penetrates the atmosphere to reach and warm the earth's surface, but outgoing long-wavelength terrestrial radiation cannot penetrate the atmosphere to escape into space. Instead, atmospheric gases (mainly water vapor and carbon dioxide) absorb the long-wave terrestrial radiation. As a result, this long-wave radiation ends up keeping the Earth's surface warmer than it would be if the atmosphere were not present.

9. Cooling by radiation prevents the Earth's temperature from rising indefinitely.

11. Air temperature is not the factor. Solar radiation is. At high elevations there is less atmosphere above you to filter UV rays, so you are exposed to more high-energy radiation.

13. Although directions are variable, on a non-spinning Earth surface winds would still blow from areas of high pressure to low pressure. On the real Earth at 15° S latitude we are in the region of the doldrums where the air is warm and the winds are light. In this region the light winds blow from east to west.

15. Jet streams are usually found between elevations of 10 and 15 kilometers, although they can occur at higher and lower elevations. As a swiftly flowing westerly wind, the jet streams greatly influence upper-air circulation as they transfer heat from polar regions to tropical regions. As a westerly wind, air travel is faster from west to east and slower from east to west. Thus, flights from San Francisco to New York are shorter in time than the return trip from New York to San Francisco.

17. Water has a high specific heat capacity thus it retains heat longer than a substance with a low specific heat capacity (like rock or soil). The fact that water takes a long time to cool and that it resists changes in temperature affects the climate of areas close to the oceans. Look at a globe and notice the high latitude countries of Europe. If water did not have a high specific heat capacity, the coastal countries of Europe would be as cold as the northeastern regions of Canada, for both are at the same latitude.

19. Evaporation exceeds precipitation.

21. The ocean acts to 1) moderate the temperature of coastal lands; and 2) provide a reservoir for atmospheric moisture.

23. The polar ice caps are on land and do not displace any water. If they melt, the water added to the sea is "new" water and sea level will rise as "new" water is added.

25. Seawater does not freeze easily but when it does, only the water freezes, and the salt is left behind. Thus the seawater that does not freeze experiences an increase in salinity.

27. Tropical regions receive greater amounts of solar radiation. With greater amounts of solar radiation one would expect evaporation to exceed precipitation causing an increase in salinity. Although this is a good assumption, in reality evaporation and precipitation tend to pretty much balance each other. In fact, viewing the world as a whole, 85% of the atmosphere's water vapor is water evaporated from the ocean, with 75% of the atmosphere's water vapor precipitated back to the oceans. The 10% difference is negligible in its effect on salinity as ocean water is able to circulate worldwide. In a more-or-less closed sea system, such as the Mediterranean Sea, salinity is increasing as the circulation of water is impeded by land barriers.

29. The midlatitudes are noted for their unpredictable weather. Although the winds tend to be westerlies, they are often quite changeable as the temperature and pressure differences between the subtropical and polar air masses at the polar front produce powerful winds.

Solution to Chapter 31 Problem 1

1. The density of the air in the tank is 1.25 kilograms/cubic meter. The mass of this air is found by multiplying by the tank volume: kg/m^3 × 0.0100 m^3 = 0.0125 kg

Chapter 32: Weather
Answers to Exercises

1. Weather is the state of the atmosphere with respect to temperature, moisture content, and atmospheric stability or instability at any given place and time. Climate is the consistent behavior of weather over time.

3. As moist air is lifted or pushed upslope against a mountain it cools adiabatically. As rising air cools, its capacity for containing water vapor decreases, increasing the relative humidity of the rising air. If the air cools to its dew point, the water vapor condenses and a cloud forms. Stable air that is forced upward forms stratus type clouds whereas unstable air tends to form cumulus type clouds.

5. The ground and objects on the ground are often cooler than the surrounding air. As air comes into contact with these cold surfaces it cools and its ability to hold water vapor decreases. As the air cools below its dew point, water vapor condenses onto the nearest available surface.

7. Warm, dry air holds more water vapor than cold dry air. The wind keeps the air above the glass dry by blowing away the moist air formed from evaporation. Hence, a glass of water will evaporate more readily on a windy, warm, dry summer day.

9. The change in environment from cold to warm. As you leave the air-conditioned room the warm air outside comes into contact with the cold surface of the sunglasses. During contact the cold surface cools the air by conduction and the warm air's ability to hold water vapor decreases. As the air cools to its dew point water vapor condenses onto the sunglasses.

11. Yes! The temperature of an air mass can change without the addition or subtraction of thermal energy—this is adiabatic expansion or compression.

13. As an air mass is pushed upward over a mountain the rising air cools, and if the air is humid, clouds form and precipitation occurs. As the air mass moves down the other side of the mountain (the leeward slope), it warms. This descending air is dry because most of its moisture was removed in the form of clouds and precipitation on the windward (upslope) side of the mountain.

15. Nimbostratus. Nimbostratus clouds are a wet-looking low cloud layer associated with light to moderate rain or snow. They are generally dark gray, which makes visibility of the sun or moon quite difficult. Although cumulonimbus clouds are also associated with precipitation, they do not produce an overcast sky. You can generally see the top of a cumulonimbus cloud.

17. The formation of cumulus clouds requires hot spots of air. Over cool water the air is cool; there is an absence of warm thermals.

19. By a change in atmospheric stability. Altostratus clouds, although varying in thickness, are a layered type cloud that often covers the sky for hundreds of kilometers. Layered clouds are generally stable. If the top of an altostratus cloud cools as the bottom warms the cloud becomes unstable to the point that small convection currents develop within the cloud. The up and down motions make the cloud develop a puffy appearance—the transformation into an altocumulus cloud.

21. When two air masses make contact, differences in temperature, moisture, and pressure can cause one air mass to ride over the other, forming clouds and causing precipitation.

23. When an air mass is pushed upward over a mountain range the rising air cools, and if it is humid, clouds form. As the air mass moves down the leeward slope of the mountain, it warms. This descending air is dry because most of its moisture was removed in the form of clouds and precipitation on the windward side of the mountain. Because the dry leeward sides of mountain ranges are sheltered from rain and moisture, rain shadow deserts often form.

25. Tornadoes evolve from thunderstorms that form in regions of strong vertical wind shear. Rapidly increasing wind speed and changing wind direction with height cause the updraft within the storm to rotate. Rotation begins in the middle of the thunderstorm and then works its way downward. As air rushes into the low-pressure vortex, it expands, cools and condenses into a funnel cloud. As air beneath the funnel is drawn into the core the funnel cloud descends toward the surface. When the funnel cloud reaches the ground surface it is called a tornado.

27. They simply have more moisture.

29. Texas through Oklahoma, Kansas, and Missouri, a zone known as Tornado Alley.

Solution to Chapter 32 Problem 1

1.

$$\frac{\text{amount of water in air}}{\text{maximum amount of water vapor in air at 50°F}} =$$

$$\frac{\text{amount of water in air}}{9 \text{ g/m}^3} = 0.4$$

amount of water in air = 3.6 g/m³
So the mass of water vapor is 3.6 g.

Chapter 33: The Solar System
Answers to Exercises

1. The connection is that the ratio of pole shadow/pole height is the same as Alexandria-Syene distance/Earth radius. Both are 1/8, which is no coincidence.

3. Because then he knew the angle between a line joining the sun and moon was at 90° to the line joining the moon and Earth. Knowing the moon's distance, he needed only measure the angle between the moon and sun to calculate the sun's distance.

5. Erosion hasn't occurred on the moon, so craters have not been covered up. Another way of saying the same thing is that the moon wears no makeup.

7. There are no atmospheric distortions of air to contend with on the moon.

9. The fact we see one side is evidence that it rotates; if it didn't rotate, we'd need only wait till it completed a half orbit to see its opposite side.

11. Observations are made during the new moon part of the month, when the sky is moonless. It makes a difference because moonlight is not there to be scattered and obscure a good view.

13. Extend the bite to complete a circle, and the patch of the Earth's shadow appears to be a circle with a diameter 2.5 moon diameters. Does this mean the Earth's diameter is 2.5 moon diameters? No, because the Earth's shadow at the distance of the moon has tapered. How much? According to the tapering that is evident during a solar eclipse, by 1 moon diameter. So add that to the 2.5 and we find the Earth is 3.5 times wider than the moon.

15. The sun's output of energy is that of thermonuclear fusion. Because fusion in the sun is the result of gravitational pressure, we can say the prime source of solar energy is gravity. Without the strong gravity, fusion wouldn't occur.

17. It has more surface area in the disk shape which allows it to radiate more energy not re-radiated.

19. In star interiors.

21. The Jovian planets are large gaseous low-density worlds, and have rings. The terrestrial planets are rocky and have no rings.

23. A planet like Earth rotates through an axis that is slightly non-perpendicular to the orbital plane. This means that the angle that the sun's rays make with a given part of its surface depends on the time of the planet's year. A slight tilt results in slight changes of season. Uranus, however, is enormously tilted, with its polar axis nearly in the plane of its orbit. Its seasons are very exaggerated, so that when the polar axis is aligned with the sun, a full summer is at one pole and a full winter at the opposite pole.

25. It would appear like any other comet! Tails and all!

27. A comet continually orbits the sun.

29. Quite simply, the sky is BIG. A far-away comet occupies a pinpoint in the sky, and there are oodles of pinpoints!

Chapter 34: The Stars and Beyond
Answers to Exercises

1. He didn't know that the constellations are not always overhead in the sky, but vary with the Earth's motion around the sun.

3. Figure 34.2, which shows that the background of a solar eclipse is the nighttime sky normally viewed 6 months earlier or later.

5. Twelve hours. In 24 hours it makes a complete cycle.

7. The gold in any ring was made in the death throes of stars during supernovae explosions.

9. Too low a mass, and gravitational pressure in the inner core is insufficient to provoke thermonuclear fusion. No fusion, no star.

11. A protostar is not yet a star, and is made up of an aggregation of matter many times more massive than the sun and much larger in size than the solar system.

13. Thermonuclear fusion is caused by gravitational pressure, wherein hydrogen nuclei are squashed together. Gravitational pressures in the outer layers are insufficient to produce fusion.

15. Just as a spinner skater slows down when arms are extended, a spinning star in formation similarly slows down when material that forms planets is extended. Thus, a slow-spinning star has more likely extended material as planets than a fast-spinning star.

17. There is insufficient gravitational pressure within the sun to initiate carbon fusion, which requires greater squashing than hydrogen to fuse.

19. Blue stars are hottest, red stars are coolest. White hot stars have surface temperatures in between.

21. Gravitational force on you would be enormous, but more important, the differences in gravitational forces between your near part to the hole and your far part would also be enormous and stretch you apart before you'd make impact.

23. The radius decreases as the mass of the hole increases.

25. Yes, the central bulge of the Andromeda Galaxy, which covers an area about five times that of the full moon, can be seen with the naked eye on a clear night. The Magellanic clouds are two galaxies visible to the naked eye in the southern hemisphere.

27. Because they are the most distance stellar objects detected.

29. Radiation at the time of the Big Bang has been bouncing to and fro in the expanding universe, stretching out just as sound waves bouncing from a receding wall stretch out. The amount of stretch conforms to the Big Bang event some 15 billion years ago.

Chapter 35: Special and General Relativity
Answers to Exercises

1. The speed is the same, c.

3. In the case of a light beam shining from atop a moving freight car, the light beam has the same speed relative to the ground as it has relative to the train. The speed of light is the same in all reference frames.

5. No, for light has speed c only in a vacuum or void. In Chapter 12 we spoke of "average" speed.

7. There is an upper limit on speed, but no upper limit on the Lorentz factor, and accordingly no upper limit on either the momentum or kinetic energy of a particle. Momentum can grow without limit, even though m is constant and v is limited. Similarly, kinetic energy can grow without limit. As p gets larger, so does KE.

9. If a person travels at relativistic speeds—that is, very close to the speed of light—distances as far as those that light takes thousands of years to travel (in our frame of reference) could be traversed well within an average lifetime. This is because distance depends on the frame of reference in which it is measured. Distances that are quite long in one frame of reference may be quite short in another.

11. Yes, as strange as it sounds, it is possible for a son or daughter to be biologically older than his or her parents. Suppose, for example, that a woman gives birth to a baby and then departs in a high-speed rocket ship. She could theoretically return from a relativistic trip just a few years older than when she left to find her "baby" 80 or so years old.

13. In contrast to the previous exercise, if you were monitoring a person who is moving away from you at high speed, you would note a decrease in his pulse and a decrease in his volume. In this case, there is very definitely a velocity of the observed with respect to the observer.

15. Elongated like an ellipse, longer in the direction of motion than perpendicular to that direction. The Lorentz contraction shortens the long axis of the elliptical shape to make it no longer than the short axis.

17. The stick must be oriented in a direction perpendicular to its motion, unlike that of a properly-thrown spear. This is because it is traveling at relativistic speed (actually $0.87c$) as evidenced by its increase in momentum. The fact that its length is unaltered means that its long direction is not in the direction of motion. The thickness of the stick, not the length of the stick, will appear shrunken to half size.

19. As with the stick in the preceding exercise, the momentum of the rocket ship will be twice the classical value if its measured length is half its normal length.

21. If you were traveling with the electrons, no matter how fast they and you were moving, you would see nothing out of the ordinary. In your frame of reference, the electrons would just be "sitting there." (The v in the Lorentz factor would be zero.) They would have zero momentum and their normal rest energy mc^2.

23. Just as time is required for knowledge of distant events to reach our eyes, a lesser yet finite time is required for information on nearby things to reach our eyes. So the answer is yes, there is always a finite interval between an event and our perception of that event. (There is even a time interval between touching your finger to a hot stove and feeling the pain!)

25. Yes, by centripetal acceleration as occurs in a rotating system. In a uniformly rotating giant wheel, inhabitants could feel normal g on the inner rim, providing the rotational speed was correct for the radial distance of the wheel.

27. The separation distance of two people walking north from the Earth's equator decreases, and if they continue to the north pole their separation distance will be zero. At the north pole, a step in any direction is a step south!

29. We say that a tightened chalk line forms a straight line. It doesn't. We say the surface of a still lake is flat and that a line laid across it is straight. It isn't. But these approximate the straight lines in our practical world. A much better approximation, however, is a beam of light. For distances used by surveyors, a beam of light is the best approximation of a straight line known. Yet we know that a laser beam is ever-so-slightly deflected by gravity. In actual practice, however, we say that a laser beam of light *defines* a straight line.

31. Faster on Jupiter because it is in a stronger gravitational field.

33. The photons of light are climbing against the gravitational field and losing energy. Less energy means less frequency. Your friend sees the light red shifted. The frequency she receives is less than the frequency you sent.

35. Yes. For example, place the sun just outside one of the legs in Figure 35.20.

Solutions to Chapter 35 Problems

1. Putting $v_1 = 0.80c$ and $v_2 = 0.50c$, we get $V = (0.80c + 0.50c)/[1 - (0.80)(0.50)] = 1.30c/1.40 = 0.93c$. The drone moves at 93% of the speed of light relative to the Earth.

3. Open ended.

5. When 1 kg of uranium undergoes fission, the loss of mass is 1 g, or 0.001 kg. We note here that c^2 is 9.0×10^{16} J/kg

(recall that 1 J = 1 kg m²/s²). So the energy released by this loss of mass is $E = mc^2 =$ kg)(9.0×10^{16} J/kg) = 9.0×10^{13} J, or 9.0×10^7 MJ (megajoules).

Multiply this energy by $0.03 per MJ and you find that the energy in one gram of matter is worth $2.7 million dollars! (Note: Three cents per MJ corresponds to about 11 cents per kWh.)